FROM EVERY PEOPLE AND NATION

FROM EVERY PEOPLE AND NATION

The Book of Revelation
in *Intercultural* Perspective

Edited by DAVID RHOADS

FORTRESS PRESS
MINNEAPOLIS

FROM EVERY PEOPLE AND NATION
The Book of Revelation in Intercultural Perspective

Unless otherwise noted, Scripture quotations are from the New Revised Standard Version Bible, copyright © 1989 by the Division of Christian Education of the National Council of the Churches of Christ in the USA, and are used by permission.

Chapter 2: Scripture quotations are from the Revised Standard Version of the Bible, copyright (c) 1946, 1952, 1971 by the Division of Christian Education of the National Council of the Churches of Christ in the USA. Used by permission.

Chapter 3 and 10 use the authors' own translations.

Chapter 5: Scripture quotations are from *The New Jerusalem Bible,* copyright (c) 1985 by Darton, Longman & Todd, Ltd. and Doubleday, a division of Bantam Doubleday Dell Publishing Group, Inc. Reprinted by permission.

Cover art: *A Great Multitude* by Anne C. Brink, with color by Kevin van der Leek
Cover design: Kevin van der Leek Design Inc.
Interior design: Zan Ceeley

Library of Congress Cataloging-in-Publication Data

From every people and nation : the book of Revelation in intercultural perspective / edited by David Rhoads.
   p. cm.
Includes bibliographical references.
ISBN 0-8006-3721-6 (pbk : alk. paper)
1. Bible. N.T. Revelation—Criticism, interpretation, etc. I. Rhoads, David M.
BS2825.52.F76 2005
228'.06—dc22
                         2005001883

Manufactured in the U.S.A.
09   08   07   06   05   1   2   3   4   5   6   7   8   9   10

Contents

Acknowledgments   vii

About the Contributors   viii

Introduction   1

1. The Witness of Active Resistance:
The Ethics of *Revelation* in African American Perspective
Brian K. Blount   28

2. *Revelation*: Clarity and Ambivalence:
A Hispanic/Cuban American Perspective
Justo L. González   47

3. Coming Out of Babylon:
A First-World Reading of *Revelation* among Immigrants
Harry O. Maier   62

4. Polishing the Unclouded Mirror:
A Womanist Reading of *Revelation* 18:13
Clarice J. Martin   82

5. Power and Worship: *Revelation* in African Perspective
James Chukwuma Okoye   110

6. The Heroine and the Whore:
The *Apocalypse of John* in Feminist Perspective
Tina Pippin   127

7. Reading the *Apocalypse*:
Resistance, Hope, and Liberation in Central America
Pablo Richard   146

8. For the Healing of the World:
Reading *Revelation* Ecologically
Barbara R. Rossing   165

9. *Revelation* 13:
Between the Colonial and the Postcolonial, a Reading from Brazil
Vítor Westhelle   183

10. Hope for the Persecuted, Cooperation with the State, and Meaning for the
Dissatisfied: Three Readings of *Revelation* from a Chinese Context
K.-K. (Khiok-khng) Yeo   200

Appendices
1. Intercultural Bible Study: Three Principles   223
2. Intercultural Bible Study: Some Suggestions for Group Interaction   232
3. Reading Profile: Cultural Identity/Social Location/
   Personal Perspectives   241
4. *From Every People and Nation:* A Study Guide for Ten Sessions
   of Two Hours   243

Bibliographies
1. Intercultural Bible Study   249
2. Cultural Interpretation   252
3. The *Book of Revelation*   261

Acknowledgments

■ ■

I would like to thank the Lilly Foundation for their support of the initial work on this volume during the 2000–2001 academic year. The Lutheran School of Theology at Chicago, and in particular Dean Kadi Billman, also supported and encouraged this project from its inception. And I am grateful to Mark Thomsen, Director of the Chicago Center for Global Ministries, for his eagerness to sponsor the conference on "The Bible in Multicultural Perspective" that launched the project.

I especially express my appreciation for the contributors to this book, for their commitment to it from beginning to end, and for the high quality of their work. A working group comprised of James Okoye, Barbara Rossing, Vítor Westhelle, and K. K. Yeo met early on to assist in the conception of the project. I am particularly indebted to Jae Won Lee and Jose Irizarry, both of McCormick Theological Seminary, and my colleague Connie Kleingartner along with Harry Maier, James Okoye, Barbara Rossing, and Vítor Westhelle, all of whom gave very helpful feedback to my contributions to the book. I am indebted to Carmen M. Rodriguez and José Rodriguez for translating the essay by Pablo Richard.

Sandy Roberts and Joanna Dewey have been extremely helpful as personal editors. Britt Leslie, my student assistant, and Zan Ceeley of Fortress Press have done stellar work in putting the manuscript into user-friendly form. As with previous projects, I have benefited greatly from the encouragement, professionalism, and friendship of K. C. Hanson, the Fortress editor with whom I worked.

Finally, I wish to express my gratitude to those I have mentioned and to my students for all that I have learned through this project.

About the Contributors

Brian K. Blount
Richard D. Dearborn Professor of New Testament Interpretation at Princeton Theological Seminary in Princeton, New Jersey. He is author of numerous books and articles, including *Cultural Interpretation: Reorienting New Testament Criticism* (Fortress Press, 1995), *Then the Whisper Put on Flesh: New Testament Ethics in an African American Context* (Abingdon, 2001), and *Can I Get A Witness? Reading Revelation through African American Culture* (Westminster John Knox 2005).

Justo L. González
A popular lecturer and author based in Atlanta, Georgia. He has published many books and articles, including the widely translated *Story of Christianity* (two volumes, HarperSanFrancisco) and the *History of Christian Thought* (three volumes, Abingdon), as well as *For the Healing of the Nations: The Book of Revelation in an Age of Cultural Conflict* (Orbis, 1999), and (with Catherine Gunsalus González) *Revelation* (Westminster John Knox, 1997).

Harry O. Maier
Professor of New Testament Studies at Vancouver School of Theology. His publications include *The Social Setting of the Ministry as Reflected in the Writings of Hermas, Clement, and Ignatius* (Wilfred Laurier, 2002) and *Apocalypse Recalled: The Book of Revelation after Christendom* (Fortress Press, 2002).

Clarice J. Martin
Jean Picker Associate Professor of Philosophy and Religion at Colgate University in Hamilton, New York. Her publications include *Pentecost 2: Interpreting the Lessons of the Church Year* (Fortress Press, 1996) and numerous articles in journals and col-

lections, including "Womanist Interpretation of the New Testament" in *Feminism in the Study of Religion: A Reader* (Continuum, 2001).

James Chukwuma Okoye

Associate Professor of Biblical Languages and Literature at the Catholic Theological Union in Chicago. Originally From Nigeria, he is interested in biblical interpretation from a cross-cultural perspective. In addition to his book, *Israel and the Nations: The Hermeneutics of Mission in the Old Testament* (Orbis, forthcoming), he has published several articles, including "African Theology," in the *Dictionary of Mission: Theology, History, Perspective* (Orbis, 1997) and "Mark 1:21-28 in African Perspective" in *Bible Today* (1996).

Tina Pippin

Professor of Religious Studies at Agnes Scott College in Decatur, Georgia. She has authored books and articles, including *Death and Desire: The Rhetoric of Gender in the Apocalypse of John* (Westminster John Knox, 1992) and *Apocalyptic Bodies: The Biblical End of the World in Text and Image* (Routledge, 1999). She is working on a book on apocalyptic space.

David Rhoads

Professor of New Testament at the Lutheran School of Theology at Chicago. He has authored numerous articles and several books, including *Israel in Revolution 6 to 73 c.e.* (Fortress Press, 1976), *The Challenge of Diversity: The Witness of Paul and the Gospels* (Fortress Press, 1996), *Mark as Story: An Introduction to the Narrative of a Gospel* (co-author, 2nd ed., Fortress Press, 1999), and *Reading Mark, Engaging the Gospel* (Fortress Press, 2004). He also offers dramatic performances of biblical writings, among them the "Gospel of Mark" and the "Book of Revelation."

Pablo Richard

Chilean priest and theologian, Professor of Scripture at the Universidad Nacional in Costa Rica and the Latin American Biblical Institute, and Director of the Departamento Ecumenico de Investigaciones devoted to the formation of pastoral agents. He is also the author of articles and books in Spanish and English, including *Apocalypse: A People's Commentary on the Book of Revelation* (Orbis, 1995).

Barbara R. Rossing

Professor of New Testament at the Lutheran School of Theology in Chicago, Illinois. She is author of *The Choice between Two Cities: Whore, Bride, and Empire in the Apocalypse* (Trinity Press International, 1999) and *The Rapture Exposed* (Westview, 2004), in addition to numerous articles on the *Book of Revelation,* including "River of Life in God's New Jerusalem: An Eschatological Vision for Earth's Future," in Rosemary Radford Ruether and Dieter Hessel, eds., *Christianity and Ecology* (Harvard University Press, 1999).

Vítor Westhelle
Professor of Systematic Theology at the Lutheran School of Theology at Chicago, Illinois. He is in demand internationally as a lecturer. Originally from Brazil, he is the author of numerous articles in several languages, including articles on "Liberation," "Liberation Theology," "Religious Socialism," and "Theory and Praxis" for the fourth edition of the encyclopedia *Die Religion in Geschichte und Gegenwart*.

K.-K. (Khiok-khng) Yeo
Holds the Harry R. Kendall Chair as Associate Professor of New Testament at Garrett Evangelical Theological Seminary in Evanston, Illinois. He is author of numerous articles and books in Chinese and English, including *What Has Jerusalem to Do with Beijing? Biblical Interpretation from a Chinese Perspective* (Trinity Press International, 1998) and *Chairman Mao Meets the Apostle Paul: Christianity, Communism, and the Hope of China* (Brazos, 2002). He edited *Navigating Romans through Cultures: Challenging Readings by Charting a New Course* (T. & T. Clark, 2004).

Introduction

■ ■

David Rhoads

The *Book of Revelation* offers a passionate critique of the oppressive political, economic, social, and religious realities of the Roman Empire. It also unveils the vision of a world-in-the-making, a vision of justice and peace embodied in a new heaven, a new earth, and a new Jerusalem. And it delivers a rhetorically charged challenge for believers to withdraw from the Empire and to live even now in the worship and service of the God who is making all things new. The writers of the essays in this book share a similar passion. These authors enter into dialogue with the *Book of Revelation* about matters of great consequence. In whatever ways the authors embrace or resist particular dynamics of *Revelation*, they oppose oppression in all its forms in our world and express the longing to create a world free of injustice, racism, patriarchy, destruction of the environment, economic exploitation, and empire. Taken together, these essays present a challenge to create a different world.

The purpose of this book is to put forth that challenge by giving voice to biblical scholars and theologians from different cultural contexts with diverse reading perspectives as they interpret and appropriate the *Book of Revelation* for our time. The title—*From Every People and Nation*—is drawn from the *Book of Revelation*. It alludes to the fact that the earliest Christians came from "every tribe, language, people, and nation." This volume seeks to embody that diverse cultural reality. It offers ten interpretations of the *Book of Revelation* as seen through ten distinct cultural lenses.

Encountering interpretations from diverse cultural/social locations can be a startling experience. It can transform the way people understand the Bible, the way they see their own interpretations, and the way they appropriate the Bible for their own life and cultural context. The experience can also empower people to clarify

1

their own cultural location and thereby find their distinctive voice in reading and interpreting the Bible. And, most important, it can enable people to find solidarity with others who share passion and commitment for a new world.

The purpose of this introduction is to set the stage for the essays that follow by (1) identifying who we are, (2) introducing cultural interpretation, (3) sharing the format of the essays and our approach to biblical studies, (4) naming some of the cultural and personal factors that shape reading experiences, (5) reflecting on the dynamics of power involved in cultural interpretation, (6) introducing the *Book of Revelation*, and (7) previewing the ways in which the essays in this volume place the *Book of Revelation* in multicultural perspective.

Who We Are

In this section, I will share my cultural/social location and explain the occasion for this project. Other contributors will share their cultural/social context in their essays.

I am a white male of Anglo-Saxon descent. I grew up in a middle-class family of the 1940s and 1950s in central Pennsylvania, in the United States, where my father was a Lutheran pastor. Like many European American males of my era, I have gone through successive, often wrenching experiences of being disoriented and then slowly reoriented by encounters that have challenged me with other perspectives. These experiences have subverted my identity and led me to embrace new beliefs and values that have changed my life and commitments. Two years of graduate study at Oxford University in England overturned my political, economic, and religious certainties. Participating in the civil rights, anti-war, and feminist movements of the sixties and seventies made them a personal as well as a societal revolution. Foreign travel in the seventies and eighties punctured my ethnocentrism and introduced me to liberation theologies—seeing poverty in the barrios of Peru and Bolivia; visiting a camp of displaced persons in Brazil; preaching in Latvia under the Soviet Union; talking with Palestinians in East Jerusalem; participating in an interfaith conference in Indonesia. I encountered in these places not only rich cultural differences but, more important, tragic manifestations of suffering. As a result, I have grasped more clearly the ways in which I and my country/culture are implicated in the global injustice, indifference, exploitation, and oppression that have contributed to such suffering.

In the last two decades, cultural interpretation of the Bible has opened me up in new ways. In 1992, I attended a biblical conference that featured thirty-some lectures by people from as many cultures around the globe speaking about their way of reading the Bible.[1] This experience changed everything about the field of New

Testament studies for me. I realized the riches that lay outside my present cultural purview, the relative and particular nature of my own efforts at biblical interpretation, and a vision of what the future of biblical studies could be. Furthermore, becoming familiar with the dynamics of colonialism and anti-colonialism through the postcolonial literature of the last decade has profoundly transformed my view of the Bible and its interpretations and led me to realize the complex power dynamics that exist in every aspect of individual and corporate life.

In the spring of 2001, I helped to plan the World Mission Institute at the Lutheran School of Theology at Chicago, entitled "The Bible in a Multicultural Context: Reading the Book of Revelation from Your Place." The conference included presentations by Clarice Martin and Pablo Richard and workshops by James Okoye, Barbara Rossing, Vítor Westhelle, and K.-K. Yeo. I contributed by giving a dramatic performance of the *Book of Revelation*. The purposes of the conference were several: to display the various ways people read the Bible from different cultural contexts; to show the relative and contextual nature of each perspective; to demonstrate the insights that come from learning with people who interpret the Bible from cultural locations that are different from one's own; and to see the devastating effects that some interpretations of the Bible have had on people. The process opened up new vistas to Bible study as participants representing many international cultures and United States ethnic groups came to learn from and be challenged by the interpretations of others.

At the end of that conference, the leaders met and decided to produce a book together that would enable a wider audience to experience the same fruits as those who had participated in the conference. We expanded the number and range of contributors to include Brian Blount, Justo González, Harry Maier, and Tina Pippin. And we discussed ways in which to frame the book so as to foster intercultural Bible study among readers.

As will be apparent from the following essays, there is much more to the complex social location and reading perspective of the contributors than simply an identification of country of origin, culture, and gender. Yet the following list gives a sense of their diversity. They include (in the alphabetical order in which they appear in this book) African American male, Hispanic, Cuban American male, European Canadian male, African American female, Nigerian male, European American female, Chilean/Costa Rican male, European American female with an ecological perspective, Brazilian male, and Chinese American male. Eight of us have formal training as biblical critics, the other three as theologians. For the most part, the writers of the essays seek to express their point of view out of their native cultures, even though all contributors except Pablo Richard currently reside and teach in the United States and Canada.

Cultural Interpretation

In the last decade or so, there has arisen a discipline variously called "cultural interpretation," "cultural exegesis," "intercultural criticism," "contextual study," and "scripture criticism."[2] They all deal in somewhat different ways with the dynamics involved in reading the Bible out of one's cultural context. The following explication of cultural interpretation is an approach to the discipline that seeks to provide a framework for the essays in this book. Inevitably, it represents a perspective out of my own cultural/social context, and interpreters in my own cultural/social context are certainly among the many audiences I seek to address here. I share it with an invitation for dialogue and critique.

Cultural interpretation of the Bible includes the theories, strategies, practices, and results of interpreting the Bible self-consciously out of one's cultural location. The goal of cultural interpretation is to foster justice, transformation, and liberation through the process of interpretation. It seeks to do this by reflecting on the ways in which interpreters from diverse cultural and social locations give responsible *interpretations* of biblical interpretations and responsible *appropriations* of those writings for relevant contexts in the contemporary world. It also reflects on the power dynamics of this dialogue with the Bible and of the interactions among interpreters.

Cultural interpretation seeks to make explicit the fact that *every interpretation is a cultural interpretation*. There are no neutral, value-free interpretations. Whether the interpreter is aware of it or not, interpretations are situated in and informed by the interpreter's cultural/social location. Interpretations have ethical dimensions *and* ethical consequences. Interpretations involve power dynamics vis-à-vis groups that are internal and external to the cultural/social locations from which they originated. Interpretations serve purposes. They are offered by someone, addressed to others, and given on behalf of others—whether those dynamics are explicit or not. As means to explicate all these dynamics, cultural interpretation makes use of cultural studies, historical disciplines, ideological criticism, liberation theologies, and postcolonial studies, along with postmodern theories of reading and studies in the ethics of reading.

Cultural interpretation seeks to locate the place in life from which one interprets the Bible. The concept of "culture" in use here refers to the diverse expressions of particular communities of people in relation to the patterns of life, the values, the beliefs, and the stories/myths that hold a society or ethnic group together.[3] A culture has enough coherence to distinguish it from others, but cultures are not homogeneous. Cultures are living realities that change in relation to internal conflicts and forces and in interaction with external forces. A culture is often but not always coterminous with nationality. Also critical to cultural interpretation is the place people have within their culture—referred to as the "social location"—in terms of race, gender, age, social class, economic level, political position, education, religious affiliation, sexual orientation, health, and so on. Personal experiences and commitments also inform interpretation. Culture, national identity, social location, and personal perspective are all laden with power dynamics in relation to other groups within and outside the culture.

Cultural interpretation recognizes that all expressions of Christianity are culture specific. There are no Christian beliefs, values, practices, or views of Scripture that are not embodied or embedded in the interests and dynamics of a particular culture. People from dominant cultures are often not aware of the degree to which their understanding of Christianity is culturally conditioned and tend to think their beliefs are universal.[4] For example, dominant cultures in the West often present the idea that "Jesus died for our sins to be forgiven" as *the* fundamental gospel for all people. But this is not the good news that people in suppressed cultures who are primarily "victims" of sin need to hear. They may instead respond to a gospel that proclaims Jesus' death as an event that overcomes the forces causing their misfortune and suffering. Such diverse cultural expressions of Christianity are already present in the New Testament itself.[5] On this basis, cultural interpretation in principle honors diverse cultural manifestations of Christianity in our contemporary world as well.

Likewise, all biblical interpretations are culture specific. Cultural interpretation values the contributions to the understandings of the Bible that come from diverse reading perspectives. The experiences people bring to interpretation from diverse places can be tremendously illuminating. However, the purpose of cultural interpretation is not only to expand the range of interpretations. People interpret the Bible in order to make a difference in the world. People who speak from positions of oppression, exploitation, and marginalization, for example, may interpret the Bible in order to claim their dignity, to find the power of God in their world, to develop strategies of survival, to find an empowering vision that will overcome discrimination, domination, injustice, and the harsh realities of empire. People who read self-consciously from cultural positions of dominance in the world may read to overcome their privilege and their part in oppression, to counter materialism and the resulting exploitation of people, to resist complacency and cultural arrogance, and to counter destruction of the environment. All may read in different ways for personal renewal and communal transformation. Cultural interpretation stresses the value of interpreting with purpose and of making those purposes explicit. It also recognizes the importance of countering the appropriation of interpretations of the Bible that contribute to injustice and oppression or that sustain the status quo.

Hence, whether we do it consciously or not, we interpret with interests, dynamics, and concerns specific to our cultural/social context. Being aware of cultural/

social location puts interpreters in a better position to recognize the ways in which their location affects their understanding of the text. Bringing an interpreter's context to awareness also enables interpreters to see more clearly when texts and their interpretations contribute to oppression or to justice. The task of identifying an interpreter's cultural location, therefore, serves a liberating praxis both for dominant and for suppressed cultures.

Cultural interpretation burst onto the European American male world of biblical scholarship in the last decades from the explosion of scholarship coming into that world both from suppressed groups within the West and from scholarship coming into the English-speaking world from countries and cultures all over the world. For centuries, men and women all around the world, including women and men from suppressed groups within the Western world, were excluded from Western biblical studies because white, male, Christian (predominantly Protestant and clergy), European and European American, middle- to upper-class scholars dominated the presses, the teaching positions, the academic journals, and the scholarly societies. Because these scholars all came from the same general cultural/social location and reading perspective, there was a tendency to assume that agreement meant objective truth. Although Western scholarship has historically been aware of the biases of religious doctrine and the presuppositions of a modern scientific worldview,[6] most scholars were generally unaware of the extent to which fundamental factors of cultural and social location had shaped, distorted, and limited their interpretations and their methods. Furthermore, because of the power of Western societies, these situated interpretations have been appropriated to justify conquest, destruction, and domination over cultures, subcultures, and social groups both within and outside the Western world.

Meanwhile, biblical interpretation from other cultural locations has been carried out in many languages for centuries. Nevertheless, it went unnoticed by Western interpreters due to ethnocentrism, arrogance, and language barriers. In the last several decades, however, the introduction of biblical scholarship from many different cultures into the English language has begun to reconfigure the nature of biblical studies in the West. It is the Western world that has needed to learn about cultural interpretation—its own and others. Traditional Western scholars are now beginning to interpret openly out of our cultural location, to see the relative nature and the power dimensions of our interpretations in new light, and to sit at the table with biblical interpreters from many cultures with a common commitment to struggle against scholarly (and societal) hegemony.

The break with cultural hegemony and homogeneity in biblical studies in the West began in the 1950s and the 1960s. Jewish scholars after the Holocaust challenged views about Jews and Judaism in Christian histories of early Christianity. The emergence of European American women into New Testament studies led to a foundational reconsideration of the history of early Christianity and of traditional interpretations of the New Testament writings.[7] Men and women of color in the West—African Americans, Hispanic/Latino Americans, Native Americans, and Asian Americans—identified racism, oppression, and marginalization in the Bible and its interpretations and have provided fresh and liberating interpretations from perspectives at the margins.[8] All of these groups have brought experiences that raise new avenues of investigation for uncovering the meaning of texts in their original contexts. Even more crucial, their liberating efforts have been counter-cultural, as they have exposed and contested the biases and the hegemony of Christian, white, male, European American scholarship and its impact on society.

Meanwhile, base communities in Central and South America, Africa, and elsewhere were reading the biblical materials from the perspective of the poor and oppressed.[9] It was a revelation to Western scholarship to discover that impoverished, oppressed, and "uneducated" readers could discern dynamics in the biblical materials that had been virtually ignored by generations of scholars—biblical dynamics having to do with solidarity with the poor and marginalized, the condemnation of oppression and elitism, the call for liberation from political domination, the encouragement to resist oppression, and so on. More recently, readers of the Bible from countries and cultures of every continent emerging from colonial domination and suffering under neocolonialism are exposing the imperialistic and anti-imperialistic dynamics in the Bible and condemning the ways in which Western interpretations of the Bible have justified imperial domination.[10]

As a result of all these developments, the biased ways in which cultural/social location has been shaping traditional Western scholarship and the destructive influences of some traditional appropriations upon the larger society/world have become patently clear.

As far as I know, the first formal efforts in English to articulate the overall dynamics of cultural interpretation in the West were addressed at a conference at Loyola Marymount in California in the early 1990s, in which more than thirty scholars from as many countries and social locations shared their respective approaches to biblical studies. Daniel Smith-Christopher published papers from this conference under the title *Text and Experience: Towards a Cultural Exegesis of the Bible*.[11] This event was followed by two conferences at Vanderbilt University organized by Fernando Segovia and Mary Ann Tolbert, who edited two volumes from these conferences under the title *Reading from This Place*, one volume that included diverse voices from the United States and another comprised of global voices.[12] Many other scholars have now added their contributions to the development of methodologies and critical reflections that comprise the discipline of cultural interpretation.[13] The bibliography on "Cultural Interpretation" at the end of this volume identifies many of these resources.

There is still a very long way to go. Traditional biblical scholarship has indeed gone through changes in response to these developments. Also, a look at publishers' offerings of books and articles on the Bible by diverse contributors and a glance at faculty makeup and course offerings at many religion departments and seminaries show promise. Yet it is profoundly difficult to de-center the traditional ethnocentrism and power dynamics in Western biblical studies. Nevertheless, it may be helpful to keep a vision before us. A vision for New Jerusalem in our midst might be one in which the dominant culture will no longer be European American with multiple subordinate cultures. Rather, the common culture would be the experience of people from many cultures and social locations interacting with each other in new forms of community. Biblical studies would be genuinely intercultural and interclass, with people making their diverse interpretations of the Bible and commonly seeking to dialogue with the Bible and with each other in such a way as to overcome injustice, oppression, and imperialism wherever it occurs and to promote life, health, and wholeness where possible.

The goal of cultural interpretation goes beyond a *multi*cultural dynamic to an *inter*cultural (and *intra*cultural) dynamic. A multicultural dynamic imagines many cultures working side by side, with each culture making its contribution but not necessarily interacting with others. The more challenging image is that of an ethnic roundtable of interpreters where many people are *interacting with each other* around the study of the biblical texts.[14] The goal of such interaction is not just that people accept each other and engage their interpretations but that they are changed by the interaction—seeing the Bible through the eyes of others, having one's own interpretations affirmed and/or challenged, learning the life-giving and dehumanizing effects of different interpretations—so that, as a result, some new configuration of communal sharing and common commitments may emerge from the process.

Ideally, at an ethnic roundtable, no one would be privileged and none would be marginalized. No interpretation of the Bible would be held sacrosanct, and none would be dismissed. Each interpretation would be respected, explored, and weighed in dialogue by diverse critical and ethical norms. In the absence of an ideal situation and in order to move toward some equity in the present, the message for those of us who are Western scholars in dominant positions may be captured by a play on some words of John the Baptist: "They must increase, and we must decrease."[15] This attitude would represent a "preferential option" to listen to voices from cultures and groups that have been suppressed and to learn from them. Such an approach would help to dislodge the (often unconscious) Euro-centric power dynamics of privilege and, at the same time, to counteract the larger societal/global forces that privilege those who have traditionally held power.

About Our Format and Approach

Our hope is that this volume will make a contribution, however small, to the new intercultural atmosphere by fostering a challenging and transforming experience of the Bible from many cultural perspectives. For the most part, published collections on cultural interpretation have tended to include essays that offer interpretations of many different biblical writings. The contribution of the present volume is that it *includes diverse cultural interpretations of one and the same biblical text, namely the Book of Revelation.*[16] In this way, scholars, teachers, and students, pastors and laity who read this book will be able to compare and contrast in one volume the differing ways people from diverse cultural locations approach the same biblical book—thereby enhancing and potentially transforming the reader's engagement with the *Book of Revelation.*

To facilitate comparison and contrast, contributors agreed to a format that included, although not in any set order or with the same weight, the following elements in each of the articles:

1. *Cultural Location and Reading Perspective*: Personal/cultural information about the contributor to help the readers see in what ways the interpretation of each contributor has been informed by their cultural context, their social location, and their personal commitments.

2. *Methods of Interpreting*: An explanation of the primary method or methods that each contributor uses to interpret *Revelation*, how those methods are shaped by their cultural perspective, and what each interpreter is looking for when they read.

3. *An Interpretation of Revelation*: The bulk of each article is an interpretation of some dimension of the *Book of Revelation* in its first-century context as understood through that interpreter's perspective and lens for reading.

4. *The Purpose and Goal of Interpretation*: How each contributor embraces and/or resists *Revelation* as a means to address contemporary issues such as race and gender oppression, economic exploitation, environmental devastation, and colonial/neo-colonial domination. This element represents the challenge that each contributor gives to readers.

The contributors to this volume commonly embrace historical approaches to *Revelation*; that is, we make a distinction between, on the one hand, our constructions of what *Revelation* might have meant for its own time and place and, on the other hand, how *Revelation* might be relevant for contemporary times and places—however fraught with difficulties that distinction may be and despite the fact that in practice the two are never fully separate. As such, the essays here do not include a millenarian approach that would see the *Book of Revelation* directly describing events that are taking place progressively from the time of the first century up until our time, nor do they take an allegorical approach that would see *Revelation* as referring not to the first century at all but directly to contemporary time. Large portions of the Christian church take millenarian and allegorical approaches to *Revelation,* and by this means they determine meanings for their cultural contexts. By contrast, the scholars in this collection accept to greater or lesser degrees and in different ways a western academic approach and should be read with this social/ cultural influence in mind.

While the historical approaches in this volume may differ from each other, they share the point of view that *Revelation* was addressed to people in the first-century. Contemporary readers "overhear" *Revelation* as a vision and a voice of protest in the first century Roman Empire. Potential impacts we discern from *Revelation* for today are drawn in part by analogy from that ancient text and context—as we see how the author depicts God's work and the dynamics of human history in *his* time and as we consider the commonalities and differences of that depiction by analogy to similar situations in *our* time. And we also experience the contemporary impact of *Revelation* when analogy breaks down and something unexpected occurs—through cognitive dissonance, the power of mythic language, ironic insight, openings for reader involvement provided by the author's rhetoric, or the subversion of our cultural constructions of the world—some meanings and challenges may emerge that are genuinely new.

The commitment to formulate plausible historical (re-)constructions of the past involves respect for the text, an attempt to allow the text to speak on its own terms, seeking interpretations that make the best sense of the text, and using history as a key guide to infer the range of interpretive options. Carrying out this commitment involves the use of various methods to formulate scenarios of first-century meaning—textual criticism, linguistic analysis, form criticism, genre criticism, inter-textual studies, rhetorical analysis, narrative analysis, socio-historical reconstruction, and cultural anthropology, among others. Comparing *Revelation* with other similar writings of the time, placing the text in various possible historical contexts, using other (Jewish and Greco-Roman) literature to illuminate *Revelation* and its context, and seeing the text of *Revelation* within developing Christianity—all contribute to the effort to interpret *Revelation* in its original context. In general, cultural interpretation recognizes these methods as valuable results of the Enlightenment. Nevertheless, the choice of methods, the understanding of them, and the application of them differ with each culture and with diverse purposes for reading the Bible.

Cultural interpretation not only adapts historical methods, but also critiques fundamental interpretive assumptions that underlie the use of these methods in the West. Since the Enlightenment, biblical studies have tended to operate on the following assumptions about determining the meanings of a text: a single meaning lies in the written text; it is possible to be objective about finding this meaning; objectively discerning this one meaning results from an effort to detach oneself and one's presuppositions from the interpretive process; discerning this objective meaning results from the application of methods that assure objectivity; there is only one valid interpretation and it has universal significance; and this interpretation is relevant and appropriate for all people in all times and places. Although Western scholars themselves have differed in their interpretations in relation to each other, nevertheless, the assumed framework for these differences reflects a competition to determine one true objective meaning. Although this list of assumptions is somewhat of a caricature, it does basically reflect the Enlightenment approach to history in general and to biblical studies in particular.

These Western assumptions have inhibited the acceptance of multiple valid readings from diverse cultural perspectives. When those who hold power in academic circles claim that only one interpretation can be correct, then their methods and their interpretations become normative and universal—a situation that thereby grants them the right to impose these views on others. Furthermore, the focus on objectivity by scholars from dominant cultures has obscured the subjective, biased, and interested dimensions of their own interpretations. The exclusive focus on an object (the text) obscures the ways in which cultural context and social location inform the subjectivity of interpretation. The failure to bring these factors to light in the interpretive process has led Western interpreters to marginalize and dismiss interpretations from other cultures and social locations (where these factors are usually made explicit) as having "an agenda" that prevents objectivity—as if having an agenda were something wrong or even avoidable. In so doing, this attitude has also resulted in the rejection of biblical interpretations that challenge the political, economic, social, and religious hegemony both within U.S. society and from the West generally.

Newer understandings of the dynamics of interpretation both challenge and qualify these assumptions.[17] There are three main theoretical reasons why cultural interpretation questions the idea that there is only one objective meaning to a text. The first reason has to do with the nature of texts. Recent linguistic studies have shown that language cannot be easily reduced to one meaning or one valid interpretation. This is because language is polyvalent and often bears the potential, within a certain range, for multiple meanings.[18] Texts have the potential for multiple meanings that transcend even the intentions of the author. There may be much about a text that interpreters can agree upon. Nevertheless, words, sentences, and compositions that comprise a text allow for multiple valid interpretations. This is especially true of a text like *Revelation* with its mythic, metaphorical, and highly symbolic language. Besides, many New Testament writers apparently envisioned complex audiences in multiple social situations and wrote to address them in different ways by means of the same writing. Consider, for example, the composite audiences of the seven churches in Asia Minor to which John addressed *Revelation*.

The second reason has to do with the dynamic nature of reading. A text does not have meaning embedded within it as though meaning were a "thing" to be excavated or extracted. Rather, the meaning of a text is always a combination of the marks on the page *and* the mind of the reader at work. That is, meaning exists only as readers read. There is nothing else. We cannot read or hear a text apart from interpreting it. And we cannot interpret a text apart from reading it. When a reader sees the words on the page or hears them, each one imagines the meaning of it in different ways as they seek to construct first-century reading/hearing scenarios. Furthermore, authors make assumptions of their readers. And language itself is never adequate to describe or explain something exhaustively. Therefore, there are holes, gaps, breaks, tensions, and contradictions in the language—all of which will be filled by interpreters in different ways as they imagine its first-century meaning. So when interpreters are seeking to determine a valid understanding of the text in its first-century context, there will be multiple interpretations that are supported by a careful and rigorous reading of the text in context.

The third reason has to do with the nature of readers. Because meaning results from the interplay between text and interpreter, different interpreters bring the images, experiences, analogies, and dynamics from their cultural/social location to make the best sense of the text. Even with the use of methods designed to secure so-called objectivity, interpretation inevitably involves an imaginative investment by interpreters out of their own cultural context. If we think we are able to detach or disengage from ourselves and our contexts, we are gravely mistaken. This assumption only blinds us to the ways our culture unavoidably informs our interpretations anyway. The best approach is to bring ourselves and our contexts to consciousness so as to understand how they affect the ways we read—so that we do not remain captive to our biases but grow in critical awareness of them. This will also better enable us to avert the undesirable consequences of our interpretations for contemporary times and places.

We can use the awareness of our cultural context, therefore, to construct responsible interpretations. Efforts to construct the meaning of a first-century text from any cultural location will come from a combination of *differentiation* and *engagement*. For example, to understand *Revelation* in its own time and place, we in the West do indeed need, on the one hand, to see the ways in which our modern, individualistic, post-industrial, urban, imperial, economic, political, religious, and psychological assumptions and patterns of life are *differentiated* from first-century life. On the other hand, it is by empathetic *engagement* with the text that our feelings, imagination, and cultural understanding can be enlivened to construct scenarios of meaning for *Revelation* in John's time—based on our careful reading of the text, on our knowledge of the ancient world, on analogies from our cultural experiences, and on our efforts to discern what may be distinctive or novel about *Revelation*.

In this way, a wide range of interpreters from different cultures will enhance the understanding of the Bible. People from diverse cultures with diverse imaginative experiences will notice what others have not seen and configure in a new way what has been seen before. Interpreters from diverse cultures are drawn to distinctive features of a text—themes, passages, lines of argumentation, uses of language, means of persuasion, and so on—as ways to focus and organize interpretation. People who come to the text with cultural experiences similar to the cultural dynamics of the ancient Mediterranean world—cultures with honor as the core value, collectivist societies, societies marked by a spirit world or issues of purity, or economies based on patron/client relationships—are able to gain a better grasp of the text and the way it was received in the first century. People in marginal circumstances similar to the social location of many early Christians may grasp the rhetorical thrust of the text in new ways. Such contemporary experiences will also enable people to discern more clearly the dynamics of oppression and marginalization inscribed in the biblical writings themselves.

Hence, there is no single, "objective" reading. There are differing particular readings that aim to be valid readings. Instead of "either-or" there may be "both-and." We can hold diverse, even mutually exclusive, interpretations in relation to each other—in tension and contradiction with each other—as a way to grasp the text's potential for meaning. Differences in the interpretation of a writing like *Revelation* will be due to many factors: the use of the methods, the criteria of the methods, the way interpreters construct the context of a writing, the choice of other texts as background, the ways of configuring the themes and coherence of the text, the organizing focus they have, the cultural lenses through which they view the text, and their purposes and commitments in reading.

Since interpreters are responsible for giving interpretations that are faithful to first-century texts based on a rigorous analysis of the text in context, how do we determine validity? Cultural interpretation seeks to avoid misuses and abuses of the text. In principle, the text and context constrain interpretation. Therefore, not every interpretation is equally valid. Interpretations can be explored and weighed for their literary cogency and their historical plausibility. Yet the limits or boundaries of what is valid will be contested, partly because they are adjudicated by the same interpreters who propose differing interpretations and partly because interpreters from diverse cultures will negotiate those boundaries in different ways.

But in cultural interpretation there is another level of adjudicating texts that comes into play with cultural interpretation, and that has to do with the evaluation of texts for appropriation in contemporary life.[19] When there are multiple valid interpretations, other factors become critical, particularly ethical factors. Interpretations may be weighed by their ethical impact on various contemporary contexts—in what ways they may promote justice, respect, and liberation and in what ways they may lead to injustice, exploitation, and oppression. In this sense, again, clearly one interpretation is not as good as another. Interpretations that foster patriarchy, racism, or colonialism, for example, must obviously be renounced in regard to appropriation. Also, an interpretation that is good for one culture/group may be destructive for another. Adjudications about these matters are made by people situated in various cultures and places of power/powerlessness. And those who make these adjudications need to be open about these power dynamics and explicit about the criteria they are using to assess interpretations—and to present them for discussion and critique as well.

Having an explicit purpose for reading a biblical text does not mean that the interpreter will distort the text to serve that purpose. Rather, the explicit purpose gives focus and insight to the effort to interpret responsibly. With regard to appropriation, some interpreters may choose valid historical interpretations of a text that promote life in contemporary contexts—interpretations that are, in the words of *Revelation*, "for the healing of the nations." Other interpreters may be convinced that the most historically valid interpretation will only foster oppression in contemporary contexts, and they will reject its appropriation. When we consider the *Book of Revelation*, for example, we may question its violence, its stereotypical depiction of female figures, its stark dualistic contrast between good and evil, and its glorification of suffering. In this regard, interpreters may well acknowledge these destructive features, denounce them, and warn against their appropriation for contemporary contexts. Whatever the approach may be, it is ethically important that interpreters take responsibility both for the validity of their interpretations *and* for their potential impact in contemporary contexts.[20]

Factors of Cultural/Social Location and Reading Perspective

Identifying cultural, social, and personal factors is designed not to categorize people but to suggest some exemplary and inconclusive hints that will bring to awareness key factors shaping interpretation.

Culture encompasses the language, values, beliefs, and patterns of behavior into which one receives primary socialization—whether of a nation or a subculture within or across nations. *Nationality* includes internal dynamics as well as the place of the nation within the larger community of nations—as a first-world or third-world nation, privileged or impoverished; a (neo-)colonial power or a (post-)colonized country. *Geographical location* includes climate, environmental conditions, devastations caused by natural disaster or ravaged by war, a landscape devoid or rich with natural resources. *Historical ethos* also shapes interpretation and may include the characteristics of an era, such as scientific developments and issues of environmental justice. Relevant *historical circumstances* include such conditions as war or peace, civil conflict or stability, political oppression or freedom, terrorism or nuclear threat, discrimination or ethnic cleansing, plagues or epidemics (AIDS).

Interpretation is profoundly influenced by the *social location* of individuals/ groups embedded within a culture or nation. Social locations identify the way people experience privilege and power and the way people are exploited, marginalized, or oppressed. Social locations include *race and ethnicity, gender, age, economic level, religious community, political stance, social class, occupation, education* (formal and informal), *sexual orientation, health, disabilities, legal status,* among other things. This list has primarily U.S. society in mind. For people from other cultures, the list will need to be changed and expanded, because structures of social location differ with each culture.

Cultural interpretation also takes account of the fact that many people are *out of place.* The poor, the homeless, those in prison, and the non-literate have no status and no voice in most cultures. And they are usually out of range of most people who do academic interpretation of the Bible, although there is now a movement among some scholars to "read with" those who have no voice in academic circles or in society.[21] People with same-sex orientation, those with alien status, people who do not speak the dominant language, and people with illness or disabilities experience dislocation. Scholars who converse in a second language struggle daily through a sense of displacement from their native tongue. People interpret not only from their "place" but also from their perspective of being "out of place." Profound insights into the Bible come from people whose dislocation puts them in a position similar to some early Christians, including biblical writers.[22]

We are formed not only by our social location/dislocation but also by our *personal perspectives*—originating from experiences, beliefs, and commitments—which may well run counter to certain aspects of our cultural/social location.[23] Personal experiences (abuse, poverty, illness, friendships, religious experiences, good fortune), ideological commitments (personal morality, justice issues such as feminism, environmentalism, socialism, economic equity), individual abilities and talents (gift for learning languages, fascination with other cultures, community organizing, analytical abilities), and beliefs (religious or non-religious convictions, scientific views, liberation theology) will all influence what one sees in a text, what one misses, and how one configures/interprets in certain ways. We come to reading with our own longings and hopes for ourselves and for our world. Furthermore, readers bring to the text a method of reading shaped by their education, their church experiences, and their views of Scripture. Among scholars and students, the particular training—disciplines they have studied and the methods within those disciplines—obviously shapes the way they interpret.

Not only do we interpret with certain lenses, but we also communicate our interpretations in relation to *communities of interpretation*—with whom we interpret, to whom we speak, and on behalf of whom we speak—such as an ethnic group, a religious community, base communities, the scholarly academy, a racial or gender group. Some interpreters may establish solidarity with communities of interpretation other than their own, perhaps with those who are oppressed or marginalized.

Identifying factors of cultural location does not imply an "essentialist" approach to readers or their communities. Readings differ among those within the same social location. There may be characteristic African American or Korean approaches to interpretations, but there will be no homogeneous or unchanging approach. There is no one feminist or womanist approach. Similarly, an individual's perspective cannot be reduced to their cultural/social location or treated as though their perspective does not change. People may choose to read against the grain of their communities. Readers change, communities make transitions, cultures go through transformations, and new social and historical circumstances emerge. Hence, while some readings may typify certain groups or communities, the identification of such communities cannot ever serve as a basis to stereotype a person or community in an essentialist or static way.

Moreover, many interpreters have a complex or compound cultural/social location. For example, people interpret at different times with different interpretive audiences in mind, such as a nation or an oppressed group or a religious community or a scholarly association. Many interpreters are oppressors as part of their social location and at the same time are oppressed in another part of their social location. For example, someone may be part of an oppressed group within U.S. society, but to other cultures they are perceived as an oppressor by virtue of being an American—an observation that must not relativize the force of the oppression involved. Many individuals have "hybrid" identities with more than one cultural community, either because they are part of a culture that is hybrid or due to intermarriage or migration. Some groups experience multiple forms of oppression in their social location. African American women, for example, labor under racism, economic classism, and sexism.

All these factors, then, will affect our interpretations, some more than others. We can hardly take any of them for granted. To imagine that they do not exist will give them greater power in the interpretive process, because they will influence us in ways of which we are not aware. People from dominant cultures/groups tend to take their cultural/social location for granted and do not make it explicit. Explicitly identifying the cultural/social traits and personal commitments that shape our interpretation will alert readers that we are conscious of the relative and limited nature of our interpretations. In this way, others can take into account our reading perspective and social location in assessing the validity of our interpretations and the rightfulness of their appropriation for contemporary contexts.

Finally, it is crucial that the awareness of our own cultural location makes us also aware that each writing in the New Testament has its own distinct cultural/social location as well—the author, the audience, and the interests served by the text itself in that culture. Social profiles can be made for the authors, audiences, and writings of the New Testament. We ignore these at our peril. If we ignore *our cultural/social location*, we are in danger of reading the text in terms of social dynamics that do not reflect the first-century realities. Likewise, if we ignore the *cultural/social location of the text*, we are in the same danger of assuming that our social location is similar to that of the author. Responsible interpretation insists that we assess the similarities and differences in the socio-cultural location of the text and our own socio-cultural location. In so doing, we will have a better chance of interpreting a biblical writing plausibly for its own time and a better chance of making ethical appropriations of the text for our time.

Dynamics of Power

Dimensions of power have been integral to every part of our exploration of cultural interpretation. Because of their importance, a brief restatement of them is in order. At an ethnic roundtable, dimensions of power include the power of the text, the power of interpreters in relation to the text, the power among interpreters in relation to their culture/audience, and the power dynamics between interpreters from differing cultural/social locations.

Cultural interpretation employs ideological criticism to make explicit (often-obscured) power dynamics by asking: What is the cultural/social location of the interpreter? Of the audience? Whose interests does the interpretation serve? What cultures/groups in society will benefit from it? In what ways? What cultures/groups may be ignored or diminished or marginalized or oppressed or harmed by this interpretation? In what ways? What cultures/groups are challenged by the interpretation? These and other questions assess the power of an interpretation and its potential impact.

1. The biblical writings have power, especially in their status as scripture—as moral compass, source of religious experience, vision for society, insights into life, an experience of solidarity, empowerment for liberation, place for healing and inspiration, among other things. Because of the status we give to them, these writings

have the power to affect and shape individuals, churches, and society. Furthermore, the Bible can interpret—illuminate, critique, challenge—those of us who are interpreters *and* our cultures. By doing ideological analysis of these writings in their first-century context, we can better discern the power—for good and for ill—that a biblical text may have exerted in its own time and that it might exert today.

2. Interpreters have power in relation to the text. Entering imaginatively into the world of the first century is a *cross-cultural* experience. Interpreters are "immigrants" or travelers into ancient times in their efforts to discern the author's social construction of the world and the potential impact that the writing may have had on hearers.[24] In such a cross-cultural experience, interpreters have an ethical responsibility not to distort or dominate or control the text but to use their power respectfully in discerning potential meanings of the text in its original context.

3. Interpreters have power in relation to other interpreters in the cultural/social communities of interpretation out of which and with whom they may speak. As people with positions of status in a culture, academic interpreters have the responsibility to promote interpretations that are life-giving. Sensitive to these power relationships, some academic interpreters are intentional about "reading with" (rather than "speaking to") those who have no voice in their culture and then writing on behalf of (rather than "speaking for") them—so that their insights and cries can be brought to the table.[25]

4. There are complex power dynamics between representatives of different cultural/social locations, particularly in conversations about differences between interpretations, adjudications of validity of interpretations, and criteria for assessing them. In these interactions, there comes into play the power dynamics between empires and nations, between dominant cultures and subcultures, between men and women, and between people of different races and ethnic groups. The goal of these interactions is to interpret and appropriate the Bible so as to overcome destructive power dynamics and to promote an empowerment ethic for liberation and justice both among biblical interpreters and in the world.

Again, if the model of cultural interpretation is an ethnic roundtable, we are naïve to think that we are on a level playing field. With the history and background, the assumptions and presuppositions, the power differentials in the influence and voice of the diverse groups represented, a level field is not possible now. Therefore, there is a need to unpack the complex dynamics that exist between individuals and groups. If we ignore these dimensions, we diminish the validity of our interpretations, we jeopardize the possibilities for reconciliation that may come in the very act of interpreting together, and we risk losing the opportunity for interpreters of the Bible from every people and nation to work cooperatively for a just world.

Introducing the *Book of Revelation*

My own Lutheran tradition gave little attention to *Revelation*. Martin Luther generally dismissed *Revelation* and counted it, along with the *Letter of James*, as one of the "other writings" of the New Testament. Teaching *Revelation* gave me some familiarity with it. But in the mid 1990s, when I decided to get serious about understanding the meaning and rhetoric of *Revelation*, I memorized it and began performing it dramatically. That has proven to be an astounding experience for me. What follows is a brief accounting of some key features of *Revelation* as I have come to understand them.

More than any other New Testament writing, *Revelation* is a cosmic drama of conflict between God and the Roman Empire. It is, on the one hand, about the imperial domination over nations, economic exploitation, and political idolatry and, on the other hand, political protest, a religious determination to stand resolutely against injustice, and the call for people from every culture under heaven to join the resistance. It is filled with larger-than-life mythic language that sweeps over the hearers until they are caught up in a drama that brings them through an apocalyptic transformation and shows them a new vision to live for. It is obvious why the *Book of Revelation* has attracted so many interpreters from cultures around the world. Doing cultural interpretation in relation to *Revelation* makes for a powerful combination.

Although views about the *Book of Revelation* are contested, there seems to be general agreement among contributors to this volume that *Revelation* was probably written in the mid-nineties of the first century, late in the reign of the Roman Emperor Domitian (81–96), at a time when he was claiming divinity. It was composed by an early Christian prophet named John who wrote to seven churches in seven different cities of Asia Minor—"seven" being a number of completeness symbolizing the whole church. Presumably because of his Christian testimony, John himself had been exiled by regional agents of the Roman Empire to Patmos, an island off the coast of Asia Minor. John reports that while on Patmos he saw in a series of visions a great conflict emerging between the God of the spreading Christian movement and the colonial power of the Roman Empire—a conflict that would result in many people martyred for Jesus Christ by the Romans but with the ultimate victory belonging to God.

In John's view, the worldwide Roman Empire had seduced (by its wealth) the kings of the earth and coerced (with its armies) the nations of the world to give to Rome an idolatrous allegiance that rightfully belongs only to God. By such means, Rome had oppressed and exploited people from many nations and cultures. In addition, Rome had suppressed all who stood in opposition to it. John wrote this account of his experience in the form of letters, symbolic visions, powerful auditions, mythic figures, and allegorical narratives. John sought to expose the evils of the Roman Empire and to envision the emerging new world under God. He challenged the churches to withdraw from participation in the oppressive economic, social, and political life of the Roman Empire, to refuse to bow down and worship the emperor, and instead to bear faithful witness to the lordship of Jesus, the king over all kings and lord over all lords—even if it meant martyrdom.

John believed that the life, death, resurrection, and risen presence of Jesus was liberating people of every tribe, tongue, people, and nation from the fear of Roman domination and empowering them to worship and serve the true God and to witness to Jesus in spite of the persecution that would surely follow. John believed that a circular, spiraling process—a repetitive and intensifying sequence comprised of Christian witnessing, Roman persecution, and punishment by God designed to provoke imperial repentance—would eventually come to completion in the utter destruction of Rome, the end of the present cosmic order, and the appearance of a new (renewed) heaven, a new (renewed) earth, and a new Jerusalem characterized by peace and justice in the immediate presence of God. John exhorted followers of Jesus that they must be on the right side of this conflict when the impending conflagration occurred. In John's view, the faithful witness of followers of Jesus made them "conquerors" of Rome, because the commitment to die for Jesus was in fact hastening the day when the vision of a new world would be brought to completion.

The genre or "type of literature" of *Revelation* is "apocalyptic," a genre shared in common with other literature in the ancient world, particularly in Judaism and early Christianity. The Greek word "apocalypse" means "uncovering" or "revealing." Hence, the various names for our text—the *Apocalypse* or the *Apocalypse of John* or the *Book of Revelation*, or just *Revelation*—are drawn from the first words of John's writing: "The *revelation* of Jesus Christ . . ." An ancient apocalypse revealed, often in cryptic language, a scenario of the events and dynamics that would unfold as God began to destroy the evil in the world and bring about the final age of justice and peace. The *Book of Revelation* was one expression of a larger "apocalyptic movement" in early Christianity whereby people expected the end of the current world order to occur soon. Furthermore, we can speak of an "apocalyptic ethos" of heightened anticipation of imminent catastrophic transformation. Different interpreters, including those represented in this volume, explain this phenomenon in different ways.

An apocalyptic stance is more radical than a prophetic stance. Prophecy calls for reform of the current order. Apocalyptic literature challenges readers to question the core values that make the society work and dares its readers to imagine a different world. The Roman Empire, with its wealth, power, and glory, surely looked as if it were blessed by God. But John urges his readers to see it as an evil, idolatrous, oppressive, and destructive empire empowered by Satan. John envisions an end to this present evil order and the appearance of a world in which God will wipe away every tear from the eyes of those who have been persecuted and oppressed. Such an image of the future that John projects gives readers the hope to struggle, the courage to resist, and the faith to endure. Although apocalyptic is about the future, it has everything to do with the present. The first-century hearers of *Revelation* were invited into a vision by which they were called to live *now* as if that vision of the future were already occurring in the present.

We can discern from *Revelation* the cultural/social location of the author and his audience. John was a male Christian prophet, perhaps originally from Israel, perhaps a refugee from the Roman-Judean War of 66–70 c.e., steeped in the Jewish writings, whose native language was probably not Greek, likely a resident alien in Asia Minor, anti-imperial, and sent into exile on the Isle of Patmos by the Romans. He identified with poor and marginalized people, perhaps as a person of some means who had chosen to withdraw from all participation in the Roman economy and who refused to defer to Rome in any way. John's audiences were quite mixed, as the clues in the letters to the seven churches imply—Judean Christians, Gentile Christians, wealthy and poor, Roman accommodators and Roman resisters, and some ready to die as witnesses for Jesus. A construction of the social location and "hearing" perspective of these audiences enhances the understanding of *Revelation* and its rhetorical power

We can also discern John's ideology, because it is quite clear whom and what he favors and whom and what he condemns. John calls on the authority of his prophetic role to recount his visions—which he sees as the truth about things that have already happened, things that are presently happening at the time of writing, and things that will happen soon after. He invokes the authority of God as well as the visions and words given him by Jesus as means to challenge those in the churches to be faithful to the one true God and to resist the Empire. In his visions, he portrays male and female figures, depicts the role and fate of nature, sanctions certain kinds of violence and condemns others, and lays bare his own image of what life should be like. The ideology of the text definitely does not serve the interests of the Empire or those inside and outside the churches who cooperate with the Empire. Rather, the author enjoins those who will heed him to withdraw from social, economic, political and religious affiliation with the Empire in the confidence that they will populate the New Jerusalem when it comes.

Revelation in Multicultural Perspective

For those who wish to preview the essays in this book, the following brief sketches summarize the interpretations of *Revelation* offered by the authors and the challenges they offer to readers.

Chapter One deals with "The Witness of Active Resistance: The Ethics of *Revelation* in African American Perspective." In this essay, Brian Blount views *Revelation* through the lens of African American slave narratives and spirituals. By using the call to activism implicit in these traditions, he demonstrates how the author of *Revelation* calls upon the oppressed communities of Asia Minor to emulate the witness borne by Jesus—even though it will lead to conflict with Rome and perhaps to death. Far from advocating an escapism that waits passively for rescue from the present circumstances, John calls for people to witness to the kingship of Jesus in the face of the imperial claims of Rome and thereby to refuse to assimilate. With this "witness of active resistance," *Revelation* provides an ethic for African Americans today, an ethic that stands against accommodation to the dominant culture in America with its racist patterns of domination and discrimination and that leads to the enactment of John's transformative vision now in the present.

Chapter Two is "*Revelation*: Clarity and Ambiguity: A Hispanic/Cuban American Perspective." Reading out of his mixed religious and cultural heritage, Justo González illuminates the hybrid identity of the author of *Revelation* and the challenge he offers to his readers. Rejecting any fundamentalist interpretation, González discerns in *Revelation* patterns of the way God relates to God's people. He details clearly the idolatrous geopolitical order of the Roman Empire and the dynamics of its economic exploitation. He also explores the contrast between Rome's tyrannical seduction of all "peoples and nations" and God's will to liberate all nations for a new world of justice. González offers readers the difficult challenge to emulate these patterns in our world today. He speaks for many first-world people when he acknowledges being torn between the benefits of the dominant culture and solidarity with the oppressed "peoples and nations" of worldwide Christianity.

Chapter Three focuses on the experience of "Coming Out of Babylon: A First-World Reading of *Revelation* among Immigrants." For his interpretation of *Revelation*, Harry Maier draws upon the conflicted experience of his hybrid German and Canadian identity—on the one hand, his German heritage of flight from persecution in Eastern Europe after World War II and, on the other hand, the pressure to assimilate into Canadian first-world culture. This "double" cultural location leads him to read *Revelation* from the perspective of a wealthy person in Laodicea, where John warns readers who think of themselves as rich and satisfied that they are really poor, blind, and naked. In opposition to popular interpretations of *Revelation* such as the Left Behind series, Maier explores how John calls people out of the social and economic exploitation of Rome in order to enter even now into the New Jerusalem. He argues that John's vision of God's reign, rather than replicating the imperial dynamics of the Roman Empire, actually turns the whole idea of "empire" on its head.

Chapter Four engages in "Polishing the Unclouded Mirror: A Womanist Reading of *Revelation* 18:13." With a self-conscious, womanist lens of interpretation and in solidarity with the Africana diaspora, Clarice Martin sees the painful history of African Americans mirrored in the Seer's critique of the commodification of slaves by the Roman Empire. She explicates the ancient view of slaves as dominated, alienated, dishonored, and "defectively souled." Drawing upon the use of subversive language in her heritage of "the signifying monkey trope," she clarifies how John "signifies" on Rome by portraying Rome as Babylon on trial, by equating Rome with the ancient evil empire of Tyre, and by a devastating attack on Rome for trading in "human souls." She concludes with stories that illustrate how the ancient system of slavery was every bit as severe as the slave system of the American South.

Chapter Five is a treatment of "Power and Worship: *Revelation* in African Perspective." A native of Nigeria, James Okoye sees power and worship as the heart of an African reading of *Revelation*, observing that, in *Revelation*, one worships either the power of the beast in the form of the Roman Empire or the Lord God on the throne of heaven. Representing the dialogue between traditional African culture and the intrusive cultures of globalization, he identifies problems most Africans will have with *Revelation*: the glorification of martyrdom, which suppresses resistance; the rejection of the state and the culture, which inhibits dialogue between traditional African culture and Christianity; and the focus on violence as a form of justice. Yet he sees many African correlations with the worldview of *Revelation*: the interrelationship of visible and invisible spheres of life; a holistic, earth-oriented vision; and the view of Christ as conqueror of evil forces. The essay culminates in an appreciation for the worship of God so richly displayed in *Revelation*.

Chapter Six deals with "The Heroine and the Whore: The *Apocalypse of John* in Feminist Perspective." Drawing on insights from studies of fantasy literature and with a feminist hermeneutic, Tina Pippin reads *Revelation* for its archetypal gender codes, in which images of women are blurred, stereotypical, marginal, and/or conspicuously absent. She shows how John's visions of an alternative political order may well have subverted the Roman Empire, but it nonetheless perpetuated the same degraded, stereotyped, and subordinate roles of women. She demonstrates how the female figures of *Revelation*—whether god or evil, heroine or whore—are all treated either as objects of desire or objects of violence. In the final visions, women are simply absent. Pippin concludes that the misogyny of the *Apocalypse* makes it a tale that is not for women and that women should resist it and create other positive apocalyptic tales to chart their liberation.

Chapter Seven is "Reading the *Apocalypse*: Resistance, Hope, and Liberation in Central America." Using his work in biblical training among the poor and exploited in Costa Rica, Pablo Richard outlines ten keys to interpreting *Revelation*, including: its resistance to the Roman Empire; the commitment to an alternative world in the present; the historical nature of its myths and symbols; and the call to a transformative praxis of history-making. He then illustrates these principles by explicating the core of the letter (12:1—15:4), showing how myths and symbols offer hope for the community and impetus for it to act. This passage exposes the Roman Empire's structures of oppression, and it culminates in a song—the exodus song of the lamb—of liberating faith and optimism. Richard concludes by identifying the empire of our time as the world global market led by the United States, which is exploiting poor nations and their people and destroying nature at an alarming rate.

Chapter Eight interprets *Revelation* "For the Healing of the World: Reading *Revelation* Ecologically." As an avid environmentalist and out of a commitment to a liberating theology, Barbara Rossing believes that we need the earth-healing perspective of the *Book of Revelation* as a means to address our present global environmental justice crisis. In contrast to a fundamentalist reading of *Revelation* that leaves earth behind along with our responsibilities for it, Rossing shows how *Revelation* expresses a lament for the earth and how it threatens plagues as a means to get the Roman Empire to repent of its devastations of earth. The end envisioned by John is not the end of the world but the destruction of "the destroyers of the earth," leading to visions of a new heaven and a new earth, including a New Jerusalem with its river of life and a tree of life that is a healing for the nations—and God dwelling among the people. For Rossing, the whole *Book of Revelation* affirms an ethic of responsible renewal of earth rather than an escape from it. She concludes with a contemporary explication of the powerful image of "the water of life."

Chapter Nine offers an interpretation of "*Revelation* 13: Between the Colonial and the Postcolonial: A Reading from Brazil." As a pastoral worker among landless peasants in Brazil in the late 1980s, Vítor Westhelle conducted a Bible study on *Revelation*. In his account of that experience, he depicts both the Brazilian context and the context of *Revelation* in terms of an apocalyptic ethos—a state inbetween colonial hegemony and postcolonial liberation, a state in which the oppressed must use the tactics of dissimulation to carve out space for resistance. For Westhelle, John the Seer uses the tactic of dissimulation to expose the dynamics of oppression to insiders covertly so that they (and we) can name the beasts in our midst—not only those beasts that oppress us from the outside but also (and often surprisingly) those beasts that are internal to our communities and that are of our own making. He challenges readers to name the beasts in their world.

Chapter Ten explores *Revelation* as "Hope for the Persecuted, Cooperation with the State, and Meaning for the Dissatisfied: Three Readings of *Revelation* from a Chinese Context." Writing from the perspective of his native China, Khiok-Khng (K. K.) Yeo discerns three different readings of the *Book of Revelation* that have successively evolved during the changing social and political situation in China during and after the era of Mao Tse-tung. An early interpretation saw *Revelation* as a source of comfort and empowerment for those who resisted in the face of state persecution. A subsequent reading developed for those who sought cooperation with the Chinese state because of the similarity of Mao's vision for society compared with that of a Christian vision. This reading resisted the wholesale dualistic rejection of the Roman state in the first century by the author of *Revelation*. Finally, now, in the face of capitalist seduction and democratic utopia of a wholly secular society in China, a third reading meets the needs of those who are intellectually dissatisfied by showing how *Revelation* offers a vision of renewal for China, a vision of the future that is holistic and communal. These readings illuminate in a fresh way the original purposes of *Revelation* and the audiences to which it was first addressed.

Conclusion

The purpose of this book is for readers to be transformed by encountering diverse cultural interpretations of the Bible. I have lifted up a model for doing intercultural interpretation, namely the model of an ethnic roundtable. Such a model serves both as an *explanation* of the dynamics of these offerings and also as an opportunity for *exploration* by others. In so doing, we hope that the diverse voices expressed here will give encouragement for readers to explore how and why you read—what you look for, how you understand, what you notice and what you ignore, how you are faithful in discerning original meanings, how you appropriate interpretations for contemporary contexts, and in what ways interpretations may be problematic. In short, we encourage readers to be aware of your cultural/social location in reading and to find your voice. We encourage people intentionally to read in community with others from diverse social locations, to learn from others who are reading from their place, and in so doing to be changed by the process.

Notes

1. The Casassa Conference at Loyola Marymount College in Los Angeles, California.

2. See, for example, Daniel Smith-Christopher, editor, *Text and Experience: Towards a Cultural Exegesis of the Bible*; Brian K. Blount, *Cultural Interpretation: Reorienting Biblical Criticism*; Fernando Segovia, "Toward Intercultural Criticism: A Reading Strategy from the Diaspora," in *Reading from This Place*, volume 2, edited by Fernando Segovia and Mary Ann Tolbert, 302–30; Daniel Patte, et al., *The Gospel of Matthew: A Contextual Introduction for Group Study*; Gerald West, *Contextual Bible Study*; and Christina Grenholm and Danielle Patte, editors, *Reading Israel in Romans: Legitimacy and Plausibility of Divergent Interpretations*.

3. This is in distinction to a definition of "culture" as the universal fact of human life in contrast to other animals and in distinction to culture as the expression of arts and letters among elites in a society. See Kathryn Tanner, *Theories of Culture: A New Agenda for Theology*, 25–58.

4. Justo González, *Out of Every Tribe and Nation: Christian Theology at the Ethnic Roundtable*, 31.

5. For further reflections on the diversity of the biblical writings, see Justo González, *Out of Every Tribe and Nation: Christian Theology at the Ethnic Roundtable,* and David Rhoads, *The Challenge of Diversity: The Witness of Paul and the Gospels.*

6. See, for example, Rudolf Bultman, "Is Exegesis Without Presuppositions Possible?" 289–96 in *Existence and Faith: Shorter Writings by Rudolf Bultmann,* edited by Shubert Ogden.

7. See, for example, the groundbreaking works of Elisabeth Schüssler Fiorenza, particularly *In Memory of Her: A Feminist Reconstruction of Christian Origins*, and Mary Ann Tolbert, editor. *The Bible and Feminist Hermeneutics.*

8. See, for example, Cain Hope Felder, *Troubling Biblical Waters: Race, Class, and Family;* Cain Hope Felder, editor. *Stony the Road We Trod: African American Biblical Interpretation;* Virgilio Elizondo, *Galilean Journey: The Mexican American Promise*, among other works in the bibliography on Cultural Interpretation.

9. See, for example, Ernesto Cardenal, *The Gospel in Solentiname*, Four Volumes, translated by Donald Walsh; Gerald West and Musa Dube, editors. *The Bible in Africa: Transactions, Trajectories, and Trends,* and S. S. Sugirtharajah, editor. *Voices from The Margins: Interpreting the Bible in the Third World.*

10. See, for example, Musa Dube, "Postcolonialism and Scriptural Reading," in Laura Donaldson, editor, *Postcolonial Feminist Interpretation of the Bible*, Fernando Segovia, *Decolonizing Biblical Studies: A View from the Margins*; R. S. Sugirtharajah, editor, *The Postcolonial Bible*; R. S. Sugirtharajah, *Postcolonial Reconfigurations: An Alternative Way of Reading the Bible and Doing Theology.*

11. Daniel Smith-Christopher, editor. *Text and Experience: Towards a Cultural Exegesis of the Bible* 35.

12. Fernando Segovia and Mary Ann Tolbert editors, *Reading from This Place*, volume 1: *Social Location and Biblical Interpretation in the United States* and *Reading from This Place*, volume 2: *Social Location and Biblical Interpretation in Global Perspective.*

13. In addition to the works cited in footnote 2 above, see, for example, Brad Braxton, *No Longer Slaves: Galatians and African-American Experience*; Elisabeth Schüssler Fiorenza, *Rhetoric and Ethic: The Politics of Biblical Studies*; and R. S. Sugirtharajah, *Postcolonial Criticism and Biblical Interpretation.*

14. The image of an ethnic roundtable is from Justo González, *Out of Every Tribe and Nation: Christian Theology at the Ethnic Roundtable.* I urge readers to consult this for a stirring account of an intercultural roundtable of twenty-eight participants and seventeen observers meeting over the course of several years and the discoveries and transformations that took place among them. I have adapted the image for use in this context.

15. This analogy was suggested by Mary Ann Tolbert, "Afterwords," 347–61 in *Reading from This Place:* volume 2: *Social Location and Biblical Interpretation in Global Perspective*, edited by Fernando Segovia and Mary Ann Tolbert.

16. Others of which I am aware include Musa Dube and Jeffrey Staley, editors. *John and Postcolonialism: Travel, Space and Power*; Fernando Segovia, editor *What Is John? Readers and Readings of the Fourth Gospel*; Fernando Segovia, editor. *What Is John? Literary and Social Readings of the Fourth Gospel*; K.-K. Yeo, editor. *Navigating Romans Through Cultures: Challenging Read-*

ings by Charting a New Course; Christina Grenholm and Daniel Patte, editors. *Israel in Romans: Legitimacy and Plausibility in Divergent Interpretations.*

17. George Aichele et al. *The Postmodern Bible: The Bible and the Culture Collective*; A. K. M. Adams, *What Is Postmodern Biblical Interpretation*; A. K. M. Adam, editor, *Handbook of Postmodern Biblical Interpretation*; A. K. M. Adam, editor, *Postmodern Interpretations of the Bible—A Reader*; David Jobling, Tina Pippin, and R Schliefer, editors, *The Post Modern Bible Reade*; and Edgar McKnight. *Post-Modern Use of the Bible: The Emergence of Reader-Oriented Criticism.*

18. On the issue of multiple valid meanings, see Charles Cosgrove *The Meanings We Choose: Hermeneutical Ethics, Indeterminacy, and the Conflict of Interpretations*; and Robert Robinson and Robert Culley, editors. *Textual Determinacy: Part Two.*

19. See, especially, Charles Cosgrove, *Appealing to Scripture in Moral Debate: Five Hermeneutical Rules* and Charles Cosgrove, editor. *The Meanings we Choose: Hermeneutics, Ethics, and the Conflict of Interpretation.*

20. For bibliography and further reflections on the ethics of reading, see David Rhoads, "The Ethics of Reading Mark as Narrative," in *Reading Mark, Engaging the Gospel*, 201–19.

21. See Gayatri Spivak, "Can the Subaltern Speak?" 277–13 in *Marxism and the Interpretation of Culture*, edited by Cary Nelaon and Lawrence Grossberg. In biblical studies, see, for example, Gerald West and Musa Dube, editors, "'Reading With': An Explanation of the Interface Between Critical and Ordinary Readings of the Bible;" Pablo Richard, "Interpreting and Teaching the Bible in Latin America," 378–86; and Daniel Patte, et al., *The Gospel of Matthew: A Contextual Introduction for Group Study.*

22. See, for example, Robert Goss and Mona West, editors, *Take Back the Word: A Queer Reading of the Bible* along with works in the bibliography on Cultural Interpretation by Ken Stone.

23. See Ingrid Rosa Kitzberger, editor, *The Personal Voice in Biblical Interpretation*; Ingrid Rosa Kitzberger, editor, *Autobiographical Biblical Criticism: Between Text and Self*; and Janice Capel Anderson and Jeffrey Staley, editors. "Taking It Personally: Autobiographical Biblical Criticism" *Semeia* 72. Atlanta: Scholars Press, 1995.

24. I owe the suggestion for the metaphor of biblical scholar as "immigrant" to Jose Irizarry.

25. See footnote 21 above.

1
The Witness of Active Resistance:
The Ethics of *Revelation*
in African American Perspective

■■■■■■■■■■■■■■■■■■■■■■■■■■■■■■■■

Brian K. Blount

Introduction

I am a product of the African American church. I grew up as a regular attendee and very involved member. Eventually, I became the pastor of a local black congregation. As a pastor, I longed for the kinds of reading material that would support the preparation and presentation of sermons and Bible studies geared to a predominately African American audience. I returned to a Ph.D. program and a career in teaching and writing with the hope that I could help contribute to the production of such research resources. It is for this reason that I enjoy interpreting and engaging New Testament texts through a conscious African American lens. This reading of *Revelation* is one such interpretive effort.

I propose to interpret *Revelation* through the lens of the religious experience of African American slaves. We all know that slavery did not really end with the civil war and the Emancipation Proclamation. Even today, most African Americans experience a "psychological occupation" due to colonization within the United States, where they are disproportionately plagued by circumstances of poverty, inequality, injustice, and deprivation. Focusing in retrospect on the actual experience of slavery as an interpretive lens helps to clarify the ethic of *Revelation*, an ethic of active resistance that I believe sharpens our grasp of a religious resistance to the oppressive reality that foments such conditions—in John's time and in our own.

The Religious Response to Slavery
Slaves lived in a context of horrific social and political oppression. Despite this context, when they heard the biblical story, they experienced an exodus God of

political as well as spiritual liberation. They discovered a Jesus who had suffered as they did and whose life, death, and resurrection shattered the principalities and powers of enslavement. Their religion *was* their resistance.

Methodology

We all read and interpret from our particular context, from the language that expresses the culture of our context. I want to do this kind of reading explicitly and self-consciously. I want to explore the socio-linguistic recognition that John's text, like any other, does not have a single meaning. Rather, it has "meaning potential." That potential will be developed differently by people of different social and linguistic backgrounds.

Unfortunately, however, the Euro-American culture has read the Bible with a domineering, middle-class, white lens that has pushed other culturally determined readings to the interpretive margins. I propose to resist this exegetical trend by seeking out the interpretive margin of the slave narratives (spirituals, autobiographies, oral histories, interviews, etc.) and then by reading the *Book of Revelation* consciously from that margin.

Correlating the Witness of Slaves and the *Book of Revelation*

There are important correspondences between the African American slave situation and the circumstance of John's reading community. I do not make these connections in an uncritical way. Obviously, millennia separate them; they were people of vastly different circumstances, needs, and cultural dynamics. Nevertheless, there are also striking parallels between John's prophecy and his audience and the slave songs/ narratives and their audiences. John believed that he was writing to a people whose occupied lives were threatened at every turn; the creators of the spirituals and of the slave narratives justifiably believed the same.

The Suffering of the People

John's language about the suffering of God's people can be striking. Consider the prophecy about the fate of two key witnesses who proclaim the lordship of Christ over against the lordship of Rome.

> When they have finished their testimony, the beast that comes up from the bottomless pit will make war on them and conquer them and kill them, and their dead bodies will lie in the street of the great city that is prophetically called Sodom and Egypt, where also their Lord was crucified. For three and a half days members of the peoples and tribes and languages and nations will gaze at their dead bodies and refuse to let them be placed in a tomb; and the inhabitants of the earth will gloat

over them and celebrate and exchange presents, because these two prophets had
been a torment to the inhabitants of the earth. (11:7-10)

Evidently, this was the fate of many who would dare make such a witness:

> When he opened the fifth seal, I saw under the altar the souls of those who had
> been slaughtered for the word of God and for the testimony they had given; they
> cried out with a loud voice, "Sovereign Lord, holy and true, how long will it be
> before you judge and avenge our blood on the inhabitants of the earth?" (6:9-10)

There is language just as striking in the historical ledgers of the slave narratives.
Consider the recounting of one Solomon Bradley who, when he was interviewed in
South Carolina in 1863, was a twenty-seven-year-old slave who had recently joined
a Union Army regiment.

> I went up to [Mr. Farrarby's] house one morning from my work for drinking water,
> and heard a woman screaming awfully in the door-yard. On going up to the fence
> and looking over I saw a woman stretched out, face downwards, on the ground her
> hands and feet being fastened to stakes. Mr. Farrarby was standing over and strik-
> ing her with a leather trace belonging to his carriage-harness. As he struck her the
> flesh of her back and legs was raised in welts and ridges by the force of the blows.
> Sometimes when the poor thing cried too loud from the pain Farrarby would kick
> her in the mouth. After he had exhausted himself whipping her he sent to his house
> for sealing wax and lighted a candle and, melting the wax, dropped it upon the
> woman's lacerated back. He then got a riding whip and, standing over the woman,
> picked off the hardened wax by switching at it. Mr. Farrarby's grown daughters
> were looking at all this from a window of the house through the blinds. The punish-
> ment was so terrible that I was induced to ask what offence the woman had com-
> mitted and I was told by her fellow servants that her only crime was in burning the
> edges of the waffles that she had cooked for breakfast. The sight of this thing made
> me almost wild that day. I could not work right and I prayed the Lord to help my
> people out of their bondage. I felt I could not stand it much longer.[1]

Similar to *Revelation*, there are also very poignant accounts in the slave narratives
that relate a devastating connection between witnessing to the Lord and persecution
on account of that witness. The matter of the would-be slave preacher James Smith
is a case in point.

> He was finally received into the church and baptized. Not long after this, he felt
> loudly called upon to go out and labor for the salvation of souls among the slave

population with whom he was identified. At this conduct his master was much displeased, and strove to prevent him from the exercise of what the slave considered to be his duty to God and his brethren, on the Sabbath day. He was sometimes kept tied all day Sundays while the other slaves were allowed to go just where they pleased on that day. At other times he was flogged until his blood would drip down at his feet, and yet he would not give up laboring whenever he could get an opportunity, on the Sabbath day, for the conversion of souls. God was pleased to bless his labors and many were led to embrace the Savior under his preaching.

At length his master sold him to a slave trader, who separated him from his family and carried him to the State of Georgia. His parting words to his wife were that if they proved faithful to God, He would bring them together again in a more free land than Virginia.[2]

Visions of the Future

There is also a correspondence between the way John and the spirituals addressed their respective audiences. Both offered powerful visions of hope for world-weary people.

> My Lord, what a mornin',
> My Lord, what a mornin',
> My Lord, what a mornin',
> When de stars begin to fall.

> You'll hear de trumpet sound,
> To wake de nations underground,
> Lookin' to my God's right hand,
> When de stars begin to fall.[3]

Like John of Patmos, the slave singer-songwriters looked to the future because the present was so abhorrent. In fact, much of the slave imagery about the future is imagery from the *Book of Revelation*: trumpets sound, stars fall, nations crumble, a Lamb arises, an altar appears, and a beaten, bloodied people sit vindicated upon it. Finally!

> John saw, Oh, John saw,
> John saw the holy number,
> Sitting on the golden altar,
> On the golden altar.

Worthy, worthy is the Lamb,
Is the Lamb, Is the Lamb,
Oh, worthy, worthy is the Lamb,
Sitting on the golden altar.

Mary wept, an' Martha cried,
Martha cried, Martha cried,
Oh, weeping Mary weeps no more,
Sitting on the golden altar.[4]

Perhaps in a world where desperation and death are intimate and where hope keeps promising to visit but never does, all that people have are dreams and visions. Perhaps those dreams are like an opiate. Perhaps what John saw on Patmos had no clear connection to the lives of his people, except to divert their attention. Perhaps the spirituals simply averted the gaze of their listeners for a time without doing anything to change the horrors haunting their historical horizons. Perhaps John spouted painkiller prophecies, and the slaves arranged for artistic, antebellum inoculations. Perhaps.

Transformation of the Present Time
I do not buy it. And I do not buy it because the people who lived the symbolic language also lived lives of opposition contrary to the political and religious powers in their respective worlds. John was on Patmos because he had himself witnessed to the very cause the visions were now urging upon others. So, too, is the case with the slaves who created and sang the spirituals. Harriet Tubman used them as a signal on the outlawed Underground Railroad. She used them to engage, encourage, and inspire those who risked their lives to flee their enslavement. Nat Turner created and sang spirituals like "Steal Away to Jesus" in order to arouse black anger until they fought back against white oppression. These were not folk given to escapist tendencies; these were folk used to retorting, running, and rebelling.

Both John and the writers of the spirituals employed their visions as weapons in a war of resistance; they unleashed them so as to unbind a people from their fear. A people who are assured of their standing and existence in the world-to-come are more likely to risk their standing in the present in order to secure their future. This, I believe, is what John and the slaves were doing; they were envisioning the future in the hope that their people would be emboldened by the vision they saw of the future to paint that very vision into their present history—to hope, to endure, and, ultimately, to resist now, in the present.

In other words, the visions do not just suggest a new future; they also create the future within the present. Indeed, what George Cummings says about the slaves and their spirituals, he might well say about John and his revelation.

> The common black experience of tragic suffering lived in and through the dialectic
> of hope and resignation is set on a powerful journey in the context of worship,
> where a qualitative shift in the community's consciousness takes place and serves to
> liberate momentarily and keep alive the hope of permanent liberation.[5]

It is as though a people occupied by the power and force of Rome can—even now
in the present moment of worship when they heard John's *Revelation*—sense the
liberation that God's triumph will bring. Just as a people devastated by slavery
could, even as they worked the fields, tended the master's home and children, or
endured the master's sexual and vindictive fury, be free in imagination in the North
at the very moment they were shackled in the South. Both John and the slave singers
knew that a *taste* of freedom is a powerful inducement for the solicitation of freedom.
That is what those visions and these songs were all about.

New Age Coming
In both situations, the authors pray not for spiritual escape but for a new age of
historically engineered vengeance and transformation. It is clear when we read
Revelation, for example, that John envisions two powerful world eons. The present
eon is controlled by the forces of Satan; the future eon will be controlled by God
(chapters 21–22). In this age, Satan had been (and will be) allotted power and rule
(12:12; 20:7); in the future, however, the rule of Satan will be forever curtailed.
Followers of God who live in the present must take heart in their knowledge of this
truth that one day soon Satan and Satan's forces would be overthrown (12:9; 20:1-
15). This knowledge was the basis upon which John called upon them to resist
those forces and to maintain their allegiance to God.

  This kind of dualistic worldview also pervaded the thinking of the slaves. They
knew that human beings are meant by God to be free, and that God is in control
of history, and yet, unbelievably, they were not free. Nevertheless, the present age
looked very different in light of the imminently approaching future age.

> Children, we shall be free,
> When the Lord [as Messiah] shall appear.
> Give ease to the sick, give sight to blind,
> Enable the cripple to walk;
> He'll raise the dead from under the earth,
> And give them permission to talk.[6]

Just as John expressed his vision for the coming triumph, so too do the narratives of
the slaves use powerful visions of the future to induce hope for real transformative

change in the present. As was the case with John, what the slaves see in their minds has implications for what God will soon do in their historical circumstance.

What was anticipated was divine judgment that would transform the human historical landscape. In John's vocabulary, it was the symbolic language of a fallen Babylon (chapters 17–18); in the slave narratives, it was the portent of the Civil War. As monstrous an event as it was in the life of the United States of America, the slaves had prayed fervently for it, believing it to be the only form of judgment that could punish the system that had enslaved them. At the same time, it would wipe that system of slavery out forever. As Dwight Hopkins notes, "Various slave stories, accordingly, attribute the success of the Yankee forces over the Confederates to God's will." He quotes a certain Charles Grandy as a case in point.

> Den a gra' big star over in de east come right down almos' to de earth. I seed it myself. 'Twas sign o' war alright. Niggers got glad. All dem what could pray 'gin to pray more 'n ever. So glad God sendin' de war.[7]

As this following interchange between Robert Smalls, a twenty-four-year-old slave interviewed in South Carolina in 1863, indicates, the slaves were most eager to participate with God in this historic enterprise.

> Q. Have the colored people any general idea of fighting for their liberation?
> A. They have a great idea. If they had a chance there would be no difficulty in raising a military force. If our headquarters were in Charleston we would have ten or fifteen regiments. The people there have been constantly praying for this day.[8]

This is not the language or imagery of an escapist people who look to otherworldly visions to "drug out" their historical realities. Just as John foresaw a new earth as well as a new heaven (21:1), the slaves believed that God's accomplishments in the heavenly realm could and would lead to liberation on the earthly one. The war and the emancipation of slaves validated the slave's belief that God acts in human history, as the spiritual shows: "Shout the glad tidings o'er Egypt's dark sky/ Jehovah has triumphed, his people are free."[9] This is why they could sing in images that talked about other worlds but in their essence challenged the structures of this world and, even more important, beckoned their participation in that challenge.

> Singin' wid a sword in ma han', Lord,
> Singin' wid a sword in ma han',
> Singin' wid a sword in ma han',
> Singin' wid a sword in ma han.'

> Purtiest singin' ever I heard,
> 'Way ovah on de hill,
> 'De angels sing an' I sing too,
> Singin' wid a sword in ma han',' Lord.[10]

This is the language of resistance, not escapism. It is the kind of language that I believe characterizes the slave narratives[11] and corresponds with the ethical exhortation that John wanted his visionary imagery to impress upon his first-century hearers. In fact, the lens of the spirituals and the slave narratives helps us to see more clearly the way in which John's apocalyptic language encourages "a witness of active resistance." It is to this that we now turn.

Reading *Revelation* through the Lens of the Slave Experience

A Christian believer in one of John's churches might rightly ask: "Who is in control? God? Or the emperor and Rome?" In John's world of Asia Minor (1:4), where the pagan attraction to the emperor cult was at its strongest,[12] the truthful answer appeared to be: "The emperor and Rome." John even acknowledged this "truth" in his portrayal of Rome as the great and mighty "Babylon," whose unrivaled wealth and power were idolized by the entire world.

John's truth, though, is an alternative to this one, a hidden truth amid the mighty claims that Caesar is lord and that Rome rules. Rome's public truth drowns out all other truths and, with the might of the Roman legions, declares them all to be lies. But John offers his visionary prophecy anyway. This is the message his mythology brings: despite what you see in this world, where the powers and forces of chaos and destruction seem to be victorious at every turn, the truth is that *God is in control* (see 1:5, 8; 2:12, 26-27; 3:21; 11:15; 19:15-16) and God is stronger than Rome. To any objective observer the claim is a ludicrous one.

Of course, one would first want to ask: "Whose God? Whose God is stronger than Rome?" John will reply: "It is Jesus' God." That is where it really becomes ridiculous. Jesus' God? Jesus, the same Jesus who died on the cross? His God? Precisely. His God! That is the truth. His God is stronger than Rome. John's vision seems to turn the apparent truth of Roman power on its head. John's vision gives to Jesus the symbolic characteristic of a lamb, a helpless animal used as an offering of sacrifice. Yet it is precisely such a lamb that served as a paschal offering for the liberation of the people from their historical captivity to the apparently all-powerful nation of Egypt.

It is not all that odd, then, that this lamb has the character of a lion. Notice how John opens his discussion of Jesus' role in God's plan: "Then one of the elders said to me, 'Do not weep. See, the Lion of the tribe of Judah, the Root of David, has conquered, so that he can open the scroll and its seven seals.'" The elder points out a Lion, a conquering Lion who wields the power of almighty God. But when John looks, what does he see? "Then I saw . . . a Lamb standing as if it had been slaughtered, having seven horns and seven eyes, which are the seven spirits of God sent out into all the earth."

The ironic message is clear: *looks deceive*. The Lamb has all the markings of one who was slaughtered. But the slaughtering did not take. For the Lamb apparently rose beyond the slaughtering—but with the markings intact in order that his followers who believed in him might be consoled and in order that his enemies who slaughtered him might become afraid. It is clear, despite how it looks, that this Jesus is a conquering Lion. The fact that he now wields the seven spirits of God is proof of that. This Jesus, along with the God whose plan he represents, is the one in control of human history. The Romans who slaughtered him are not. In using this imagery, John's goal was to show the truth of what his people believed, namely, that despite how it appears on the surface, God rather than Rome is in charge.

To demonstrate this truth, John imagined two key polar oppositions, God and Satan. On the heavenly or mythological level, these two were at war, and, despite how it seemed at times, God was destined to win. In fact, in the future that John foresaw, that victory had already taken place. On the ground, here on earth, that mythological battle had direct human, historical referents. God was represented by Christ, the slaughtered Lamb with the conquering power of a Lion. Satan was represented by the beastly portrayals of Rome and the conquering power of her Caesars. Rome's dominance, however, is only an appearance, an illusion, a mirage. That is the truth *Revelation* says is out there—the truth that the satanic forces who support Rome do not want the believers to find out.

The Temptation to Accommodation

Why is it so important to Rome that the Christian believers not find out the truth? Because Rome wants the Christian, out of a fearful desire to protect this physical life and the things that go with it, to be willing to compromise his or her beliefs and accommodate them to the belief structure offered by Rome. All of this tells us something important about the community to which John was writing. Socially, politically, and economically, these were people of some means.[13]

John's audience was comprised of people with enough local standing and money to want to avoid losing it. As such, and here is the issue, they were prone to accommodate to Roman rule. This tendency was acute in relation to religion. Rome allowed subject peoples to pay homage to their own gods and goddesses as long as their worship *also* included appropriate recognition of Roman deities. Refusal to participate in Roman cult worship attracted suspicion and hostility. An impulse to accommodate resulted because people who refused to participate in the cult risked the loss of economic security and political standing.

John realizes that his hearers are coming before a situation where they will have to decide whether to progress societally, politically, and economically or to declare themselves followers of Christ—at the risk of losing everything! He is afraid that the time might come when they would sacrifice their Christian commitment and allegiance to God's future in a futile attempt to conserve their status in the present by buying into the Roman economic way of life, by participating in cultic-societal gatherings that may require them to compromise their faith, or even by denying their faith if declaring it would risk loss of property, privilege, or life.

This is why John creates a narrative-symbolic world that presents an alternative truth. In John's eye of faith, as ridiculous as it may seem, the truth is that God and God's Christ are in control. This, John reveals, is not only an alternative truth; this is *the* truth. And it is on the basis of this truth and of the historical circumstances of the hearers that John fashions an ethics of active resistance.

An Ethics of Active Resistance: Witnessing

John promotes an ethics of active resistance by means of "witness." He does so by witnessing to an alternative truth and by seeking this same witness from those who, like him, follow the Lamb and attest to the truth that the Lamb, by the power of God, is in control of human history. By so doing, believers also witness against the false truth that Rome is lord and master of human history. I turn, then, to the language of witness in several key passages early in John's prophecy as a means to explicate John's ethics.

Revelation 1:1-3
In this opening passage, we learn how the concept of witnessing is central to John's whole work. This passage is an action text in which a revelation is delivered along a chain of figures from God to Jesus to the angel and then to John. The language John uses to build the chain suggests a literary equivalence between the term "revelation" and the formula "word of God and witness of Jesus Christ." Furthermore, the revelation of God's word is the same revelation as John's written prophecy (1:3). A kind of literary equation has developed: the revelation of Jesus Christ *is* "the Word of God and witness of Jesus Christ," each of which is also in turn the written prophecy that John's audience is to hear. This audience is to *keep* that witness.

But what is the "witness of Jesus Christ" that the believers are supposed to keep? Here David Aune's translation helps us: " . . . the message from God, that is, the witness borne by Jesus."[14] In this translation, "the witness of Jesus" expresses and specifies one aspect of the nature of "the word of God."[15] But what exactly is the witness of Jesus Christ, who is the spirit of prophecy? (19:10). We can say that it is not the believer's witness about Jesus, but, as Aune correctly translates, it is the witness "borne by" Jesus himself (cf. 1:9; 11:7; 12:17; 19:10; 10:4). When John talks about the "witness of," he is referring to the "witness borne by." And the prophecy John is now writing is in turn the witness to the truth that was borne by Jesus Christ. John here characterizes his entire work as the witness borne by Jesus.

What does this have to do with John's ethics? The answer lies not in *what* John says but in *how* he says it, namely with the language of blessing: "Blessed is the one who reads (aloud) . . . and blessed are those who hear . . . and keep it (the witness borne by Jesus Christ)."[16] John makes it known that he, along with God and Jesus Christ, considers that the person who reads this witness aloud (so that others may hear it) and the persons who hear and keep this witness are indeed blessed. And this is the action John wants his readers to perform, namely, to proclaim and to keep the witness that is borne by Jesus Christ, a witness so powerful and true that it is, for them, in their circumstance, the Word of God. They may not know yet precisely what that witness is (this becomes clear as the prophecy unfolds), but right from the start they know that they are to keep it by *emulating* it.

Throughout his book, John reinforces the importance of "keeping" this witness (3:3, 8; 14:12; 16:15; 22:9), and he promises eschatological victory to those who do so (2:26-29; 3:10). At the end of the book, John even pronounces the same blessing again on those who hear and keep the witness (22:7).

Revelation 1:4-8

In this passage, we learn that keeping the witness of Jesus will place the believer directly in conflict with Rome. John's language contributes to this conflict. He writes in the symbolic language of apocalyptic, which is characteristically resistance language.[17] Furthermore, as Allen Callahan has argued, John deliberately uses grammar that has Semitic features, and he makes Old Testament allusions, both of which demonstrate John's refusal to accommodate his "Greek" to that of the Romans.[18] As such, John's grammar is a symbol of the social and political resistance his people must wage. In addition, as we shall see, John describes God and Jesus in such a way as to be provocative in relation to the claims that Rome makes for itself and its gods.

For example, John writes that the God of Jesus Christ is "the one who is, who was, and who is coming." This is a direct challenge to the gods of the Greco-Roman world, because a similar three-fold formulation was a commonplace way of celebrating a deity's eternity and immutability: "Zeus was, Zeus is, and Zeus will be."[19] John testifies that this notoriety belongs to God. Furthermore, he claims that God is not only the eternal one, but also the "coming one." And God is coming for a purpose. John hints at that purpose when he adds to this three-fold formulation that God is "the Almighty one." God is the true and supreme power in the cosmos, and God is coming to establish God's power. In the eastern provinces of John's seven churches, where Rome was also making the claim to be the supreme power in the cosmos, an announcement of God's impending arrival as the Almighty One was bound to cause conflict.

John heightens the probability for that conflict in his description of Jesus Christ as "the faithful witness, the firstborn of the dead, and the ruler of the kings of the earth." These phrases allude to *Psalm* 89, where the terms "faithful witness" and "firstborn" are both associated with kingship, with "the unending reign of David's seed on his throne" (cf. also *Psalm* 88:30). John applies the phrase directly to the Messiah's own faithful witness, which has led to the establishment of his eternal kingship.[20] In John's passage, each phrase builds on the previous one. The image of universal kingship clarifies what it means for Jesus to be firstborn of the dead, and, in turn, both these phrases clarify what it means for Jesus to be a faithful witness. By bringing together all these phrases from *Psalm* 89, John fosters the establishment of a secure and abiding kingship.

Indeed, the reference to "firstborn" in the psalm is directly associated not only with kingship in general but with the highest kingship on the earth. That is exactly the kind of kingship John envisions here for Jesus Christ: "I will make him the first-born, the highest of the kings of the earth." Just as God is the Almighty One (the ruler of all creation), so Jesus is ruler of the entire human realm (the ruler over the kings of the earth). This is the revelation of Jesus Christ.

This is a revelation bound inevitably for conflict, particularly in a context in which Rome already lays claim to ultimate kingship. Indeed, "kings of the earth" is a phrase used throughout *Revelation* to refer to opponents of God's kingdom (6:15; 17:2; 18:3, 9; 19:19; cf. 16:14).[21] Jesus' kingship, by claiming to be the one abiding and universal kingship, necessarily resists the already established kingdoms that are making the same claim. In John's context there is only one kingdom to be resisted, namely, Rome.

This passage commends the characterization of Jesus as the faithful witness to the behavior of his hearers (cf. also 3:14). "The phrase 'the faithful witness' points to Jesus, not only as the revealer from heaven but as the one who also, like the Christians in John's churches, once stood before the Roman authorities. He had borne his witness, even at the cost of his life."[22] This is the part of the description that Christians can emulate. Although they cannot be the firstborn of the dead or the ruler of the kings of the earth, nevertheless they can, like Antipas (2:13) and like

John himself (1:2), be faithful witnesses to the witness that Jesus himself bears—that God is the Almighty One and that Jesus Christ is his coming king. In their cultural context, to bear such witness is also to broker a very dangerous form of political as well as religious resistance.

Revelation 1:9-11

Here we see how John commends his own witness to his hearers. John declares himself to be on the island of Patmos "on account of the word of God, that is, the witness borne by Jesus." A clarification of John's language is important here. The phrase "on account of" could mean either "in order to" (bear the witness borne by Jesus) or "as a result of" (bearing the witness borne by Jesus). Eugene Boring points out that the phrase "on account of" is always used in *Revelation* "for the result of an action, not its purpose. John has been banished to Patmos *because* he had been preaching the Christian message."[23] That message is Jesus' own witness to his universal and abiding kingship.

John is here commending his own actions, lifting himself up as a model to be imitated. And therein also lies the text's ethics. John calls himself his hearers' partner; in doing so, he also challenges them to live up to the standards of that partnership. As he held to the witness borne by Jesus, despite the consequences, so must they. Such a witness is an *active* resistance. To witness that Jesus Christ is king in a world that actively proclaims the lordship of Rome and Caesar is to act obstinately. It is to resist, to refuse to fit in. Even more, if you add to that declaration of witness the belief that God is coming soon to inaugurate Christ's kingship and to make a kingdom of Christ's followers, you invite "tribulation." In such a context, endurance cannot mean passive waiting in the face of what Rome is doing. Rather, it means a continued resolve to keep witnessing even though this witness, by its very nature, provokes an angry Roman response.

Revelation 2:12-17

John's letter to Pergamum provides a good example of his call for active resistance. In Pergamum, a hostile response to the witness of Jesus' universal and exclusive Lordship would be expected. Pergamum was the capital city of the Asian province, a hotbed of pagan cults and emperor interest, "a citadel of Hellenistic civilization in Asia"[24] and "the center of imperial worship for the whole region."[25]

The particular issue at hand was the eating of meat sacrificed to foreign deities. Participation in feasts where such food was available was one of the key ways in which members of a community integrated themselves into the larger populace. John believed that such "integration" came at too high a price. He believed that followers of Christ needed to make a stand. If they truly believed that Jesus was the Lord of history, then they must live in a way that showed it. He therefore demanded that they refuse to partake of any rite or to eat any food consecrated to any other person's or power's lordship—no matter what the consequences.

And so, through his portrayal of Antipas as one who was executed in Pergamum, he commends resistance rather than accommodation. John commends Antipas by describing him, like Jesus, as "that faithful witness of mine" or "the faithful witness of me." That suggests not only that Antipas witnessed to what Jesus witnessed to (the kingship of Jesus) but that he died "because of" it, and it makes his tragic character worthy of emulation. Indeed, John commends those who have behaved like Antipas (2:13) and condemns those who have not (2:14-16). John celebrates those who have held fast, even though such defiance in such a place can lead to the kind of end that claimed Antipas.

The directive is clear: The community at Pergamum, in spite of the consequences, must be what Antipas had been—a faithful witness to the kingship of Christ. They must resist the temptation to acquiesce to the demands of the Roman cultic/political infrastructure, demands that stemmed from the foundational belief that Caesar is Lord and Rome is the universal and abiding kingdom. In other words, the language of witness, whether it is related to Jesus Christ, John, or one of John's fellow believers, calls for an active resistance to contemporary cultic and political expectations. Such resistance is so controversial and provocative that it can lead to death. Hence, John is not commending believers to act passively but to act oppositionally—to resist any devotion to the lordship of Rome and its many client deities. He is asking them to testify to the Lordship of another and, in so doing, to put themselves directly in harm's way.

Revelation 6:9-11

Here John has a vision of the souls of martyrs waiting beneath the altar in heaven. The formula "the word of God, which is the testimony borne by Jesus," is repeated here. This time John makes a causal connection perfectly clear; it is "because of" their witness to Jesus' Lordship that believers have suffered. Witnessing to the Lordship of Christ has caused their physical deaths.

And this is why the souls are crying out for justice. They want God to vindicate their testimony that Christ is King. For as long as justice is delayed, those who deny this witness will continue to believe Rome's lordship instead. So they wait beneath the heavenly altar for God's action. However, their passive waiting in heaven does not imply that they had waited passively on earth. They are slaughtered souls in heaven precisely because they had actively witnessed to the testimony that Jesus is the ultimate Lord of human history in a world where Rome laid vicious claim to its own witness of ultimate authority.

Ironically, the witness that caused the deaths of the faithful also participates in the historical transformation that it seeks. Even as the souls cry out for God to act, their earthly compatriots continue the transformative effort they began. The souls in heaven have but a little while to wait for justice, just until the deaths of witnesses like themselves have come to a completion. In this way, then, the deaths actually contribute to the coming of God's kingdom.

John is not, however, commending death. He is instead commending witness, even though he knows that such witness will inevitably lead to tribulation and perhaps death. A progressive formula becomes clear. The witnessing leads to the death of the witnesses, and the death of the witnesses in turn leads to the coming of God's justice. The active witnessing, not the dying, is in the primary position. It is the witnessing that believers can control. They cannot control whether Rome will respond with censure, appropriation of property, denial of social privilege, exile, or death. But they can control whether they will witness to the Lordship of Jesus Christ. The more who witness, the more intolerable will become the word that is witnessed, and the more belligerently Rome will be forced to act. It is the provocative witnessing that brings on Rome's response, which in turn will result in God's action against it.

It is the witnessing, then, that leads to the coming of God's justice. Dying is a result; witnessing is the cause. It is witnessing that John commends. For it is witnessing that plays a synergistic role with God's own efforts to accomplish the universal and abiding Lordship of Jesus Christ. This is the revelation of Jesus Christ.

Final Discourses: Completing the Case

Chapter 12 provides another example of witness material that is to be read in light of earlier passages. The reader sees that the key characterization here is neither the divine child, the supernatural woman, nor the aggrieved dragon. It is instead the almost anonymous "them" (12:10) who become the active "they" (12:11). "They" are the people who "keep the word of God, which is the testimony borne by Jesus" (12:17). Again, the relationship between witnessing and suffering is causal: *because* they keep witnessing, they are continually hounded by the power that denies that testimony. But the passage says something more, something that on the surface seems startling, but for which the reader has been prepared: What they do will have a transformative effect. "They" will conquer the dragon. "They" will break the back of the force that is behind Rome. "They" will shatter its claim to lordship.

Once again John uses the language of instrumentality.[26] The relationship between witnessing and transformative victory is causal. "They" will conquer "because of" the blood of the Lamb. Here, of course, "they" are dependent upon divine action in Jesus that they themselves cannot emulate. Though their blood too will spill, it cannot have the redemptive and victorious effect of the blood of the Lamb. But John does not stop here. He continues with another "because of" statement that places them in partnership with God: because of their witness, they will conquer.

John's language leads to a crucial conclusion: by obstinately proclaiming the Lordship of Christ, they help to bring that Lordship about, *even* in a world that believes in and prosecutes the lordship of Rome. As Walter Wink wrote:

> We must not fail to observe the implications of this. If it is right to say that the basis for a new order of society is God's word of judgment pronounced in Christ, then it follows that the witnesses who proclaimed that word to challenge the prevailing political order, were not acting anti-politically at all, but were confronting a false political order with the foundation of a true one. We must claim John for the point of view which sees criticism, when founded in truth, as genuine political engagement.[27]

This is witness that serves not only as active resistance but also as triumphant cultic, social, and political transformation. *This* is the revelation of Jesus Christ.

Some Concluding Thoughts: Reclaiming the Language of Apocalyptic

For the African American church the apocalyptic language of resistance in the *Book of Revelation* ought to be an integral part of the personal and corporate language of faith in a contemporary way. It is the language of the powerless, the language of future hope presently realized. It is the language of the future because the present often speaks in such destructive ways.

African American churches hear the present destructive news of our collective circumstances—racial profiling, the return of extensive re-segregation of our nation's schools, the revival of hate groups that target people based on ethnicity and race, the pervasive preponderance of the impoverished and the destitute, the cries of the hopeless in our inner cities, and the wave of political conservatism that exhorts accommodation to United States society. Because most African Americans in this country still count themselves among the most impoverished and oppressed,[28] John's message to resist, to refuse to accommodate to the present social, economic, and political way of life, is still a necessary message. His language of resistance, as the slaves rightly understood in their time, must remain a vital part of the African American language—if African American Christian language is to remain the language of hope for the future in the midst of an unbearable present.

African American Christians must therefore reclaim the language. Unfortunately, in much of our middle- and upper-class Christian circles, *Revelation* sounds creepy and misguided, violent and deranged. And so, through its lack of use, the language has been surrendered to extremists like David Koresh or fundamentalist groups who misuse it as a literal plan for their kind of future. The crazier the people who use the book, the crazier the book itself seems to be. That is because we are looking at the book through the lens of *their* realities and issues. We allow those issues to determine how we should understand the book and whether the book should be preached and taught. Like the early Christian search for a canon, many contemporary African Americans are not sure *Revelation* should be a part of our heritage. To be sure, there is some good prophetic imagery there (chapters 1–3, the letters to the churches, talk of a new heaven and a new earth), but all the rest—the sevens and the twelves, the seals and the bowls and the trumpets, the whores and the madonnas, the Lamb and the blood, the lakes of fire and the 144,000 saved from it—all of that seems too far out and too inexplicable except to those who have an extremist or fundamentalist agenda.

But the messages for the African American community are all too relevant. Among middle- and upper-class African Americans who have attained a measure of freedom, there is the danger of accommodation. Like the listeners in the churches of Asia Minor who had much to lose by resisting Rome, so also many African Americans today may be tempted to accommodate to the dominant culture in such a way as to abandon others who continue to suffer the brunt of discrimination and oppression. The question becomes: Are they going to accommodate, or will they choose to resist the oppressor and thereby voluntarily enter a situation in which they too might risk loss and oppression? The perspective and vision of *Revelation* can enable people to see clearly the dynamics of the present oppression and motivate them to embrace solidarity with those who suffer.

I am suggesting that the apocalyptic imagery we find in *Revelation* can be the foundation of a potent social and political ethics, if we will engage its symbolic potential through the lens we find in the slave narratives. Through such a lens, the language of *Revelation* clearly promotes an ethics of social, religious, and political resistance.

John's text, then, has a particular ethical agenda in mind. He wants the hearers and the readers of this text to do something. To endure. To witness. To resist accommodation to the practices and trends of their time and culture, no matter how much it costs them, and to do so in a way that helps precipitate the rushing in of the kingdom. He shows them a future where "what ought to be," God in charge and God's people vindicated, has become "what is."

This is why I say that *Revelation*, like the slave narratives I have used as a lens, is a "historical" apocalypse. Though it envisions the future and the heavenly world, it does not encourage its hearers and readers to escape there. Rather, the visions are encouragement to do the kinds of things that are necessary, in history, to transform the world. That is what the imagery and symbolism are about.

What Zora Neale Hurston said about the spirituals, that they were really only spirituals when sung in the context of the oppression that birthed them, should also be said about *Revelation*. To understand *Revelation*, we must view it from John's perspective, namely, "from below"—from the point of view of the suffering ones who are resisting oppression. Otherwise it sounds vengeful, spiteful, and escapist. Elisabeth Schüssler Fiorenza makes a helpful analogy between *Revelation* and Martin Luther King Jr. She points out that the outcry for divine justice in *Revelation* is borne out of the experience that no Christian who was denounced by his or her neighbors could receive justice from a Roman court. Similarly, she argues, Martin Luther King Jr.'s *Letter from a Birmingham Jail* "addresses experiences and hopes similar to the theology of *Revelation*. . . . His indictment of racist White America cannot be construed as 'hatred of civilization' or as 'envy' deficient of Christian love for one's enemies, if the dehumanizing power of racism is understood as evil."[29]

Does *Revelation* have a place in our present world? Absolutely, as long as we understand the book in light of its context and apply it to those current situations that correspond with that context, namely, situations "from below." For in situations "from below," the powerful imagery of *Revelation* may well have the same provocative effect for us as it did for John's first hearers—to encourage endurance and to provoke a transformative witness that can make "what should be" into "what is." Such power is available to us. That is the truth of *Revelation*. That is the truth out there.

Notes

1. John Blassingame, editor, *Slave Testimony: Two Centuries of Letters, Speeches, and Autobiographies*, 372.

2. Ibid., 276–77. The hoped-for reunion took place seventeen years later in Canada.

3. James Weldon Johnson, ed. *The Book of American Negro Spirituals*, 162–63.

4. Ibid.

5. George C. L. Cummings, "The Slave Narrative as a Source of Black Theological Discourse: The Spirit and Eschatology," 65.

6. James H. Cone, "The Meaning of Heaven in Black Spirituals," 60, in *Heaven*, edited by Bas Van Iersel and Edward Schillerbecks.

7. Dwight Hopkins, "Slave Theology in the 'Invisible Institution,' " 14–15.

8. Blassingame, *Slave Testimony*, 378.

9. Cited by Albert L. Raboteau, *A Fire in the Bones: Reflections on African-American Religious History*, 12.

10. Johnson, *The Book of Negro Spirituals*, 86–88.

11. For further discussion of the spirituals as resistance language, see Brian K. Blount, *Cultural Interpretation: Reorienting New Testament Criticism*, 55–69.

12. See Elisabeth Schüssler Fiorenza, *Revelation: Vision of a Just World*, 54. Under the Flavian emperors, particularly Domitian, "the Asian Provinces strongly promoted the imperial cult."

13. Only two of the seven churches are depicted as poor. Note also how this implies their economic non-participation in the wealth described in chapter 18.

14. David Aune, *Revelation 1-5*, 6.

15. Ibid., 7.

16. Eugene Boring, *Revelation*, 67.

17. See also Adela Yarbro Collins, "The Political Perspective of the Revelation to John," 241–42, and Pablo Richard, *Apocalypse: A People's Commentary on the Book of Revelation*, 18–19.

18. Allen Callahan, "The Language of the Apocalypse," 453–70.

19. Boring, *Revelation*, 75.

20. Gregory Beale, *The Book of Revelation: A Commentary on the Greek Text*, 247; cf. 192.

21. Ibid, 191.

22. Boring, *Revelation*, 76.

23. Ibid., 82.

24. Schüssler Fiorenza, *Revelation*, 54.

25. Richard, *Apocalypse*, 57.

26. Beale, *The Book of Revelation*, 663–64.

27. Walter Wink, "Biblical Theology and Social Ethics," 90.

28. Blount, *Go Preach!*, 199–267; Mark Lewis Taylor, *The Executed God: The Way of the Cross in Lockdown America*.

29. Schüssler Fiorenza, *Revelation*, 11–12.

2

Revelation: Clarity and Ambivalence,
A Hispanic/Cuban American Perspective

■ ■

Justo L. González

Introduction

A Matter of Perspective

When an artist paints a landscape, the resultant piece has much to do with the artist's perspective and interests: Is the artist standing on this hill or on another? Is her primary interest in colors, in shapes, in light, or in textures? The answers to such questions help us to understand the manner in which the artist "reads" the landscape. Likewise, when someone interprets a text, that interpretation is significantly affected by the interpreter's perspective, experiences, and questions. It is for this reason that I begin this essay with a few words about myself, my perspectives, and my method of interpretation.

As I was growing up, the *Book of Revelation* was very seldom read or used in our church. We were Protestants (Methodists) in a country (Cuba) that was, at that point, almost entirely Roman Catholic, at least nominally. There were fewer than ten thousand Methodists in the entire country, which had an overall population of more than six million people. Other "mainline" denominations (Presbyterians, Episcopalians, Baptists, Lutherans) were even smaller, or not much larger than ours. In total, between 5 and 7 percent of the population of Cuba were Protestants. The typical and stereotypical images that my classmates had of Protestants were derived either from the rather conservative Catholic priests and nuns who taught in many schools or from their encounters with radical Protestants who claimed to know exactly when the Lord was coming, who the Beast was, and whether we were on the fifth or the sixth trumpet.

47

Given that situation, it is not surprising that we tended to shy away from the *Book of Revelation*, with its weird visions, multi-headed monsters, and words of woe. We did not want to be lumped together with people like the apparently mad man who stood at the entrance to our high school and predicted the rolling up of the sky and the coming of the great tribulation. The result was that, besides our knowing that it was a strange book, just about all we knew of *Revelation* were a few phrases taken out of context, such as "Behold, I stand at the door and knock." We also sang many hymns inspired by passages in *Revelation*, although we did not know that!

Then, through a series of circumstances and after some time teaching in Puerto Rico, I came to live in the United States. In my new context, as in my former one, the *Book of Revelation* was often used as the happy hunting ground for people with strange ideas. The Beast was Mao. The Beast was the Soviet Union. The Beast was the European Common Market. The Beast was the Mid-East oil cartel. Much of this was very similar to what I had heard in my own homeland, and it did little to increase my interest in *Revelation*.

And, once again, I was a minority, but now I was no longer a religious minority. Now I was a minority because of my ethnicity, my culture, and my accent. In the dominant culture, I generally belonged, by virtue of being a Protestant, to the religious majority. Yet within my ethnic minority, the Latino community, I was still in the religious minority—again because I was a Protestant! In both the Latino community and the wider society, people who paid much attention to the last book of the New Testament and who sought to decipher its meaning for the present were generally considered to be quite strange and profoundly alienated both from the mainstream of society and apparently also from themselves! I had no desire to be counted among them, and therefore I had little interest in the visions of *Revelation* or in its beasts and cups of wrath.

Those were the years of the so-called Cold War—which may have been "cold" in the United States and in the Soviet Union, but not in Vietnam, in Central America, or in Angola. While generally agreeing with the need to stop the ravages of totalitarianism in various parts of the world, I also became profoundly aware of—and angry at—the apparent inability of American foreign policy to understand the dreams, the pain, and the aspirations of other peoples. When such aspirations challenged the vested interests of large corporations, it sufficed to raise the specter of communism, and all sorts of mayhem seemed to be justified—much as today the specter of terrorism is employed to justify egregious violations of national and international law. Then came the welcome collapse of the "evil empire" of the Soviet Union, with the not-so-welcome implication that the remaining empire (the United States) was good and that it could do no evil—and that therefore any who resisted or criticized it, from Osama bin Laden to Jacques Chirac, were evil.

At a more personal level, it was also during those years that I became deeply and existentially aware of the enormous importance that culture plays in all our lives and of the difficulties and ambiguities of life in multicultural settings such as the United States. I had always considered myself fairly bilingual and bicultural. Yet I soon discovered that such self-perception was much easier when I saw myself as a visitor in the dominant culture than when I became a more permanent resident within it. I soon learned that the interaction among cultures is a complex and often painful process, that cultures are not fixed realities, that they always exist and develop within the context of encounters with other cultures, that they both require and resist change, and that there is an inherent tribalism in all of us that tends to obscure these realities. The ambiguities of being a Latino in the United States is typically expressed in images such as *mestizaje*[1] and "living on the hyphen." It then occurred to me that in a way my experience was similar to John's as he was writing *Revelation*. As a Jew, he had had the experience of being a minority in a society dominated by other cultures and other religions. Then as a Christian he had the experience of being marginalized within his own Jewish community. And now, as he is given a word from God, he must deliver to these mostly Jewish Christian congregations a message that transcends the limits of their horizons.

I was working on these issues when the United Methodist Women asked my wife and me to write a study book on *Revelation*. It was to be a simple book, designed for a series of Bible studies.[2] But the task of writing it was not so simple, for it became apparent that *Revelation* had much to say to our present situation and that the reasons why so many of us tended to ignore it were subtle and complex. Later, we were asked to write a fuller commentary on *Revelation*, thus continuing a process that had begun long before.[3]

It is through the lenses of these experiences and concerns that I have come to read the *Book of Revelation*. But I also read it with a particular method, grounded on a theological perspective that I must now clarify.

A Method of Interpretation

At this point, I must begin by declaring that my interest in the book of *Revelation* is not merely historical. I am certainly interested in matters such as who wrote the book, why, where, and what the author's sources may have been. But all of this is of secondary importance, since I read *Revelation* first of all as an authoritative book, as part of a canon through which God's will is manifested, not only to me but also to the church at large.

Having said that, I must add that this does not mean that I am siding with the apparently mad fanatic who stood at the door of my school shouting words of doom, nor that I see any value in any of the various readings that today tell us that the beast is Saddam Hussein or Osama bin Laden or that we are now on the sixth trumpet or that the restoration of the state of Israel is a sign of the impending end. Throughout history there have been many such interpretations, and up to now all have been proven wrong by the mere passage of time![4]

This, however, is not the only reason why I find little value in any such interpretations. Another reason is that they contradict the repeated biblical injunction that the dating of the end-times is none of our business (*Mark* 13:32; *Acts* 1:7). Another is that, in spite of all that we are told to the contrary, were we to be able to date the end, this would not make us any more obedient, but rather less. If I know, for instance, that the Lord is coming ten years from now, I have a few more years before I really have to worry about making things right. (I remember that when I was a child and our parents would leave us at home with a number of tasks, telling us when to expect them, we simply postponed the assigned tasks to the last possible minute.)

A much more important reason to reject such interpretations is that they are based on a misconception regarding the meaning of the word "prophecy." *Revelation* refers to itself as a book of "prophecy" (1:3), and on that basis these interpreters turn it into a sort of crystal ball through which they can look into the future and foretell the order of events to come. But in biblical usage, "prophecy" does not refer necessarily to foretelling the future. A prophet is anyone who speaks for God, and a prophecy is any such speech. Thus, *1 Corinthians* 13 and *Romans* 7 are prophecies as much as *Revelation* 17.

However, the main reason why any such interpretations fall short is that by making *Revelation* into a sort of program for the latter days, they rob the book of any value or relevance for any other time. A *TV Guide* is very useful for a particular week. During that week, we can use it to find out what will be happening next, or where we have to look to see a particular program. But it is practically useless both before and after that particular week. After its date, the best use to be made of it is to tear it up and recycle the paper. Before its date, it is also useless, for the "Thursday" to which it refers is not my "Thursday."

Likewise, when *Revelation* is turned into a sort of program for the latter days and the claim is made that we are living in those latter days, the implication is that when Martin Luther read this book in the sixteenth century and when John Wesley read it in the eighteenth, this book was supposed to tell them only that the end would come in the twenty-first century. Even worse, such interpretations imply that when John in his exile on Patmos wrote to the suffering and perplexed churches in Asia, all he had to tell them was that at some distant point in the twenty-first century the seventh trumpet would sound and the end would come—in other words, John's book was scarcely a word addressed to the very real and immediate needs and concerns of his readers.

How, then, are we to interpret *Revelation*? Simply—just as we interpret the rest of Scripture. When we read, for instance, that God called Moses, that God used him to liberate Israel, and that God gave him the Law, we do not turn these accounts into an announcement of future events. We read the text as historical narrative. And yet, we read it for more than mere—and even questionable—historical information. We read it as depicting a pattern of the way God relates with God's people. As Christians have read this story of Moses through the centuries, they have come to the conclusion that God calls, that God frees, and that God commands.

It is in this manner that the New Testament frequently uses the Hebrew Scriptures. Thus, for instance, the Gospel writer says that Jesus and his family fled to Egypt and that thus the prophecy was fulfilled, "Out of Egypt I called my Son" (*Matthew* 2:15). The author of *Matthew* is quoting *Hosea* 11:1, which actually refers to the story of the exodus out of Egypt and speaks of the people of Israel as God's "son." The Gospel writer knew that the words of Hosea referred to Israel and to the exodus. But even so, they referred also to Jesus and to his flight to and return from Egypt.

One of the verses in the Hebrew Scriptures most often quoted in the New Testament is *Psalm* 118:22: "The stone which the builders rejected has become the head of the corner." This is an ancient psalm in which the people of Israel praised God for the vindication of the weak and the despised. In the Gospels (*Matthew* 21:42; *Mark* 12:10; *Luke* 20:17), Jesus quotes this line in the context of the parable of the wicked laborers in the vineyard. At least in *Matthew* and *Luke*, Jesus quotes these words as a sign that the owner of the vineyard will give it to others; for just as a builder may take a rejected stone and turn it into the most important one, so can the owner of the vineyard take it away from its present keepers and give it to others. In *Acts* 4:11, Peter quotes the same text, but now applying it to Jesus: "This is the stone which was rejected by you builders, but which has become the head of the corner." And in *1 Peter* 2 it is also applied to Jesus, but now with the further purpose of claiming that Jesus' followers, even though themselves rejected and despised, are living stones in God's great edifice. In these various interpretations, the pattern is the same: rejection by the builders, and acceptance and vindication by God.

What we have here is a sort of interpretation that takes history seriously. History is important because it does not repeat itself; it is always new. And yet history is worth studying, because there are patterns that appear repeatedly and because by looking at those patterns we may draw some guidance for our particular moment in history.

It is in this manner that I choose to interpret the book of *Revelation*—not as a sort of *TV Guide* for future events that had nothing to say to John's contemporaries and not just as a specific message for a particular group of churches in Asia Minor at a particular time, but rather as a message that, precisely because it spoke concretely to besieged believers in the late first century, also speaks concretely to believers early in the twenty-first century.

This means that one way to show the relevance of *Revelation* for our day and our setting is to relate the context of *Revelation* to our own context, to see how *Revela-*

tion deals with its own context, and then to see how this may provide guidance for our own life in our present context.

Three Fields of Interest

By relating what I said at the beginning to what I have just said about my method of interpretation, the reader will understand why part of what I find significant in the *Book of Revelation* is its basic attitude in relation to its context, namely, its critique of the existing political order and its resistance of it—even in hope against all hope. The reader will also understand why in most of my work on *Revelation* I focus my attention on three related dimensions of the original context of *Revelation*, which are paralleled by similar dimensions in my context. These have to do with (1) the geopolitical order, (2) the economic order, and (3) cross-cultural encounters. While much could be said about each of these, the limitations of this essay compel me to focus my attention on just a few of the passages that relate to these various contexts.

The Geopolitical Order

The region that John knew as Asia Minor (which today we know as Turkey) had long been torn by the conflicting interests of mighty empires. In the glory days of Greece, it was here, in Ionia, that Persian imperialism most often clashed with Greek culture, traditions, and independence. Now, in John's time, the entire region was the meeting point of the two mighty empires of Persia and Rome. Toward the east, the kingdom of Armenia subsisted with difficulty as a buffer state between Rome and Persia. While clearly within the bounds of the Roman Empire, Asia Minor was sufficiently close to the Persian border that there was always the fear of spies and infiltration. This was one reason why loyalty to the Roman emperor was so important. In order to bolster and to express such loyalty, temples to Rome as a goddess had been built, and emperor worship was stressed—as is seen in the correspondence between a regional Roman official by the name of Pliny and the Emperor Trajan, penned just a few years after John wrote *Revelation*.

In such circumstances, any criticism of Rome, her government, or her policies could easily be construed as treason or at least as pro-Persian sentiments, just as in the late twentieth century in Central America any criticism or opposition to the overwhelming presence of the United States was labeled communist. From the point of view of Roman authorities, whoever did not support them was clearly an enemy, a subversive element, and most likely an agent of Persian policies and ambitions. Nevertheless, in *Revelation*, John levels major critiques against the Roman Empire and calls for resistance to it.

In *Revelation*, John shows no love or admiration for Persia. Indeed, the first of the famous "four horsemen of the Apocalypse" most likely refers to Persia, whose armies consisted mostly of cavalry armed with bows and arrows: "And I saw, and behold, a white horse, and its rider had a bow; and a crown was given to him, and he went out conquering and to conquer" (6:2). But then we come to the second rider, which represents a different empire: "And out came another horse, bright red; its rider was permitted to take peace from the earth, so that men should slay one another; and he was given a great sword" (6:4).

If the first rider represents Persia, this second rider represents Rome. The "great sword" that this rider carries is not a military weapon. In Greek there are two different names for a sword. One word refers to the short and relatively light sword carried by the legionaries. The other, which is the word used here, refers to the large and fairly unwieldy sword of the executioner, which was also used as a symbol of the higher Roman magistrates' authority to condemn to death—the "authority of the sword" or *jus gladii*. Significantly, while Rome boasted of the great peace it had brought to the world, the famous *Pax Romana*, John tells us that this horseman, the one who wields the sword of imperial authority, goes out to take peace away from the earth. At this point, it is good to remember that the so-called Roman peace was greatly resented by many of the subjugated peoples and that at least every few years rebellion broke out in one province or another—and quite often in more than in one province at a time. These rebellions were crushed by military might and by the wholesale application of the "authority of the sword" represented by this "great sword," which the second rider carries—although death by decapitation was reserved for citizens and other privileged cases, while the rest were often crucified or killed in other cruel fashions.

In short, while John did not believe—as some probably did—that liberation from Roman oppression would come through Persian might, this did not keep him from naming the evil brought about by Roman rule.

Similar reflections are prompted by the much debated "beast from the sea" that first appears in chapter 13: "And I saw a beast rising out of the sea, with ten horns and seven heads, with ten diadems upon its horns and a blasphemous name upon its heads." There has been much discussion about the meaning of the ten horns and seven heads, which has also led to many a depiction of this beast as having the appearance of a horrible monster. This, however, is a misinterpretation of symbolic imagery, for the Lamb of God is also depicted as having seven horns and seven eyes (5:6). Numbers seven and ten are numbers of perfection. This means that the beast from the sea is depicted as apparently having the fullness of power and of government. It is, therefore, not an unattractive beast. But then, this apparent perfection is contradicted in that it has "a blasphemous name upon its heads." The beast is not frightening in its appearance, but even so, it is blasphemous—it is insulting to God.

Who or what, then, is this beast? For readers in Asia Minor, generally looking out upon the Aegean Sea, Rome and its might came from the sea. By sea came the provincial governors, and by sea came also the legions, particularly when unrest or the threat of rebellion required the rapid movement of troops. By sea came the tax collectors, and the sea seemed to swallow much of the wealth of the land. The beast from the sea is none other than Rome itself and its imperial might: powerful (as with ten horns) and apparently indestructible (as with seven heads), but still carrying a blasphemous name and still opposing the will of God. By such symbolism, John exposes the evil of the Roman Empire.

In addition, John critiques local authorities who collaborate with the Romans. We see this in the beast out of the earth: "Then I saw another beast which rose out of the earth; it had two horns like a lamb and it spoke like a dragon" (13:11). This beast also looks as if it is one thing (a lamb) while in truth it is something else (a dragon). John makes it very clear that this beast has no real power on its own but is subservient to the beast from the sea, whose power and policies it serves. In Asia Minor, apparently springing out of the earth itself, there was an entire native structure that served Rome. Indeed, much of the area had become part of the Roman Empire through a bequest from the king of Pergamum, making Rome his heir. And thereafter, not only in Pergamum, but also in Smyrna and several other cities, there was a vast cadre of natives who survived and flourished by collaborating with Rome as tax collectors, minor functionaries, and magistrates. (Something similar happens today in many countries subjected to the neocolonialism of the twentieth and twenty-first centuries, where a cadre of military, merchants, and others—often called "Herodians" by those who oppose them—prosper as a result of their collaboration with the neocolonial system.)

It is, however, in chapter 17 where John makes it most clear that his symbolism is referring to Rome and to its misuse of its might. This is the well-known depiction of the great harlot, drunk with the blood of the martyrs. As a side note, it is interesting, illuminating, and tragic to observe that, while practically all Christians are aware of the image of the great harlot of chapter 17, the woman clothed in the sun who appears in chapter 11, which is a very positive figure, has been practically ignored in the popular imagery of *Revelation*—except in some traditional depictions of that figure as Mary, the mother of Jesus. I find this interesting, illuminating, and tragic because it shows the degree to which biblical interpretation and the selection of passages to be studied have been marred by stereotypes of gender, such that feminine figures with negative connotations are much more studied than their positive counterparts.

There would have been little doubt for a first- or second-century reader that the image of the great harlot referred to Rome, sitting on seven mountains (17:9) and clothed in imperial purple (17:4).[5] In addition, "the kings of the earth have committed fornication" with her (17:2), and she is given the symbolic title of "Babylon the great, mother of harlots and of earth's abominations" (17:5). The point here is so obvious that it needs no further explanation. For John, Rome has become a new Babylon, a harlot drunk on the blood of the martyrs, and a tool of the Dragon. And this does not mean simply the urban center that was called Rome. It is important to remember that in the context of first-century Greek, a *polis* ("city") was both an urban center and a state. Thus, "Rome" is the city itself, but it is also its system of government, its imperial power.

Significantly, the *Book of Revelation* is in a sense a tale of two cities: the city of Rome and the new city that John sees coming down from heaven. These cities are not just urban centers; they represent entirely different ways of organizing life—or, as we would say today, conflicting world orders. *Revelation* is therefore a radical critique of Rome's geopolitical order—and, by extension, of every world order that falls short of John's vision of the heavenly city. This is a word that is particularly relevant for Christians living in any society—including ours—that claims divine sanctions for its socio-political order.

The Economic Order

The second dimension of the context of *Revelation* that I wish to highlight is the economic order. World orders do not exist independently of economic orders. Organizing the world in a particular order implies also distributing its resources in a particular order. Imperial Rome is not just a political empire, in which various nations are now ruled by the center; it is also an economic empire, in which the resources of the conquered lands are made to flow toward the center. Rome's rule over its provinces is also Rome's economic exploitation of its provinces.

In the passage about the great harlot, *Revelation* alludes to this connection between political rule and economic exploitation. The harlot Rome is depicted as "seated upon many waters." This is a traditional image that often depicts a rich and powerful city as standing amid rivers or on the seashore. The reason for this symbolism is that in the ancient world most long-distance trade took place over waterways—rivers and seas—rather than by land. A few luxury items, such as silk from the Orient, did travel overland in caravans, but trade on a large scale was much more feasible over water than across land. It was much more difficult and expensive, for example, to carry tons of wheat to Rome by oxcart over the Apennines than to carry the same load by ship from Sicily or from Egypt. For this reason, one way to say that a city was wealthy was to speak of it as standing among the waters—at the crossroads of trade. Consider, for example, what *Jeremiah* 51:13 proclaims about Babylon: "O you who dwell by many waters, rich in treasures, your end has come."

In *Revelation* 17, this imagery from Jeremiah of a rich and powerful city as living by many waters appears once again, but now with a new twist. The angel tells John that "the waters that you saw, where the harlot is seated, are peoples and multitudes and nations and tongues." In other words, Rome is rich because she sits over the peoples of the earth like so many waters, and the riches of the world flow toward her. John condemns the imperial order of Rome, not only because Rome persecutes Christians and Rome blasphemes against God, but also because Rome has become rich by exploiting the peoples of the earth. The geopolitical system of government is yoked with an economic order in which riches flow from the provinces to the center, from the conquered to the conquerors.

John's critique of the existing economic order—or disorder—is not limited to this particular passage. Since I referred above to the first two "horsemen of the Apocalypse," it may be well to refer now to the third. This rider emerges when the third seal is broken. Following the first rider carrying a bow and the second rider carrying a mighty sword, one would expect this rider to carry an instrument of destruction. And he does. But it is a subtler weapon of destruction. This rider carries a balance, a symbol of trade. This does not seem as deadly a weapon as the bow of the first rider or the sword of the second, and this may be why in the case of the third rider a voice is heard that explains how this rider brings about death and destruction. Indeed, as this rider emerges, a voice is heard: "A quart of wheat for a denarius, and three quarts of barley for a denarius, but do not harm oil and wine" (6:6).

To understand the significance of these words—which would have been obvious to John's readers in Asia Minor—one must take into account what was happening in Asia Minor in terms of agriculture and economics. When this region was annexed by Rome, it was self-sufficient in the production of food. But then Roman capital moved in, and the very fertile lands of the province were bought by senators and other wealthy Romans, who soon discovered that land devoted to vineyards and to olive groves yielded greater profits than land devoted to cereal grains. The result was that very soon, while the rich in the province accumulated wealth, the poor found it very difficult to buy the wheat that was at the center of their daily diet. Domitian sought to remedy the situation by limiting the production of wine and oil and thereby forcing landowners to plant cereals. But the outcry was so great and the influence of the powerful was so strong that the project was abandoned. The result was greater inflationary pressures on the price of cereals—and greater hunger among the population at large. The prices that the voice in *Revelation* quotes represent a twelve-fold rise in the cost of wheat and an eight-fold rise in the price of barley—which in normal times was seldom eaten by people but was used rather for animal fodder. A denarius was the typical daily wage for a laborer, before taxes. Thus, even apart from taxes and other expenses, the most wheat that a laborer could buy in a day was roughly a quart of unhulled grain—just about enough for a rather small loaf of bread.

Thus, the geopolitical order is not just a matter of world politics, of empires and kingdoms; it is also a matter of people going hungry, of families not being able to sustain themselves, and of the rich and the powerful making sure that the system continues working for the benefit of those in power, even if it means hunger and starvation for others.

This is why John comes to the point where he is actually calling on his readers to resist the existing economic order by opting out of it: "Come out of her, my people!" (18:4). He explains to them that in order to participate in the Roman economic order, they must have the mark of the beast: "it [the Roman beast] causes all, both small and great, both rich and poor, both free and slave, to be marked on the right hand or the forehead, so that no one can buy or sell unless he has the mark, that is, the name of the beast or the number of its name" (13:16-17). In other words, the economic order has been organized by the political beast, and it results in exploitation such that a quart of wheat costs a denarius. So, in John's view, what the faithful are expected to do is to resist by opting out, to refrain from participating in that order.

It is impossible to know what John's alternative was. Was he actually calling on Christians in Asia Minor to opt out of all exchange, to withdraw into a self-sufficient community, growing all their food and producing whatever else the community might need? It is difficult to imagine how they could do that, particularly since John is writing to urban churches, most of whose members made a living as craftsmen and day laborers. Perhaps what he intended was to have them resist the large-scale economic order by reverting to a barter, limited-scale economy. In any case, what is clear is that his book includes both a vehement protest against the existing economic order and a call to believers to refrain from its apparent benefits—which are really losses when seen within the context of the economy of God's reign or, in John's imagery, of God's city.

Cross-Cultural Encounters

Imperial systems of government and of economy invariably lead to greater cultural exchange and conflict. In the first century of the Christian era, the city of Rome was being flooded with people and ideas from all over the Roman Empire. Tacitus's complaint is well-known, that Rome had become "that cesspool for all that is base and sordid from every corner of the earth."[6] Suetonius comments that during the reign of Claudius, unrest among the Jewish population in Rome reached such a level that the emperor expelled them from the city.[7] And it was not only humans that were invading the city of Rome; the gods from all over the empire were also coming to the city. Tacitus refers, for instance, to the case of the aristocratic woman Pomponia Graecina, who was accused of "foreign superstition"—whatever that may have meant.[8] At approximately the same time that *Revelation* was written, the emperor's cousin Flavius Clemens and a former consul, Acilius Glabrio, were executed for "falling into Jewish practices" and for denying the gods, and Flavia Domitilla, the emperor's niece, was exiled under the same charges—which some scholars believe to be an indication that Flavius and the rest had become Christians.[9] Not only Christianity, but also other religions from the East, such as Judaism, the worship of the Magna Mater from Syria, the mysteries of Isis and Osiris, and others, were criticized by many who considered themselves "true Romans." And sometimes these religions were banned or placed under severe legal restrictions.

When we look at the persecution of Christians in this light, it is clear that many of those who persecuted Christianity—Trajan, Marcus Aurelius, Decius, Diocletian—saw their actions as measures to restore the classical glory of Rome, to return to the ancient gods and values, and to stop the growth of "foreign superstition." Even though Eusebius of Casearea, in his efforts to show the compatibility between the Empire and the church, claimed that most persecutions were the result of evil schemes on the part of misguided authorities, the fact is that the worst persecutions were led by rulers who sought to restore the glories of ancient Rome. In other words, they persecuted Christianity not because they misunderstood this new religion but rather because they understood it all too well—and saw it as subverting the traditional order and culture of the Empire.

At the same time, not all Romans rejected everything that was foreign. The very fact that cults and practices from the East had to be repeatedly suppressed is an indication that these cults and practices held an appeal for many Romans. Emperor Marcus Aurelius, who deplored the "superstition" of Christians, was nevertheless a staunch follower of the maxims of Stoicism—which after all was also an import from Greece. Among the learned in Rome, the Greek language (and culture) was often preferred to Latin. As is so often the case, cultures in apparent conflict influenced and penetrated each other, thus making cultural conflicts at once more bitter and more polarized.

The *Book of Revelation* acknowledges the variety of cultures and traditions in its context. Seven times in the book one finds variations of the phrase—ultimately borrowed from the book of Daniel—"every tribe, and language, and people, and nation." Sometimes this phrase appears in negative contexts, and sometimes in positive ones. For example, the throng who worship the lamb is comprised of people from "every tribe and tongue and people and nation," but the same is also true of those who worship the beast.[10]

A particularly illuminating use of this phrase appears precisely in the passage about the great harlot who sits on many waters (that is, who is rich), for we are told that "the waters that you saw, where the harlot is seated, are peoples and multitudes and nations and tongues" (17:15). In other words, the great harlot is rich because she sits on many peoples and multitudes and nations and tongues. Rome may believe itself to be rich because of its hard work, its superior skills, or the productivity of its labor force, but the truth is that Rome is rich because it has devised a system to exploit the wealth of other nations and peoples.

That being the case, there is nothing surprising about these various nations and languages and peoples being present in the city of Rome—turning it, as Tacitus would say, into a "cesspool." There is no doubt that where the rivers of wealth flow, there also flow the rivers of population. Some conservative elements in Britain and France today may deplore the high level of immigration from Africa and may even speak of being "invaded" by Africans, but this is simply the result of a colonial system, and later of a neocolonial system, so devised as to produce a flow of wealth from Africa to Britain and France. Some people in the United States may complain that they are being overrun by immigrants, that the borders are too porous, that their traditional culture and values are being challenged, but this is simply the result of economic and international policies so devised as to produce a constant flow of wealth from Latin America and other poor nations into the United States. It is not surprising that so much of the wealth of Mexico flows into the United States legally over the bridge and, at the same time, many Mexicans cross illegally under the bridge. Where the rivers of wealth flow, there too flow the rivers of population, and it is very difficult to promote one flow while stemming the other.

In this context, what I find fascinating about the *Book of Revelation* is precisely its acknowledgment—and perhaps even its reluctant acknowledgment—that the various peoples, nations, and tribes are part of a single plan of God—and that this is true of these tribes and nations not separately but jointly. There is probably no writer in the New Testament that is as deeply immersed in traditional religion, literature, and culture of Judaism as is John of Patmos. Practically every verse in his book contains at least one allusion to Jewish literature and practices. While all the other New Testament authors quote the Hebrew Scriptures from the existing Greek tradition (the Greek language version called the Septuagint), John uses his own translation.[11] The congregations to which he writes must also be mostly Jewish, for otherwise they would find it difficult to follow this book so full of allusions to Jewish traditions— just as we ourselves would find it difficult to understand *Revelation* if we were to ignore the origin and significance of those allusions. And yet this Jewish Christian, writing to congregations that are comprised mostly of Jewish Christians, announces a future in which "a great multitude which no one can number, from every nation, from all tribes and peoples and tongues" (7:9) will stand singing praise before the throne and before the Lamb.

In this regard, the passage that I find most poignant is the eating of the small scroll in chapter 10. This is clearly patterned after *Ezekiel* 2, where the prophet is also given a book to eat. However, in contrast to Ezekiel, who finds the book sweet, John finds it also to be bittersweet. He finds it sweet because it is God's promise, but he also finds it bittersweet because God's promise involves telling his own people that they are not particularly privileged before God, telling them about the many peoples and nations and languages and kings that have also been made heirs to the promise to Abraham.[12]

Today, many North American readers find themselves in a strangely dual situation. On the one hand, they are citizens of the most powerful and rich nation in the world, and in that nation they belong to the dominant culture. Thus, their experience is similar to Tacitus and many others, enjoying the fruits of empire, but pained by the manner in which the imperial order itself undermines the culture and traditions of the center. On the other hand, in contrast to those early Romans, these North American readers are Christians. As Christians in the dominant culture, they have long stood at the apparent center of the church, providing missionaries, financial resources, teachings, and so on to the rest of the worldwide church. Yet the time has come when the centers of Christian vitality are no longer in the North Atlantic, nor are they in the traditionally Christian nations of the dominant culture. In this respect, North American readers must often feel as John must have felt, having to tell his mostly Jewish congregations in Asia Minor (who were benefiting from the dominant Roman culture) about the many tribes and peoples and nations that had also become part of God's people—and that they themselves were no longer privileged or so central. On the contrary, they were being called to a solidarity with these oppressed and persecuted Christians throughout the Roman world. It is not an easy situation to be in. It is a situation that requires great understanding and patience on the part of other Christians.

Indeed, it is in many ways this strangely dual situation in which I too find myself, for I am very much a part of the dominant culture, and I benefit greatly from being part of that culture. Yet as a Christian, I stand at odds, in many ways, with the dominant culture. I am part of a church that has long had the support of the surrounding dominant society but that is now having to learn how to live and how to be obedient without such support—a lesson long ago learned by poorer churches in poorer countries. My location at the "center" of the church is being relativized by the emerging churches in many impoverished and colonized parts of the world, a situation that is placing me in radical solidarity with them. So I am being torn between the benefits I have as a result of being part of the dominant culture and my solidarity with a worldwide Christianity that challenges the political and economic policies of the dominant, imperial society.

It is this strangely dual situation that stands at the root of our ambivalence toward *Revelation*. The problem is not really that the book is too difficult to understand. The problem is rather that we use its difficult imagery and our perplexity over the meaning of this or that metaphor to hide from its message—which is altogether too clear. We are ambivalent about *Revelation* because we are ambivalent about our discipleship. We are ambivalent about our discipleship because we are quite comfortable in the present order—and yet claim to yearn for another. As a scholar, I benefit from an economic and social order that gives me the means and leisure to analyze texts and to write books. As a Christian, I know that there is much wrong with this order. As an American citizen, I benefit from the riches of our libraries and enjoy delving into the literary background of the *Book of Revelation*. As a Christian, I am challenged by its vision. I do not wish to bear the mark of the beast, and yet I am quite pleased with my ability to buy and to sell in the present order. With John and with *Revelation*, I pray "thy kingdom come," and "come, Lord Jesus!" Yet with many Christians through the ages, and even today, I also add "but not just now!"

Notes

1. A *mestizo* is a person of mixed breed—usually the descendant of Spanish and Indian fore-bears. The *mestizo* is neither Spanish nor Indian, and yet is both. In Latino theology in the United States, the classic discussion of this subject is Virgilio Elizondo, *Galilean Journey: The Mexican-American Promise*.

2. Catherine Gunsalus González and Justo L. González, *Vision at Patmos: Studies in the Book of Revelation*.

3. Catherine Gunsalus González and Justo L. González, *Revelation*.

4. There is a review of a number of such "prophecies" in Arthur W. Wainwright, *Mysterious Apocalypse: Interpreting the Book of Revelation*. See also my essay, "Los últimos tiempos en la historia de la iglesia," 87–110.

5. J. Massingberde Ford, *Revelation*, in the series The Anchor Bible, has argued that most of the *Book of Revelation* did not originate among Christians, but rather in the circle of John the Baptist, and that the great harlot is not Rome, but Jerusalem. This theory has found little support among New Testament scholars.

6. *Annals*, 15.44.

7. *Life of Claudius*, 25.4.

8. *Annals*, 13.32.

9. Dio Cassius, *Epitome*, 67.14.

10. I have discussed this quite fully, as well as how the encounter of cultures relates to the economic and geopolitical order, in *For the Healing of the Nations*. What is said above regarding the relationship between cultural encounters and economic orders is for the most part a summary of what I explored in that book.

11. It is commonly said that John is using a translation that is unknown to us. I am more inclined to think that he is simply translating from memory as he goes. I find myself doing this quite often when speaking extemporaneously in English. A Bible reference comes to my mind, and, since I know it by heart in Spanish but not in English, I simply translate it in my mind. The result is a quotation that my English-speaking listeners will recognize but that is not quite the same as any existing English translation.

12. For a fuller argument showing this to be the case, see *For the Healing of the Nations*, 85–91.

3
Coming Out of Babylon:
A First-World Reading of *Revelation* among Immigrants

■ ■

Harry O. Maier

Introduction

The truism that "you get out of something what you put into it" is, for biblical texts, nowhere more apt than in the *Book of Revelation*. John's *Apocalypse* is famous for its wide diversity of interpretations resulting from audiences of different times and places, using various exegetical tools, representing a host of social, cultural, and historical contexts, and crossing the gap separating text and interpreter in different ways to arrive at a compelling understanding.

Take the well-known example of *Revelation* 13:18, with its widely recognizable "Mark of the Beast." Here John asserts that this cryptic reference "calls for wisdom," and he says that he will "let those with understanding reckon the number of the beast, for it is a human number; and its number is six hundred and sixty-six" (13:18; see also 17:9). Whatever candidate our author had in mind when writing these words, the text has come to function as a kind of exegetical blank check, where interpreters representing their own cultural, geographical, and historical biases fill in the name that best addresses their context. Generations of biblical interpreters over two millennia—as socially and religiously diverse as Hippolytus of Rome, Joachim of Fiore, Martin Luther, Daniel and Philip Berrigan, and David Koresh—have done the math and made their own nomination for the award of "best hated": Nero, Domitian, the Holy Roman Emperor, the Pope, Napoleon, Adolf Hitler, Communism, the American government, a still-to-come one-world-ruler of the United Nations, and global capitalism. Add to this *Revelation*'s potent symbols, strange creatures, grotesque monsters, sacredly charged numerological patterns, and larger-than-life heroes and villains, each of which in its own way "calls for wisdom." The result is a text that people can—and do—make of what they want, sometimes without very noble intent.

This, alongside its extreme violence, is perhaps why less apocalyptically minded people have tended to shy away from the Bible's last book, challenged enough by the mysteries of the present and the past to let the promised mysteries of *Revelation* unfold as they may. But if statistics are anything to go by, non-readers of John's *Apocalypse* are the minority, especially in North America. Tim LaHaye and Barry B. Jenkin's twelve-part Left Behind series (a fictional telling of the end of the world as scripted by a pre-millennial chronicle based on *Revelation*) has sold over 32 million books in the United States, displacing even John Grisham from the number one spot on the *New York Times* best seller list. Three in five Americans believe that *Revelation* forecasts coming events, while two in five believe that those events are now unfolding.[1]

To the truism that "you get out of something what you put into it" may be added a second, more sobering one, that "what you expect usually happens." In other words, while many may be happy ignoring *Revelation*, this is a text that ends up not ignoring very many. The themes and tropes of *Revelation* echo through first-world popular culture in blockbuster films like *Armageddon, The Matrix,* and *The Terminator* series, even as they resound through the halls of political power as speech writers and decision makers draw on the millennial metaphors from *Revelation* to give voice to national dreams and international visions.[2]

The "War on Terrorism," to cite a potent first-world example, with its holy war rhetoric promising to rid the world of evil, is evidence that *Revelation* is alive and well in first-world political culture, shaping the public imagination and its expectations. The September 11th Memorial Service in the National Cathedral in Washington, D.C. had as its hymn of the day "The Battle Hymn of the Republic," that nineteenth-century warhorse based on the militaristic and gruesomely violent scene of *Revelation* 19:15: "He is trampling out the vintage/ Where the grapes of wrath are stored;/ He hath loosed his fateful lightning/ Of his terrible swift sword;/ His truth is marching on." This was the musical backdrop to President George W. Bush's memorial address, which included a series of apocalyptically charged promises that the victims' deaths would be avenged, foreshadowing the darker promises of the weeks and months ahead. "Just three days removed from these events, Americans do not yet have the distance of history," he said, "but our responsibility to history is already clear; to answer these attacks and rid the world of evil."

"Responsibility to history," to "rid the world of evil": this is a political millennialism (a utopianism instructed by apocalypse), certain of America's divinely appointed role to be a light to the nations, inspired to take action by the Bible's last book, which washes the world in red on the way toward the inevitable victory of good over evil. "They have attacked America because we are freedom's home and defender," President Bush would later say, his speechmakers playing on popular pieties and millennial motivations. In the days that followed, he would herald the War on Terrorism as "the first war of the new millennium." And, like those late medieval theologians similarly inspired by the Bible's last book to throw the infidel out of Jerusalem, he called it a crusade.

The Bush administration's first crusade of the new millennium (beginning now with the twenty-first century) with its justifications en route to a utopian world order, however, seemed in its historical certainty strangely similar to earlier crusades, themselves no less millennialist and arguably inspired by *Revelation*. A racially purified Christianity wedded to a thousand year Reich to realize German Manifest Destiny, the proletariat toppling the bourgeoisie in the historically appointed destiny of the worker rising victorious over the owners of the means of production, the inevitable victory of global industrial capital over the state-controlled economies of Communism and Democratic Socialism, utopia as the systematic spreading of materialism—each of these, however distant the family resemblance, bears the genetic trace of John's Apocalypse in its own narration of history and conflict leading toward a happy ending.[3] The "new" War on Terrorism is in fact old news. To adapt a quotation, those who ignore the *Book of Revelation* are likely to find themselves repeating it—usually without knowing it.[4]

Hence this essay. I am no exception, and neither are you. We are tethered to a shared fate of being read in innumerable and sophisticated ways by John's *Apocalypse*. For some it gives voice to our greatest hopes; for others, our worst nightmares. Pay close attention to the media: you will discover it regularly invoked in headlines, on the radio, and on TV. You may hate the last book of the Bible with its rivers of blood, its condemnations of the wicked to never-ending torment in a lake of burning fire, its gender stereotypes of whores and warriors, virgins and victors, its manichean dualisms of lambs and beasts, angels and demons, and its disposal of the old creation along with all the environmental holocausts that go with that transformation. You may stop reading *Revelation* and command your friends to do likewise—seal it, shut it, and bury it deep in a chest in your grandmother's attic, or throw it into the burning pit of Mount Doom. No matter. For the foreseeable future, the *Book of Revelation* is here to stay, if for no other reason than that your neighbor or your neighbor's neighbor is reading it.

This is a matter of ethical urgency, especially for first-world people. And here is my point: when the citizens of the most powerful nations and economies on the planet—indeed, in history—are having their civic and religious imaginations shaped by a book as complex and violent as the *Book of Revelation*, it is critical for them to understand as much as possible their entanglements with John's *Apocalypse*. Further, in interpretation generally and in biblical interpretation in particular, we tend to see what we are looking for. It is important, therefore, to reflect on the eyes—better, the I—doing the seeing, as a means to come to a more self-critical appraisal of *Revelation*. In this way, we will not become trapped like Narcissus by our own reflection.

Finally, because *Revelation* is read aloud in church, sung in its hymns, and chanted in its liturgies, those vouchsafed with the task of focusing the eyes of worshipers on particular aspects of the text are obliged to be as shrewd as serpents when joining text and context and when unleashing the potential of this apocalyptic book to shape our lives. This is especially so because amid first-world political and popular culture in matters related to John's *Apocalypse* and to apocalypse in general, the competition is fierce. When the going gets rough, the tough get exegetical.

Now it is no small or easy task to become critically acquainted with the biases and interpretive lenses we bring to the interpretation of Scripture or to the interpretation of anything, for that matter. The case for the Enlightenment notion of the individual—as one who has access to a-cultural, a-temporal, and a-historical categories integral to the means of reason and who could use these categories to measure and know the world—has disintegrated before the critique that social context and historical location affect every act of interpretation. With it has gone the idea of biblical interpretation as an exact objective science in which exegesis registers what a text says, like a photographic plate marking the traces of electrons emitted in a vacuum, before the work of taking up what it all means comes into play. The cool, detached, analytical exegete in his lab coat distancing himself as much as possible from his many prejudices that might influence the interpretation of data has been replaced by the sweaty exegete in her street clothes leaving her fingerprints all over the evidence. Culture, social location, tradition, experience, the history of the way we have come to think about things the way we do, the things that in a given time and place pass for common sense, the methodological tools and technologies used to analyze and express them, what we choose to see in a text and to ignore—these are the "street clothes" and "fingerprints" of our latter-day interpreter. They shape the questions and interests we bring to the interpretation of texts, and they shape the answers we find in them. How vicious the resulting hermeneutical circle becomes depends upon how conscientious we are willing to be in engaging the factors just listed. The circle becomes a spiral when we learn to pose new questions and open ourselves to the possibility of different kinds of answers.

To return to *Revelation*: in what follows I offer a reading of John's *Apocalypse* conscious of my own first-world social location as a privileged white male Canadian enjoying the material benefits and the security of living next to the United States. I take notice of a spiral journey from context to text and back again to draw readings from *Revelation* relevant to my own social location. What the text impresses upon me has my fingerprints all over it, sweaty reader that I am. While there may be overlap, they are not your impressions or fingerprints. I write hoping you will take note of yours, how they came to be, and how your readings and judgments of *Revelation* urge you to live.

Apocalypse 1945–Apocalypse Now

I am the son of German refugees who were evicted from Eastern Europe after the Second World War as a consequence of what today we would call ethnic cleansing.[5] I was born less than a decade after my family's arrival in Canada when the trauma of expulsion was still fresh and family members were struggling to adapt to the dominant English-speaking culture of western Canada. I grew up surrounded by a German-Canadian community of similarly expelled people who claimed all the rights and benefits of Canadian citizenship but who urged a critical distance from its Anglophone culture. Having suffered the betrayal of National Socialism, the shame of defeat, and brutalization by victors, like many of the expellees I have come to know, my family was suspicious of the people and culture around them. Though Canadian, I was urged, "Vergiss nie deine Heimat!" ("Never forget your homeland.") As I was growing up in the 1960s and 70s and the horrors of the Holocaust and the Nazi era were fresh topics in the popular media, I was nevertheless urged to be proud of my German heritage and to demonstrate my cultural superiority to "Canadians" by dressing well, working hard, excelling at school, and pursuing a career.

Such exhortations were intended to distance me from Canadian culture; ironically, they helped me to assimilate to its English-speaking culture and to benefit from its post-war economic prosperity. On the other hand, the language voicing these exhortations to responsibility and success—the first language I learned as a child—was a strange mixture of poor English and half-forgotten German. Regular conversations recalling the loss of homeland and recounting traumatic memories of rape, executions, and torture, told in the strangely inflected tones and queer grammar of immigrants, created in me a kind of "double-talk." Such experiences meant that, however much I assimilated to the dominant culture, the memory of dislocation and loss would accompany me as I grew into an adult. I would always be in some way an outsider looking on or listening in—both on the trauma I did not personally experience and on the nationalist hopes and dreams I was encouraged by the culture around me to embrace as my own. To borrow a phrase from Julia Kristeva, the language that spoke me into cultural consciousness made me "a stranger to myself," articulating within me an irreducible foreignness.[6]

In postcolonial political theory, this experience of being a stranger is called "hybridity," a term deployed variously by different theorists but in its most general formulation used to describe the complex social processes that result when dominant and subjugated cultures interact and define themselves against one another.[7]

As the horticultural metaphor implies, hybridity describes the mutation of both colonizer and colonized in the process of exchange.[8] To be hybrid is to be a cross-species, to have a double identity even as a single face is presented to the world. The not-quite-English/not-quite-German that was my first language created an in-between identity to occupy the ambivalent space of the hyphenated German-Canadian citizen. Ambivalent space here refers to a double social location; it also refers to an unease with the protocols of industry, self-sacrifice, and commitment to the social order demanded by a burgeoning Canadian economy and commended by German ethnic identity. The German efficiency, know-how, and strict adherence to law and order celebrated by the immigrant culture in which I grew up certainly resulted historically in technological advance, economic growth, and social stability. Rarely admitted, however, was how these same values contributed to the deadly efficiencies of the Holocaust and other state-orchestrated terrors of the Nazi era.

Industry and efficiency similarly translated into North American material prosperity as new immigrants contributed to the economic development of post-war Canadian society. Absent, however, was an ethical analysis of the dependency of that prosperity on the industrial-military order south of the border or of how North American economic development and military policy affected the rest of the world. The apocalypse of 1945 with my family's traumatic tales of state betrayal, expulsion, and privation might have given rise to cultural- and self-critique. Instead, it occasioned an anxiety, on the one hand, to *remain invisible* and "not make waves" (by imagining the unlikely possibility of another expulsion) or paradoxically, on the other hand, to *become visible* (by proving ethnic and cultural superiority through material success).

Still, the doubled vision of being German-Canadian invited a refocusing of cultural lenses and a cross-examination of prevailing ideals. As I grew up and learned about the fascist horrors of the Nazis and about the economic, military, and environmental horrors of the capitalist West, such rehearsed trauma from Apocalypse 1945 led me to take a closer look at the surrounding social order and familial patterns of adaptation. Stories of homelessness invited a reappraisal of being at home in the post-war Canadian socio-economic order and of the exhortations to seek refuge in the German immigrant adaptation to it. The effect of these stories was to nurture a posture of being critically "in between"—a product of both, irreducibly neither, critically distant from either.

This is the social location that shapes me to be a particular reader of *Revelation*. I grew up hearing stories of traumatic endings and hopeful new beginnings. I have been urged by the social order around me to believe in a secular millennial vision of endless economic growth that will achieve global prosperity and national security. John's *Apocalypse* is not the sole determinant in making either my family story or that of the secular West compelling. Still, it is a sacred text that has shaped

Western consciousness in sometimes overt, more usually subtle ways, and it would be imprudent to ignore its influence. It certainly has left its mark on the immigrant culture in which I grew up.

For example, in my family's recollection of their experience of the years leading up to and following the war, themes and metaphors from *Revelation* were often invoked: Adolf Hitler first as a Messiah bringing stability and prosperity and then as Antichrist bringing horror, betrayal, and persecution; the German-Soviet battlefield as Armageddon; the destruction of Germany as divine punishment for idolatry; Canada as New Jerusalem, land of promise; material blessing as reward for faithfulness, hard work, and commitment. Such a reading of *Revelation* "at home" mirrors a more public influence. *Revelation* has been a key text in shaping the multiple European and North American subcultures that comprise the Christian/post-Christian West, and it continues to furnish the leaders of Western states with a narrative mythos for interpreting the world, envisioning the future, and understanding daily experience.

What is *Revelation* if not a tale of tragic endings and promising beginnings—the prototypical North American immigrant story? How does it end if not in a vision of a prosperous future with roads paved in gold and the rulers of the earth forever bringing their endless wealth through the bejeweled gates of a secure Heavenly Jerusalem (21:15-26)—the capitalist millennial dream? Does it not promise reward and victory over adversity to those who endure (2:9; 3:10; 7:13-17; 12:10-11)? Without an unquenchable hope in a happy ending, my family would have perished in the undertow of trauma. For the reward of ever-greater prosperity, Western citizens of the first world are willing to endure hundred-hour work weeks, to commit global suicide in exploiting the last drop of the earth's non-renewable resources, and to allow the state to break international law abroad while restricting civil liberties at home.

Given the kind of gravitational pull *Revelation* continues to exert on Western culture, I find myself complaining with Luther that "my spirit cannot fit itself into this book."[9] And yet when I scratch the surface of my social location I find its spirit staring me in the face. Like many others, I see much in John's *Revelation* and its history of interpretation that troubles me—its dualisms, its militarism and violence, its gender stereotypes, its visions of ecological destruction. These notions are hardly conducive to living constructively in a global village torn apart by conflict and perched precariously at the edge of environmental collapse.

However, *Revelation* also troubles in more positive ways—in its critique of imperial power, its call to steadfast witness, its analysis of the interrelation of politics and worship, and its cross-examination of economic exploitation and the politics of domination. Reflection on my particular social location has led me to a reading of *Revelation* in which I see John of Patmos urging his audience to take up a provocative position of resistance to and witness against the forces of economic exploitation and military domination of the Roman Empire.

As we shall see, *Revelation* offers a double view as John takes up images and ideology borrowed from the imperial cult of the emperor in order to reverse them by applying them to the victim of imperial power, the slain lamb, the crucified Jesus of Nazareth. John cross-examines the promises of Roman imperial ideology to deliver peace and security, and he urges upon his audience a posture of critical counter-imperial witness. Such a reading urges resistance to competing readings of *Revelation* that are at home in North American popular culture and that are influential in the shaping of American civil religion. In my reading, *Revelation* is neither a script for a best-selling series forecasting pre-millennialist doom nor a motivation-booster to assure a bruised nation of its historical destiny. Rather, it is a form of resistance literature urging its audience to see the world through the lens of a hybrid double vision, and by learning from what one sees to become a stranger to oneself in the cross examination of culturally favored millennial schemes and utopian ideologies.

Reading from Laodicea

Apocalyptic literature is often accounted for as a response to suffering or disappointed expectation. The phrase "cognitive dissonance" is a technical term used by social historians to explain the source of apocalyptic scenarios and expectations.[10] The phrase describes the conflict of identity that arises when a group that is convinced of its elect identity has its expectations shattered by suffering or oppression. Since suffering and oppression can take many forms—including the mere threat or even imagination of persecution—some analysts of apocalyptic use the phrase "relative deprivation" to take account of the social and psychological dimensions that entail disappointed hope.[11] On this account, the cognitive dissonance arising from (relative) deprivation is overcome by an appeal to an apocalyptic narrative in which deprivation is seen as part of a larger divine plan wherein God battles the forces of evil, with divine victory and the vindication of religious hope assured from the outset.

The theory of cognitive dissonance thus interprets apocalyptic literature generally and the *Book of Revelation* in particular as a form of theodicy. Applied to *Revelation*, this approach theorizes that John wrote his apocalypse as a means to shore up disappointed religious expectation arising from imperial persecution and religious oppression. John composed *Revelation* to comfort Christians in Asia Minor who were being oppressed as a consequence of their refusal to acknowledge the divine claims of the emperor or to participate in his imperial cult. John thus urged them to hold fast, and he held up for them the promise of divine reward for faithful endurance.

Revelation does indeed address itself—at least through narrative representation—to disappointed expectation, and it offers comfort to the persecuted and oppressed. There is a lively debate in scholarship on *Revelation* concerning just what form the historical persecution took, if there even was any, that lies behind this book.[12] In the world of the text, if not in the world behind it, John portrays characters either directly harassed or anxious about their future. John encourages members of the churches of Smyrna and Philadelphia to remain faithful in the face of direct or threatened persecution (2:8-11; 3:7-13). His vision of the martyrs who are gathered below God's heavenly altar crying for justice and who are given white robes and told "to rest a little longer until the number of [your] fellow servants and [your] brethren [is] complete" (6:11) assures those who are suffering that God is in control and remains faithful. That affirmation is implicit in his confident exhortations to endurance (2:2,19; 3:10; 13:10; 14:12), as well as his visions of the glorified white-robed martyrs divinely rewarded for their faithful suffering (7:1-17; 12:10-11; see 14:13; 15:2-4; 20:1-4, 6; 22:1-5). If John's audience was experiencing persecution or anxiety about its future, such passages must have been comforting to them, just as these passages have offered comfort as well as inspiration and hope to so many over the two thousand years that they have made their way into the hymnody, spirituals, and sacred liturgies accompanying the faithful through difficult times.

But this is only half of *Revelation*'s story. John addresses seven churches in *Revelation*, and five of them (2:1-7, 12-17, 18-29; 3:1-6, 14-22) are neither encouraged nor comforted; rather, they are warned. John criticizes the church of Laodicea for being lukewarm and for trusting in its wealth: "For you say, I am rich, I have prospered, and I need nothing; not knowing that you are wretched, pitiable, poor, blind, and naked" (3:17). Members of two of the churches (Pergamum and Thyatira—2:14-15, 20) are charged with idolatry and eating food sacrificed to idols. John complains that Christians in Ephesus have lost their first love (2:1-7) and that those at Sardis are half-dead (3:1-6). Thus, if *Revelation* functions as comfort for the suffering believers, it offers prophetic admonition for the rich and self-satisfied who are tempted by idolatry. *Revelation* promises vengeance on behalf of the slain righteous ones who are waiting for justice below God's heavenly altar; it pledges despair and dismay to the wealthy rulers of the earth and to the merchants and shipmasters who prosper for a time from economic relations with Babylon (that is, Rome) but who are destined to lament her inevitable divinely appointed destruction (18:1-19). As we shall see in what follows, those darker omens are no idle threats. John paints his portraits of despair for maximum effect. The lamenting rulers and merchants of chapter 18 act out before the rich and self-satisfied of Laodicea, the idolatrous of Pergamum and Thyatira, and the fickle of Ephesus the drama that awaits them unless they repent.

For the patiently enduring Smyrnaeans and Philadelphians, the apocalyptic visions that unfold from chapter 5 onward function to shore up hope and invite the faithful to hold fast in anticipation of God's promised coming. But for the impenitent among John's audience, John offers a darker future. The visions in which the impenitent idolaters (9:20; 16:9,11) and the earth's powerful and wealthy rulers (6:15-17; 17:4,15-18; 19:17-21; 20:7-10) suffer horrifying and gruesome scenes of divine punishment function as a kind of mirror with which they are to consider themselves. Readers will misunderstand these visions if they read them only as descriptions of the fate of the persecutors of the seven churches. These visions form the central plank of John's rhetorical strategy to persuade his listeners not so much that persecutors are doomed, but that certain members of his audience of believers are also doomed if they continue along a certain path. The line separating the idolatrous from the faithful is drawn not around the churches but through their center. Six times he warns his audience to repent (2:5,16, 21, 22; 3:3, 19), and then he shows what will happen to those who do not.

Recent scholarship has analyzed John's complaints against the civic, economic, and religious imperial culture of first-century Asia Minor in order to come to a fuller understanding of John's charges of idolatry and his criticism of the Laodiceans.[13] Whereas in contemporary Western secular society religion operates more or less separately from politics and economics, in ancient society they were inextricably interwoven. In the first-century Roman Empire of John's *Apocalypse*, the stability of the economic and political order was believed to rely on proper religious observance and ritual. One of the chief obligations of the reigning emperor was to preserve the *Pax Romana*, the Roman peace, by assuring the blessing of the *Pax deum*, the peace of the gods, through the proper performance and protection of traditional religious ritual.[14] The economic and political order of imperial provinces and local cities was similarly believed to rest on correct religious observance and ritual—whether conducted by ruling elites in fulfilling civic obligations of governance or by family members in securing the blessing of household gods on the hearth or by leaders of the Empire's countless trade guilds and clubs to secure divine patronage in business enterprises. The genius of Roman political administration was its ability to adapt itself to and to appropriate local religious and civic festivals in a way that mutually benefited imperial rule and local rulers. The cult of the Roman emperor shrewdly positioned itself in provincial and civic cultures, adapting itself to local religious beliefs, but reconfiguring them as a means of celebrating the divinely appointed rule of Caesar.

And it was as shrewdly welcomed. In first-century Asia Minor, for example, where the imperial cult was practiced at both the provincial and municipal imperial level, popular enthusiasm for the cult of the Roman emperor offered opportunities for local elites to win honor and promote their social standing by winning elections as high priests and acting as caretakers (*neokoroi*) of the cult's temples.[15] This arrangement translated into social stability for the imperial regime and the integration of elites, together with the cities and provinces they governed, into the Empire. For the rank and file members of provincial municipalities, participation in civic religious celebrations was a means of expressing civic pride and securing the social and economic well-being of cities by winning divine, not to mention imperial, favor. Devotion to the imperial cult was a way for provinces to benefit locally through guarding and promoting the well-being of the Empire as a whole. There was no shortage of ancient authors on hand to praise the socio-religious and political order of imperial rule as the source of unparalleled economic and social advantages and to conclude that such advantages were proof of divine blessing and of the piety of the imperial overlords.[16]

Thus, when John complains that some members of his audience were promoting the consumption of food offered to idols, that specific charge makes sense when read against the backdrop of imperial civic culture and the religio-social means its citizens used to preserve it. The criticism that the Laodiceans are rich and need nothing possibly reflects what John judges to be a too enthusiastic endorsement of the material goods arising from the socio-religious and economic order of imperial Asia Minor. In such an interpretation, it is significant that John narrates the destruction of Babylon (18:9-19) in the provocative form of an after-the-fact lament voiced in the first person by governing elites (vv. 9-10), then by merchants (vv. 11-17), and finally by maritime traders (vv. 16-19)—each of whom gaze upon the city's ruin and express their loss. These were precisely the ones who were gaining the most from the Empire's political, economic, and religious arrangements and who therefore had the most to lose from the Empire's demise.[17] Nor is it an accident that John's famous vision of the "Mark of the Beast" (13:11-18) interweaves religion (here idolatrous worship of the image of the beast: vv. 14-15) with economics (the ability to buy and sell: vv. 16-17).[18] In doing so, John seeks to expose a benighted *Pax Romana* as an impious sham and to urge his audience toward a more critical appraisal of its surrounding culture.

John was not the only inhabitant of the Roman Empire critical of the social order around him.[19] *Pax Romana* describes the often brutal military and economically exploitative rule of "pacified" peoples by a conquering power, and there were many ancient observers on hand to offer a frank appraisal of the inconsistencies between the lived reality of the vast majority of the Roman Empire's inhabitants and the official representation of the *Pax* they were invited to celebrate.[20] Even a panegyrist of the Roman order like the first-century pagan philosopher and moralist Plutarch had to remind elites aspiring to public office that they were subjects living in states controlled by Rome and that it was prudent "not to have great pride or confidence in your crown, since you see the boots of Roman soldiers just above your head."[21]

John's *Revelation* is unique, however, for the way it combines the imagery and ideals of Roman imperial rule with the literary form of an apocalypse. *Revelation*'s criticism of Rome is idiosyncratic for the way it inverts reigning socio-religious, economic, and political ideology by applying that ideology's imagery to the victim of empire, the slain lamb Jesus Christ. This results in a highly ironic reading of empire even as the Roman Empire is mimicked in portraits of divine power and heavenly blessing. *Revelation* creates a kind of double-vision and hybridity as the Empire's utopian *Pax* is unveiled as a demonic counterfeit, and as the victim of empire looks ever more imperial as John's visions unfold.

Parodies of Empire

There is a lively debate over whether John's *Revelation* replaces one form of imperial domination with another and whether his lauded hero, the slain lamb, is an emperor in sheep's clothing.[22] I side with those who argue that John's application of imperial metaphor to the slain lamb does not resolve in an alternative politics of domination. On this account *Revelation* destabilizes domination by offering a cross-examination of attempts to achieve utopian bliss through the application of imperial might, even that form of utopia apocalyptically guaranteed by divine omnipotence.[23] John's *Apocalypse* offers us a lamb in emperor's clothing and, in doing so, turns empire and conventional notions of divine omnipotence on their head.

My preference for this reading arises from a close exegesis of the text. But it is also rooted in my own hybrid social location as a son of immigrants who were expelled from one empire only to find themselves resisting the embrace of another. As I indicated above, the effect of this was to create a sense of being "in between" cultures. Like many children of immigrants, the dislocation of being neither one nor the other and yet equally both nurtured a sense of ironical detachment from the powerful cultural and economic forces surrounding me.[24] Linda Hutcheon, surveying the contribution of first-generation immigrant literature to Canadian culture, observes what she calls "the subversive doubling within and against the dominant."[25] The *Book of Revelation*, I am arguing, offers a form of ironical detachment that takes the shape of active cultural resistance—indeed a subversive doubling against the dominant culture of imperial Rome. It is an interesting question whether exegesis alone would have convinced me of this reading, especially since I also see the alternative account in many ways persuasive. The interpretation of *Revelation* is conditioned by socio-cultural location.

Recent studies have shown that an important source for the imagery and narratives of John's apocalyptic visions reflect the ideology, the iconography, and the pagan mythology associated with Roman rule and the imperial cult; indeed, they mirror the actual rituals in the imperial throne room. John seems, for example, to model his vision of the heavenly throne room (4:1—5:14) after the imperial one. Repetitive acclamations of praise shouted by subjects and court attendants to the emperor, torches of fire, bowls of incense, dignitaries surrounding the throne, the luxuries of dress and architecture, *proskynesis* or ritualized obeisance to the divine ruler, the opening of a scroll to read a decree—all of this belongs to the drama and ritual of the Roman court.[26] John applies this imagery in his throne room vision. However, instead of putting a powerful emperor at the center of these representations of imperial might, he places the victim of empire, the slain lamb (5:6, 9, 12).

Furthermore, from this throne room with imperial praise ironically being offered to this unlikely character, thunder and lightning issue forth, either directly or indirectly by characters and events originating there (4:5; 6:1; 8:5; 10:3,4; 11:19; 14:2; 16:18; 19:6). This is more than apocalyptic light and sound effects—it is pointed imperial politics. Imperial iconography regularly depicts emperors using lightning imagery as a means of representing their divine descent from Jupiter, whose emblems were thunder and lightning.[27] The resulting juxtaposition of imperial acclamation and iconography with a vision of "a Lamb standing as though it had been slain" (5:5) creates an exceedingly rich narrative tension that the rest of *Revelation* seeks to exploit. That juxtaposition poses a provocative question for those members of John's audience at home in the Roman Empire. Is it from a Roman imperial throne room with Caesar at its center that a divinely appointed order streams forth? Or is it from an alternative one, with a slain lamb standing at its center? If it is the latter, what does that order look like? How are people at home in the Roman Empire invited by this vision to interpret the social order surrounding them? How are they to respond to it?

A further inversion of political ideology appears in the apocalyptic drama and visionary imagery associated with the dragon and the beasts of chapters 12–13 and 17–18. Chapter 12 plays directly on imperial propaganda. The chapter replicates the narrative structure of a widely shared ancient myth associated with Python, Leto, and Apollo, and with Seth, Isis, and Horus.[28] Broadly outlined, these myths recount a dragon/giant/monster (Python/Seth-Typhon) pursuing a female figure (Leto/Isis), the defeat of the antagonist by a combat figure (Apollo/Horus), and the restoration of order. In Greek and Roman mythology, Apollo is the son of Zeus/Jupiter. Since imperial ideology and imagery represented Caesar as a divine son of Jupiter, the combat myth of Apollo's victory over Python was invoked in coins and other imperial media as a political celebration of imperial order brought about through Jupiter's divine descendants—successive Roman emperors—vanquishing anti-Roman challengers (the dragon, Seth-Typhon).[29] Imperial propaganda favored depictions of the emperor as Jupiter vanquishing the forces of chaos, restoring social order, and guaranteeing peace and concord.

In *Revelation*, however, Caesar takes up the role of Python, not Apollo. Far from representing a *Pax deum*, a peace of the gods, Caesar's rule arises as a consequence of war in heaven (12:7-12). And in the apocalyptic narrative of chapters 13 and 17, Caesar's rule becomes the means by which the dragon that was cast from heaven to earth pursues and destroys (God's people?) (12:4,12,13-15,17). Imperial rule, provocatively represented as beasts of the sea and of the land (13:1-10, 11-18), does not represent a divinely blessed civil and economic reign. It is, rather, a blasphemous (13:5-6) and idolatrous rule (13:4,8,12,15) made possible by the dragon (13:2). In Roman religion, a chaste protector of Rome at the furthest remove from the chaos symbolized by Python, Roma becomes in John's rhetorical program the great whore of Babylon (17:1-6) astride the mythological dragon (cf. 12:3), committing adultery with the rulers of the earth and drunk on the blood of those who worship God rightly—John's saints and martyrs unwilling to compromise with imperial rule.

Further, John applies imperial imagery to describe the victorious battles over God's enemies. *Revelation* 19:11-21—the proof text for the Battle Hymn of the Republic—offers a vision of apocalyptic destruction that draws from the combat imagery of the Hebrew Bible (especially *Isaiah* 63:1-6) depicting Yahweh as a mighty warrior victorious over Israel's enemies. However, the warrior—astride a white horse with a red robe and captions of military might inscribed on his thigh and leading a host of finely dressed soldiers—is also recognizably Roman; this image draws upon the iconography associated with the military culture of imperial Rome.[30] At first glance, as the glorious strains of the famous Battle Hymn suggest, this is a vision of conquest and of a mighty emperor exercising vengeance over the wicked. But a closer look reveals a profound destabilization of such military ideals. The robe the rider wears is red not with the blood of enemies, but his own, shed on account of his faithful testimony.[31] Earlier in *Revelation*, there is a similarly oxymoronic juxtaposition in which John sees the mighty rulers, generals, and elites of the Roman Empire (very similarly listed in 19:18-19) fleeing for their lives from the "wrath of the Lamb" (6:15-16). The warrior lamb thus becomes a burlesque of imperial might and power and urges a reappraisal of what power is and where it resides. Again, an irreducible hybridity flows forth from the surplus of apocalyptic metaphor that refuses to be contained either by imperial ideology or by traditional apocalyptic visions anticipating the destruction of the wicked. If it is a lamb dressed in warrior's clothing who charges forth to slay by being slain, then what will count as dominion and victory in this world? If his army is comprised of the nonviolent who defeat evil by nothing other than word of mouth, how are we to measure power? If apocalypses offer visions of endings and new beginnings, what kind of ending and beginning is being offered here?

Finally, John's vision of the heavenly Jerusalem (21:1—22:5) carefully parallels by way of contrast the vision of Babylon (17:1—18:24). The two visions play with ancient utopian civic ideals, but in a way that is destabilizing and disruptive. John furnishes both visions with identical introductions (17:1, 2; 21:9,10), and then systematically contrasts them. The whore Babylon clothes herself in orientalizing luxury to seduce her paramours (17:4); the chaste bride Jerusalem is adorned and bejeweled for her husband (21:3, 9-11, 19). The whore Babylon makes the saints suffer (17:6); Jerusalem is a city of healing for the nations, where there is no more suffering (21:2; 22:2). The kings of the earth gather to war against Babylon (17:16), and traders mourn the loss of their commerce with her (18:9-19); the kings of the earth bring their "glory and honor" into Jerusalem's gates and so show their allegiance to the heavenly city (21:24, 26). Babylon herself is impure and gathers fornicators (later her murderers) about her (17:2, 4, 5,16); Jerusalem bars murderers, fornicators, and idolaters from entering (21:8; 22:15). Babylon the "great/mighty city" (18:9, 16, 18, 19, 21) is outsized by giant Jerusalem (21:15-17). After Babylon's destruction, the city lies in darkness (18:23); night never falls in Jerusalem (21:23, 25; 22:5). The empty city Babylon bereft of all sounds of weddings (18:23) contrasts with heavenly Jerusalem descending in wedding celebration (21:2,9). In sum, John's depiction of Jerusalem re-sketches Babylon, but as a reversed image.

More than this, with its pastoral picture of a city situated around the green space of the tree of life (22:1-5), it offers a vision of a realized civic utopia promised in Greco-Roman political ideology but not delivered.[32] And it does so on terms foreign to pagan civic ideology—there is no temple in the city, symbol of civic pride and identity in the pagan polis and guarantee of the presence of the gods and access to their blessings. More to the point, there is no Sebasteion—the temple complex dedicated to emperor worship. Instead, "its temple is the Lord God the Almighty and the Lamb" (21:22), the latter having become in the course of John's visions an ironizing imperial double. It is to this Jerusalem, the reversal of Babylon, that wealth and peace come (21:22-26), a procession which, in the civic imperial ideology of the day, is the sign of divine blessing. The Laodicean of 3:17, boasting of wealth and prosperity gained from participation in an idolatrous Empire, is bound to be disappointed. Here is the place of solace and reward for the faithful Philadelphian (3:12) who has resisted Babylon's lure. The idolaters of the seven churches are destined to lament over Babylon's ruin; those who hold fast will reign over the nations in the City of God (2:26).

By this time in the *Apocalypse*, however, we may well wonder what the promise of being given "power over the nations" entails. John has trained us by the time we reach the ending of his apocalypse not to take anything at face value, and this includes its representations of power, wealth, might, and victory. John's Jerusalem is not a Rome *redux* with cleaner streets and safer neighborhoods. In contrast to an empire that deals in "human souls" (18:13), the New Jerusalem exists for the healing of the nations (22:2); if in the portrayal of Babylon luxury goods (18:12-13) flow from outlying areas to feed the appetites of elites with "dainties and splendor" (*ta lipara kai ta lampara*—18:14), in Jerusalem all enjoy the water of life "without price" (*dorean*—21:6; 22:17). The heavenly host earlier hail this order acclaiming, "The kingdom of the world has become the kingdom of our Lord and of his Christ, and he shall reign for ever and ever" (11:15). This is in fact what John's *Apocalypse* shows repeatedly—one kingdom/empire becoming another—but the Lord and Christ's *basileia* is no Doppelgänger, or phantom double. If it borrows the Empire's words and images, their content is all changed.

Coming Out

"Come out of her, my people," John's angel urges his audience in anticipation of Babylon's destruction (18:4). Indeed, John's apocalypse is a "coming out" tale and an invocation to be "queer." It is a call to emigration and the taking up of an ironically charged apocalyptic hybridity of exile by means of "a subversive doubling against the dominant." Replaying Empire so as to revise it, the *Book of Revelation* urges an irreducible foreignness upon the inhabitants of their first-century imperial order. Once led out by John's hermeneutical suspicion of the Roman order, however, it is not so clear where his ironical juxtapositions—of slain lamb as conquering emperor, of faithful witness-unto-death as victory, and of powerful rule as healing of nations—will in fact lead. What is clear is that his apocalypse does not envision a New Jerusalem in a utopia that is, as the etymology of the word suggests, "nowhere," or in the sweet hereafter. It is into the imperial present of John's first-century readers that John's narrative pitches the tent of a city where the nations come for healing and all are welcome without price. John's visions, however much they are famous for their future, insist upon the present: "Now the salvation and the power and the kingdom of our God and the authority of his Christ have come. . . ." (12:10).

As many commentators have pointed out, the plot of *Revelation* is not a straight line from past to present to future; rather, it is a spiral bringing future to the present and urging a reappraisal of contemporary preoccupations in the light of the paradoxically remembered hope of a future vision told in the past tense.[33] In *Revelation*, this paradoxical present is realized in worship—John receives his vision while "in the spirit on the Lord's Day" (1:10). And as his visions unfold revealing the things that "must soon take place" (1:1), John interjects portraits of heavenly worship told in the present tense (4:1—5:14; 7:1-12,15; 11:15-18; 12:10-12; 15:2-4; 19:1-8). Worship itself, then, is a place where "Jerusalem happens." Here, however, first-world readers must be careful, accustomed as we are, on the one hand, to the strict separation of church and state and, on the other hand, to a civic religion uncritically millennialist in its promotion of a global order.

Over a century ago, Alexis de Toqueville, observing the evangelical revivalism then sweeping the United States, remarked that however devout Americans were, their religious devotion was usually parochial—confined to the private recesses of the heart, removed from economic analysis and political activism, except in the inculcation of virtues designed to keep the machinery of capital running.[34] John's visions of worship do not allow such parochialism, nor do their ironic recapitulations of empire allow any straightforward millennial application. They are pitched against the worship that legitimizes the socio-religious political order of empire, and they call for a clear, even life-threatening choice as they call for witness that protests against an exploitative economic and military order. The protagonists of John's *Revelation* are witnesses to the alternative order presented by the slain lamb. John offers what one author calls a "martyr christology"; in *Revelation*, Jesus is "the faithful witness (*martys*)" (1:5), and those John celebrates are the ones who similarly bear testimony (*martyria* 6:9; 11:7; 12:11,17; 19:10; 20:4; see also, 2:13; 11:3; 17:6).[35]

However much his visions may be used in popular American religious culture to sell books and films portraying the imminent advent of a coming one-world government whose citizens must bear the Beast's indelible mark to buy and sell, *Revelation* will not so easily allow first-world citizens off the hook. It is not something future it unveils; it is something present it unmasks. To read *Revelation* in the contemporary first-world comfort of the middle class—that group for whom religious apocalyptic entertainment is marketed—is to risk coming away with the sinking sense that one is a Laodicean.[36]

The immigrant German-Canadian culture with which I grew up, which borrowed metaphors and themes from *Revelation* to give expression to what would otherwise have remained unspeakable horror, also offered "coming out tales." Invocations of John's *Apocalypse* were raw and visceral—its symbolism of evil was called upon to describe the extremities of human cruelty and ruin as millions fled for their lives. However, reading *Revelation* among immigrants adapting themselves to the capitalism of Canadian society meant overhearing only part of its message. New Jerusalem was uncritically slipped into Western capitalist comfort. Having fled one Babylon these immigrants seemed to fall into the embrace of what increasingly appears to be another. Still, the sense of uprootedness lingered in the rehearsed stories of Apocalypse 1945. The feeling of being foreign that came with it offered the possibility of an ironical double-vision of the hybrid. No longer German, not entirely Canadian, the double identity of being not really one and being complexly the other and of the distinctive testimony of being in the middle—from my own distinct first-world context, *this* has given me ears to "hear what the Spirit says to the churches" (2:7, 11, 17, 29: 3:6, 13, 22).

Notes

1. Nancy Gibbs, "The Bible and the Apocalypse."

2. For accounts of apocalyptic and John's *Apocalypse* in contemporary popular culture and the philosophical backdrop of modernity, see the highly readable accounts of Mark Kingswell, *Dreams of Millennium: Report from a Culture on the Brink*, and Eugen Weber, *Apocalypses: Prophecies, Cults and Millennial Beliefs through the Ages.*

3. For the relation of the *Apocalypse* to Marxist ideals, see Ernst Bloch, *The Principle of Hope*; for a millennialist appraisal of democratic capitalism, see Francis Fukuyama, *The End of History and the Last Man*, especially 287–339.

4. See Catherine Keller, *Apocalypse Now and Then: A Feminist Guide to the End of the World*, 1-20, who argues for the continuing usually unconscious hold of John's *Revelation* on contemporary Western culture.

5. Between 1945 and 1950, at least 8 million (some estimate as many as 15 million) ethnic Germans emigrated or were expelled from Eastern Europe, the largest mass migration of people in recorded history. For an account in English with citations, see Alfred M. de Zayas, *Nemesis at Potsdam: The Expulsion of Germans from the East*. For an account of emigration to Canada and Canadian immigration policies of the period, see Modris Ecksteins, *Walking since Daybreak: A Story of Eastern Europe, World War II, and the Heart of Our Century.*

6. Julia Kristeva, *Strangers to Ourselves.*

7. For a general overview see Bill Ashcroft, Gareth Griffiths, Hellen Tiffin, *Post-Colonial Studies: The Key Concepts*, 118–21.

8. See especially Homi K. Bhabha's essay, "Signs Taken for Wonders," in *The Location of Culture*, 102–23, at 110–16.

9. Martin Luther, "Preface to Revelation" in his 1522 Translation of the New Testament, *WA Bibel* Bd. 7, 404.

10. For cognitive dissonance in contemporary millenarian groups, see Leon Festinger, Henry W. Riecken, and Stanley Schachter, *When Prophecy Fails: A Social and Psychological Study of a Modern Group that Predicted the Destruction of the World*; for application to the *Book of Revelation* see John G. Gager, *Kingdom and Community: The Social World of Early Christianity.*

11. Thus, for example, Adela Yarbro Collins, *Crisis and Catharsis: The Power of the Apocalypse*, 104 5.

12. Theories range from no persecution and the use of persecution motifs rhetorically to fashion communal self-definition (Leonard I. Thompson, *The Book of Revelation: Apocalypse and Empire*, 95–167), to an insistence on *Revelation* as response to direct assault by imperial repression (Elisabeth Schüssler Fiorenza, *The Book of Revelation: Justice and Judgment*, 126–27, 193), to a latent fear of persecution arising from earlier persecutions under Nero and the martyrdom of Antipas (2:13) and sense of powerlessness in the face of Roman rule (Collins, *Crisis*, 160–61).

13. In particular, see the excellent study by Paul B. Duff, *Who Rides the Beast? Prophetic Rivalry and the Rhetoric of Crisis in the Churches of the Apocalypse*, as well as the earlier study by Thompson, *Revelation.*

14. For further discussion, see Karl Galinsky, *Augustan Culture: An Interpretive Introduction*, 288–31; Paul Zanker, *The Power of Images in the Age of Augustus*, 101–35, 167–238.

15. See the excellent study of Steven J. Friesen, *Imperial Cults and the Apocalypse of John: Reading Revelation in the Ruins*, 23–131; also S. R. F. Price, *Rituals and Power: The Roman Imperial Cult in Asia Minor*, 101–33, 234–48.

16 For references and discussion, see J. P. V. D. Balsdon, *Romans and Aliens*, especially his chapter "A Generally Good Press for Rome," 193–213.

17. For a fuller discussion of the socio-rhetorical significance of chapter 18 against the backdrop of imperial commerce and Asia Minor trade, see Richard Bauckham, *The Climax of Prophecy: Studies on the Book of Revelation*, 338–83; J. Nelson Kraybill, *Imperial Cult and Commerce in John's Apocalypse*.

18. For the promotion of the imperial cult in ancient trade associations, see Philip A. Harland, *Associations, Synagogues and Congregations: Claiming a Place in the Ancient World*.

19. Again, Balsdon, *Romans*, nicely gathers and summarizes the views of detractors who exposed the gap separating official ideologies of peace and tranquillity and daily life for the vast majority of the Empire's inhabitants; see, especially, "A Bad Press for Rome," 161–92.

20. See Klaus Wengst, *Pax Romana and the Peace of Jesus Christ*, 7–54; Gerardo Zampaglione, *The Idea of Peace in Antiquity*, 131–84.

21. Plutarch, *Praec. gerend. reipubl.* 17.813E.

22. Persuasive cases are offered by Robert M. Royalty Jr., *The Streets of Heaven: The Ideology of Wealth in the Apocalypse of John*; Stephen Moore, "The Beatific Vision as a Posing Exhibition: Revelation's Hypermasculine Deity," 27–55; Tina Pippin, *Death and Desire: The Rhetoric of Gender in the Apocalypse of John*.

23. Similarly, Loren L. Johns, *The Lamb Christology of John: An Investigation into Origins and Rhetorical Force*; Ronald L. Farmer, *Beyond the Impasse: The Promise of a Process Hermeneutic*; Friesen, *Imperial Cults*, 185–91, 197–201; David L. Barr, *Tales of the End: A Narrative Commentary on the Book of Revelation*, 145–47; Sophie Laws, *In the Light of the Lamb: Imagery, Parody, and Theology in the Apocalypse of John*.

24. Smaro Kamboureli, *In the Second Person*.

25. Linda Hutcheon, *Splitting Images: Contemporary Canadian Ironies*, 8.

26. For full discussion and cross-references, see David E. Aune, "The Influence of Roman Imperial Court Ceremonial on the Apocalypse of John," 5–26.

27. For Jovian theology and the cult of the emperor, see J. Rufus Fears, *Princeps a diis electus: The Divine Election of the Emperor as a Political Concept at Rome*, 220–22; "The Cult of Jupiter and Roman Imperial Ideology," 3–141.

28. Adela Yarbro Collins, *The Combat Myth in the Book of Revelation*.

29. See Jan Willem van Henten, "Dragon Myth and Imperial Ideology in Revelation 12-13," 508–9.

30. For detailed exegesis and cross-references, see my analysis in *Apocalypse Recalled: The Book of Revelation after Christendom*, 187–90 and notes.

31. Earlier in 7:13-14, John associates being clothed in fine linen and white clothing with being washed in the blood of the slain lamb—those who have been faithful to death even as Jesus was and who thus conquer as he did. The representation of the rider as "the Word of God" (19:13) who smites nations with a sharp sword issuing from his mouth refers to the faithful witness of Jesus to death, which in the rhetorical program of John's apocalypse is the means by which evil is vanquished (12:10-11).

32. For readings sensitive to John's appropriation and reconfiguration of imperial ideals in his vision of Jerusalem, see Klaus Wengst, "Babylon the Great and the New Jerusalem: The Visionary View of Political Reality in the Revelation of John," in Henning Graf Reventlow, Yair Hoffman, and Benjamin Uffenheimer, editors, *Politics and Theopolitics in the Bible and Postbiblical Literature*, 189–202; *Pax Romana*, 129–31; Dieter Georgi, "Die Visionen vom himmlischen Jerusalem im Apok 21 und 22," in Dieter Luhrmann and Georg Strecker, editors, *Kirche, Festschrift Günther Bornkamm*, 351–72; Barbara R. Rossing, *The Choice between Two Cities: Whore, Bride, and Empire in the Apocalypse*.

33. For a detailed discussion of *Revelation*'s transformation of the lived time of the reader through its uses of narrative past and telling of the future through retrospective reporting, see my treatment in *Apocalypse Recalled*, 123–63, as well as the thoughtful presentation of Barr, *Tales of*

the End; for *Revelation*'s plot as (hermeneutical) spiral; Schüssler Fiorenza, "Composition and Structure of the Book of Revelation," 344–66; and Collins, *Combat Myth*, 5–55.

34. Alexis de Toqueville, *Democracy in America*, 345–63, 652–58. De Toqueville's observations have been repeated by more recent observers of American religiosity: Peter Berger, *The Noise of Solemn Assemblies: Christian Commitment and the Religious Establishment in America* offers a representative, if dated, account.

35. See Mitchell G. Reddish, "Martyr Christology in the Apocalypse," 85–95.

36. In the Left Behind Series, for example, the protagonists resisting the Beast and the forces of evil are upper-middle-class Americans—the most to lose, of course, from an inability to buy and sell. For the marketing of popular apocalyptic media to relatively educated middle-class America, see Stephen O'Leary, *Arguing the Apocalypse: A Theory of Millennial Rhetoric*, 143–46. This is not to deny that many post–1945 premillennialist dispensationalists have been critical of political ideologies, including capitalism (Paul Boyer, *When Time Shall Be No More: Prophecy Belief in Modern American Culture*, 250–53, 263–67), only to point to the irony of how unwittingly premillennialists play into the very socio-political order and consumerism they decry as they look forward to a new heaven and earth.

4

Polishing the Unclouded Mirror
A Womanist Reading of *Revelation* 18:13

████████████████████████████████

Clarice J. Martin

And the merchants of the earth weep and mourn for her, since no one buys their cargo anymore, cargo of gold, silver, jewels and pearls, fine linen, purple, silk and scarlet, all kinds of scented wood, all articles of ivory, all articles of costly wood, bronze, iron, and marble, cinnamon, spice, incense, myrrh, frankincense, wine, olive oil, choice flour and wheat, cattle and sheep, horses and chariots, *slaves—and human lives* [*or slaves and human souls* / kai sōmatōn, kai pseuchas anthrōpōv]
— *Revelation* 18:11-13[1] (italics mine)

The past is what I cannot pass
It is the future's looking glass.
— Reuel Denney,
The Connecticut River and Other Poems[2]

There's nothing in the world that clings
As does a memory that stings;
While happy hours fade and pass,
Like shadows in a looking glass
— Georgia Douglas Camp Johnson,
The Heart of a Woman, and Other Poems[3]

Mirrors have been numbered among the most fascinating items of humanity's treasured objects. Whether originally crafted from polished metals such as bronze or from layered sheets of glossy metal foil or from the sleek surface of glass, they exhibit an incomparable capacity to reflect, distort, and reproduce both reality and illusion.[4] The twentieth-century poet and scholar Reuel Denney reminds us that the images of a historical past are always reflected in the concaves of a mirror's present, gathering light—if we would but perceptively take note of it. Georgia Douglas Camp Johnson (1866–1966), one of the first widely recognized African American women poets, similarly utilizes mirror or "looking glass" symbolism to contrast the tenacity of painful memories with more cherished, happy ones. The latter are woefully transient and fleeting, like shadows that light briefly upon the even surface of a mirror—and then quickly disappear.

In this essay, I examine the way in which *Revelation* 18:11-13, with its reference to "slaves and human lives," functions for African American readers as a "mirror" or "looking glass" into their own history. In addition, I suggest how such a reading might shed new light on the rhetorical and ideological functions of *Revelation* 18:13 in its first-century socio-historical and rhetorical context.

An African American Face in the Looking Glass

Until the lions have their historians, tales of the hunting will always glorify the hunter.

—Kenyan proverb

I am preoccupied with the spiritual survival, the survival *whole* of my people. But beyond that, I am committed to exploring the oppressions, the insanities, the loyalties, and the triumphs of black women.

—Alice Walker, *In Search of Our Mother's Gardens*[5]

My project rises from delight, not disappointment. It rises from what I know about the ways writers transform aspects of their social grounding into aspects of language, and the ways they tell other stories, fight secret wars, limn out all sorts of debates blanketed in their text. And rises from my certainty that writers always know, at some level, that they do this.

—Toni Morrison, *Playing in the Dark*[6]

Reading the climactic words of *Revelation* 18:13, usually translated from the Greek as "slaves and human souls" or "slaves and human lives," brings me face to face with an unclouded mirror. And the image refracted back to me on the surface of the glass is not mine alone. The African American female face is there, to be sure, but it is compressed about by a "great cloud" of African American witnesses who have shared the inexhaustibly fertile and rich cultural matrix and experience of those who are interminably linked by the four-hundred-year-long history of slavery within the United States. This is a history that began with the "indelicate" experience of the overseas slave trade to the Americas, including the devastating genocide of the Middle Passage and chattel enslavement in America, all of which resulted in the tragic loss of what Pulitzer Prize–winning laureate novelist Toni Morrison calls "The Sixty Million and More."[7]

The stark, refracted reflections of the mirror flash out the movements of ancestors in every decade of every century advancing on freedom's tortuous path. The path is marked by treks through unholy vales of racial violence, Jim Crow segregation and politics, protest marches of men, women, and children amid menacing mobs, and the passionate rhetoric and legal forays of the Civil Rights Movement—all contested markers of hard-fought gains and liberties. These gains and liberties are deposits whose yields are yet to be attained in full. The aesthetic images of this mirror reflect the glimmering flashes of a continuing story of liberation, with certain strides toward the prize of justice and freedom. A womanist reading of *Revelation* seeks to further the gains of resistance, struggle, and liberation on this journey to freedom.

A Womanist Method for Reading *Revelation*

My self-consciously womanist method for a critical analysis of *Revelation* 18:13 is based on four theoretical assumptions. First, all interpretations are relative. My philosophical approach, hermeneutical stance, and reading strategy are grounded in the conviction that biblical writers, biblical texts, and all interpretations of those texts are ideologically contingent and relative. That is, I affirm that meaning does not reside in texts as such—as though meaning were a solid, immutable kernel to be "excavated" or recovered from a text. On the contrary, in agreement with the premises of ideological criticism in the past twenty years, I maintain that meaning emerges in the interaction of author, text, and reader. As such, "value-neutral" interpretations of the meaning of a text do not exist. Rather, meaning-in-interpretation arises from a dialogical, rhetorical struggle among multiple voices and between often-competing ideologies.[8]

Second, my interpretive lens is "womanist." As a womanist, my project foregrounds the hermeneutical lenses, epistemic assumptions, and cultural matrices of African-American people in general and of African American women in particular. The term "womanist" derives from the acclaimed novelist Alice Walker's use of the term in her book, *In Search of Our Mother's Gardens* (1983),[9] and from the ground-breaking and creative development in theological thought called "womanist theology." Womanist theology emerged out of the watershed Black Theology movement of the 1960s and 1970s. The Black Theology movement demonstrated empirically what theologians had accepted theoretically, namely, that all theology or "God talk" is ideologically and culturally conditioned. This affirmation exploded the prevailing myth of rational objectivity in the theological enterprise and challenged the ideological and racial hegemony of traditional Euro-centric thought that had pervaded traditional theology. In so doing, it established the legitimacy of interpreting the Bible through other cultural lenses.

As a culturally coded concept that provides an alternative interpretive lens, the term "womanist" identifies Black women as courageous, audacious, knowledgeable, and extraordinarily creative as purveyors of culture, as cultural readers, and as critics. Womanist thought privileges and foregrounds Black women's wisdom, intellectual traditions, sites of agency, resistance and struggle, and their function as creative, constructive, life-sustaining, and ennobling agents within their families, their communities, and the world.

Out of their identity and experience, womanist interpreters challenge the gender-exclusive hegemony of male-articulated understandings of the Christian faith. They affirm the significance of reading the Hebrew Bible and New Testament within the context of women's experience. As such, womanist interpreters advance and struggle against the idolatry of both androcentrism and patriarchy—those twin evils that foster gender subordination, passivity, and oppression. And at the same time, womanist interpreters also advance in solidarity with Black male interpreters against the idolatry and the hegemony of White supremacy in traditional religion—the idolatry and the hegemony that foster the evils of racist domination, ideology, interpretation, and oppression. Hence, womanist theory and analysis seek to dissolve and to dismantle the three-fold tyrannies of gender, race, and class as among the overarching and interlocking structures of domination in their lives.

Womanist interpreters reject the hegemony of the life-nullifying tyrannies of gender, race, and class within the lives of Black peoples. They do this in proactive ways through life-ennobling ideologies and ideals, critical transformative discourses, the recovery of subjugated knowledge, and dynamic activist commitments. These proactive efforts bring about revolutionary and liberating wholeness at the personal, communal, ecclesial, and socio-political levels on behalf of Black peoples in particular and on behalf of the larger human family in general (after all, a womanist is a universalist by temperament).[10] As ethicist Joan Martin so cogently observes, womanist thought is rooted in neither decontextualized "truth claims" nor lofty idyllic suppositions, nor is it traced to abstract philosophical musings; rather, it is rooted in the lived experience of African American women. A womanist worldview is as concerned with activist moral agency as it is with resistance to oppression. And it promotes constructive cultural discernment as a means to reclaim full humanity and embodied human freedom:

the starting point [for womanist thought] is the spiritual and the religious, the historical and the economic, the social and the cultural, the personal and the diverse, the complex and the simple experience of African-American women. This experience, critically and constructively reflected on, is central for our understanding of what it means to be human and how to act so that we reach our full humanity.[11]

Third, I interrogate *Revelation* 18:13 from within an extended community. As an African American female biblical scholar by training, I am invested within a larger Black feminist and womanist[12] community of activism. This activist community is comprised of generations of Black women within the United States who are with and without formal academic training. I have also chosen to be part of a larger conversation of Africana women, including women who are African, African American (geographically located within the United States), and Caribbean—in short, women of African descent in the global diaspora.

My womanist method assumes that Africana diasporic identity in general is characterized by distinct grammars of disclosures and culture experiences that set it apart from other cultural identities. Nevertheless, a sustained engagement with Africana women does not require the presumption of an essentialist identity or a conflated "homogeneity" of Africana women's experience. Africana identity is multiple and diverse, and its boundaries are permeable and fluid. Furthermore, the rhetoric of hermeneutical reflection, theologizing, and emancipatory practice is markedly enlarged by the cross-fertilization of Africana women's commonly shared legacies of enslavement, colonialism, and diasporic consciousness.

My reading of *Revelation* 18:13 is therefore but one of many readings of sacred texts on a richly broad continuum of Africana biblical scholars, theologians, ethicists, sociologists, literary critics, classicists, and political scientists. These women of African descent represent an expansive multidisciplinary and interdisciplinary community of interpreters who interrogate, affirm, contest, and resist ancient and contemporary readings of and engagements with both oral traditions and narratives (in this case, apocalyptic traditions and narratives) in light of the Black experience.[13]

Fourth, my method deals with John's critique of slavery. The essay will document the ways in which a womanist critical reading enlarges our understanding of the social critique leveled by the author of *Revelation*[14] against the ethical-political commitments of the Roman Empire relative to ancient slavery. "John," or "the Seer" as he is often called, rendered a sharply polemical indictment of the pervasive and baleful commodification and trafficking of human beings throughout the Roman Empire. His indictment represents one of the most striking, if under-examined, critiques of slavery in a society where slavery's ubiquitous presence and the hierarchies of power that sustained it were integral features of the Greek and Roman socio-cultural, political, and religious milieu. As such, we must "tilt the mirror" of historical and hermeneutical inquiry a bit so as to glimpse, in the words of Toni Morrison, the ways in which the author of *Revelation* alludes to "secret wars" reflective of a particular "social grounding" and political commitment within his historical context. In this essay, I seek to "limn out" some of the "debates blanketed within the text" of *Revelation* 18:13, to hear the cry of subaltern (oppressed and marginalized) lions whose voices are muted by the thunderous victory chants of the (Roman) hunters, and to explore the rhetorical and political implications of a womanist critical reading and critique—all oriented toward the creation and "mirroring" of a liberationist vision and practice within the lives of Black women and within the lives of all who have suffered imperialist and colonialist marginalization and domination.

Clouding the Mirror: The Realities of the Slave Systems

If historians are to understand the
Less attractive and deeply buried aspects
Of slave society, the scales will have to fall
From their eyes.

> —Nell Irvin Painter, *Soul Murder and Slavery*[15]

The alternative to seeing someone as a robot is to see them as human, to see them as *ensouled*. . . . The master's failure to see the humanity of his slaves is not simply a lack of insight, but rather a way of seeing that obscures their humanity: he "sees certain human beings as slaves, takes them for slaves." In consequence, he sees his slaves as something different from human beings like himself: . . . we might conclude that seeing humans as slaves is a perfect example of *soul blindness*, i.e., seeing the robotic, slavish aspect of a person but not the soul.

> —Malcolm Bull, *Seeing Things Hidden:*
> *Apocalypse, Vision, and Totality* (italics mine)[16]

When, as a womanist interpreter, I suggest that reading *Revelation* 18:13 is akin to having a panoramic panoply of African American history reflected back to me as truistic culturally coded scenes on an unclouded mirror, I do not thereby imply that the Seer's reference to "slaves and humans lives [human souls]" (18:13) mirrors with exactitude the American slave system of later centuries. The reflection in the looking glass refracts historical parallels to the slave systems of Greece and Rome that are only partially commensurate with the American slave system. Nevertheless, the relative differences cannot diminish the often striking and conspicuous, albeit culturally differentiated, similarities.

Dissimilarities

Prima facie evidence for the *dis*similarities between ancient slavery and slavery on the American landscape should be noted. For example, ancient slaves could not be identified by "ethnic" or "racial" criteria. In ancient times, slaves came from almost every part of the Mediterranean world and in a variety of ways—through capture in warfare, military campaigns, kidnapping, piracy, brigandage,[17] and, in desperate situations, self-indenture. Further, slaves usually worked "side by side" with free or "freed" women and men, performing work that ranged from the most menial tasks to some highly intellectual responsibilities as business managers and secretaries. Classicist William Fitzgerald reminds us that slave ownership was "spread across the population" such that even slaves could own slaves.[18] Sociologist Orlando Patterson has shown that the Greeks did not require their slaves to wear special clothes and that, among the Romans, the slave population often blended easily into the larger proletariat. By contrast, in the Americas, obvious racial distinctions between slave and free made it unnecessary to require standardized clothing protocols as indicators of slave status.[19]

Similarities

At the same time, these stark differences between the slave systems of antiquity and slavery in the Americas cannot obfuscate striking parallels in the master-slave relationship of these chronologically, ideologically, and socially discrete slaves systems. Orlando Patterson has demonstrated these parallels with an analysis of the structure and dynamics of tribal slavery, ancient slavery, pre-modern slavery, and modern slavery in sixty-six societies—including Greece, Rome, medieval Europe, China, Korea, the Islamic kingdoms, Africa, the Caribbean Islands, and the American South. He documents three constituent elements of slavery that typify master-slave relationships in all these societies.[20]

First, slavery was unusual in the extremity of power involved. That the master exercised total domination over the slave was normative, such that a constituent feature of this relationship was the use of various forms of coercion. Force, violence, and might served both to maintain and to perpetuate slavery. When slaves died or were freed by manumission, the master considered it necessary to repeat the original, violent act of transforming yet another free man or woman into a slave. "Whipping was not only a method of punishment. It was a conscious device to impress upon the slaves that they were slaves; it was a crucial form of social control particularly if we remember that it was very difficult for slaves to run away successfully."[21]

Second, the slave relationship with the master in all these societies is characterized by what Patterson calls the slave's "natal alienation." That is, the slave, however recruited, was a socially dead person. "Alienated from all 'rights' or claims of birth, he [or she] ceased to belong in his own right to any legitimate social order. All slaves experienced, at the very least, a secular excommunication."[22]

Third, slaves were persons who were dishonored. Their former status no longer mattered, and their present status as slaves held no honor. Indignity, indebtedness, and the absence of an independent social existence reinforced the sense of dishonor. The slave was without power except through another. She or he had become objectified, commodified, and rendered thoroughly disposable—the "ultimate human tool."[23]

Slaves: "Defectively Souled" and "Live in Hiding"

To Patterson's identification of powerlessness/coercion, natal alienation, and dishonor as constitutive and persistent features of servile relationships within slaveholding communities and societies, we would like to add a persistent, constitutive notion of enslaved persons as "defectively souled." People who embraced the view of slaves as "defectively souled" often treated the opposite view—the idea that slaves were fully human—as scandalous and opprobrious. In an inversion, the author of *Revelation* 18:13, by referring to the Roman enslavement of "human souls," reverses this attitude and levels a biting critique against the view that slaves are defectively souled.

The Greek phrase "*kai sōmatōn, kai pseuchas anthrōpōn*" is usually translated "slaves and human souls," with the terms "*sōmatōn*" (bodies), and "*pseuchas anthrōpōn*" (souls of people) functioning as synonyms for "slave." With this equation, John was affirming the full humanity of the vast number of people who were sold and held as slaves.

Apprehending the full-scale humanity of enslaved persons was often like looking into a "clouded mirror." In this regard, we need to consider Aristotle's (384–322 B.C.E.) views on slavery, because Aristotelian philosophy has exerted a profound influence on slavery in Western culture. Not only did Aristotle's views about slavery function as the underpinning for the medieval concept of dominion, they also provided arguments for the enslavement of indigenous Americans in the Renaissance and, later, for the enslavement of Africans in the Americas.[24]

Malcolm Bull sheds helpful light on Aristotle's views about slaves. Bull correctly highlights a paradoxical and puzzling feature of ancient slavery. On the one hand, slavery was an integral feature of ancient society. On the other hand, slavery was viewed as a "subhuman" condition, and, as a consequence, slaves were considered to be subhuman. But if, as we noted above, there was no clear distinction of ethnicity or other external criteria to legitimate the condition of the enslaved—people could become slaves in so many different ways—then on what basis was slavery justified?[25]

Aristotle proposed that slaves had a "dual identity," one as a slave and one as a human being. First, as slaves, they functioned like a "soulless body" or tool, with their mechanicity (like that of tools and domestic animals) as paramount. In this sense, slaves were akin to what we would call "robots," that is, instruments of action or, in the words of Orlando Patterson, the "ultimate human tool."[26]

Second, as human beings, the slaves possessed a soul, but they were not "ensouled" in the way free humans were ensouled. In Aristotle's view, the master's humanity "took the place" of the slave's humanity. Aristotle's analysis did not fully obliterate the humanity of an enslaved person *qua* human being, but it did legitimate the enslavement of persons whose humanity was considered to be incomplete.[27] In this relationship, the unrestricted domination of the master and the extreme inequality of the slave's status together functioned as the defining features of the master-slave dialectic. This was a relationship in which the slave "lives in hiding" in the master's shadow.[28]

It is important to acknowledge Aristotle's distinction between natural slaves and legal slaves. In Aristotle's view, "natural slaves" were characterized by the "incompleteness" of their soul; specifically, they were thought to lack deliberation, spirit, and rationality. That is to say, they "possessed" the capacity for reason only in a simplistic, childlike fashion, rather than being able to function as persons capable of original, critical thinking and sustained intellectual discourse. Such a view obviously upholds the presumed intellectual superiority of masters. Because of their "natural" inferiority, these slaves were considered by nature fitted for slavery. "Legal slaves," on the other hand, are those who had become enslaved by chance but who are really "natural citizens." For Aristotle, it follows that "the only true slaves are natural slaves legally enslaved; natural citizens who are legally enslaved ought to be freed, and natural slaves who are legally freed ought to be enslaved."[29]

In Aristotelian philosophy, therefore, the scaffolding is in place for an ideology that maintains that natural slavery was not contrary to nature and, moreover, that real freedom was freedom of the "spirit" only. This view was echoed by the Roman senator Seneca (5 B.C.E.–65 C.E.), who proposed that slavery bifurcates human beings, with the body belonging to the master but the soul functioning freely and autonomously, unable to be held by any prison.[30] These views about slaves and slavery found in Aristotle and Seneca were widespread in Roman imperial ideology and practice. It is against the backdrop of such ideology and practice in the Roman Empire that we now turn to the *Book of Revelation*.

The *Book of Revelation:* Preliminary Observations

A few preliminary observations are in order regarding the authorship and social setting of the *Book of Revelation* in anticipation of our focus on *Revelation* 18:13. Scholars have traditionally dated *Revelation* between 92 and 96 C.E., during the latter years of the reign of the Emperor Domitian. This was a period of systematic propagation of the cult of Caesar by Domitian. Domitian's widespread campaign to promote the Roman cult of emperor worship is well attested in the historical annals.[31] As a strategy for solidifying power, Domitian expected to be addressed as *Dominus et Deus Noster* ("our Lord and God"). Of course, this imperial declamation was to be offered by Roman subjects as a test of loyalty, with all the appropriate sacrifices and acts of deference. Although there is no evidence for a Domitianic edict against Christians in particular, this campaign by Domitian to promote the cult of Caesar established the conditions for the persecution of Christians.

The danger for those who scorned the imperial edict and cult, including Christians who confessed Jesus alone as "Lord and God," is immediately apparent. In a politically and religiously charged climate, Domitian gave free reign to observant informers to bring charges against those who balked at and resisted imperial power, domination, and cult. And he executed as "atheists" those who failed to worship the gods of Rome, including "gods" such as himself. Such executions were a continuation of the brutal practices of some of his imperial predecessors, including the Emperor Nero. The result was brutal suffering and persecution reminiscent of the Neronian persecution in Rome in 64 c.e.

It is essential to recognize that the Seer's social and world vision functioned as "protest" literature with a particular advocacy stance over against the Roman imperial context. John's vision of protest was cast in the dramatic mold and cadences of Christian apocalyptic-prophetic traditions that emerged in the Christian communities of Asia Minor. As is often characteristic of apocalyptic literature, *Revelation* reflects the standpoint of persons or groups who were marginalized and powerless and who appealed to visions, trances, and revelations to secure legitimation and status enhancement.[32] As such, *Revelation* is, in the words of Leonard Thompson, a "minority report." This minority report reflects "deviant knowledge" because it has a radically distinct character as the "revealed knowledge" of Christian insiders in contradistinction to the hegemonic "public knowledge" of "outsiders" with imperial ties and allegiances.[33]

In other words, John has drawn a proverbial line in the sand. As a member of a deviant community, which Thompson refers to as the "cognitive minority," the Seer rejects the symbolic universe and worldview of the "cognitive majority," with its knowledge, rhetoric, ethical-political values, and social mores—including its false divinity, its sexual excesses, its politics of domination and oppression, and its self-indulgent boasting and lies. In short, the author of *Revelation* utterly repudiates the hegemonic imperialist prescription of "what the world is really like" with its organizing grid of relationships and power structures.[34]

The truculent rhetoric and oppositional ideological stance of the cognitive minority is emblematic of the subversive intonations of resistance literature. For John, the foundation for this social protest and resistance is rooted in the purposes of the true God and Lord of all creation who ushers in the radical aegis of "a new heaven and a new earth"—both as a present reality and as a future hope for Christian believers. The ideological stance of the majority toward the "deviant" minority shifts precipitously across the spectrum of invested imperialist ideals and commitments—from the one extreme of "bemused" patronizing irritation and curiosity to the other extreme of imperialist violence and persecution, which John had doubtless witnessed and decried. As sociologist Peter Berger observes, the cognitive majority would most certainly refuse, in any case, "to accept the minority's definitions of reality and knowledge."[35] Thompson aptly summarizes the Seer's prophetic critique and program:

> In contrast to the writings of Paul or to 1 Peter, the seer of Revelation rejects any recognition of the empire as a godly order. In both style and content the writer of the Book of Revelation sets his work against the public order. More accurately, he reclaims all the public order for himself, incorporating the whole of the empire and everything else in his vision of what the world is really like and how one should live in it. His revealed knowledge, not public knowledge, integrates religious, social, economic, political, and aesthetic aspects of the world properly. Here John is unambiguous. Within his vision of reality, he and all those who wear the white garments are pitted against the evil empire.[36]

The exigency of *Revelation*'s theological, ethical-political, and rhetorical situation can only be maintained if *Revelation* is correctly perceived as a prophetic-apostolic letter that proposes an alternative symbolic universe for its audience. Written for those who "hunger and thirst for justice" in a socio-political situation characterized by injustice, suffering, and dehumanizing power, John's vision functioned in at least two ways. First, for Christians in Asia Minor, John's vision provided encouragement, despite fear of Rome, to decide for the worship and power of God over against the worship and power of the Emperor. Second, John's vision insisted that Jesus Christ is the true Lord of the world, who "has created an alternative reign and community to that of the Roman Empire ... in order to strengthen Christians in their 'consistent resistance' (*hypomonō*) to the oppressive power of the Roman Empire."[37]

Subversive Language: The Signifying Monkey Trope

> There's a whole heap of them kinda by-words. . . . They all got a hidden meanin' jus' like de Bible. Everybody can't understand what they mean. Most people is thin-brained. They's born wid they feet under de moon. Some folks is born wid they feet on de sun and they kin seek out de inside meanin' of words.
> —Zora Neale Hurston, *Mules and Men*[38]

So how does John express a minority opinion in the face of the hegemonic, oppressive powers of the Roman Empire? Based on an analogy from African American traditions, I would like to suggest that John does this by "signifying on Rome." Here I draw upon the path-breaking work of Henry Louis Gates, *The Signifying Monkey: A Theory of African-American Literary Criticism*,[39] which examines the relationship between the African and African American vernacular traditions and Black literature (inclusive of mythological and poetic traditions in African, Latin American, and Caribbean cultures). Gates presents the "Signifying Monkey" trope as the central rhetorical principle in African American vernacular and rhetorical discourse—as the trope par excellence of literary revision. Signifying was a verbal means for marginalized, oppressed, and vulnerable people to expose the truth about oppressors and to subvert the arrogant assumptions of those in power over them. The signifying is usually done in verbally cryptic and clever ways in order to protect the oppressed signifier from the oppressor being signified upon—such that the insiders can discern the "inside meaning of words," while the outsiders, who are the oppressors, will encounter indirection, innuendo, and obfuscation.

Gates traces the extensive literature and tales about the Signifying Monkey back to slavery. Pervading jazz lyrics, Black verbal language games, and literature, the Signifying Monkey figure has given rise to "signifying" as a mode of figuration in Black discourse—characterized by techniques of indirect argumentation and persuasion, the obscuration of apparent meaning, implication, the use of gesture, and even trickery. The signifier often appropriated the discourse of the master and revised it to his or her benefit. For example, enslaved Black Americans revised and re-appropriated the racist image of Black people as "simianlike" into stories about a signifying monkey who could outwit the powerful. By means of the figure of the Signifying Monkey and his language of "signifying," they created extraordinary rhetorical conventions and practices, including profoundly creative language rituals. These conventions gave rise to a rich and multifaceted corpus of mythological narratives and imaginative literature that embodies potent and wide-ranging signifying aesthetics.[40]

Of particular importance in the densely structured discursive practice of signifying is the role of the signifier herself or himself. The signifier who undertakes the signifying act (that is, the Signifying Monkey) utilizes with quintessential skill an arsenal of rhetorical tropes such as metaphor, metonymy, synecdoche, hyperbole, litotes, rhyme, repetition, and displacement, producing a rhetorically ingenious sequence of signifiers in service of the construction of meaning. "Signifying turns on the play and chain of signifiers, and not on a supposedly transcendent signified. As anthropologists demonstrate, the Signifying Monkey is often called the Signifier, he who wreaks havoc upon the Signified."[41] The signified is usually someone in power who is arrogant. As we shall see, the exiled author of *Revelation* uses a variety of such verbal indirections to "signify" on Rome.

The Signifying Monkey tales illustrate the rhetorical genius of the monkey as master signifier. Signifying Monkey tales are comprised of three stock characters: the Monkey, the Lion, and the Elephant, with the Monkey functioning as the trickster figure, intent upon subverting the Lion's unquestioned presumption of his status as King of the Jungle. As a trickster figure who beguiles and combats the truth, he tricks the Lion into entanglements with the Elephant—who is the true King of the Jungle to those in the animal kingdom. The Monkey's rituals of verbal dexterity routinely trounce and undermine the Lion's pretentious claims. By signifying on the Lion through a series of articulate language tropes, including innuendo, the Signifying Monkey demystifies the Lion's self-imposed status as King of the Jungle.[42]

An example of the Signifying Monkey's effective "signifying artistry" as a trickster can be seen in the narrative poem by writer, producer, and composer Oscar Brown Jr.[43] In this story, the Monkey, from the safety of his treetop home, taunted the arrogant Lion with fictitious gossip about how the Elephant was talking about "yo momma in a scandalous way." Boasting of his powers and letting out a great roar, the Lion went off to take on the Elephant, who was surprised by the Lion's hostility. One thing led to another, and the Elephant "whupped that Lion for the rest of the day." Thoroughly defeated and deflated, the Lion dragged back to the Monkey, who proceeded to gloat over the Lion's humiliation with great glee. The Monkey celebrated so much that he fell off his safe place in the tree, whereupon the Lion pounced on him. The Monkey immediately signified on him again: he apologized and told the lion he would tell him "something he really needed to know." When the Lion backed off to hear what it was, the Monkey slipped away and scampered back up the tree to continue taunting him—noting that the Lion better not pick on him or "he would sic the Elephant on him again." Brown's poem illustrates how a vulnerable monkey could use clever language to subvert the arrogance of the powerful lion and at the same time protect himself.

The African American anthropologist Claudia Mitchell-Kernan describes signifying as "essentially a folk notion that dictionary entries for words are not always sufficient for interpreting."[44] It may or may not involve humor, but it often involves some form of indirection:

> A particular utterance may be an insult in one context and not another. What pretends to be information may intend to be persuasive. The hearer is thus constrained to attend to all potential meaning-carrying symbolic systems in speech-events—the total universe of discourse. *The context embeddedness of meaning is attested to by both our reliance on the given context and, most important, by our inclination to construct additional context from our background knowledge of the world.*[45] (italics mine)

An example of signifying that illustrates the power and efficacy of indirection in the use of this trope is a story told by Mezz Mezzrow, a popular jazz musician. In his autobiography, *Really the Blues,* Mezzrow recalls an episode in which Black patrons in a bar "signify on" some White patrons whose reputations as gangsters and criminals are widely known. Using terms like "killer" and "murder" in their conversation with one another, the Black patrons "signify on" the gunmen with verbal language play:

> He could have been talking about the music, but everybody in the room knew different. Right quick another cat spoke up real loud saying, "That's *murder,* man, really murder," and his eyes were *signifying* too. All these gunmen began to shift from foot to foot, fixing their ties and scratching their noses, faces red and Adam's apples jumping. Before we knew it they had gulped their drinks and beat it out the door, saying good-bye to the bartender with their hats way down over their eyebrows and their eyes gunning the ground. That's what Harlem thought of the white underworld.[46]

A final example of the efficacy of signifying artistry comes from Zora Neale Hurston, whose cultivated anthropological skill as a detective of "the inside meaning of words" in Black culture is well-known. She was perhaps the first scholar to define the trope of signifying.[47] She herself is a celebrated literary artist whose mastery of signification and circumlocution is well attested in her numerous writings.[48] John Lowe describes her book, *Moses, Man of the Mountain* (1939; reprint 1991), as an example of her skill at "signifying on God." This compelling allegorical narrative recasts the biblical Moses tradition by viewing it from the perspective of the Black experience of slavery in America. Utilizing the Moses/Exodus/Promised Land typology so prominent in slave narratives and Black oral traditions (including preaching), Hurston convincingly signifies upon all forms of authority in the biblical narratives, including the portrayal of a deity who resembled (in the tradition of pro-slavery apologists) a "White, Old, Massa-like God."[49] Hurston rewrites and revitalizes the biblical traditions in a restorative act of "cultural translation," giving God a "remodeling job" by signifying on the Bible—or at least on the White version of the Bible.[50]

Signifying on the Roman Empire

In a similar way, the marginalized author of *Revelation* "signifies" on the mighty Empire of Rome. This is my conclusion as a womanist biblical interpreter who, in Hurston's words, "seeks the inside meaning" of John's words—the nuanced significance of the words limned and blanketed within his text. When I "tilt the hermeneutical mirror" and align it with his apocalyptically framed, rhetorically charged indictment of Babylon/Rome, one of the images refracted back to me is that of John as "historian and spokesperson" for the oppressed and the marginalized who provides both social critique and religious revision of the events of history within his socio-cultural milieu. Here, the uniform function of early Jewish and apocalyptic literature becomes most evident, for it represents the mixture of protest and hope on the part of oppressed believers against unjust or imperial powers.[51] As *Revelation* 18:11-13 attests, the imperial powers viewed the enslaved as "defectively souled" and as chattel, whose value was bested by cattle and horses in Roman imperial commerce. And some of these slaves would have been numbered among the holy ones, apostles, and prophets who rejoiced (18:20) when God rendered judgment against Babylon/ Rome in the universal court drama—for New Testament evidence about partici-pants in the Jesus movement and in the "communities of the saints" throughout the Mediterranean world amply attests to the presence of slaves.[52]

Thus, to say that John "signifies on Rome" suggests that, by critiquing the com-mercial sale of human beings, John is using language in indirect and covert ways to critique the larger hegemonic, imperial power arrangement of what he deems to be the "evil empire," including all power arrangements arising from the subjugation of human beings in slavery. Note how John employs incredible verbal dexterity in his attacks on Rome. John never directly names the oppressor he is attacking. Attacks on Rome are all achieved masterfully through the use of indirection, symbolism, allegory, irony, inter-textual allusions, and the strategic arrangement of narrative ele-ments. The most obvious example of indirection is the author's address to the city of Rome as "Babylon," whereby he associates Rome not in terms of her own image of glory and honor but in terms of the tyranny and evil of a fallen empire of the past. But there is much more.

I would like to suggest four ways in which John, in the passage under consid-eration (18:11-13), signifies on Rome: (1) by placing descriptions of Rome in the frame of a courtroom scenario of judgment, (2) by inter-textual associations with evil empires of the past, (3) by arranging material so as to intensify its message, and (4) by affirming that those whom Rome has enslaved are indeed "human souls."

Signifying on the Empire: Judgment on Rome

First, John signifies on Rome by portraying her as the condemned defendant in a criminal trial. *Revelation* 18:13 is located more immediately within the literary context of *Revelation* 17:1—18:24, a section that details God's judgment on Rome, here metaphorically (and indirectly) described and addressed as "Babylon." For the author of *Revelation*, Rome is widely recognized as the seat of evil resistance to God and the political embodiment of godless power that draws all nations into its web of idolatry (14:8). In *Revelation* 17 and 18, John's compositional technique skillfully frames the angelic dirge over Babylon/Rome in the imagery of a political contest held within a lively universal courtroom wherein a class action lawsuit is adjudicated against Babylon/Rome.[53]

The Plaintiffs in the universal court drama represent a diverse group of "all who have been slaughtered on earth," including Christians who are depicted as "the saints," "the witnesses of Jesus," and "the prophets" (17:6; 18:24). The discredited Defendant, namely Babylon/Rome, is charged with moral bankruptcy arising from arrogant domination, reckless violence, the radical perversion of justice, the oppression of the powerless, an insatiable appetite for luxury, and wanton murder in the interests of power and self-aggrandizement (18:9, 10, 11-17, 24).[54] Roman imperial rulers (the "seven kings" in 17:9 likely referring to emperors from Julius Caesar to Domitian) and their client rulers and subordinates (the "ten horns" in 17:12) all stand indicted before the bar of justice. As presiding judge, God has decreed that Babylon/Rome has lost the lawsuit (14:8).

While Christians and the heavenly court rejoice over the verdict and the punishment of arrogant Rome (18:20-24), those who grieve the loss of Babylon/Rome break into wails, lamentations, and mourning (18:9-19). *Revelation* 18:11-19 foregrounds the lamentations of merchants, shipmasters, seafarers, and sailors who were notoriously enriched by the maritime commerce of the Roman Empire. All of them had much to lose by the demise of Rome. Although travel by sea was a particularly dangerous enterprise in antiquity, it was also extremely profitable for the merchants who plied their trade in luxury goods—including slaves. By indirect use of the courtroom imagery, John succeeds—for those who catch the inside meaning of his words—in exposing arrogant Rome as a pathetic criminal guilty of the most heinous crimes and receiving appropriate punishment.

Signifying on the Empire: The Evil Empire of Tyre (*Ezekiel*)

Second, John signifies on Rome by associating Rome with evil empires of the past. Here he uses intertextual associations to mirror Rome's egregious transgressions with those of imperial predecessors. The most obvious intertextual associations are those that equate Rome with Babylon. But here we want to focus on a more extensive way in which John signifies with intertextual associations and revisions in relation to an earlier prophetic passage of judgment on the ancient empire of Tyre. John's indictment of those who trafficked in the buying and selling of human lives (*pseuchas anthrōpōn* of 18:13)—who were "soul blind" to the full humanity of the enslaved—becomes clearer with an examination of the "intertexual" relationships of *Revelation* 18:9-19 (in which the indictment of slavery is embedded) and *Ezekiel* 27.

Intertextual analysis illuminates this section by looking at the ways in which the author of *Revelation* has repeated, revised, and reconfigured the words, structure, and dialogue of *Ezekiel* 27. In his groundbreaking study of socio-rhetorical interpretation, *Exploring the Texture of Texts: A Guide to Socio-Rhetorical Interpretation*, Vernon Robbins presents intertextual analysis as a comparative literary tool that seeks to identify four narrative features of texts: (1) reference ("with what texts and textual traditions are these phrases in dialogue?"); (2) recitation (including the "rehearsal of attributed speech in exact, modified or different words from other accounts of the attributed speech, and rehearsal of an episode or series of episodes, with or without using some words from another account of the story"); (3) recontextualization ("the placing of attributed narration or speech in a new context without announcing its previous attribution"); and (4) reconfiguration (modification of a word, phrase, topic, or theme).[55] Based on these categories, we can look at the intertextual relationships of *Revelation* 18:9-19 with *Ezekiel* 27, the textual tradition with which the Seer is most conversant in this section.

John here signifies on Rome with indirection—without ever mentioning Rome explicitly—by modeling the three dirges over the fallen city of Babylon (Rome) after Ezekiel's lamentation over the downfall of the prosperous city of Tyre. Tyre was the leading island city of Phoenicia that fell to the Babylonian king Nebuchadnezzar after a siege of thirteen years. John uses the same three groups of mourners as Ezekiel does to provide the framework for the dirges: (1) mariners (*Ezekiel* 27:29-30 par. *Revelation* 18:17), (2) kings (*Ezekiel* 27:35 par. *Revelation* 18:9), and (3) merchants (*Ezekiel* 27:36 par. *Revelation* 18:11, 15). John also repeats Ezekiel's list of luxury goods and commodities, even though he omits the place of origin of the goods. In this list, fifteen of the twenty-nine luxury goods and commodities in *Revelation* 18:12-13 are also found in *Ezekiel* 27:12-22.

Hence, by means of recitation, revision, and recontextualization in these dirges, John likens Babylon/Rome to Tyre, a nation who similarly engaged in arrogant, idolatrous, and swaggering boasting about her domination over peoples and nations. Tyre "imposed terror" on others (*Ezekiel* 27:17). Tyre is self-identified as a "merchant of the peoples on many coastlands . . . perfect in beauty" (*Ezekiel* 27:1-3; *Revelation* 17:1-2; 18:1-3). Like Babylon/Rome, many peoples and nations were enriched by Tyre's corruption and commerce. And like Babylon/Rome, Tyre traded "human beings" as slaves for merchandise (*Ezekiel* 27:13). In addition, the dirges suggest, Babylon/Rome will also be like Tyre in that it too, for all its power and wealth, will fall.

Insiders familiar with *Ezekiel* will discern the ways in which parallels to *Ezekiel* 27 expose John's apocalyptically embedded social critique of the abusive system of Roman domination. Like Tyre, Rome used its dominant power to expand economic exploitation as a means to benefit the ruling elite. And like Tyre, hubris and self-glorification were integral features of Babylon/Rome's oppressive reign of terror (17:6; 18:4-7; cf. *Ezekiel* 27:17).

Signifying on the Empire: Slaves as the Least Valued Commodity

Third, John signifies on Rome by his reconfiguration of Ezekiel's references to slaves in the list of commodities that have enriched Rome and her clients. Strikingly and notably different in the Seer's taxonomy of luxury goods and commodities is

John's reversal of the location of the enslaved in his list of commodities compared to that of Ezekiel's list. In Ezekiel's list, slaves were itemized among the *first* group of wares and luxury items, preceding horses, gold, and precious stones (27:12-25). In *Revelation*, however, slaves are listed in a *descending order of value—and at the nethermost level of the list* (18:12-13). Hence, the Seer has intentionally placed enslaved women, men, and children at the nadir of the list of items that Rome utilized and exploited with gluttonous, idolatrous excess. This placement functions as a strategically crafted social critique of the widespread and "taken for granted" practice of the slave trade in the pre-industrial, urban-agrarian Mediterranean world of John's day. This strategic placement has received little notice in the commentaries on *Revelation*.[56]

To understand fully John's reference to the commodities of "slaves and human souls," it is crucial to see the relationship between the grieving merchants of slavery and the thriving slave trade. The ancient geographer Strabo (64 B.C.E.–21 C.E.) attests to this situation when he reports of the bustling activity on the island community of Delos, perhaps the largest nerve-center of the trans-Mediterranean slave trade of the Roman republic. Straddling the trade routes between Italy, Greece, and Asia, Delos provided the Roman Republic with enormous revenue. Pirates who plundered the Roman fleet (piracy was second to war as a source of slaves in the Roman Empire) captured passengers and crews, even kidnapped people from towns and villages along the coast, and then sold them all into slavery. Piracy was, in effect, a "cover name" for the slave trade.[57] Strabo describes the profitable commercial trafficking in human lives in Delos in 146 B.C.E. as a kind of partnership between pirates and merchants. Cilician bandits of the late republic would discharge great quantities of enslaved victims in the port of Delos, where traders swiftly redistributed them to the far regions of the Empire. Delos could receive and send away ten thousand slaves on the same day. As a result, a proverbial saying that signified the readiness of merchants to purchase imported slaves was commonplace in the Mediterranean world: "Merchant, sail in, unload your ship; everything has been sold" (*Strabo* 14.5.2).

Nicholas K. Ruah has documented the lifestyles of the "rich and *in*famous merchants" at Delos in the Hellenistic period. The historical evidence certifies that merchants were notorious perjurers, in spite of the fact that some of them invoked the names of Hercules and Mercury, the Roman gods of trade. In regard to the reputation of merchants as rich profiteers, part of their stock-in-trade was a notorious propensity for deception, fraud, and perjury. Like slave-dealers, they were typically held in contempt. The Roman poet Ovid (43 B.C.E.–17 C.E.) narrates a striking example of the merchants' contradictory practice of making pietistic overtures to the gods (whose statues filled the marketplaces and sea ports) while at the same time exploiting commerce for economic gain. He records a startling scene of Roman merchants washing in the waters of the sacred spring at the Porta Capena in Rome in order to cleanse themselves from perjured oaths, while at the same time invoking the gods to grant them the ability "to commit fresh perjuries tomorrow" for the "joy of profits made."[58] Obviously, there was little remorse about the slave trade among merchants.

By putting slaves at the end of the list of commodities, the author of *Revelation* "signifies" on Rome's devastating and dehumanizing treatment of slaves for profit. As an act of signifying, John's critique is a prophetic public witness, embedded within a context of dirges that exposed imperial excesses and violence within a commercial maritime ethos. As Mitchell-Kernan observed of "indirection" as a mode of signifying: "What pretends to be information [a mere list of commercial goods in *Revelation* 18:11-13] may intend to be persuasive."[59] In 18:13, John underscores Rome's profane treatment of the enslaved by thus placing them at the nadir—the "rock bottom"—of a laundry list of luxury goods and material items. Lamentably, they are even bested by livestock of "cattle and horses" in the repertory of estimable vendibles. The author's strategic placing of slaves at the nethermost point of a taxonomy of commodities is a rhetorically effective strategy for intensifying the critique on the utterly degrading effects of the violence against enslaving human beings—both in wide-scale and in more local or domestic contexts.

Signifying on Rome: The Enslavement of "Human Souls"

Fourth, and most emphatically, John signifies on Rome with the Greek phrase "*kai sōmatōn, kai pseuchas anthrōpōn.*" This phrase is usually translated "slaves and human souls," with the terms "*sōmatōn*" (bodies), and "*pseuchas anthrōpōn*" (souls of men) functioning together as a synonym for "slaves." The phrase would be considered a classical figure of speech in which two words/phrases connected by a conjunction are used to express a single idea—a hendiadys, typically expressed by an adjective and a substantive. By contrast, William F. Arndt and F. Wilbur Gingrich describe the occurrence of these Greek terms as "a unique combination" and translate the phrase as "slaves and bondsmen" (compare *Ezekiel* 27:13), as though the two terms referred to two different groups.[60] However, in light of the common imperial (Aristotelian) ideology that considered slaves to be "defectively souled," it is much more likely that John is signifying on that ideology by referring to slaves emphatically as "human souls" or "human lives."

The force of the Seer's construction is rhetorically and ideologically catastrophic. After placing slaves at the bottom of the list of commodities, John adds the final devastating blow: those whom you have enslaved are human souls! This slam on Rome at the climax of the list of commodities represents one of the most emphatic critiques of Roman ideology in *Revelation*—namely, that it is an empire that enslaves human souls. A fuller lexical analysis of the uses of *pseuchē* in ancient literature will doubtless shed additional light on the rhetorical-ethical significance of its function in *Revelation* 18:13 as an emphatic critique of imperialist ideology.

It is apparent why *Revelation* 18:13 functions as an "unpolished mirror" for Black Americans. Ancient slavery's rhetorically descriptive imagery of human beings as commodified chattel—living tools whose bodies, lives, and labor were exploited for the social and economic well-being of merchants and others for economic profit—mirrors key aspects of slave regimes in America. The gilded mirrors created by purveyors of slavery in both the ancient and the American slave regimes were purposely "clouded," refracting broken and fractured images of enslaved humanity, with contested ideals about them as "soulless, living instruments" whose wills were easily co-opted by masters.

The Mirror: The Severity of Ancient Slavery

The severity of John's signifying on Rome in regard to slavery enables us to address one final issue in studies of ancient slavery. Some have argued that ancient slavery was relatively sanguine compared to the American institution of slavery. The thesis of slavery's relatively innocuous character is a thesis the Seer himself seeks to challenge within the context of imperially sanctioned abuses of power. The intensity of John's critique of ancient slavery is thus itself evidence that ancient slavery was more normatively severe and cruel. The combination of ways John signifies on Rome reinforces the intensity and the extent of his critique. The criminal indictment and punishment of Rome, the association of the Roman Empire with Egypt, Babylon, and Tyre, and the location of slavery as the last and least of the goods all serve to witness to the idea that John himself considered slavery in the Empire to be a horrendous, cruel, and dehumanizing institution.

The long-held thesis of its relatively sanguine character, that it was not and could not be a "severe and cruel institution," has been helpfully challenged in recent years.[61] For example, classicist K. R. Bradley offers a cautionary note against presumptions of a sanguine intimacy between masters and slaves. While "simple, constant animosity between slave and slave master is too naïve a concept to have had universal applicability or meaning," the less human side of Roman slavery should not be romanticized. Harmonious relations between slaves and their masters were possible, in some instances, but the brutality of the slave experience in Roman social relations must be acknowledged.[62] Roman slave owners may have treated their slaves generously, but generosity alone did not secure the elite ideal of *fides* and *obsequium* (faithfulness and compliance/submission) required to maintain power. Force and fear were deemed to be requisite elements to reinforce domination over all slaves—agricultural, mining, and domestic slaves alike. Moreover, distinctions of status, function, age, and gender were no protection against arbitrary punishment.[63]

Diodorus Siculus' *Historical Library*, compiled from 60–30 B.C.E. during the Late Republican period of Rome, surveys the period of *domi militiaeque* when

Rome ruthlessly plundered city and countryside at home and abroad.[64] As he portrays it, the wholesale enslavement of thousands of men, women, and children had long been a standard feature of Roman empire-building. In one episode, he describes the procurement of slaves in war that took place at Panormus, Sicily in 254 B.C.E. during the First Punic War.[65] Once the city had been conquered, the survivors fled to the heart of the city and sent ambassadors to plead for their lives. As Diodorus Siculus depicts it, the Romans agreed that those people who paid two *minae* each would go free. As a result, "fourteen thousand people found the money and met the terms of the agreement and were released. The rest, thirteen thousand in number, were sold by the Romans as booty along with the other loot."[66] This was standard military practice.

The visual modalities both of enforced subjugation, on the one hand, and of slave resistance and flight, on the other hand, were everywhere visible. Metal identification collars, collars with identification tags, and the branding of slaves on their faces were a common hedge against slave flight. One such collar read: "I am Asellus, slave of Praeiectus, who is an administrative officer of the Department of the Grain Supply. I have escaped from my post. Capture me, for I have run away. Return me to the barbers' shop near the temple of Flora."[67] It is evident that Asellus and others like him had the odds stacked against them, for the detailed inscription on the collar would provide professional slave catchers or others with the "name, rank, and serial number" of the master's identity and geographical place of origin.

The Roman satirist Juvenal (60–128 C.E.) is known for writing acerbically critical satires detailing the corruptions and decline of the Roman Empire in the late first century and early second century C.E. Despairing of ever improving or reforming Roman moral laxity, his narrative assault painted searing images of Roman depravity, cruelty, and hypocrisy. In Book 1 of the *Satire*, Juvenal's indignant speaker condemns the decadence of the Roman elite as prime examples of moral corruption. In Satire 2 and 4, the Emperor Domitian is portrayed as a sexual hypocrite and autocrat—one who displays abusive powers, such as humiliating his courtiers.[68]

At one point, Juvenal describes an episode about owners and slaves that provides a glimpse of domestic power relations in the ancient slave system—one that would be repeated centuries later in the antebellum slave system of America. *Satire* 6 chronicles the brutality of elite Roman women and men against the enslaved women who worked within the household. Enslaved women were fully subject to the sexual whims and excesses of their masters and mistresses. Because they were considered to be "property," they had no authority over their own bodies. As a result, they were often brutalized by the wife of the slave master who might be jealous of a slave to whom the husband was attracted. In this account, Juvenal narrates an instance in which a suspicious wife, ignored by her husband in bed, immediately assumes he is in a sexual liaison with the household secretary (a slave) and has her repeatedly whipped. The punishment does not forestall the enslaved woman's responsibilities to tend to her mistress's hair:

> If her husband turns his back on her in bed at night, his secretary suffers! . . . Some women hire a torturer on a yearly salary. He whips, while she puts on her makeup, talks to her friends, and examines the gold thread of an embroidered dress. He lashes, while she looks over the columns of the account book. He lashes, and is exhausted by lashing—until she bellows out, "Go away." . . . Poor Psecas, whose own hair has been torn out by her mistress, and whose clothing has been ripped from her shoulders and breasts by her mistress, combs and styles her mistress's hair. "Why is this curl so high?" the mistress screams, and at once a whipping punishes Psecas for this crime of the curling iron and a sin of a hairstyle.
> —Juvenal, *Satires* 6.475–76, 480–84, 490–94[69]

Juvenal's account of power arrangements between slave mistresses and enslaved women refracts familiar images in the unclouded mirrors of Black peoples in America and the diaspora with shared legacies of enslavement and colonialism. Indifferent to any kind of accountability for their uses and abuses of power, slave masters and mistresses typically exacted their will on the enslaved with impunity. Consider how James Curry, an African American enslaved in the early nineteenth century, describes a slave mistress who beat a nine- or ten-year-old child nearly to death, presumably for breaking a haircomb:

> She took her in the morning, before sunrise, into a room, and calling me to wait upon her, had all the doors shut. She tied her hands and then took her frock up over her head, and gathered it up in her left hand, and with her right commenced beating her naked body with bunches of willow twigs. She would beat her until her arm was tired, and then thrash her on the floor, and stamp on her with her foot, and kick her, and choke her to stop her screams. . . . She continued this torture until ten o'clock, the family waiting breakfast meanwhile. She then left whipping her; and that night, she herself was so lame that one of her daughters was obliged to undress her. The poor child never recovered. A white swelling came from the bruises on one of her legs, of which she died in two or three years. And my mistress was soon after called by her great Master to give her account.[70]

Juvenal's description of the Roman mistress's unbridled rage recounted above also recalls the experience of the enslaved Black woman writer, abolitionist, and reformer Harriet Jacobs (1813–1897), as she narrated it in her now classic autobiographical slave narrative, *Incidents in the Life of a Slave Girl, Written by Herself*, published in 1861 under the pseudonym "Linda Brent." Born a slave in Edenton, North Carolina,

Jacobs provides extensive reflection and analysis about the devastating effects of both racial oppression and sexual exploitation in the lives of enslaved women. Living in the home of Dr. and Mrs. Norcom since childhood, she experienced the periodic torture of Dr. Norcom's violation of her physical body and Mrs. Norcom's punishing bouts of jealousy and rage:

> But I now entered on my fifteenth year—a sad epoch in the life of a slave girl. My master began to whisper foul words in my ear. Young as I was, I could not remain ignorant of their import. I tried to treat them with indifference or contempt. He was a crafty man, and resorted to many means to accomplish his purposes. . . . He tried his utmost to corrupt the pure principles my grandmother had instilled. He peopled my young mind with unclean images, such as only a vile monster could think of. I turned from him with disgust and hatred. But he was my master. I was compelled to live under the same roof with him—where I saw a man forty years my senior daily violating the most sacred commandments of nature. He told me I was his property; that I must be subject to his will in all things. My soul revolted against the mean tyranny. But where could I turn for protection? No matter whether the slave girl be as black as ebony or as fair as her mistress. In either case, there is no shadow of law to protect her from insult, from violence, or even from death; all these are inflicted by fiends who bear the shape of men. The mistress, who ought to protect the helpless victim, has no other feelings towards her but those of jealousy and rage. The degradation, the wrongs, the vices, that grew out of slavery are more than I can describe. . . . I would rather drudge out my life on a cotton plantation, till the grave opened to give me rest, than to live with an unprincipled master and a jealous mistress.[71]

These stories of the treatment of ancient slaves and enslaved African Americans illustrate the harsh realities of both systems and provide evidence for the severity of slavery under the Roman Empire. The intensity of John's critique of slavery witnesses to the harsh realities of Roman slavery, and it confirms the parallels we have drawn in seeing the African American experience in the mirror of John's testimony.

Conclusion

This essay has foregrounded three central approaches to a womanist critical reading of *Revelation* 18:13. First, a womanist critique places the interpreter in solidarity with the oppressed and marginalized—in this case, slaves—in the world of *Revelation* and leads the interpreter to discern John's writing as a minority protest against the devastating domination of the Roman Empire. African scholar Musa Dube has cogently underscored the necessity of vigilance in challenging the ideological strategies and effects of imperial structural forms in any age. She writes that "the pervasiveness and persistence of imperial rhetoric in reality and texts, through ancient and current times and over different people and places [must be] recognized, studied, and called into question."[72] Serious interpreters must acknowledge and reckon with a biblical writer's rhetorically transgressive critique of imperialist ideologies and practices in ancient biblical narratives and contexts. And, just as astutely, they should engage and heed the transgressive critiques of imperialist ideologies and practices by oppressed, subjugated, and colonized peoples who are on the "receiving end" of dominant and abusive power in contemporary contexts. The Seer's critique mandates a radical revision of social ideals and power arrangements—not acquiescence to an evil, "business-as-usual," imperial status quo.

Second, a womanist critique draws upon the Black tradition to reveal the way in which the author of *Revelation* registers his protest; namely, the Seer insolently "signifies" on Roman imperial power, including its de-humanizing and "desouling" effects on the enslaved as a flash-point of his critique. We have seen the variety of language skills and strategies of indirection and association by which the author names for insiders the true nature of their plight. Quite consonant with the literary and rhetorical functions of apocalyptic literature, the Seer "discloses, unmasks, and uncovers" (the Greek term *apocalypse* means to "uncover" or reveal) the evils and violence of the imperial politics of subjugation and dominance. Like the Signifying Monkey who uses language tropes with defiance to subvert the Lion's hegemonic claims to authority as the unquestioned "King of the Jungle," so the author of *Revelation* subverts the hegemonic, imperialistic political-ethical social mores that render human beings of less value than material goods and livestock.

Finally, a *womanist* critical standpoint and reading allow one to discern with more nuanced hermeneutical insight and to relumine with more theoretical precision additional secret wars limned beneath the Seers' critique in *Revelation* 18:13. For when the mirror of *Revelation* 18:13 is tilted for interpretive clarity, some of the images refracted back to Black women not surprisingly mirror some of their own historical experiences of subjectivity—including violence at the hands of both slave mistresses and masters and the rendering of their bodies and persons into manipulable and disposable commodities.

For those who have experienced racial or colonial oppression, marginalization, and domination, it takes no "daring hermeneutical leap" to recognize the intrepid rhetorical nuances of signification on and resistance to morally and philosophically flawed and untenable views about the integrity of human personhood. Black women have similarly engaged in activist, prophetic critiques and resistance against the kind of domination we see etched in *Revelation* 18:13. This fact is registered quite explicitly in the oppositional rhetoric of Black women like the nineteenth-century political writer and activist Maria Stewart, who equated America's easy tolerance of racial injustice with Babylon's abominations, immorality, and idolatry.[73] If Black women's unclouded mirrors refract struggle, they also refract untrammeled resistance and fearless resolve in pursuit of the liberated life. On this point, the Seer and womanist thinkers would be in agreement.

Notes

1. All citations are taken from *The New Oxford Annotated Bible, New Revised Standard Version with the Apocrypha,* 3rd ed., edited by Michael Coogan (Oxford: Oxford University Press, 2001). For *Revelation* 18:13, see New Testament, 443.

2. Reuel Denney, "The Poet and the Scholar," *The Connecticut River and Other Poems,* 23.

3. Georgia Douglas Camp Johnson, "Inevitably," *The Heart of a Woman and Other Poems,* n.p.

4. Cf., Mark Pendergast, *Mirror, Mirror: A History of the Human Love Affair with Reflection*; Sabine Melchoir-Bonnet, *The Mirror. A History.*

5. Alice Walker, *In Search of Our Mother's Gardens: Womanist Prose by Alice Walker,* 250.

6. Toni Morrison, *Playing in the Dark. Whiteness and the Literary Imagination,* 4.

7. Toni Morrison, *Beloved,* frontispiece (dedication page).

8. The literature on the subject of ideological criticism and the politics of meaning is extensive. Cf., A. K. Adam, *Handbook of Postmodern Biblical Interpretation*; Brian K. Blount, *Cultural Interpretation. Reorienting New Testament Criticism*; Musa Dube, *Postcolonial Feminist Interpretation of the Bible*; Elisabeth Schüssler Fiorenza, *Rhetoric and Ethic: The Politics of Biblical Interpretation*; Fernando F. Segovia, *Decolonizing Biblical Studies: A View from the Margins.*

9. See my discussion of the history of the term in Clarice J. Martin, "Womanist Biblical Interpretation." *Dictionary of Biblical Interpretation.* Vol. 2, John H. Hayes, ed., 655–58.

10. Walker, *Our Mother's Gardens,* xi–xii.

11. Joan M. Martin, "A Sacred Hope and Social Goal: Womanist Eschatology." *Liberating Eschatology: Essays in Honor of Letty M. Russell,* 211.

12. As Patricia Hill Collins observes, we cannot essentialize Black women's self-definitions. Black women's analyses of their activist commitments both within the United States and across the continuum of Black diasporic feminist thought betray notable fluidity. See Patricia Hill Collins, *Black Feminist Thought, Knowledge, Consciousness, and the Politics of Empowerment,* 97–121, 236–37.

13. The following works are illustrative of the range of contributions providing scholarly analysis of apocalyptic traditions from the perspective of the Black experience: Allan A. Boesak, *Comfort and Protest. The Apocalypse from a South African Perspective*; Susan Bowers, "*Beloved* and a New Apocalypse"; Katie G. Cannon, "Race, Sex, and Insanity: Transformative Eschatology in Hurston's Account of the Ruby McCollum Trial" ; Maxine Lavon Montgomery, *The Apocalypse in African American Fiction.*

14. Tradition ascribes the authorship of *Revelation* to "John" or the "Seer." For helpful historical overviews and discussions of the authorship of the *Apocalypse,* consult Wes Howard-Brook and Anthony Gwyther, *Unveiling Empire: Reading Revelation Then and Now*; Elisabeth Schüssler Fiorenza, *The Book of Revelation: Justice and Judgment,* 85-113; Jürgen Roloff, *The Revelation of John.*

15. Nell Irvin Painter, *Soul Murder and Slavery,* 30.

16. Malcolm Bull, *Seeing Things Hidden: Apocalypse, Vision and Totality,* 200, 205.

17. Brigands were runaway slaves or ex-soldiers who were often recaptured and sold to slave dealers, who might then sell them to the slave barracks of landowners.

18. William Fitzgerald, *Slavery and the Roman Literary Imagination. Roman Literature and Its Contexts*, 3.

19. Orlando Patterson, *Slavery and Social Death: A Comparative Study*, 58.

20. Ibid., 1–2.

21. Ibid., 3.

22. Ibid., 5.

23. Ibid., 7.

24. On the other hand, opponents of slavery also appealed to Aristotle in their abolitionist critique. Bull, *Seeing Things Hidden*, 207.

25. Ibid.

26. Patterson, *Slavery and Social Death*, 7.

27. Bull, *Seeing Things Hidden*, 210.

28. Ibid.

29. Ibid., 208.

30. Bernard Williams, *Shame and Necessity*, 115, 116. See also Seneca, De Beneficiis, 3.20.

31. Cf., Adela Yarbro Collins, *The Apocalypse*; Colin J. Hemer, *The Letters to the Seven Churches of Asia in Their Local Setting*; Pablo Richard, *Apocalypse. A People's Commentary on the Book of Revelation*; Schüssler Fiorenza, *The Book of Revelation*.

32. For a helpful summary of the character of apocalyptic discourse see Greg Carey, "Apocalyptic Discourse, Apocalyptic Rhetoric"; Schüssler Fiorenza, *The Book of Revelation*, 1–4.

33. Leonard Thompson, *The Book of Revelation: Apocalypse and Empire*, 186.

34. Ibid., 193.

35. Ibid.

36. Ibid., 192.

37. Schüssler Fiorenza, *The Book of Revelation*, 2–8.

38. Zora Neale Hurston, *Mules and Men*, 135–36.

39. Henry Louis Gates Jr., *The Signifying Monkey: A Theory of African-American Literary Criticism*.

40. Ibid., 51-54.

41. Ibid., 52.

42. Ibid., 56.

43. Linda Goss and Marian E. Barnes, eds. *Talk That Talk. An Anthology of African-American Storytelling*, 456–57.

44. Claudia Mitchell Kernan, "Signifying, Loud-Talking and Marking," 311.

45. Ibid.

46. As cited in Gates, *The Signifying Monkey*, 69.

47. Gates, *The Signifying Monkey*, 196. On Hurston's narrative art, see also Houston A. Baker Jr. *Workings of the Spirit: The Poetics of Afro-American Women's Writing*, 77–79, 82–99.

48. The library of Hurston's prolific legacy is too extensive to narrate here. Cf. Michael Awkward, ed., *New Essays on Their Eyes Were Watching God*; Ayana I. Karanja, *Zora Neale Hurston: The Breath of Her Voice*; Cheryl A. Wall, *Zora Neale Hurston: Novels and Stories*.

49. John Lowe, *Jump at the Sun: Zora Neale Hurston's Cosmic Comedy*, 206-9, 249–50.

50. Ibid.

51. That *Revelation* fantasizes a "new space" for those experiencing earthly "dislocation" is illustrated aptly by Catherine Keller. See Keller, *Apocalypse Now and Then: A Feminist Guide to the End of the World*, 145, 171.

52. Cf. the very helpful study by Jennifer A. Glancy, *Slavery in Early Christianity*; Sandra R. Joshel and Sheila Murnaghan, eds., *Women and Slaves in Greco-Roman Culture: Differential*

Equations; Wayne A. Meeks, *The First Urban Christians: The Social World of the Apostle Paul.*

53. Tina Pippin is correct to decry the symbolic portrayal of Babylon/Rome as a prostitute—for the centuries-old misogyny it reifies. The vision of what she describes as the "grossly exaggerated vision of death and desire" is one of the most misogynist passages in the New Testament. Tina Pippin, *Death and Desire: The Rhetoric of Gender in the Apocalypse of John.* On *Revelation* 18:1-24 as reflecting a "universal courtroom drama," see Elisabeth Schüssler Fiorenza, *Revelation. Vision of a Just World*, 99.

54. Schüssler Fiorenza, *Revelation*, 99.

55. Vernon K. Robbins, *Exploring the Texture of Texts: A Guide to Socio-Rhetorical Interpretation.* See also the discussion by L. Gregory Bloomquist, "Methodological Criteria for Apocalyptic Rhetoric: A suggestion for the Expanded Use of Sociorhetorical Analysis," 181–203.

56. While I am not the first to suggest the possibility of implicit rhetorical-ethical critique of ancient slavery in *Revelation* 18:13, I am struck by the dearth of any extended commentary about the allusion to the enslaved in critical commentaries on *Revelation*. The very negligible commentary about slaves on the list of commercial goods is exceeded only by sporadic, passing references to possible rhetorical or ideological functions of *kai sōmatōn, kai pseuchas anthrōpōn* within *Revelation* 18:13 for John. Cf. M. Eugene Boring, *Revelation*; G. K. Beale, *The Book of Revelation. A Commentary on the Greek Text.* Beale provides a helpful, but brief discussion of vv. 12-13, more than most commentaries; Robert H. Mounce, *The Book of Revelation*; John Sweet, *Revelation*; Jürgen Roloff, *Revelation.* Jennifer Glancy's analysis is helpful in *Slavery in Early Christianity*, 85–86.

57. Nicholas K. Ruah, *The Sacred Bonds of Commerce. Religion, Economy, and Trade Society at Hellenistic Roman Delos*, 166–87 B.C.E., 41–49. For the historical quote from Strabo 14.5.2., see Ruah, 43.

58. Ibid., 172–73.

59. Mitchell-Kernan, "*Signifying, Loud, Talking and Marking,*" 311.

60. Bauer, Arndt, and Gingrich, *A Greek-English Lexicon of the New Testament*, 902. A fuller analysis of what I call a "homonymic critique" within the particular context of *Revelation* 18:13 is in order. Cf. the fuller discussion of *pseuchē* and its cognates in Gerhard Kittel and Gerhard Friedrich, eds., *Theological Dictionary of the New Testament*, volume 9, 608–66.

61. See especially the excellent survey by Richard A. Horsley, "The Slave Systems of Classical Antiquity and Their Reluctant Recognition by Modern Scholars," 19–66.

62. K. R. Bradley, *Slaves and Masters in the Roman Empire: A Study in Social Control*, 13–14. See also my discussion in "Womanist Interpretations of the New Testament. The Quest for Holistic and Inclusive Translation and Interpretation."

63. Ibid.

64. Shelton, *As the Romans Did: A Sourcebook in Roman Social History*, 163.

65. Ibid.

66. Diodorus Siculus, *The History of the World* 23.18.4 and 5. See Shelton, *As the Romans Did*, 164.

67. Ibid., 177; *Corpus inscriptonum latinarum* 15.7172 (*ILS* 8727).

68. According to some legends, Juvenal was exiled until Domitian's death, although some scholars question the merits of even this supposition since they argue the *Satires* are not historical reconstructions but merely sophisticated literary constructions. See Susanna Morton Braund, "Juvenal," 386–87.

69. Ibid., 178–79.

70. As cited in Clarice J. Martin, "'Somebody Done Hoodoo'd the Hoodoo Man': Language, Power, Resistance, and the Effective History of Pauline Texts in American Slavery," 220.

71. Harriet Jacobs, "Incidents in the Life of a Slave Girl, Written by Herself," 773–76.

72. Musa Dube, *Post-Colonial Feminist Interpretation of the Bible*, 28–30.

73. Clarice J. Martin, "Biblical Theodicy and Black Women's Spiritual Autobiography: 'The Miry Bog, The Desolate Pit, A New Song in My Mouth,'" 13–36. Among the many pathbreaking texts on the subject of Black women's activist resistance to racism, and their constructivist ethic of empowerment and hope are the following: Cheryl Townsend Gilkes, *If It Wasn't for the Women: Black Women's Experience and Womanist Culture in Church and Community*; Joanne Marie Terrell, *Power in the Blood? The Cross in the African American Experience*; Emilie M. Townes, *Breaking the Fine Rain of Death: African American Health Issues and a Womanist Ethic of Care*; Traci C. West, *Wounds of the Spirit: Black Women, Violence, and Resistance Ethics*.

5
Power and Worship:
Revelation in African Perspective

■ ■

James Chukwuma Okoye

The Drama of Revelation

From an African perspective, the *Book of Revelation* is about power and worship. It is the drama of two reigns in conflict and of two opposing modes of worship, one ministering to life and the other to death. The drama opens with the throne liturgy in heaven (chapters 4–5), where all living things in creation—everything that lives in heaven and on earth and under the earth and in the sea—were crying out,

> To the One seated on the throne and to the Lamb,
> Be all praise, honor, glory and power, forever and ever. (5:13)

This is the true reality of creation: at the heart of all things, God rules in majesty, with the present and the future securely in God's hands. In *Revelation*, whenever prayers are mentioned (5:8; 8:3-4), the sphere is heavenly. The twenty-four elders who pray, "we give thanks to you, Almighty Lord God" (11:17), are in heaven and belong to that sphere.[1] On earth below, in the meantime, matters are quite different. Another throne holds sway over the earth, the throne of the beast, with one of its centers located in Pergamum (2:13).

These differing conditions in heaven and on earth begin with war in heaven, when Michael and his angels attack the dragon and his angels and cast them down from heaven to earth (12:7-8). Now on earth, the dragon continues the war, but he continues it against the woman and her offspring, God's people. And the dragon does this through proxy, for he has a political representative on earth, the beast from the sea, (the Roman Empire), to whom he hands over his immense authority and his throne (13:3). This beast, in turn, extends his authority to a second beast, the beast that emerges from the land (the religious and political apparatus that enforces the divine authority of Rome). This second beast has horns like a lamb, but he makes a noise like a dragon (that is, he imitates the Lamb, but he is really a dragon). This second beast erects a statue of the first beast and makes the whole world worship it, such that anyone who refuses to worship the statue is to be put to death (13:15). Furthermore, no one is to buy or sell unless branded on the right hand or on the forehead with the mark of the beast (13:17). The Roman state had become "goddess Roma," and the emperor Domitian had become "our Lord and God Domitian." God's response was to mark the servants of God on their foreheads with the seal of the living God (7:3). So the earth was now divided into two camps: those who were marked for the beast (and who worshiped the beast) and those who were marked for the living God.

When John wrote, things had not quite come to this critical point, but John had no doubt that this scenario would soon become reality. He thus set down his visions and sent them as a book to the seven churches of Asia Minor in order to disclose to them the real meaning of their experiences and of the history they were about to undergo (chapters 1–3) and as a means to encourage them to stand fast unto death and, in this way, to "conquer." John made it clear that no compromise was possible: either one is marked for the beast and for ultimate destruction in the lake of sulfur, or one washes one's garment in the blood of the Lamb (dies in martyrdom) and is welcomed into heaven. In 11:1-13, John portrays the role of the church in these circumstances: the two witnesses are prophet-martyrs who die on account of their witness, but whose death and resurrection provoke soul-searching and repentance among the nations.

However, this situation will not continue for too long. God has already assured those who have been killed on account of the Word of God (6:9) that the total number of those faithful who were going to be killed would soon be completed. God would then break God's silence and "destroy the destroyers of the earth" (11:18). At that time, "the kingdom of the world [will] become the kingdom of our Lord and his Christ, and he will reign for ever and ever" (11:15). Chapters 6–18 portray three measures of increasing intensity that God will take as means to remedy the situation and also to lead the nations to repentance. The first measure (the seven seals) destroys a quarter of the earth. The second measure (the seven trumpets) destroys a third of the earth. However, the survivors of these first two measures do not repent. Instead, they refuse to stop worshiping devils, and they refuse to give up their murdering, their witchcraft, their fornication, and their stealing (9:20-21). Finally, a third measure, a universal plague of destruction (the seven bowls, chapter

16), ushers in the end and opens the way for "a new heaven and a new earth" to appear (21:1) and for the holy city to come down out of heaven from God. Of this city it is said,

> The throne of God and the Lamb will be in the city;
> his servants will worship him,
> they will see him face to face,
> and his name will be written on their foreheads. (22:3-4)

The drama has come full circle. "Throne" begins and ends the visions; in between is the process by which a chaotic world is brought under the compass of divine sovereignty.[2]

An African Reading Perspective

"What we see depends on where we stand,"[3] and "every reading bears the stamp of who reads."[4] A text is not a "meaning-container" but only a "weaving,"[5] that is, it has potentialities of meaning that can be actualized by different readers coming to it from different backgrounds. A reader makes choices among various potential readings of the text, identifying with what is particularly significant for his or her context and situation.[6] Cultures generally have a perspective on some texts, and sometimes they have themes that they find particularly apposite. Different epistemologies attune readers to different voices. By reading the text from a particular focus or perspective, aspects of the text are highlighted as problematic or meaningful for the particular situation of the reader. The potential for diverse, contextual readings is especially present with regard to apocalyptic language, because apocalyptic language is highly symbolic. Symbols can bear multiple meanings; hence, symbols lend themselves to ever-new configurations of meaning.

In my reading experience, the particular lived reality of the African culture and context enters into dialogue with the text of *Revelation*, with its rich potential for meaning and with its received readings (no text is ever innocent of reading traditions). I am an African who has studied and worked on three continents. Born in Nigeria, I have lived and worked in Rome, Italy and now live and teach in the United States. My experience has made me especially aware of the similarities as well as the differences among cultures. I cannot represent traditional Africa; in fact, I do not believe that the traditional Africa of even fifty years ago still exists. Cultures are constantly changing, all the while remaining themselves. However, I dare to believe that I represent the dialogue of African culture with other cultures in an increasingly globalized world. In what follows, I try to represent the average African torn between traditional culture, on the one hand, and imported meanings and values, on the other hand. Space does not allow me to delineate elements of the African culture and context (beyond what is adduced in this paper); those who are interested can find abundant material on that subject.[7]

I also mention that I belong to a religious congregation dedicated to serving the poor and oppressed. The Congregation of the Holy Spirit was founded in 1703 in Paris by a young lawyer, Venerable Poullart des Places, who was concerned for the material and spiritual well-being of chimney sweeps and poor seminarians (because they could not afford boarding fees). His original group developed into a seminary and an Institute that sent priests to the French Colonies, where they were especially concerned about the slaves. In 1848, this congregation merged with the Congregation of the Immaculate Heart of Mary, which had been founded by Venerable Francis Mary Libermann, a converted Jew who was concerned for blacks. The Congregation has an international membership of priests and brothers and currently works in over sixty countries of the world. Certainly, oppression and marginalization are universally accepted as experiences that have shaped African cultures. Yet my participation in this congregation has further sharpened my African sensitivity to oppression, marginalization, and exclusion.

What follows, then, is an effort to unpack elements of a reading experience from the perspective of the African culture and context. I will proceed by reflecting on aspects of *Revelation* that are difficult for Africans and then follow this by identifying aspects of *Revelation* that are positive and challenging for Africans.

Challenges for an African Reading

I would like to reflect here on four problems that African people may have with the *Book of Revelation*. These problems represent aspects of Revelation that may have negative consequences for African people.

The Glorification of Martyrdom

First, the glorification of martyrdom in *Revelation* may encourage people to accept supinely an oppressive situation. There is a subtle twist in the way *Revelation* uses the verb *nikaw* (to conquer); namely, that the Christian "conquers" by being a martyr. The Christian is simply *ho nikōn* (2:7, 11, 17 and passim), that is, "one who conquers" as Christ conquered (3:21). At 12:11, it becomes clear that the Christian "conquers" by the blood of the Lamb and the witness to the word of God that may lead to death. To die for witnessing to the Lamb is to conquer—and the victim is the victor. As Bonhoeffer said, "when Christ calls a person, he bids him/her come and die."[8] The church of *Revelation* is called to be a church of martyrs. Between the true worship of God and its negation, the Christian cannot but choose to resist, even unto death, those who negate the true worship of God. As such, *Revelation* encourages its readers to stand fast for the true worship of God and to resist oppression. This is an abiding and universal truth; however, it would be a mistake to extrapolate directly from the situation of the church in *Revelation*, because each time and place must accept the responsibility of discerning when and how the true worship of God is at stake.

Political and economic oppression began in Africa in 1885 when the world powers of that time divided Africa into spheres of influence and set out to "pacify the natives," that is, to "civilize and educate" them. In the 1960s, the colonial era gave way to neocolonialism and to so-called *cooperation*, a situation in which Africans are oppressed by foreign powers with the connivance of native elites and rulers. Then came the Economic and Structural Adjustment Programs of the 1980s, which sapped all native economic initiatives, slanting the economies in favor of greater dividends for foreign investors. In the present time, such unidirectional globalization is the new face of imperialism. This economic imperialism seeks rapid penetration of national and regional boundaries by products, services, and images from a Western globalizing culture.[9] Thus, what we now have is oppression in the name of "globalization."

In the *Book of Revelation*, Babylon is the powerful personification of international oppression and murder carried out by Rome throughout the Roman Empire.[10] When Africans hear about Babylon and the beast from the sea, their minds turn to the powerful international forces who grow fat on the blood of Africans, who foment wars and supply arms to keep servicing their selfish interests. For example, the national foreign debt of Nigeria in 1985 was $8 billion; by the year 2000 and with no further borrowing, this had grown to $30 billion. And Africa itself has produced merciless tyrants and despots—they are the beast from the land. African people generally regard authority as sacred and expect leaders to do right. As a result, some African leaders exploit this trusting attitude toward authority in the service of tyranny and naked self-interest.

Thus, to appropriate *Revelation* for the African context as a cult of victimhood of martyrs may be dangerous. It may foreclose and inhibit every effort at redressing the unjust situations that plague Africa. In 1886, in the time of the Martyrs of Uganda[11] when Christianity was an insignificant minority, these martyrs gave priceless witness to the gospel in their own context and time. However, Christianity today has great social impact in Africa and should be a force for transformation. It will be playing into the hands of the "beasts" to elevate the martyr paradigm of Christianity in the manner in which the author of *Revelation* seems to glorify martyrdom. John's efforts to encourage *hypomonē* (endurance) among the Christians of Asia Minor must not be understood as an "incapacitating endurance" or "long-suffering," but as "staying power" and as "consistent resistance."[12] The context of Africa demands that Christians engage with and neutralize the beast, both the beast from the sea and the beast from the land.

The Total Rejection of the State

Second, the total rejection of the state in *Revelation* could be misused to work against the absolutely crucial and positive participation of Christians in the politics of African societies. In opposing what Rome had become, an idolatrous colonial empire dominating the world by economic exploitation, political oppression, and military force, John portrayed the Roman state as demonic. He opposed any participation by Christians in the civic life of Asia Minor and any significant cultural assimilation. He admonished the faithful to "Come out of her, my people" (18:4). Similarly, in the early days of the Christian mission in parts of Africa, missionaries set up "Christian villages" as a means of isolating converts from the so-called pagan cultures of Africa. For a long time, Christians were actively discouraged from entering politics because it was considered demonic, just as *Revelation* seemed to paint it.

However, this missionary approach represented a misunderstanding of traditional African politics and was a misappropriation of the *Book of Revelation*. The local politics of Africa cannot be compared to the external, colonial domination of Rome. In traditional African religiosity, the political leaders could not in any way be considered demonic. On the contrary, kings, chiefs, and other authority figures personified the order of the world and the harmony that enables the world to continue for the benefit of humankind.[13] Politics is a sacred trust from the gods and from the people, and participation in it, for those with the requisite qualities, is both a civic duty and a basis for high recognition. It was not until the 1960s and especially the 1970s, thanks to the teachings of Vatican II, that the trend to demonize African politics would be reversed and the role of Christians as leaven in the society would come to be emphasized and encouraged.

Furthermore, the politics of the Roman Empire and the political dynamics of African societies are also quite different in terms of the issue of idolatry. The summary of John's accusation against Rome was idolatry—cultic and political idolatry. The deified Empire of Rome demanded worship, and the Empire encompassed much worship of pagan idols. The African context was different. The traditional African king or queen never claimed divine status; instead, they were only considered to be intermediaries between the people and God. As for the worship of idols, no "idols" have ever been reported in African traditional societies.[14] What missionaries called "idols" were simply representations of deity that were never accorded the worship reserved for the Creator of all. Most African societies knew only the one God, the creator of all life, and the various "divinities" were merely personifications of aspects of God's being and activity. The spirits did receive sacrifices, but the spirits were never placed on the same level as the Creator (although in most cases their relation to that Creator was ambiguous).

Given this situation, *Revelation*'s contention that "behind idols stands Satanic power" is not applicable to most of Africa. Contrary to what one sometimes reads in mission journals, African traditional religion is not demon worship, but worship of the one true God (albeit with ambiguities). Unfortunately, *Revelation*'s utter repudiation of traditional religion can lead to an attitude that says, "tear down their altars, smash their standing stones, cut down their sacred poles and burn their idols" (*Deuteronomy* 7:5). In contrast to this, Christianity should be in dialogue with traditional African religions. In point of fact, African people come to Christianity "as people whose worldview is shaped according to African religion."[15] And this religious outlook encourages positive participation in the politics of African societies.

Separating Faith and Culture

Third, John's worldview is problematic for African Christianity because it manifests a conflict between faith and culture, as exemplified by his condemnation of the Nicolaitans. John accuses the Nicolaitans (along with the prophetess and her followers) of being idolaters for their participation in pagan rituals of any kind. John accuses the Nicolaitans of fornication (a metaphor for idolatry), and he labels the prophetess as "that Jezebel." Similarly, the missionaries to Africa generally adopted the same "Christ against culture" paradigm. They considered traditional African religion to be demon worship and were very strict in prohibiting food sacrificed to "idols." Even up to the 1970s, traditional ways of burying the dead were forbidden to Christians in many places. Also, for a long time, Christians could not take traditional titles (which gave them say in the affairs of the village), for these were deemed to involve demonic rituals. In contrast to the approach of the missionaries, Christianity should be in creative interaction with traditional African religions. In fact, the African church itself has now adopted "inculturation" as pastoral policy: the gospel is to become incarnate in African culture, and African culture is to be evangelized. This has been a much healthier and more appropriate approach to African traditional religion than the polarizing approach that seems to be promoted by *Revelation*.

I suspect that the Nicolaitans, along with Jezebel and her followers, were not evil in the way John portrays them. Rather, they simply had Christian views about what constituted idolatry that were different from those of John. Unfortunately, John does not give them a voice, and so they do not speak for themselves. Yet we can speculate about what their views might have been. What John saw as idolatrous worship, the Nicolaitans probably saw not as religious worship but as an expression of civic duty. To give an analogy: for African Christians with relatives who still practice the traditional religion, the act of receiving and eating meat on the occasion of festivals merely enshrines and cements the normal kinship relationships. In traditional Africa, religion is integrally embedded in culture. Therefore, every civic activity was both religious and social at the same time. In the ancient world, contact with religion was unavoidable if one wanted to participate in the life of society at all. People of the time would not have eaten meat unless it was first sacrificed to the gods. As such, meat sold in the markets was first slaughtered at the shrines. Hence, to avoid meat sacrificed to idols would have meant withdrawing oneself from all civic life. The Apostolic Decree cited in the *Acts of the Apostles* (15:29)[16] enjoined Christians to abstain from meat sacrificed to idols, but this was less a matter of orthodox practice than a means to facilitate fellowship between Jewish and gentile Christians.

Paul tried twice to tackle the same problem at Corinth (*1 Corinthians* 8 and 10), where the "strong" said that an idol has no existence and the "weak" feared that eating such meat would be idolatry. In principle, Paul agreed with the strong and decreed that meat sold in the marketplace was to be eaten with no questions asked. And he permitted Christians to eat meat offered to them as guests in the house of a non-believer (*1 Corinthians* 10:25). When Paul nevertheless said that there were occasions when the Corinthians should *not* eat such meat, his reason was based on love as the supreme basis for ethical behavior: "if food be the cause of a brother's downfall I shall never eat meat any more" (*1 Corinthians* 8:13). However, Paul did forbid in principle the act of eating in the pagan temple itself, in front of the idol. This he seemed to associate with idol worship (*1 Corinthians* 10:14). So, Paul was doing this: instead of making a blanket prohibition against all behavior related to idol worship, he was seeking to discern what things in the culture might really constitute idolatrous behavior and what things might not.

One other factor needs to be noted here. Paul associated eating meat in a temple with fornication (*1 Corinthians* 10:8). In fact, every mention of *eidōlothuta* (meat/things sacrificed to idols) in the New Testament is accompanied by references to *porneia* (fornication). There is evidence that sacred meals and sexual immorality often went together at the pagan temples.[17] However, in *Revelation*, the references to fornication seem to point to the use of fornication as metaphor for idolatry, rather than as a literal depiction of sexual activity as such. For example, when John writes that "every king on earth has prostituted himself with her (Rome)" (18:3), he is clearly referring to idolatry. As far as Africa is concerned, there is no ruler worship (as with *Revelation*'s reference to fornication) and there is no idol worship, let alone idol worship connected with sexual practices (as with Paul's reference to fornication).

Like Paul, Christians in Africa are now seeking to discern, in an ongoing manner, which traditional practices and symbols may be treated as merely social and which are to be considered contrary to the Christian faith. For this task, Paul serves as a good example, because he is more aware of and accepting of the intermingling of religion and culture in such situations. Paul's approach therefore is more helpful to Africans than the absolutizing tendencies of the strict dualism exemplified by the author of *Revelation*.

Violence and Destruction

Finally, Africans do not minimize the violence and destruction of *Revelation*, which they view as integral to the message of the book. On the one hand, they may cringe at John's description of the torture carried out in the presence of the angels and the Lamb (14:10) or at the river of blood that is five feet high and two hundred miles long (14:20) or at the locust-scorpion bites that inflict injury for five months, bites meant only to torment but not to kill—and which smack of the torture chambers on Robben Island, where Nelson Mandela was tortured by the Apartheid Regime, or of the torture chambers of totalitarian regimes. Still, on the other hand, Africans are aware that ancient sensitivities differed from modern sensitivities.

Africans will not minimize the depiction of violence in *Revelation*, as some people do who plead that the destruction portrayed in Revelation is "only literary violence"[18] or that such violence is only a vision and not real.[19] Africans consider that the violence in *Revelation* is an integral part of its portrayals and that even literary violence has a powerful effect on its readers. As Renita Weems[20] has said with regard to sexual violence as a poetic portrayal of divine retribution, one is dealing not with "only a metaphor," for metaphors have fatal attraction; they influence and mold the cultural imagination. Narration is "world-making"; a narrator weaves a web of happenings, the meaning of every part and every detail being determined by the whole sequence. As a whole, the narrative, including its depiction of violence, has an impact on hearers.

Hence, the violence in *Revelation* must be taken seriously and seen within its function in the narrative world. In the narrative of *Revelation*, violence is directed against the heavenly beings (sun, moon, and stars are not seen as inanimate) and against the portions of earth that these heavenly beings were allowed to govern. If the world becomes totally corrupt, so must the corresponding "rulers," who are above, be totally corrupt and ready to receive retribution. As such, the violent imagery of *Revelation* against humans and against nature reflects a sense of justice. In this regard, the literary violence in *Revelation* is part of its portrayal of an imaginative and alternative world from which God has removed all sin, injustice, and oppression. *Revelation* insists that there will be retribution and that in the end the oppressors will get their just desserts. *Revelation* claims that God is just in making these judgments: "they spilt the blood of the saints and prophets, and blood is what you have given them to drink; it is what they deserve" (16:6). The seven golden bowls were filled with incense from the same heavenly altar where the souls of the martyrs were praying for justice. As such, the punishments inflicted by the seven bowls were, at least in part, God's response to these prayers of the holy souls who had been killed for their faith. Those who are oppressed call for judgment, not for vengeance. And they see no dichotomy between God's love and God's justice; their uplifting hope is that "God shall reign."[21] As with Pharaoh in Egypt, God cannot achieve God's creative purposes of liberation from oppression without engaging the hardened Pharaoh.

In reflecting on revelation and violence in connection with Yahweh's order in *Joshua* 11:6 to hamstring the horses and burn the chariots in fire, Walter Brueggemann notes that revelation occurs in the concrete; that is, it rises out of the hurts and hopes of a community. The community of Israel was utterly persuaded that the God of tradition was passionately against domination and passionately for an egalitarian community;[22] they were convinced that their God did not intend their long-term subservience and destruction. The authority given to the leaders of Israel to carry out this destruction was seen as the only way to secure Israel's future. Brueggemann points out that, in similar manner,

> the affirmation of third world communities of faith is that God's great promise of land and justice is indeed linked to concrete human acts against horses and chariots. As in ancient Israel, none can persuade such communities of faith and hope that the God of justice and freedom withholds such a permit.[23]

We Africans feel deeply the anguish of our situation. On the one hand, we feel that there is a divine permit to hamstring the horses and burn the chariots. On the other hand, we are confronted with the gospel of Jesus Christ, who deliberately chose nonviolent evangelization. Yet, Christ did speak of God finally weeding sinners and oppressors out of his kingdom. It does not help to dissimulate the violence in *Revelation*, as some try to do; rather, we should take it seriously as one element in a theology of resistance still to be developed. *Revelation* contains scenes of remarkable violence. For example, in 19:15, a sharp sword proceeded from the mouth of the Word of God to strike down the nations (*pataxē ta ethnē*) and to rule them with a rod of iron. In v. 20, the "nations" ("those who had received the mark of the beast and worshiped its image") are all killed by the sword of the rider, and the birds gorge themselves on their flesh (v. 21). This image is dangerous if it is understood to divide the world along religious lines of affiliation into those fit to live (followers of the Lamb) and those to be utterly destroyed (non-followers). It would merit the strictures of Adela Yarbro Collins[24] when she characterizes such dualist division of humanity as failing to rise to the demands of Christian love.

It may be claimed that "the supposed battle scenes are not really battles at all,"[25] the weapon being a sword that extends from the Lamb's mouth, which makes it the word of God (compare *Ephesians* 6:17; *Hebrews* 4:12). But the word of the judge may send a prisoner to the gallows. As Miroslav Volf says, "the violence of the divine word is no less lethal than the violence of the literal sword."[26]

The traditional gods of Africa fought no religious wars; African traditional religion was neither missionary nor exclusive. Each of the African peoples had their gods, and these gods promoted common norms of ethics and social behavior. Now, however, since the introduction of Islam and Christianity as missionary and exclusivist religions, there are religious wars in several parts of Africa, especially between Christians and Muslims. All religions in Africa have the duty to assess critically their traditions and history with respect to the building up of peace and justice in Africa. Africa needs to find a way for all faiths to live together in peace and to promote together the good of society. For this task, the attitude of violence toward others who hold different religious beliefs, as it is depicted in the *Book of Revelation*, may be counter-productive.

The African Universe Highlights Aspects of Revelation

In addition to aspects of *Revelation* that are problematic, there are key features of *Revelation* that Africans embrace in positive ways. I will highlight four such features.

Apocalypse as Two Interrelated Spheres

The mainstream churches in the West seem to find *Revelation* to be a closed book, leaving the preaching on *Revelation* to sectarian and millenarian groups. By contrast, Africans seem to enter more easily into the genre and drama of *Revelation*. Harold Turner[27] studied the sermons of an Aladura Church (literally "Prayer Church"), one of the African Independent Churches in Ibadan, Nigeria. The order of preference for preaching materials was as follows: Wisdom, Gospels and Epistles, mythology (as in *Genesis* 1–11), apocalyptic texts (especially for the themes of warning, judgment, and deliverance), prophetic literature, historical accounts, and legal material. Notice that apocalyptic texts came before prophetic literature.

This African attraction to apocalyptic is due to the fact that the fundamental worldview of apocalypse is similar to the worldview of Africa. For the *Book of Revelation*, Christians are "at the embattled frontier between an old and a new world."[28] The war between good and evil is waged simultaneously on two interrelated spheres or levels: the struggle between Satan and God occurs at the heavenly, metaphysical level (chapter 12), while, at the same time, this metaphysical struggle is paralleled by the struggle between the Lamb and the Beast (along with his false prophet) that occurs at the human, political level (chapter 13).[29] The African view is similar and is well expressed by Patrick Kalilombe:

> the [African] world of realities consists of two interrelating spheres, the visible and
> the invisible, of which the visible is in some ways dependent on the invisible. . . .
> What goes on among the living in the visible sphere cannot be fully accounted for
> solely from a consideration of the palpable processes of the visible or physically
> observable realities, for there is a mystical interaction of forces and wills between
> the two spheres.[30]

The idea of mystical, spiritual warfare is at home in Africa. Africans are conscious
of being at the center of invisible warfare conducted through mystical power. The
existence of evil spirits who harm life is taken for granted. Evil does have a supra-
human dimension. Satan and the Beast are not merely symbols or projections of
human fear. Africans will not agree that "the abyss is a reservoir of accumulated
evil, from which come many plagues to torment humankind; but it is fed from the
springs of human sin."[31]

Africans will generally enter the world of *Revelation* precisely through the hymns
that celebrate the triumph of God in this mystical warfare. *Revelation* consists of
heavenly liturgies and dramatic narratives, which are related in such a way that the
liturgical hymns interpret the narrative visions.[32] The hymns sing of a present (invisible) reign of God, which shall become universally manifest in the world.

> The kingdom of the world has become the kingdom of our Lord and his Christ,
> and he will reign for ever and ever. . . . We give thanks to you, Almighty Lord
> God, He who is, He who was, for assuming your great power and beginning
> your reign. . . . The time has come to destroy those who are destroying the earth.
> (11:15-19)

Revelation sings of God's power and intent to renew God's world, and in this sense
it is gospel. The present order of the world is not the order willed by God, and God
will in due course eliminate all who suppress life on earth. In the order portrayed by
Revelation, God's rule is manifest only in the faithful witness of the martyrs, while
the human condition as such is still controlled by the Beast. Yet there is something
to hope and work for: God's righteous kingdom.

Revelation is important to Africans because it nurtures this vision of the future
and inspires them to action to bring the vision about. Mbiti[33] has compared and
contrasted African and Christian eschatology. He has shown that the concepts of
messianic hope, of history moving forward toward a future climax, and of a radical
reversal of humankind's normal condition are new to Africa. The fact is, however,
that these concepts have taken root, filling a felt void. Many European writers tend
to reduce the ubiquitous language of "coming" in *Revelation* to a "present" reality; they thus emphasize that dimension of the resurrection whereby it established

once for all the universal victory of God. Hence for some, "wherever a person lives by faith in Christ and bears witness to that faith without counting the cost, there is the holy city coming down from heaven,"[34] or "New Jerusalem is found wherever human community resists the ways of empire and places God at the center of its shared life."[35] However, we are reminded that "what one sees depends on where on stands." Africans tend to look more intently at the other dimension of the truth of the resurrection, namely, that the present victory of God will usher in the universal and manifest reign of God to be revealed in the future.

Holistic Vision of All of Life

For Africans, the salvation of individuals is no substitute for the complete salvation of the entire human condition. The African person is not an individual, for personality is defined by relationship. The African does not reflect the ideology that says, "I think; therefore, I am." Rather, for Africans, their reality is expressed by the saying, "I am, because we are; and because we are, I am."[36] Nor do humans as a community live their lives in splendid isolation from the rest of creation. Rather, there is an intrinsic relationship among sky, humans, and earth—and authentic human living is at the harmonious intersection of these three interdependent realms. Human beings cannot be fully saved unless the co-determinates of authentic human life are simultaneously saved. In this regard, *Revelation* reinforces the African worldview, for *Revelation* envisions a future not of isolated individuals but of a community living in the holy city and nurtured by the river of life and the tree of life.

Christology: The Lion and the Lamb

The Christology of Revelation is in dispute among scholars. At the very least, all agree that there is tension between the redemptive Lamb Christology and the warlike Lion Christology, the latter image being reinforced by the warring Word of God in 19:11-21. Some scholars argue that the Lion is really the Lamb and that his conquest is solely by redemptive sacrificial death.[37] Others argue that the Lamb has the character traits of a Lion and that Jesus is a conquering Lion now in control of human history. A third group sees the lion as symbol of victory and the slain lamb as symbol of the means of victory, namely death and resurrection.[38] Africans do not dismiss the Lion image of Christ, nor do they reduce it to the Lamb imagery; rather, both have roles to play. In fact, the Lamb imagery itself is complex: the seven seals were unleashed by the Lamb, making the entire population beg for the mountains to fall upon them and to hide them from the One who sits on the throne and from the wrath of the Lamb (6:16). In 17:14, the ten kings will war against the Lamb, and the Lamb will defeat them—this can hardly be interpreted to mean that the Lamb will convert and redeem them. One can say that, for most Africans, the cross of Christ resulted in the wielding of all power by the risen Christ. The risen Christ now uses that power in the struggle against the evil forces opposed to those who believe in him. In treating the question of how the person of Christ fits into the African conceptualization of the world, Mbiti asserts that Christ is seen in Africa primarily as *Christus Victor*, that is, as the Conqueror of all visible and invisible forces:

> the greatest need among African peoples is to see, to know, and to experience Jesus Christ as the victor over the powers and forces from which Africa knows no means of deliverance.[39]

As such, the image of the warring and victorious Lamb of Revelation has great value for the ordinary African Christian. When Jesus is called "savior," the experience of deliverance for many Africans is not primarily from sin; rather, salvation is deliverance from the power of evil principalities and enclaves of human enemies, deliverance from ill health and misfortunes of life as a means to bring wholeness and peace—the complete person saved in unity with God.[40] Hence, Christ is savior in the *present* situation of the believer more so than in the *past* event of the cross. In Africa, one often hears the phrase, "I am covered by the blood of Jesus." This refers primarily to protection against all forces that harm life and only secondarily to liberation from sin. This aspect of the victory of Christ over the dominions and powers occurs elsewhere in the New Testament as well. In *Colossians* 2:15, the author interprets one effect of the cross of Christ as the disarming of the sovereignties and ruling forces, whom Christ paraded in public behind him in his triumphal procession. The death of Christ has to do with much more than just the spiritual salvation of the soul. In this regard, Africa may help Christianity recover aspects of the New Testament doctrine of the saving work of Christ, aspects that have been in abeyance in the West. In support of this is the African reading of *Revelation* as a text that calls for deliverance from oppression by evil beings and systemic powers.

Orientation to the World

Just as the concept of the work of Christ is dynamic and present in the African context, so is the concept of God. Africa worships a living God, a God who still acts in this world in the present. The cosmos is not seen as a closed circle with immutable and self-operating laws, but a potency that is always being brought into effect by acts of divine power. Hence, miracles are nothing extraordinary; Africans expect God to intervene directly in the lives of individuals and of peoples, just as *Revelation* shows God doing with the Christians of Asia Minor.

Although *Revelation* is the most ecclesio-centric (church-centered) book in the New Testament, it is also at the same time the most world-oriented. The martyrs give their lives so that the Beloved City (20:9) of humankind may appear on earth. The dimensions of the city, a cube, represent the Holy of Holies, but the boundaries cover the entire world. The city is a mountain 1,500 miles high; that is, heaven is joined to earth. Finally, "here is the tent of God among human beings. He will make his home among them; they will be his people" (21:3). Heaven even displaces itself to earth; God brings down God's throne to dwell with humans. The river of life rises from the throne of God and the Lamb, and on its banks is the tree of life. God exists for humankind, and life flows from God to give life to every being that lives. The vision of *Revelation* could not be more African. J. V. Taylor[41] speaks of the "unbroken circle," the African sense of cosmic oneness, which includes God as the origin of the life force. For the African, the well-being of humanity consists in the mutual interaction of forces in the cosmos in harmony with the cosmic totality. The African is *"un terrien obstiné"* (a stubborn earth-dweller),[42] whose favored place for the beatific vision remains the earth: he/she obliges God to come to earth, to renew God's own closeness to humanity, to descend to earth in order that humans may avail of the life force in God.[43]

Conclusion

Worship is the first and last note of *Revelation*. This theme of worship brings us back to our initial reflections about power and worship. For behind the activity of worship is the question of power: "Who indeed is in charge of this world?" There is worship that leads to life, and there is worship that is an instrument of death. Africans are a worshiping people; worship is integral to their life. Worship reaffirms the God-given cosmic order, and it fans the hopes for fullness of life. Oppressive regimes are ever wary of true worship; in 1985, church services were banned in South Africa, and police attacked worshipers with tear gas.[44] John Le Grange, the Minister for Law and Order, warned that it was "dangerous to continue teaching that Christians should obey God more than the state." Some oppressors in Africa are seeking to take the bite out of worship by funding overly spiritualistic groups to flood whole areas with a "Jesus-is-the-answer" worship that seeks mere consolation and that dulls the will to resist oppression. True worship of God is always a threat to imperialists and rulers who would wield absolute and self-serving power.

But in the end all mediations cease, God lowers God's self to humans, and a renewed earth becomes the Holy of Holies. Worship transmutes into the beatific vision. No longer does worship consist essentially in hymns of praise and adoration; rather, the very rhythm of life and the very breath of humans become worship. *Revelation* here proclaims something more than any culture ever proposed: it challenges African religiosity (and all religiosities) to *duc in altum* (to cast the net deeper), to enter into the very embrace of God.

Notes

1. Compare M. Eugene Boring, *Revelation*, 133.

2. Compare G. B. Caird, *The Revelation of St. John the Divine*, 62.

3. Elizabeth Schüssler Fiorenza, *Revelation: Vision of a Just World*, 3.

4. Mary Ann Tolbert, "The Politics and Poetics of Location," 314.

5. Daniel Patte, *Ethics of Biblical Interpretation: A Reevaluation*, 86.

6. Daniel Patte, "Biblical Scholars at the Interface between Critical and Ordinary Readings: A Response," 269.

7. Patrick Kalilombe, "Spirituality in the African Perspective," 115–35; Laurenti Magesa, *African Religion: The Moral Traditions of Abundant Life*; Henri Maurier, *Philosophie de l'Afrique noire*; John S. Mbiti, *African Religions and Philosophy*; J. V. Taylor, *Christian Presence amid African Religion*; Dominique Zahan, *The Religion, Spirituality, and Thought of Traditional Africa*.

8. Dietrich Bonhoeffer, *The Cost of Discipleship*, 79.

9. Cf. Justin Ukpong, "Reading the Bible in a Global Village: Issues and Challenges from African Readings," 33.

10. Schüssler Fiorenza, *Revelation*, 98.

11. On June 3, 1886, thirty-two young men of the court of King Mwanga of Buganda were burnt to death at Namugongo, Uganda, for refusing to give up their new Christian faith.

12. Fiorenza, *Revelation*, 51.

13. Magesa, *African Religion*, 246.

14. Mbiti, *African Religions and Philosophy*, 71.

15. Laurenti Magesa, *African Religion*, 6.

16. Even here, Ben Witherington, *The Acts of the Apostles: A Socio-Rhetorical Commentary*, 463, gives the sense of the decree as "turn from idolatry and its accompanying acts of impurity."

17. Gordon D. Fee, "Once Again: An Interpretation of 1 Corinthians 8-10," 186. In the light of this, the translation of *Revelation* 2:14 is problematic. The NJB translated *phageiōn eiōdōlo, thuta kai porōeusai* as "they committed adultery by eating food that has been sacrificed to idols". Here "adultery" is a metaphor for idolatry. But the NRSV translates it as "so that they would eat food sacrificed to idols and practice fornication"; here it is presumed that immorality went with the sacrifices.

18. Pablo Richard, *Apocalypse: A People's Commentary on the Book of Revelation*, 35.

19. Boring, *Revelation*, 116.

20. Renita J. Weems, *Battered Love: Marriage, Sex, and Violence in the Hebrew Prophets*, xiii, 1.

21. Compare Alan Boesak, *Comfort and Protest: The Apocalypse from a South African Perspective*, 72.

22. Walter Brueggemann, *Revelation and Violence. A Study in Contextualization*, 20.

23. Brueggemann, *Revelation and Violence*, 58.

24. Adela Yarbro Collins, *Crisis and Catharsis*, 170

25. J. Denny Weaver, *The Nonviolent Atonement*, 32.

26. Miroslav Volf, *Exclusion and Embrace: A Theological Exploration of Identity, Otherness, and Reconciliation*, 296.

27. *Profile through Preaching: A Study of the Sermon Texts Used in a West African Independent Church*, 78.

28. Amos Wilder, *The Language of the Gospel*, 131.

29. E. Schillebeeckx, *Christ: The Experience of Jesus as Lord*, 450.

30. Patrick A. Kalilombe, "Spirituality in the African Perspective," 120.

31. Caird, *The Revelation of St. John the Divine*, 293.

32. Mathias Rissi, "The Kerygma of the Revelation to John"; Leonard Thompson, "Cult and Eschatology in the Apocalypse of John," 342.

33. Mbiti, "Eschatology," 180–84.

34. Caird, *The Revelation of St. John the Divine*, 55.

35. Weaver, *The Nonviolent Atonement*, 31–32.

36. Mbiti, *African Religions and Philosophy*, 108.

37. Boring, *Revelation*, 108; Richard Baukham, *The Theology of the Book of Revelation*, 75; Caird, *Apocalypse*, 69–72; Minear, *New Testament Apocalyptic*, 111.

38. Weaver, *The Nonviolent Atonement*, 32.

39. J. S. Mbiti, "African Concepts of Christology," 54–55.

40. Mbiti, *Bible and Theology in African Christianity*, 152.

41. J. V. Taylor, *The Primal Vision: Christian Presence amid African Religion*, 64–66.

42. Dominique Zahan, *Religion, Spirituality, and Thought of Traditional Africa*, 155.

43. Ibid., 17.

44. Boesak, *Comfort and Protest*, 37.

6

The Heroine and the Whore:
The *Apocalypse of John* in Feminist Perspective

▊ ▊

Tina Pippin

Introduction

I grew up in a textile mill town in the southern United States.[1] Fundamentalist Christianity was heavy in the air, although I had refuge from biblical inerrancy in a small Episcopal church. There the 1928 *Book of Common Prayer* was, for too many years, without error. Copies of the experimental prayer books were hidden in the fellowship hall, and when I was a teenager, I would borrow these forbidden and much maligned texts. But the *Apocalypse of John* barely existed in our authoritative canons, and only then in sanitized and heavily edited versions of the throne room scenes or the New Jerusalem. Mostly the *Apocalypse* remained deep in the lectionary and could be easily avoided and ignored. Of course, gender roles were strictly maintained; only males could be acolytes or priests. And Paul was sometimes invoked to argue that women's heads should be covered in church. So my childhood was a complex mix of middle-range liturgical worship, allegiances to tradition, and frequent maligning of fundamentalism. Although I was taught early on that the Bible was like a fairy tale, issues of gender were never discussed.

Throughout all my training in biblical studies, from college through doctoral work, I never had a woman professor, nor did I encounter a feminist reading in the classroom. The one exception was a seminary lecture on feminist hermeneutics, and the presenter was a guest speaker, Phyllis Trible. In my other field, social ethics, I was reading numerous feminist thinkers, and feminist concerns were central. But in New Testament studies, patriarchal readings of biblical texts served as the entry point to exegesis and interpretation. I could still argue, fairly effortlessly, that even today patriarchal methods remain normative, despite a wealth of feminist readings.

Still, it seems almost unreal that only a short time ago—the Reagan years in the 1980s—I had to find a feminist path outside of my formal biblical education.

I have always felt limited by the traditional, historical-critical readings that searched for "definite information"—like date, authorship, social context, meanings of symbols, and so forth. As a feminist reader of biblical texts drawing on various disciplines, I had to look far and wide for conversation partners as a means to delve deeper into the more evaluative, underlying dynamics of the text. I have learned from my partners—in particular, postmodernism, ideological criticism, and fantasy theory—that a biblical text, whether grounded in the canon or loosed from its canonical home, can be a dangerous thing. What I have found in my journey is that the *Apocalypse of John* is a multivalent text that lends itself to multiple interpretations. The result is that there are seemingly infinite *Apocalypses of John*, each one constructed according to the perspective of the interpreter. That is to say, instead of an approach that finds single answers to questions seeking information, I have discovered that there are many places from which to view the *Apocalypse*.

I have chosen here to search John's *Apocalypse* for gender issues and to read it looking for and identifying with the women characters. As John portrays them, the women of the *Apocalypse*, through their acts and demeanor, symbolize either good or evil. My fundamental questions are: What underlying patterns of gender are displayed in this text? What does it mean to read for and with women, both in and outside the text? What does the characterization of women in this text have to say to and about contemporary women? What are ways to resist this patriarchal text?

Methods: Feminism, Ideology, and Fantasy Literature

My methodology in this article is plural; I want to create a conversation among ideological criticism, feminist hermeneutics, and literary studies in fantasy literature. Ideological criticism involves reading for the values and assumptions in a text and ways in which the text exposes certain ways of understanding the world. For example, from an ideological point of view, John in the broader sense subverts the status quo of the Roman Empire, but at the same time he reinforces the status quo of gender stereotypes and roles. The *Apocalypse* can be liberating on many levels, especially if the interpreter is using a liberation or postcolonial approach. Feminist hermeneutics enables me to show other ways and approaches to reading this text, leading me to the conclusion that this text is not liberating for women (or for men who care about the liberation of women). In exploring the literary studies of the fantastic I have discovered insights into reading about "other worlds" of the magical and mythical and about how the "fantastic" has traditionally categorized women as either good or evil, but in either case inferior to men.

Fantasies of the Future:
The Function of the Female in the Apocalypse

In responding to the science fiction writer Joanna Russ, Robert Scholes states, "Maybe an all-female world is the only hope for the future of the human race. It's worth considering."[2] Women readers responding to the *Apocalypse of John* may well want to entertain a similar idea! Look, for example, at the roles of the female characters in the *Apocalypse.* The earth-bound females, both the prophetess Jezebel (2:20-23) and the Whore of Babylon as the symbol of Rome (17:1-19:6), are immoral and seductive, and they help the evil males in the destruction of earth. Both face destruction themselves. Although the Woman Clothed with the Sun (12:1-17) is able to function positively in bringing about a political utopia, even she appears to be left out of the utopian city of the New Jerusalem, which is represented by the Bride (19:6-10; 21:1-2). As such, the role of the female is clearly subordinate to males in the *Apocalypse.* And once female figures are used or abused by male figures in the story, either there is no further need for them in the future world of this text or else any reference to their future presence and function is omitted.

Reading the text as a woman demands reading for the gender codes in the narrative, both in terms of where women appear and where they are noticeably absent. If Joanna Russ is correct in her analysis of science fiction, there are no realistic portrayals of women there, only stereotypical "images of women." As with science fiction, the female in fantasy literature in general is a stereotypical image. So also, in the *Apocalypse*, the images of women are blurred or they are stereotyped or they are conspicuously absent altogether. Women are either marginalized on "the edge of time" (to borrow from novelist Marge Piercy), or they are completely displaced from time.

In the enchanting and disenchanting world of the *Apocalypse of John*, the role of the female is present but displaced to subordinate roles. This displacement occurs in two spheres, the political sphere and the religious sphere. Thus, women are displaced twice; namely, they are "double-bound" to subordinate roles in both the political and the religious worlds. John's text portrays and displaces two contrasting female archetypes: the Heroine figure (queen-mother of heaven, the Woman Clothed with the Sun) and the Whore figure (Babylon-queen-mother of hell, representative of Rome). The subversive text of the *Apocalypse* subverts the status quo of the political realm and the status quo of the religious realm—the political and religious realities of the Roman Empire—but it subverts Rome without subverting or changing or challenging the typical gender relations in the culture and without empowering the "collective female." Such a dynamic is not atypical. In fact, studies in fantasy literature and in folk and fairy tales provide interesting parallels to the apocalyptic imagination evident in John's text.

In terms of the conspicuous absence of women in the *Apocalypse*, consider the description of the 144,000 who are on Mount Zion and who bear the name of the Lamb and the name of the Lamb's Father on their foreheads. They have learned a new song, and no one else can learn that song except these men "who have been redeemed from the earth." And they are clearly males only, for the author adds: "It is these who have not defiled themselves with women, for they are virgins" (14:4). The 144,000 represent the whole number of the faithful, and they are men. It is not just that males alone are present but that women are explicitly excluded. Adela Yarbro Collins notices that this passage employs sacrificial language and reflects purity laws. Her point is that women's bodies are seen as negative and capable of defiling men through intercourse or the blood of menstruation. Yarbro Collins observes that this passage "assumes that the model Christian is male."[3]

However, she fails to make full use of the logical inference—namely, that the New Jerusalem, God's future world, will exclude females! It is not just that males are the models and women are to imitate them. Rather, in order for the candidates for heaven to remain "spotless"—indeed for heaven itself to remain spotless—women will be displaced from it. Furthermore, the 144,000 are described in this way: "And in their mouth no lie was found; they are blameless" (14:5). This description removes the power of discourse from women. It assumes that only male speech is significant. And male speech, including that of John in this passage, is depicting women as a defiling force. Male is the subject; female is the object—the object of desire that must be displaced in order for men to remain undefiled!

Thus, the subject-object split is in place, a split that places the male as subject and the female as object either of desire or violence or both. This subject-object split as male/female is the same split as the dialectic of body/mind, nature/culture. Male is the "dominant subject" of the split and is associated with mind and culture, while female is the "subordinate object" of the split and is associated with body and nature. The *Apocalypse* reinforces rather than overcomes this subject-object split. In other words, to read the *Apocalypse* is to be drawn into the author's perspective that views females as objects. In the *Apocalypse*, the narrative as "socially symbolic act" (Jameson) retains the sexual oppression and stereotypes of woman as object of violence and desire. Concerning this split, Gayatri Spivak says that in order to take the female object and make her a female subject, "The collective project of our feminist critique must always be to rewrite the *social* text so that the historical and sexual differentials are operated together."[4] A feminist hermeneutic, therefore, does not take for granted the world of the text but rather re-reads the narrative for its gender codes. Two key questions to address this issue are: Who is the female? And what are her powers and plays in the *Apocalypse*?

A tension exists in the narrative of the *Apocalypse* between two different archetypes of the female: the Heroine and the Whore. This dialectic of archetypal material can be explained in several different ways—by the subject-object split or in terms of dualistic, binary oppositions or by means of the concept of displacement. Spivak's concern is with the concept of difference and, in particular, of sexual difference, which is of course based upon her reading of the deconstructionist Jacques Derrida. The issue is: What is the similarity or difference between the female stereotypes in the society and the treatment of the female in the text? The female that is displaced from subject to object in the political fantasy of the *Apocalypse* is the female that reflects (mirrors or mimics) aspects of the prevailing social order (both good and evil) and of the prevailing ideology.

Fantasy theorist Lance Olson's definition of postmodern fantasy further clarifies the deconstructive mode of fantasy literature in subverting (or not) the prevailing social order:

> Often fantasy begins in the realm of the mimetic, then disrupts it introducing an element of the marvelous, the *effect* being to jam marvelous and mimetic assumptions. In other words, fantasy [like apocalyptic] is that stutter between two modes of discourse which generates textual instability, an ellipse of uncertainty. Its result is the banging together of the *here* and *there* so that neither the reader nor the protagonist knows quite where he [*sic*] is. That is, fantasy is a deconstructive mode of narrative.[5] Hence, the fantastic is a mode designed to surprise, to question, to put into doubt, to create anxiety, to make active, to make uncomfortable, to disgust, to repel, to rebel, to subvert, to pervert, to make ambiguous, to make discontinuous, to deform. It is a mode whose premise is a will to deconstruct.[6]

That is to say, fantasy subverts the current order of things by presenting something that is out of the ordinary—the fantastic or the marvelous. In this regard, the *Apocalypse* has elements of both the mimetic (in which "the way things are" is presented just as they are) and the fantastic, the supernatural, or, according to Tsvetan Todorov, the "marvelous" (in which "the way things are" is subverted by another way to see things). Clearly, by means of the visions of heaven and the image of the fantastic New Jerusalem, the *Apocalypse* subverts the "reality" of the way things are in regard to political and religious domination by the Roman Empire. But the images of the female reflect only the mimetic and not the fantastic. They simply perpetuate the way things are in the dominant society. In the case of the *Apocalypse*, the images of the female archetypes are presented in reverse, because the images are turned inside-out. That is to say, what Rome considers to be evil (Christians), the *Apocalypse* presents as good (the Heroine). And what Rome considers to be good (the Roman Empire!), the *Apocalypse* considers to be evil (the Whore). But while the political realities represented by these images are subverted and reversed, the stereotypes of female figures in themselves remain unchanged and unchallenged.

All of this is at the archetypal level of the narrative and may remain obscure to readers noticing only the surface level of the narrative. Because the *Apocalypse* simply mirrors hidden dimensions of gender patterns in the culture, those patterns continue to remain hidden in the *Apocalypse*. Fantasy scholar Rosemary Jackson may be correct in saying, "The fantastic traces the unsaid and the unseen of culture: that which has been silenced, made invisible, covered over and made 'absent.'"[7] If it is true that the fantastic exposes the oppressions that are hidden, then the *Apocalypse* falls far short of complete subversion of the social order. The political order of Rome and the religious order that supports Rome are obviously exposed and subverted, but not the gender order. Its dynamics remain hidden and unchanged from the culture to the text. The domination of male over female in the culture remains the same and is even reinforced by the *Apocalypse*. The female is still "absent," even though she is represented in both powerful and powerless modes of being and acting. She is "absent" as a subject because she remains an object, an "image of female." In this text, the female is still "other," still marginalized, still banished to the edges of the text.

Females are present in the text, but at the same time they are absent as subjects of their own lives. They are simply objects of male desire and violence. "Jezebel" is a seductive object of desire to those who follow her and are misled into "fornication." She is an object of violence to the author who prophesies that she will be destroyed (by the male god). The Heroine is an object of good desire as one who gives birth (to the messiah, no less). The Whore is an object of evil desire to those who are seduced by her purple clothes and gold jewelry and who are led to "commit fornication" with her. The Whore is an object of violence to the author who depicts the celebration of her utter desolation and burning. The Bride is an object of good desire as the wife of the Lamb. This final female image is connected with a male, the Lamb, and is described "as a bride adorned for her husband" (21:2). The Bride is woman as desired object, adorned and passive; the New Jerusalem is the image of the seductive, the object of erotic desire.

While these images make the female absent as subject but present as objects, in the end all the female figures become completely removed from the world of the story. The prophetess Jezebel and her unrepentant followers will be thrown upon a bed and will die (2:22-23). The Whore of Babylon is dethroned and made desolate and totally destroyed, as the ceremonial line proclaims: "Fallen, fallen is Babylon the great!" (18:2). Even the Woman Clothed with the Sun is "banished" for protection and safekeeping to the wilderness, "to her place where she is nourished for a time, and times, and half a time" (12:14). The Bride figure (the New Jerusalem) alone is left standing, but only briefly, for she is replaced by the imagery of the city. The female—whether depicted as the cause of evil or as the cause of good in the world of the story—is nonetheless in the end erased from the text. Hence, all the females in the *Apocalypse* are victims; they remain objects either of desire or of violence, because they are all stereotyped, archetypal images of the female and not subjects—not the embodiment of power and control over their own lives or over either the real or the fantastic worlds.

The subjection and displacement of the female in the *Apocalypse* comes out of the unconscious. This unconscious is expressed in the imagined order of things in the world of the text. Imagination is not fixed but fluid. The unconscious desire for the new social and political order is very evident in the *Apocalypse*, but at the same time this unconscious desire does nothing to improve the status of women. The imaginary is ideological, and the ideology of gender types in the text is controlled by the sexual imagination of the male. The imagination that is operating in the text of the *Apocalypse* involves the image of the virginal male controlling (desiring/displacing/destroying) the female images. This is the case because of the hierarchal order implicit in the male imagination of the *Apocalypse*: first God and the Lamb, then the 144,000, after which come the good female images, followed by the evil female images, and lastly those males who are seduced by them. The desire of the true believer is to enter the heavenly city (the Bride), but there is erotic tension in this desire that involves a distancing from the female. On the one hand, entrance into the female (the Bride) is desirable. On the other hand, that entrance into the Bride exists only in the future, and it is possible only if the group of men desiring her remain sexually pure and undefiled by women!

Studies on women in traditional science fiction have shown how women are depicted as powerless in the future of the worlds imagined by males. The key is that the male remains the paradigm and subject of the future. One such study reports that women in science fiction function as sexual beings and "as appropriate rewards for the male protagonists who solve the problem. When a woman acts independently, she is evil; when she has power, it is intuitive or magical; when she has extra-human abilities, they are the problem."[8] In the *Apocalypse,* in order for women to be legitimate they must be granted their magical powers from male figures, from God and the Lamb; women who act on their own are defying the male-defined gender roles for women. Hence, Jezebel and the Whore, both of whom act on their own power independent of God and of the Lamb, are destroyed. Indeed, the more telling point is that these autonomous females are used symbolically by the author of the *Apocalypse* as scapegoats for *all* the evil in society.

The female with power is both desired and feared. The unconscious (or conscious) desire for the powerful, autonomous female is very strong. At the same time, the threat of a female with power over men—power identified in the form of seduction—is feared, so feared that the reaction is violence against the female. All the females in the *Apocalypse* are erotic images with potentially erotic power over men. Hence, the male must make the female into an object, displace her, marginalize her, stereotype her, destroy her, and in the end make her completely absent. Nevertheless, the desire for the powerful female is so strong that it remains even after she is destroyed. In the *Apocalypse*, men displace women by not defiling themselves with women, yet the image of a desirable female is still implanted in their minds—because now they will enter the Bride! The desire here has been transferred from the Whore to the Bride. Coming out of the Whore and entering the Bride is set up as a rite of *undefiled* men, yet the sexual fantasy about the Bride that remains is strong and alluring. The adorned Bride is an enchanting and erotic image that lures the 144,000 to the New Jerusalem.

There is another crucial point to be made before we look more closely at the contrasting images of the Heroine and the Whore in the *Apocalypse*. The dualistic, either/ or nature of the political/religious stance in the *Apocalypse* is clear. It is either Satan or God, either Rome or the New Jerusalem. But here I want to extend this claim of dualism to the sexual images as well. The erotic, enchanting female brings either birth or death. The distinct female archetypes in the *Apocalypse* represent either the way to God (rebirth in the New Jerusalem) or the way to Satan (death in the abyss).

The female images that lead to death seem to encompass many fears. Fantasy scholar Donald Palumbo makes an interesting point about the "connection between eroticism and death." In his view, our subconscious fears of the unknown (especially death) are made available to us in fantasy literature; that is, fantasy enables us to overcome death.[9] In this regard, Palumbo believes that the concern of the fantastic with sexuality gives it "psychological appeal." He summarizes his findings: "And sexuality almost always appears as the symbolic vehicle of rebirth in the nearly ubiquitous death and resurrection motifs that suffuse great fantasy literature."[10] Fear of imperialism, fear of famine, fear of disease, and fear of death itself are infused into the archetype of the seductive Whore whose erotic power over men is the most terrifying in a society that marginalizes and dis-empowers females. Females with autonomous power bring death. So, if we can overcome these females in fantasy, we can overcome our fears. Remove or completely destroy the females, and all is right with the world again.

By contrast, only those females who are connected with God, only those females adorned for the honeymoon or with wombs for use by God, that is, brides and mothers—women who have their identity by virtue of their subordination to men—are safe. These are women who are controlled by men and who do not exercise their powers on their own. Still, they too lure men, for they too are highly erotic images of desire. And the archetypes of bride and queen-mother are intended to be even more erotic, even more desirable and enchanting than the archetypes of prophetess and whore.

It is to these two contrasting images of females in the dualistic imagination of the *Apocalypse* that we now turn: the Heroine (the Woman Clothed with the Sun) and the Whore (the seductive prostitute representing Rome).

The Archetypal Heroine: The Woman Clothed with the Sun

Traditional interpretations of the Woman Clothed with the Sun in chapter 12 are so focused on the historical referent of this figure that she has almost lost her place as a character in her own right in the story. Like the Bride and the Whore who represent cities, she has been seen as representing historical institutions, namely, Israel and the church. But what is her place in the story? And how does she compare with other female figures in the *Apocalypse*? Unlike the other female figures in the text, the Woman Clothed with the Sun has no name. Whereas the fate of the other female figures is explicitly stated, her fate is undetermined (although we assume she is safe). She is set against a formidable foe, the great red dragon, but with help (from God and the earth) she is able to escape. She is speechless, without dialogue of any kind, except for her cries of pain in childbirth. And her presence is diminished—rendered barely visible—by the battle between God (Michael) and Satan, which takes place in the middle of the account about her and which overshadows her importance in the text.

If readings of the Grimms' *Kinder-und Haus Marchen* and other folk and fairy tales are any indication, then readers will identify (especially if the readers are women) with the heroine in a story. Karen Rowe offers an explanation as to how heroine identification works: "subconsciously women may transfer from fairy tales into real life cultural norms which exalt passivity, dependency, and self-sacrifice as a female's cardinal virtues. In short, fairy tales perpetuate the patriarchal *status quo* by making female subordination seem a romantically desirable, indeed an inescapable fate."[11]

The implication is that readers will transfer this mother-archetype in the *Apocalypse* to real life—whereby the female as a sexual being is affirmed only in the act of giving birth to a male child (to the messiah!). The woman in *Apocalypse* 12 is identified twice by her reproductive event: "And she gave birth to a son, a male child, who is to rule all the nations with a rod of iron" (12:5) and "the woman who had given birth to the male child "(12:13). In other words, the message is that females are productive when they are reproductive. The sexual affirmation of the Heroine in the birth process is in direct opposition to the orgy of the Whore and her followers, depicted later in the *Apocalypse*.[12] Pain in childbirth is set against the pleasure of orgasm.[13] Sexual difference in the text points out the dialectic of desire; that is, the text plays with the erotic on both sides—desire for the good females and desire for the evil females—while at the same time reaffirming traditional stereotypes of the good woman who is obedient and long-suffering (emphasis on "long").

In chapter 12 the woman is connected with nature. She is "clothed with the sun," has "the moon under her feet," with a "crown of twelve stars on her head," and she flees "into the wilderness." Sun, moon, stars, and wilderness evoke the natural order, particularly heaven, but they also open the way to God. Adela Yarbro Collins finds parallels between this Queen of Heaven figure in *Apocalypse* 12 and the goddesses Artemis (Ephesus), Atargatis (Syria), and especially Isis (Egypt and Asia Minor). Sun, moon, and stars as part of the zodiac are also used in depictions of these goddesses. Collins states, "The astral attributes with which she is endowed seem to belong to the typical depiction of a high goddess."[14] Another detail of the goddess Isis that is shared by the woman in the *Apocalypse* is that the Woman Clothed with the Sun "was given two wings of the great eagle, so that she could fly" (12:14). Similarly, Isis is represented in the form of a swallow who has power in flight. This bird motif is a typical image of the goddess. In the *Apocalypse*, the magical wings enable the woman to escape danger by flying to the wilderness. The bird motif is a powerful symbol of a high goddess. However, this positive female figure in the *Apocalypse* is not allowed to be a powerful high goddess. The evil female figure of the Whore is high goddess for a while, but she is brought down by the male god. Here is another example in literature, like the grotesque destruction of the goddess Tiamat in the *Enuma Elish*, of the death of the goddess and her replacement by the male god as head.

The Heroine in this story does not get enough credit. She gives birth on her own to the messiah child, who is immediately "snatched away" from her by God and "taken up to God and his throne" (12:5). Meanwhile, the woman flees to the wilderness two times (in 2:6 and 14), and there she is left. She enacts a kind of "traveling heroism" that is evident in women characters of fantasy literature.[15] She is an active heroine, except that she does not enact her own equality.[16] She takes the initiative in fleeing to the wilderness, yet there she is taken care of by the male God (12:6, 13). The Woman Clothed with the Sun is a goddess subdued, tamed, and under control. After her reproductive activity is completed, she is no longer useful; and so she ends up in the wilderness. The traditional female values that customarily accompany the act of mothering—nurture and caretaking—are suppressed. Instead, the child is taken immediately to live in heaven, where traditional male values of competition and separation come to the fore. While the Heroine, Jezebel, and the Whore are all three hunted in the *Apocalypse*, only the Heroine escapes. Nevertheless, her escape banishes her from the center of power to the marginal space of the wilderness. The female is de-centered, even when she is held as an ideal woman.

The irony of the function of women in the *Apocalypse* is incredible. Why even portray the Woman Clothed with the Sun with the motifs of the goddess of heaven when she will end up so marginalized? If the woman in *Apocalypse* 12 is the producer of the one who will liberate the oppressed—the mother of the messiah—then why is she not herself liberated to play a powerful role in her own right? Instead she flees to the wilderness and remains there under the male god's protection—and we hear no more of her. In the *Apocalypse*, the Queen of Heaven is condemned to silence.

Silence has an interesting function for the females of the *Apocalypse*. The model of the silent woman is a model for many heroines in fantasy and folktale. According to Eugen Weber, "it is not surprising that in a lot of folktales [the idea of] enduring in silence is one of the most common tests a heroine (or even a hero) has to pass, often connected with torment by witches or by devils."[17] Ruth Bottigheimer finds that the majority of folktales in *Grimms' Tales* condemn "women to silence during which they are often exposed to mortal danger,"[18] which is part of what Bottigheimer refers to as "textual silence and powerlessness."[19] The Heroine of *Apocalypse* 12 "cried out in her pangs of birth." So, we hear her anguish but not her words. Instead of words, she is given wings, "the two wings of the great eagle" (12:13) to fly into the wilderness. Still, she does not speak; she endures in silence in the wilderness. The two brief scenes of power where she flees and then flies into the wilderness (12: 6, 14) are quickly joined with scenes of dependency on the power of God as the ultimate protection, as the one who will take care of her, who will "nourish her" in the desert. She is a goddess with her own power, but she needs a male god to rescue her and to keep her power under control.

The textual/sexual strategies at work in the motif of the silent female are dangerous to women's consciousness. Female voice and values are suppressed. Marcia Landy summarizes the problem:

> for the most part women have concurred, have accepted the male images [of them] as their own or have created accommodations satisfactory to them [men] within the given power structure—a Virgin Queen, an Amazon, a Wielder of Power over Children and Lovesick Men—or women have agreed to see themselves as witches, demons, and deceivers. The consequences of straying from legitimized social norms were obviously too costly to entertain—deprivation of God, of man, of sociability, of economic sustenance, of biological needs.[20]

Political, economic, and religious structures are subverted in the *Apocalypse*, but women's roles and functions remain the same. The cost of straying from the traditional gender roles was apparently too great. So, women remain objects. Like the Heroine, they are to remain silent. They do not become subjects in their own right by being given speech, their own voice. The only woman who "speaks" in the *Apocalypse* is "Jezebel," and she is vicious not virtuous—and will be suppressed. The whore of Babylon is given words, but they are unspoken words that she harbors in her heart (18:7). The archetyping of the female and her narrative silence relay a powerful message to the reader/hearer of the text: all women are to remain silent, but not even all silent women are "good."

The Archetypal Prostitute: The Whore of Babylon

The Whore of Babylon is made to symbolize all the evil of the Roman Empire and, in particular, the city of Rome, with all its social, political, economic, and religious dynamics of oppression. Yet the focus of my concern here is not with what the image symbolized. Rather, I am concerned with the way in which this image of a prostitute is portrayed and used as a female symbol.

The harlot is characterized in different ways in the Hebrew tradition. In the Hebrew Bible, for example, the harlot is sometimes characterized as a heroine. Here we could point to Tamar (*Genesis 38*) and Rahab (*Joshua 2* and 6). On the other hand, the loose woman of the *Book of Proverbs* is depicted as a deceiver and a foreigner. Clearly, the Whore of the *Apocalypse* is no heroine. The name on her forehead (a sign of slavery) is Babylon, and she is the "mother of harlots and of earth's abominations" (17:5). She is the ultimate deceiver and "loose woman." The Whore is seductive; she is adorned in fine clothes and jewels and sits upon a scarlet beast. And when one looks closer, the golden cup is full of the evil of her sexual acts—her fornications—with the kings of the earth. Furthermore, as a result of her oppressions and persecutions, she is "drunk with the blood of the saints and the blood of the witnesses of Jesus" (18:6). The whole depiction of the Whore is extremely grotesque; she is a huge, exaggerated presence who is "seated on many waters" (17:1). As in chapter 12, the setting for this vision of a female is the wilderness, but in this scene, instead of being protected by God, the female ends up being brutally murdered.

This female figure has power. The thoughts of the Whore about her power are revealed to the reader: "in her heart she says, 'I rule as a queen; I am no widow, and I will never see grief'" (18:7). The belief in and expression of the powers of women are remnants of ancient beliefs in the Mother Goddess. Bottigheimer comments, "the female's original access to power through her association with nature became perverted and denied, so that more recent versions of fairy tales (e.g., the Grimms') relegate power held by females to the old, the ugly, and/or the wicked."[21] In the *Apocalypse*, the female is seductive and she has power—and she will not be tolerated. The Whore declares herself (to herself) to be a queen, and because of her egoism she will be judged and destroyed.

The destruction of the Whore in the scenes that follow is violent and total. She is hated, stripped naked, and burned up. All this is told in language that is graphic and repeated. The whole visionary scenario of the Whore of Babylon from beginning to end—from the depiction of her enthronement on the beast to her utter demise—is grotesque and larger than life. This fantastic scene, played on such a grand scale, plays out as a "parody" of the social, political, economic, and religious system of the Roman Empire.

The dialogical model of Mikhail Bakhtin is useful in reading this fantastic "parody." As Rosemary Jackson summarizes: "Unlike the marvelous or the mimetic, the fantastic is a mode of writing which *enters a dialogue with the 'real' and incorporates that dialogue as part of its essential structure.* To return to Bakhtin's phrase, fantasy is 'dialogical,' interrogating single or unitary ways of seeing."[22] Bakhtin's formalist ties show that language is subversive. Through the fantasy language of parody, the dominant ideology is "interrogated" and challenged. By parody, Bakhtin means, "the creation of a *decrowning double; it is that same 'world turned inside out.'* . . . It was like an entire system of crooked mirrors, elongating, diminishing, distorting in various directions and to various degrees."[23] Bakhtin finds parody in the New Testament

(Gospels, *Acts*, and *Apocalypse*) but notes that the "dialogic element" of satire there is expressed in a relationship of opposites (good and evil) and is thereby managed.[24]

Parody primarily is located in the genre of the carnivalesque, where it is not "managed." In medieval carnivals, there were elaborate public rituals by people in masks and costumes in which "the powers that be" were paraded, parodied, ridiculed, and destroyed in mock festivals and plays with great exaggeration and hilarity. Similarly, in the scene of the enthronement and destruction of the Whore of Babylon, indeed in the *Apocalypse* as a whole, there are clearly carnivalesque features. The carnival is used in folklore to express a "serio-comical" approach to the world.[25] Bakhtin reveals three main characteristics of the genre of the serio-comical: (1) the time of the narrative is the present reality; (2) the narrative is based on history and not legend, relying on "experience . . . and on free invention"; (3) the narrative has multiple levels, or in Bakhtin's words:

> Characteristic of these genres are a multi-tone narration, the mixing of high and low, serious and comic; they make wide use of inserted genres—letters, found manuscripts, retold dialogues, parodies on the high genres, parodically reinterpreted citations; in some of them we observe a mixing of prosaic and poetic speech, living dialects and jargons . . . are introduced, and various authorial masks make their appearance. . . . And what happens here, as a result, is a radically new relationship to the word as the material of literature.[26]

This "carnival sense of the world" as both comic and serious is found in Christian narrative. Bakhtin gives the example of the ridicule and hilarity that accompanied "the scene of crowning and decrowning" of Jesus as King of the Jews in the Gospel narratives.[27] The scene of the fall of Babylon in the *Apocalypse* is also directly carnivalesque. The Whore who is all adorned on the scarlet beast and who considers herself to be a queen is dethroned. The narrator tells us of the erotic image of the Whore as queen: "When I saw her, I was greatly amazed" (17:6). In medieval times, such a mock coronation/de-coronation scene was a ritual event that was performed in the public square and streets as a communal ritual.[28] Bakhtin describes the significance of this ritual:

> Carnival is the festival of all-annihilating and all-renewing time. This is not an abstract thought but a living sense of the world, expressed in concretely sensuous forms (either expressed or play-acted) of the ritual act. Crowning/decrowning is a dualistic ambivalent ritual, expressing the inevitability and at the same time the creative power of the shift-and-renewal, the *joyful relativity* of all structure and order, of all authority and all (hierarchical) position. . . . Birth is fraught with death, and death with new birth.[29]

Through the carnival of the *Apocalypse*, the masquerading queen is stripped of her power. The dominant ideology of power and oppression is overthrown in the carnival ritual. The mixture of poetry and prose provides a powerful sense of the eccentricity of the Whore and the shift of the structures of authority.

In the *Apocalypse*, the horror of the carnival death of the Whore is expressed in vivid terms: "And the ten horns that you saw, they and the beast will hate the whore; they will make her desolate and naked; they will devour her flesh and burn her up with fire" (17:16). In this scene, the erotic tension is heightened. The Whore is literally stripped "naked" of her fine garments and jewels. Nakedness equals helplessness. The people at the carnival "devour her flesh" (17:16). And the violent feast image is repeated in chapter 19, when the birds of mid-heaven are called to "Come, gather for the great supper of God, to eat the flesh of kings, the flesh of captains, the flesh of the mighty, the flesh of horses and their riders, and the flesh of all, both free and slave, both small and great" (vv. 17-18) "and all the birds were gorged with their flesh" (v. 21). These two grotesque depictions of a feast frame the marriage supper of the Lamb in 19:9. The menu of the marriage supper is not given.

Furthermore, the Whore is "burned up with fire." Bakhtin finds the image of fire ambivalent in carnival: "It is a fire that simultaneously destroys and renews the world" (126). Three times the burning of the Whore is mentioned (17:16; 18:8, 9), and once it says that she will burn forever (19:3). And three times it is mentioned that the destruction occurs in one hour (18:10, 17, 19). Like the dragon goddess Tiamat in the *Enuma Elish,* the Whore is disembodied. The erotic tension here points to the ultimate misogynist fantasy. All of the world's hatred of oppression is heaped on the Whore. With such violence, "Babylon the great city will be thrown down, and will be found no more" (18:21).

Everything is turned inside out in this carnival: the Whore is "drunk with the blood of the saints and the blood of the witnesses of Jesus" (17:6 and 18:24), the nations are drunk from fornicating with the Whore, the nations in turn feast on the Whore's desolate body (and in the process lose all their delicacies), and, finally, the birds of heaven feast on the nations.[30]

The utter destruction of the Whore leads to resurrection and renewal. With the death of the Whore, the Bride "has made herself ready" (19:7) and "to her it has been granted to be clothed with fine linen, bright and pure—for the fine linen is the righteous deeds of the saints" (19:8). This rebirth after the death of the Whore is a sexual rebirth, or at least a rebirth in sexual imagery (the marriage feast). The witch is burned (the hunting of the Whore is a form of witch hunt), and the heroine image is finally free.

The Whore is totally seductive. The Whore seeks to dominate totally. In *Apocalypse* 18:4, a voice from heaven says, "Come out of her, my people, so that you do not take part in her sins, and so that you do not share in her plagues." The erotic power of the Whore is all-encompassing, for the people cannot stay within her sphere of influence without being consumed by her. So they are asked to "come out of her." Then in 22:17, the word "come" is repeated to the believers: "The Spirit and the bride say, 'Come.' And let everyone who hears say, 'Come.' And let anyone who is thirsty come, let anyone who desires take the water of life as a gift." The believers who come out of the Whore are able in the end to enter the New Jerusalem, to "come" into the Bride.

Richard Kearney explains Derrida's comment on the significance of the word "come":

> "Come" is a paradigmatic figure of postmodern apocalypse because it deconstructs every conceptual or linguistic attempt to *decide* what it means. It hails from an altogether *other* world. And what it puts into play is an apocalypse *without* apocalypse—since we cannot say or know or imagine what the 'truth' of apocalypse means. Derrida thus confronts us with the word of an apocalyptic writing which can only be grasped, if at all, as an *ending without end.* . . . What is to come is, apparently, beyond the powers of imagination to imagine.[31]

The deconstructive play of apocalypse leaves the text open-ended and (temporally) shifts the object of desire from the Whore to the Bride. The narrative itself is seductive, drawing the reader to the "ending without end"—the open spaces of the fantastic vision.

The Apocalypse in American Culture

Over the past ten years, I have received interesting responses from students at other colleges who are reading something I have written on the *Apocalypse*. At one liberal arts college in the South, students in a course on the *Apocalypse* have called me on speakerphone a few times. They prepare their questions in advance, and they generally have really insightful comments, even if they think I am totally wrong in my reading of the text. But a general perception accompanies many of these student responses—that I must be a radical, feminist, lesbian separatist. For these students, a feminist reading that deconstructs and challenges a biblical text must reflect directly on the lifestyle and politics of the author. And these politics must (in their more conservative Christian minds) in turn be immoral and unpatriotic politics. It is almost as if their interpretation is based on an unwritten "Patriot Act for Reading the *Apocalypse*," with the U.S. Department of Homeland Security setting interpretive guidelines. In their view, the authoritative borders of the biblical text must be protected against exegetical terrorists such as me, and the sacred plan of the canon must be allowed to proceed on course.

I am especially intrigued by their labeling of me as a "separatist." If one objects to the violence in the *Apocalypse*, and especially to the gendered nature of the violence against women, one must have "separated" from the norm of upholding the authority and God-givenness of this final biblical text. And, for them, allegiance to this textual authority of the Bible somehow gets combined with national loyalty. To separate from a certain view of the Bible is, in their minds, to be anti-American. This attitude demonstrates to me that the *Apocalypse* helps to hold in place in America what I consider to be injustices and myths. For example, the *Apocalypse* supports the injustice of a dualistic perspective that divides the world into the saved and the damned—thereby making it acceptable to exert violence against the damned and to accept losses from among the saved as martyrs for the faith.

The chief example of a "patriotic" reading of the *Apocalypse* is the Left Behind series of novels about the tribulation period. In these novels, the Tribulation Force battles (with God's help) the Antichrist dictator of the one world order. Even though America is not the location of the future kingdom, American citizens who have been "left behind" convert to dispensationalist Christianity and then prepare for and lead the charge at Armageddon. The authors of this series, Tim LaHaye and Jerry B. Jenkins, are only the current popular purveyors of the myth of American superiority and the belief that God is ultimately "on our side."

Such end-time fantasies about world politics are always accompanied by traditional gender roles of male domination and female subordination. Although the Christian women in the Left Behind series have some leadership roles in the underground community, they follow strict heterosexual norms of relationships and family life. In the view of the (male) authors, the thousand-year reign of Jesus will be a heterotopia, in which "American" Christian values (except for democratic government and human rights!) are transferred to the Holy City. In this scenario, the Woman Clothed with the Sun and the Bride are the acceptable female, apocalyptic role models. Regarding their image of the New Jerusalem vision, God the Father rules from the throne with his Son, setting up an urban heaven on earth. But in a literal reading of the biblical text, there is no mention of women, only the 144,000 holy men. In the Left Behind series, women are added into this premillenialist vision like some *Dr. Strangelove* fantasy of ten women for every man, all of them hiding and procreating in the underground shelter after the nuclear holocaust.

Conclusion: Resisting a Violent, Male Future

Gender is always part of the equation in apocalyptic texts. The utopian political fantasy as a liberating, cathartic, revolutionary, symbolic experience is directly related to communal human experience. Liberation readings of texts have always warned against such emphasis on the general (in this case, the cosmic), because oppression and marginalization are always specific, always personal. The only female figures in the *Apocalypse* are given symbolic names and symbolic tasks; they are not allowed to speak their own identity. This technique distances the reader from the female images, leaving the women as stereotypes of good and evil and not real flesh-and-blood women. At the same time, the *Apocalypse* is a symbolic universe that is a parody of flesh-and-blood reality. Therefore, there is a relationship between the fantastic world of the *Apocalypse* and reality. And the female images are indeed a part of the larger paradigm of the final scenes of the *Apocalypse* that depict the liberation of the oppressed.

Yet, as I have argued, it is misleading and distorting to say that women are liberated in the end along with everyone else. On the one hand, in the Christian utopia of the *Apocalypse*, the broad political expectations of power and authority are reversed, such that the beasts are defeated and the Lamb rules. But, on the other hand, the reversal of these political expectations is reserved for men. And in terms of gender expectations of power and authority, women are left exactly where they were in ancient patriarchal society—excluded from the realm of power. The utopia (no place) for men is an atopia (not a place) for women. The marriage of the Bride and the Lamb brings hope (brings utopia), but this image is not an inclusive model for women. Women have historically been excluded from many areas of culture, but here they have even been excluded from the New Jerusalem! In the world of the *Apocalypse*, what happens to the female believers other than being subsumed under this image of the Bride? Here the text is silent.

In their anthropological study of female roles in culture, Judith Hoch-Smith and Anita Spring summarize the mythical representation of the female images: "The idea of female evil is transformed into specific cultural expression through *the manifestation of that culture's ideological content in art*. Female sexuality is seen as a disruptive, chaotic force that must be controlled or coopted by men, periodically purified, and at times destroyed."[32] The ideological portrayal of the female in the *Apocalypse* remains true to the dominant ideology of its culture. So when women read the narrative (especially contemporary women readers), their experience is similar to the experience described by Jonathan Culler: "When we posit a woman reader, the result is an analogous appeal to experience: not to the experience of girl-watching but to the experience of being watched, seen as a 'girl,' restricted, marginalized."[33] Likewise, women readers of the *Apocalypse* are typed, hunted, adorned, and rejected. The domination of male over female remains intact.

Fredric Jameson is correct about the class struggle in history when he points to the relationship of utopia and ideology: "ideological commitment is not first and foremost a matter of moral choice but of the taking of sides in a struggle between embattled groups . . . [and] must always necessarily be focused on the class enemy."[34] But while he is correct on the level of class conflict, Jameson's analysis falls short on the level of gender difference and conflict. Ideology is not just class-based; it is also gender-based and gender-biased. The *Apocalypse* focuses on the enemy in terms of class (Rome) but neglects the oppressed/oppressor categories of gender relations.

And, as we have seen, the class enemy is even imaged as female (the Whore). In the political realm, women are defeated or banished to the wilderness; only the submissive, sexual Bride is allowed at the utopian wedding feast of the Lamb. The image and the function of the female end up being quite ambiguous: the erotic desire at the end of the narrative may be intact with the symbol of the Bride, but the men who enter her must be ritually pure, and the female figures with any sexual autonomy (the Jezebel, the Whore, and the Heroine share this feature) are destroyed or pushed out to the edge of the narrative world.

If the writer of the *Apocalypse* is treated to the same gender critique as writers like Paul, Chaucer, and Rabelais, there will probably emerge defenders on both sides. There will be those who defend the writer "John" as "a man of his era," in which women were debased and powerless. And there will be those who accuse and dismiss the writer as continuing and reinforcing a sexist ideology that is harmful to women. A feminist reading can seek to be redemptive by focusing on the positive remnants of the goddess reflected in the winged flight of the Heroine and by grieving the murder of the Whore. Or a feminist reading can hope with Roland Barthes that the future will involve a destruction of the past "in which the potent seed of the future *is nothing but* the most profound apocalypse of the present."[35] The destruction of the past means the destruction of *all* the forces of oppression!

The Christian *Apocalypse of John* is limited in its destruction of the forces of oppression. The irony of the grotesque burning of the Whore is that the Christian utopia is itself an oppressive world (for women). In other words, for women there is no escaping oppression (except perhaps to flee to the wilderness!). Historically, by the fourth century, the church merges with the Roman state. And there Christian women seek autonomy in the monastery (in the wilderness) in a sexually exclusive environment. But in the *Apocalypse*, narrative gender oppression is left untouched by the sword of God.

The tale of the Heroine and the Whore is not a tale of the liberation of female consciousness. The *Apocalypse* is not a tale for women. The misogyny that underlies this narrative is extreme. As a result, women of the past as well as the present are going to have to be about the business of creating their own apocalyptic tales, their own utopian narratives.

Notes

1. This is a revised version of an article that first appeared in *Semeia* 60 (1992): 67–82. The article was adapted from Tina Pippin, *Death and Desire: The Rhetoric of Gender in the Apocalypse of John* (Louisville: Westminster/John Knox, 1992).

2. Robert Scholes, "A Footnote to Russ's 'Recent Feminist Utopias,'" 87.

3. Adela Yarbro Collins, "Women's History and the Book of Revelation," 90.

4. Gayatri Spivak, "Displacement and the Discourse of Woman,"185.

5. Lance Olson, *Ellipse of Uncertainty: An Introduction to Postmodern Fantasy,*19.

6. Ibid., 22.

7. Rosemary Jackson, *Fantasy: The Literature of Subversion*, 4.

8. V. Allen and T. Paul, "Science and Fiction: Ways of Theorizing about Women,"171.

9. Donald Palumbo, "Sexuality and the Allure of the Fantastic in Literature," 4.

10. Ibid., 23.

11. Karen E. Rowe, "Feminism and Fairy Tales," 237.

12. Judith Hoch-Smith and Anita Spring provide a brief summary of "chaotic female sexuality." They state emphatically: "In no religious system do women's dominant metaphors derive from characteristics other than their sexual and reproductive status. . . . Women are strikingly one-dimensional characters in mythology and ritual action. Images of women are reduced to their sexual function, women are excluded from leadership roles in most public rituals, and images of the divine are usually male" (*Women in Ritual and Symbolic Roles*, 2).

13. See Spivak on Derrida on orgasm as crime: Spivak, "Displacement," 175.

14. Adela Yarbro Collins, *The Combat Myth in the Book of Revelation*, 75.

15. Sarah Lefanu, *Feminism and Science Fiction*, ch. 3.

16. Marie Maclean, "Oppositional Practices in Women's Traditional Practices," 45.

17. Weber, "Fairies and Hard Facts: The Reality of Folktales,"110.

18. Ruth Bottigheimer, *Grimms' Bad Girls and Bold Boys: The Moral and Social Vision of the Tales*, 71.

19. Bottigheimer (*Grimms' Bad Girls*, 53) adds, "In *Grimms' Tales*, however, silence is almost exclusively female; enforced silence exists for both heroines and heroes as a precondition for redeeming oneself or others; and it also exists as a punishment for heroines (but not heroes) and as a narrative necessity for heroines (but not heroes), as in 'The Robber-Bridegroom' (74–75)". She also points to the Christian prohibition against female speech in 1 Corinthians 14:34-35 (78). In another article Bottigheimer states that "one must conclude that fairy tales offered an apparently innocent and peculiarly suitable medium for both transmitting and enforcing the norm of the silent woman serving as paradigms for powerlessness" ("Silenced Women in the Grimms' Tales," 130).

20. Marcia Landy, "The Silent Woman: Towards a Feminist Critique," 27.

21. Bottigheimer, "The Transformed Queen: A Search for the Origins of Negative Female Archetypes in Grimms' Fairy Tales," 12.

22. Jackson, *Fantasy*, 36.

23. Mikhail Bakhtin, *Problems of Dostoevsky's Poetics*, 127.

24. Ibid., 135.

25. Ibid., 108.

26. Ibid., 108.

27. Ibid., 135.

28. Ibid., 128.

29. Ibid., 124–25.

30. The juxtaposition of the feast on the Whore and the marriage feast of the lamb is described by Michael Harris, "Singing a New Song: The Literary Function of the Hymns in the Apocalypse of John."

31. Richard Kearney, *The Wake of Imagination toward a Postmodern Culture*, 294–95.

32. Smith and Spring, *Women in Ritual and Symbolic Roles*, 3; emphasis mine.

33. Jonathan Culler, *On Deconstruction: Theory and Criticism after Structuralism*, 44.

34. Fredric Jameson, *The Political Unconscious: Narrative as a Socially Symbolic Act*, 290. Jameson makes an interesting point about the semiological arrangement of the folktale: "the crucial moment for the folk tale is not that of the *parole*, but that of the *langue*. It is always anonymous or collective in essence" (*The Prison-House of Language: A Critical Account of Structuralism and Russian Formalism*, 29).

35. Roland Barthes, *Mythologies*, 157.

7

Reading the *Apocalypse*:
Resistance, Hope, and Liberation in Central America

■■■■■■■■■■■■■■■■■■■■■■■■■■■■

Pablo Richard
Translated by Carmen M. Rodriguez and José Rodriguez

- creating self-sustaining communities → utopia
↳ not from above, from grass-roots
- Revelation enables ppl to imagine an alternate world

I grew up in Chile and was ordained in Santiago as a Roman Catholic priest in 1967. After engaging in biblical studies in Rome and Jerusalem and sociology in Paris, I worked in Central America as director of the Departamento Ecuménico de Investigaciones and twenty years as professor of Scripture at the Universidad Nacional in Costa Rica. In the last thirty years I have focused my work in strengthening the biblical movement in Basic Ecclesial Communities and in the formation of "pastoral agents." The conditions of exclusion and extreme poverty in Latin America led me to a new and liberating reading of the whole Bible. In the last twenty years we have experienced the cruel and terrible experience of the Whole Market Empire, governed in a beastly way by the political and military bureaucracy of the United States of America. The *Book of Apocalypse* teaches us today to search for the spiritual and ethical power capable of destroying the Imperial Beast and to build our hope for the possibility of "another world."

The Political Context of Our Reading

My geographical and political context for reading the *Apocalypse* is Central America. I am dedicated to the Popular Biblical Movement, an interpretation of the Bible from the perspective of grassroots movements and Christian communities. While we are committed to the most scientific exegetical approach, our main objective is to be of service to God's people. We train pastoral agents and Christian leaders to become interpreters of the Bible in their own communities, cultures, and grassroots social movements. The inspiration for all our work is the theology of liberation.

Our present historical setting is an arduous and dangerous one. Our countries live in oppression and exclusion by an economic, cultural, and military system of globalization led by the United States government operating as an imperial, arrogant, and cruel power. Each day, this system generates among us greater poverty, misery, exclusion, and ecological devastation. The destruction of life in the third world is reaching 60 percent! While we recognize some positive aspects of globalization (mainly technological and electronic communications when employed in the service of human life), globalization in general is experienced among us negatively as a force that excludes the masses and destroys nature.

In this context, God's Word becomes a source of hope and life. The Word of God has been a source for survival and resistance, but most of all it is an inspiration for alternatives and utopias. Poor people who read the Bible shout with hope: "It is possible to have a different world," "we struggle for a society where all may have a place in harmony with nature," "we want life for all and a world without evil," "only if everyone can have life, will there be life for us," and so on.

The hope displayed in the *Apocalypse* is especially important for our present moment of chaos and exclusion. The similarities between the historical background of the *Apocalypse* and our present historical context make it a valuable instrument for our discernment of the God of life. While we need to resist a fundamentalist interpretation of the text (whether reductionistic or concordist), it is important to learn from the community described in this biblical witness. We can benefit from their faithful witness of hope as they met the historical and political challenges imposed by the rule of the Roman Empire at the end of the first century.

It is from this contextual background that we now suggest some keys for the interpretation of the *Book of Apocalypse*.

Keys to Interpreting the *Apocalypse*

The following ten hermeneutic presuppositions guide my historical and spiritual exegesis of the text.

1. Alternative World

The *Apocalypse* emerges at a time of persecution within a wider context of chaos, exclusion, and permanent oppression. In such a context, the biblical text works to re-construct the conscience and the hope of this embattled Christian community. The text does this by communicating a spirituality of resistance and by proposing the creation of an alternative world. The *Apocalypse* is not a confusing text of terror focusing solely on catastrophes, judgment, punishment, and the world's end. Rather, it is a liberating text that points to a historical and political utopia.

2. Apocalypse as Resistance

The *Apocalypse* is rooted in the history of the people of Israel and in the apocalyptic-prophetic experience from which the Jesus movement and the first Judeo-Christian communities emerged. The *Apocalypse* represents an important movement at the beginning of Christianity, because it gathers and transforms these apocalyptic traditions so that they function as an element of criticism and resistance within the early church—first against the Hellenization of Christianity and later against the patriarchal and authoritarian institutionalization of the church that took place in subsequent centuries. If this biblical witness had been heeded, it is unlikely that the church would have assimilated into the dominant imperial system of Rome or developed into a Christendom focused on power. The recovery of this biblical witness in the contemporary world restores a fundamental dimension of the Jesus movement and of earliest Christianity. The *Apocalypse* is not just the text of a sectarian, desperate, and marginal community. Rather, it is a universal text—in the sense that perpetually calls for a radical reformation of the church and a new expression of Christian witness in the world.

3. Present Eschatology

The eschatology of the *Apocalypse* takes place fundamentally in the present, with the death and resurrection of Jesus as the central element of historical transformation. The text is not focused on Christ's second coming or the world's end, but on the powerful presence of the risen Jesus in the community and in the world in the present time. The event of resurrection transforms our present into a *kairos*—a moment of grace and conversion, a time for resistance, for witness, and for the construction of God's reign. The central message of the *Apocalypse* is this: If Christ is risen, then the time of the resurrection and of God's reign has begun.

4. One History

The *Apocalypse* is about history. In this text, history has two dimensions: one empirical and visible (which the author calls "earth") and another deeper and transcendent (which the author calls "heaven"). There is only one history that takes place simultaneously in heaven and on earth. God and the risen Messiah affect our history by liberating us from oppression and death and by constructing an alternative world of God's reign. The utopia of the *Apocalypse* takes place, therefore, in this present historical realm by transforming oppression and death into a new historical world where God's glory becomes visible over the whole earth. This transcendent and liberating utopia of the biblical text becomes an actual presence and already guides our whole historical praxis, our mode of action in the world. The *Apocalypse* does not offer *another* world, alienated and divorced from our history. Rather, it offers an *alternative* world here and now.

5. Historical Disclosure

This biblical text aims at the historical disclosure (in Greek, *apo-kalupsis* means un-covering) of the risen Christ's transcendent and liberating presence in history. The text expresses anger and punishment at the oppressors, but good news (gospel) to those who are excluded and oppressed by the Dragon's empire. The *Apocalypse* as disclosure stands for the opposite of what we today might call ideology—ideology being that which conceals oppression and legitimizes domination. The spirit of the *Apocalypse* may be summarized in Jesus' prayer: "I thank you, Father, Lord of heaven and earth, because you have *hidden* these things from the wise and the intelligent and have *revealed* them to infants" (*Matthew* 11:25). As such, the *Apocalypse* is not an occult expression of alien beings or a neutral and abstract revelation of a God outside our history. Rather, it is the revelation of God in the midst of the world of the poor, the oppressed, and the excluded.

6. Myths, Symbols, and Visions

The text expresses itself by means of myths and symbols. The *myths* are historical. They give identity to the community and mobilize the people in times of chaos, oppression, and exclusion. They reconstruct the collective conscience and the social praxis of God's people. Myth is polysemic; that is, it carries various meanings. Therefore, it always lends itself to new interpretations. The *Apocalypse* generates liberating myths and subverts those that are dominant and oppressive. From the *Apocalypse*, we can discover the power of myth.

The *visions* in the *Apocalypse* transmit a fundamental conviction and a historical certainty. These visions should not only be interpreted; they should also be contemplated and transformed into action. Visions transmit strength and express historical spirituality. Visions are also memory and moral exhortation. The visions of the *Apocalypse* stimulate the creative imagination of the people and their quest for alternatives.

The language of myths, symbols, and visions is different from the language of concepts. It is wrong to assume that what is mythical is the opposite of what is historical. Myths reveal the deeply rooted history of people. Myths are as rational as concepts, but they express themselves differently. The failure to understand the historical dimensions of myth has led liberal and modern theologians to despise the literary genre of the *Apocalypse* because they consider apocalyptic to be a deterioration of prophetic literature. By contrast, people of the third world, especially the people of our indigenous cultures, have shown much more sensitivity to the historical, this-worldly dimensions of the myths, symbols, and visions of the *Apocalypse*.

7. Cathartic Violence

The violence in the text is more literary and rhetorical than real. The risen Jesus appears as a slaughtered lamb. His triumph is in the cross. The martyrs defeat Satan with their witness. Jesus defeats the kings of the earth with his Word. The apocalyptic praxis is the power of the Spirit, the power of conscience, the power of myths, the power of witness and of the Word—what we today would call the "spiritual power of the oppressed and their nonviolent strategy." The hate and violence that appear in sections of the *Apocalypse* express the feelings experienced by a community in a predicament of extreme oppression and anguish. The biblical text reproduces these feelings in order to provoke in the readers a catharsis (a sort of abatement and purification of their feelings) and thus to transform their rage into consciousness.

8. A Merging of the Prophetic and the Apocalyptic

John's *Apocalypse* connects the apocalyptic traditions with the prophetic traditions. The biblical text with its prophetic Spirit tempers and transforms radical apocalyptic and fundamentalist movements. Myths and symbols become instruments and criteria for a prophetic discernment of history. They provoke contemporary readers to follow John's example. Just as John reinterpreted myths and symbols from the prophetic traditions of the Hebrew Scriptures to reveal the dynamics of the Roman Empire, so today's readers can exercise prophetic discernment by reinterpreting John's myths and symbols in the context of the present empire.

9. A Transformative Praxis of History-Making

With its internal correlation between eschatology and politics, myth and praxis, conscience and historical transformation, the *Apocalypse* generates a transformative praxis oriented toward the making of history. It lacks passivity or the absence of action. As such, it is not limited just to vision, catharsis, and protest. The central historical context of the *Apocalypse* is the economic, political, cultural, social, and religious engagement of God's people with the Roman Empire and the transcendent forces of evil. In this engagement, the *Apocalypse* generates an alternative world. In this alternative world of the *Apocalypse*, history-making is not restricted to God. Martyrs, prophets, and those who resist adoring the Dragon, its image, and its mark are also makers of history: they defeat Satan, they destroy the powers of evil, they provoke an earthquake at Babylon, and they rule over the earth. The *Apocalypse* offers an analysis of reality that provides the resources—the materials and the inspiration—for the construction of a utopian future. This future is in the hands of apocalyptic communities, with the result that this utopian vision becomes enacted through the small triumphs of the present. In this way, the biblical text furnishes a decisive key for the transformation of history.

10. The Ancient Context

The *Apocalypse* should be understood in relation to the historical context from which it emerged, at the end of the first century in Asia Minor, and interpreted with the same Spirit that led to its writing. A text without a context can be used as a pretext and then manipulated capriciously. This biblical text is not a universal or eternal book, uniformly valid for all times and places. Nor does it provide an enigmatic or concise history from the time of John to the end of time. It is surely not a headline for the future or for science fiction. We reject any fundamentalist or dispensationalist interpretation of this text. We aim for a positive interpretation of the historical significance of the *Apocalypse*, along with a present understanding of its meaning—which we call "the spiritual sense of the Scriptures."

A thorough explanation of each of these ten hermeneutical points can only be fully understood through an exegesis of the entire text of the *Apocalypse*. However, we present here an example of the use of these principles as applied to the core section of the book.

The Christian Community Confronts the Beast:
Apocalypse 12:1–15:4

The section from 12:1 to 15:4 is the core of the *Apocalypse*. Here the Christian community confronts the Beast. Everything before this comes together at this core, and everything that follows is enlightened by what is here. We are not only at the literary center of the book, but also at the core of the current times. It is the right-now of God and the community; it is the time of conversion and action. What follows is a display of the chiastic patterns that give structure to this section. Chiasms are literary/oral structures of material that are similar in content and/or form and that first move forward in a series and then recur in reverse, for example, in an A B C B' A' pattern. I have included here the overall chiastic patterns for this entire section, even though space allows me to comment only on the section from 12:1 to 14:5.

The Chiastic Structure of 12:1 to 15:4

A From Heaven to Earth: 12:1-18

    a Confrontation in *heaven*: a woman and a red dragon (1-6)

        b *War* in heaven: Satan is tossed from heaven to earth (7-9)

            c **Core**: song of victory: salvation has now come (10-11)

        b' Consequences of *war*: joy in heaven and terror on earth (12)

    a' Persecution on *earth*: the dragon pursues the woman (13-18)

B On Earth: The Two Beasts 13:1-18

    a The Beast that rises from the sea (1-10)

        b The Beast that rises from the earth (11-18)

            C Core: The Community that Follows the Lamb: 14:1-5

            (The community on earth hears a song from heaven)

B' **On Earth: God's Judgment: 14:6-20**

    a Three announce judgment upon earth (6-13)

      b **Core**: the Son of Man (14)

    a' Three angels realize judgment upon earth (15-20)

A' From earth to heaven: 15:1-4

    a Another sign in heaven: Seven angels carry seven cups (which will be poured over the earth: announcement of the following section) (1)

    b The singing of those who have triumphed over the Beast, its image, and the numeral of its name (2-4)

In this large section of the *Apocalypse* we have a concentric structure. The action begins in heaven, later develops on earth, and ends back in heaven. In the first part, we have the song of victory of the martyrs in heaven at a central place (12:10-11), who have defeated the Devil thanks to the blood of the Lamb and the word of their witness. At the last part, in the same manner, we have the song of those who sing the Lamb's song of victory, that is, those who have defeated the Beast, its image, and the number of its name (15:2-4). Also at the core (14:3), the community of those who follow the Lamb listen to a song in heaven, which only that community can learn. These three songs afford a victorious liturgical character to the set: they express the conscience of the Christian community, which on earth struggles against the Devil and the Beasts.

A From Heaven to Earth (12: 1-18)

    a. A Woman and a Red Dragon (12:1-6). Chapter 12 of the *Apocalypse* has a strongly mythical character, which does not mean that it is not historical. Myth is only another way of pondering historical processes. Also, myth is not a simple reproduction of reality but a way of organizing and programming reality into one's conscience. Myth organizes the collective conscience of people. Therefore, it expresses a social practice, a hope, and a utopia.

    In chapter 12, we have two fundamental and antagonistic myths: a *woman* and a *dragon*. Both appear as signs from heaven. Signs transmit a message and counsel our action. The woman seems to be the sign of *life*: she is with child, she is about to give birth, and she then delivers a baby boy. The dragon is the sign of *death*: it is there to kill the woman's son, and it also drags down a third of the stars with its tail. Therefore, the fundamental meaning of these two myths is *the confrontation between life and death*. Life is beautiful, but fragile and weak; death is a horrible and powerful force. However, in the confrontation between life and death, life wins. As a result, the fundamental message of this mythical representation is one of *hope*.

    b and b'. War in Heaven (12:7-9 and 12:12). In 12:7-9 and its continuation in verse 12, the *Apocalypse* presents another myth: a war with Michael and his angels against the dragon and its angels. Michael's figure is drawn from the book of *Daniel*

(10:13, 21; 12:1): "At that time Michael, the great prince, the protector of your people, shall arise." The presence of Michael guarantees that, in time of tribulation, "your people will be delivered." Etymologically, Michael means "who like God." Therefore Michael, along with his angels, is a mythical figure representing the transcendental and spiritual power of the people of God (cf. *Exodus* 23:20-21). In the *Apocalypse*, Michael will now confront the transcendent and spiritual power of the Roman Empire, represented by the Dragon and its angels.

The *Apocalypse* tells us that Michael and his angels won this war and that the Dragon and his angels did not prevail, with the result that there was no longer a place for the Dragon and his angels in heaven. We have here a transcendent defeat (in heaven) of the supernatural forces of evil, personified in the figure of the ancient snake, the Devil, or Satan. The Devil is cast out onto the earth and, while there, is at war with the Christian community. But he is already a spiritually defeated demon, without any transcendent strength left. In the world of the *Apocalypse*, heaven represents the hidden and transcendent dimension of history, while earth represents the visible and empirical dimension of history. As a result of this war, heaven is now rid of obscure forces, of transcendental forces of evil. This is a reason for incredible hope among Christians on earth. The Beast (Roman Empire) has power, will make war, and will defeat the Christians, but it is already a Beast defeated in heaven, that is, a beast that is spiritually defeated.

Who is this Devil or Satan? The Devil is certainly a mythical personification of evil, of iniquity, of anomie, of sin. "Devil" is the Greek translation of the term in Hebrew for Satan. In general, it means the adversary, the accuser, and the slanderer. It is not an absolute or eternal reality who always exists like God does. Therefore, the Devil as an absolute subject does not exist. The Devil is a myth that personifies evil. Evil does exist, but it is a human creation, a social product, encompassing both personal and societal sin. Evil does not come from God, nor was it created by God. Rather, the Devil, the personification of evil, is a myth—which does not mean it is a deception or a lie. It is a historical reality: it is the expression of the supernatural forces of evil (cf. *Ephesians* 6:12).

a'. Persecution on Earth: The Dragon Persecutes the Woman (12:13-18). In 12:13-18, we have another mythical tale, which now develops on earth. It belongs with the confrontation already described in heaven in 12:1-6. The Dragon, which has already been cast down to earth from heaven and which has been stripped of its supernatural spiritual power, now persecutes the woman on earth. Just as in 12:6 and in 12:14, the woman saves herself in the desert. The desert is here the symbol of the exodus, the place where the people of God obtained their liberation and saved their identity.

c. Core: Song of Victory (12:10-11). We finally arrive at 12:10-11, which constitutes the core of chapter 12. It is the only non-mythical part of this section, and it provides the key for us to interpret the whole of chapter 12 from a historical-theological perspective. It is a liturgical hymn that places us at the heart of the Christian community and that impresses its conscience upon us.

What is central is the announcement: "Now the kingdom of God has come." For the *Apocalypse*, the terms "salvation," "power," "kingdom," and "authority" are markedly political terms. Therefore, the coming of the kingdom is a social, public, and visible act here in history, on earth. Satan's defeat in heaven is the cause for the coming of the kingdom, for he has been tossed down from heaven onto the earth. Satan has been spiritually defeated. As we have said, Satan has lost his power in the spiritual and transcendental realm. And it is the martyrs themselves who have brought about Satan's defeat.

> a *They* (*autoi*) defeated him (Satan)
>> b *by the blood* of the Lamb and
>> b' *by the word* of their witness,
> a' because *they* despised their life in front of death.

B. On Earth: The Two Beasts (13:1-18)

The central theme of chapter 12 is the defeat of Satan. In chapter 13, however, the beasts are the triumphant ones, and the Christians are defeated. Chapter 12 expresses the theological vision of the community and their faith in the defeat of Satan. Chapter 13 shows the historical reality, as it happens. The two beasts of chapter 13 act upon the earth, and here we are in real, empirical, and visible history. It is a realistic and tragic chapter, but it must be read in light of the faith and vision of chapter 12.

Chapter 13 is clearly divided into two parts. In 13:1-10, a Beast rises from the sea and, in 13:11-18, another Beast rises from the land (only here is this figure from the land called a Beast; in all other places it is called the false prophet—16:13; 19:20; 20:10). The Beast that rises from the sea is the dominant figure in all of chapter 13. It is mentioned fifteen times. It is equally the central figure in chapter 17, where it appears nine times (it is named thirty-six times overall). Here in chapter 13, we have an impressive analysis of the structure of the Roman Empire. We will first explain certain key elements necessary to reading and understanding the text, and then we will offer an interpretation of the whole chapter.

a. The Beast That Rises from the Sea (13:1-10). This Beast rises from the sea, which is a symbol of chaos, the source of evil. But the sea is also, geographically (for the churches in Asia Minor), the Western Sea—whence the Romans came! The Beast has ten horns and seven heads, the same form as Satan (compare chapter 12). The horns, heads, diadems, and names express symbolically the complexity of the Roman Empire's machinery of domination—its economic, political, ideological, and religious machinery of power. Later, the text explains that the seven heads are seven hills (the seven hills upon which the city of Rome was built) and seven emperors (17:9) and that the ten horns are ten kings (17:12).

The Beast has the characteristics of a leopard, a bear, and a lion: these are the beasts of *Daniel* 7:3-7, which also rise from the sea and represent the empires that, like beasts, have oppressed the people of God. The Roman Empire possessed the characteristics of all these beasts. This reference to *Daniel* 7 gives us a clue for interpreting *Revelation* 13. In both places, there appear the same historical design, the same theology, and the same hope.

The Dragon (Satan, or the Devil, in chapter 12) gave the Beast its "power," its "throne," and its "utmost authority." We have here an affirmation of political theology that is of paramount importance, namely, that the Roman Empire has no power or authority of its own, but only the power and authority given to it by Satan. Satan is behind the Empire. This belief was very common in all apocalyptic literature (cf. *1 Thessalonians* 2:18; *Ephesians* 6:12; *2 Thessalonians* 2:9). The worship of Satan appears in verse 4, because Satan gave his authority (*exousía*) to the Beast. We also see the worship of the Beast. The worship of the Beast is repeated in verses 8 and 12, with the added observation that the worshipers of the Beast were "inhabitants of the earth," a technical term used in the *Apocalypse* to designate the impious and the idolaters. In verse 15, the *image* of the Beast is also worshipped (the verb for "worship" appears four times).

The adoration of the Beast is expressed in two rhetorical questions that the worshipers ask themselves: "Who is like the Beast?" and "Who can fight it?" The implicit answer is obvious: no one. The Beast is an absolute and unique reality. There is no other reality like it. The logical consequence is total submission to it. Resistance and struggle against the Beast are excluded. Historically speaking, the idolaters would have said: What is against the Roman Empire? Nothing. Who can fight it? Nobody. The adoration of the Empire is thus based on its total absolutism, which results in absolute submission. Such an affirmation of total absolutism is made in the Bible regarding Yahweh as the only God: "Who is there like you, Yahweh, among the Gods?" (*Exodus* 15:11-13; cf. *Deuteronomy* 3:24). "Thus says Yahweh: I am first and last, there are no other gods besides me. Who is like me? Let them stand up and speak" (*Isaiah* 44:6-7; cf. *Isaiah* 40:12-31). The idolaters are treating the Beast like God.

The text indicates that the beast was given a mouth to speak of *greatness* and *blasphemy*. To speak of greatness is to speak insolently and arrogantly and in an exaggerated way—all conducive to blasphemous and idolatrous discourse. In Greek, "to blaspheme" is to speak badly about someone, to destroy someone with words. Oppressors and tyrants have grandiloquent, overbearing, and blasphemous discourse. Verse 6 indicates that the Beast "opened its mouth in blasphemy against God, blaspheming his name, his dwelling, and those who dwell in heaven." First, we notice that the Beast's "theological" discourse is highly dangerous, capable of destroying all of the spiritual reality of the people of God. Second, we notice that the Beast was accorded the ability to "make war with the saints and defeat them." This phrase expresses accurately the historical situation that Christians were, in fact, defeated and destroyed by the Roman Empire. Nevertheless, as we have already stated, the perspective of chapter 12 views this same event from a different perspective, namely, that the martyrs are really overpowering Satan. Further on, we will see that Satan's defeat in heaven also allows for the defeat of the Beast on earth (chapter 14 and following). Nonetheless, at this time, the overt winner is the Roman Empire, and the losers are the saints.

Third and finally, we notice that the Beast was allowed to have universal "authority over every race, people, language, and nation." In 5:9, the Lamb buys, with his blood, people of every race, language, nation, and people. Hence, Jesus' power is also universal. Jesus expresses his power in the cross, and it effects liberation by the "purchase" of freedom for people everywhere. The Beast receives its universal power from Satan, making this power an oppressive one. The four terms—race, people, language, and nation—express the universal nature of the Empire's power, and they articulate the complete character of this empire in terms of the Beast's dominance. That is, the power of the Beast is political, but it also is patriarchal, cultural, and ethnocentric. The Beast was allowed power "to act for forty-two months." This is the time God sets for the Beast. The Beast does not have unlimited and absolute time. In 11:2, forty-two months is the same time that is allotted by God to the pagans to trample the Temple's exterior court (that is, the Christian area). There are eighty-four months in a seven-year period. Forty-two months is half of that period of time (three and a half years). In the world of the *Apocalypse*, we are in the middle of present time, described as a week of (seven) years, the last week of (seven) years before the end (compare *Daniel* 9).

In verses 9 and 10, there is an exhortation to resistance and faith, an exhortation to confront persecution and to embrace martyrdom. The text takes its inspiration from *Jeremiah* 15:2 and 53:11. The intent of the exhortation here in the *Apocalypse* is not to discourage Christians with inexorable punishment, but to advise them of the risks entailed in resisting and witnessing against the Beast. Some will suffer incarceration; the sword will murder others. The Greek word "resistance" (*hupomoné*) is often translated mistakenly as "patience" or "endurance." But it really means "resistance." *Resistance based on faith* is the key to the entire *Apocalypse*. There are four exhortations in the *Apocalypse* that begin with the word "here" and that have parallel structures and functions: 13:10 calls for resistance and faith, 13:18 calls for wisdom, 14:12 calls for resistance, and 17:9 calls for wisdom and intelligence. These phrases that call for resistance, faith, wisdom, and intelligence reveal the activist ethic of the *Apocalypse*, what we today would refer to as "liberation practices." To say that there is passivity or an absence of praxis in the *Apocalypse* is false.

b. The Beast that Rises from the Land/Earth: The False Prophet (13:11-18).
This beast is really a false prophet. It is only here that it is called a Beast. Everywhere else, in 16:13; 19:20; and 20:21, it is called a false prophet. So we will refer to it not as a Beast but as a false prophet. Verses 11 and 12 describe the nature and mission of the false prophet. It has the appearance of a lamb, but it speaks like a dragon. If Satan is the one who has granted the power and authority to the Beast who had arisen from the sea, it is now Satan who speaks out of the false prophet's mouth. The false prophet exerts all the power of the Beast and is at its service. His mission is to make all the (infidel) citizens of the earth adore the Beast. The Dragon, the Beast, and the false prophet make up a perverse Trinity. Their interrelationship is like that of Father, Son, and Holy Spirit. Satan is the anti-Father; the Beast is the anti-Son; the false prophet is the anti–Holy Spirit. At the center of this perverse Trinity is the Beast. Just as the alternative world presented by the *Apocalypse* is Christ-centered, so also the oppressive structures of the Empire are Beast-centered. Later, in 16:13-14, the *Apocalypse* depicts this perverse Trinity united in purpose: "I saw . . . coming from the mouth of the dragon, from the mouth of the beast, and from the mouth of the false prophet . . . demonic spirits, performing signs, who go abroad to the kings of the whole world, to assemble them for battle on the great day of God the Almighty."

In 13:13-17, we have a description of the false prophet's "ideological domination machine." Here are the six significant features of this domination machine. (1) He produces great signs (*semeia megala*). In this regard, he achieves the ultimate prophetic miracle, the one performed by the prophet Elijah (*1 Kings* 18:38-39), namely, bringing down fire from the sky to the earth in front of all the people. (2) He deceives the inhabitants of the Earth (the infidels) with his signs, so that they will build an image of the Beast. This image was probably the same image shown on the coins, which depicted the emperors with divine features. The image could also refer to the statues (the Greek word *eikōn* can mean image or statue) of the emperors, erected in markets, temples, and professional associations. (3) The false prophet was allowed to give life to the image of the Beast—literally, to give spirit to the image. This was an image with spirit, with life. (4) The image of the Beast was given life in order for it to speak and to have those who do not worship the image of the Beast murdered. As such, the life of the image is manifested in its ability to speak and to kill. The signs made by the false prophet (the life given to the image), which are revealed in its ability to speak and kill, are not deceitful; they are not magic tricks. They are real and historical facts. Below, in our overall interpretation of this chapter, we will explain what this is and what it means.

(5) The false prophet likewise has the power to make everyone have a mark (*cháragma*) on their forehead or right hand. The text specifies that *all* are included—the small and the great, the rich and the poor, the free and the slave. The use of the article in front of each adjective indicates that these are social groups or classes. (6)

Only the one who has the sign—that is, the name of the Beast or its number—can purchase or sell in the marketplace. Only those who are so marked can take part in the marketplace to buy and to sell. Those who are not marked are excluded. The mark could be a name or its cipher. It is probably not a physical mark on the hand or forehead, such as the mark used on animals or slaves. Rather, the mark has more of a symbolic character, although it nevertheless somehow has to be visible and recognizable, social and public, allowing for an actual recognition of those that are to be included in the market. These six features, then, make up the means by which the false prophet forces its ideology of power upon people.

In verse 18, the author of the *Apocalypse* appeals directly to his listeners and exhorts them to have the intelligence to estimate the Beast's number. It is the number of a man. The number is "666." The author does not urge people to decipher the number itself but the meaning of the number. The meaning of the number "six" is imperfection or deficiency. Seven expresses perfection or fulfillment. Thus, "666" would be total imperfection or deficiency. Six is repeated three times because it is an asymptotic or infinite number, always imperfect, ad infinitum (66666666666 . . .). When someone uses the number 7, it only has to be said once, because it is a perfect number. In 13:10, the author had urged his listeners to have resistance and faith. Now in 13:18, he exhorts them to have intelligence in order to understand that the name of the Beast expresses imperfection or total deficiency. The Beast's whole system of domination is imperfect; it is not as perfect and powerful as it appears. Today, we would say that the Beast is a paper tiger.

expands his comparison

Overall Interpretation of Chapter 13

The entire chapter is a critical analysis—a fundamentally theological analysis—of the Roman Empire's structure of oppression. The depth and complexity of this analysis captures attention. This chapter expresses the Christian community's life and conscience in the context of being oppressed by the Empire. When we read it, we learn how the Christians lived, felt, and thought under the Roman Empire. They lived within the Empire, but they were excluded from its life (they could not buy or sell). They lived as people who were under a death sentence, because they did not worship the idolized Empire. The Christian community represents resistance against the Empire. They were a community of faith that discovered Satan's presence in the Empire. It is from the perspective of their resistance, their faith, and their condition of exclusion that the author makes this theological criticism of the Roman Empire. The *Apocalypse* needs to be interpreted in light of this whole context. John writes to the churches in Asia Minor at the end of the first century, yet this vision of the *Apocalypse* is also a paradigm for us and a criterion for interpreting our situation today.

The Beast is the central figure of chapter 13. There is no doubt that the Beast is a symbol or myth with which to identify, think of, and criticize the Roman Empire.

When John and the community call the Roman Empire a Beast, they demonstrate a way of thinking about the nature of the Empire. John calls it the Beast, in line with the apocalyptic tradition in general and the *Book of Daniel* in particular. Chapter 7 in *Daniel* depicts four well-defined empires, designated as four different beasts. There, the symbol of the beast represents each empire in the conscience, while the human figure (Son of Man) represents the saints of the Highest in the conscience. The empire is what is beastly in history, while the People of God is what is human. In chapter 17, the *Apocalypse* clearly identifies the Beast as the Roman Empire, and the prostitute riding on the Beast is the city of Rome, called the Great Babylon. The Beast does not represent any specific Roman Emperor, but the sum (seven heads equal seven kings) of the emperors. The Beast also represents the entirety of the imperial structure. The Beast is a complete system, universal and total, for it has power over every race, people, language, and nation. The Beast represents the whole empire, in all its economic, political, social, and, above all, religious, theological, and spiritual dimensions.

Chapter 13 highlights the fact that the Beast obtains its power, throne, and authority from Satan. We must differentiate here between the institution and the spirit of the institution. Satan is the spirit that animates and gives power to the Empire as an institution and as a system. The supernatural forces of evil are behind the Empire. In chapter 12, John showed us mythically Satan's defeat. As a result of this defeat, Satan no longer has absolute power. Now it only has power on earth, and it exercises that power through the Beast. As a consequence of its defeat, Satan is mortally wounded—although it has recovered from that wound and still lives. This wound was caused by Christ's death and resurrection. John analyzes the Roman Empire from the perspective of the resurrected Christ, who has mortally wounded Satan.

A central element in this chapter is the adoration of the Beast. The Roman Empire is idolized. It is an idol, just like Baal (the Canaanite god) or Moloch (the Ammonite god). The Roman Empire is an idolatrous system. In 13:4, as we have shown, John analyzes this absolutist or idolatrous nature of the Empire. Because the Empire is a historical structure, it has transformed into an absolute *subject* ("Who is like the Beast?"), and the worshipers of the Beast have been transformed into *objects* ("Who can fight against it?"). This is precisely what fetishism and idolatry are, namely, a dynamic in which the structures become the *subjects*, and human beings become *things*. Those who worship the Beast, those who are designated by the technical term "inhabitants of the earth," hand their subjectivity and their lives over to the Beast and become objects in submission to the Beast, who marks them.

In an extraordinary manner, John's *Apocalypse* highlights the ability of the Beast to destroy spiritual realities. John uses the concept of blasphemy to express this destruction of spiritual realities. The Beast has a mouth that speaks greatness and blasphemy. That is the Beast's spiritual pride. With its arrogant and blasphemous speech, it destroys God's name (God's essence), God's dwelling (God's presence in history), and the saints (God's people). This is the greatest danger of idolatry, namely, its capacity to destroy the spiritual.

The Beast's adoration has sophisticated and complex mechanisms. These mechanisms are portrayed in the section reserved for the false prophet (verses 11-18). The false prophet looks like a lamb (maybe it imitates Jesus), but its discourse is Satanic. He does not have his own power; rather, his power comes from the Beast, and he is at the service of the Beast. His fundamental mission is to organize the adoration of the Beast in the Roman Empire. In the *Apocalypse*, the false prophet symbolizes the full ideological structure of the Empire: priests, philosophers, teachers, magistrates, sects, massive celebrations, the circus, cultural activities in the theater (the Odeon), the hippodrome, gyms, puberty rituals, sports, Olympic games, Roman laws, Greek-Roman philosophies, the army's imperial medals, the imperial images on coins, the organization of market and commerce, and international relations. Idolatry penetrates *all of it*, and everything is at the service of the Empire's idolatry. It is not simply about the veneration of the Emperor. The Emperor is only one dimension of imperial idolatry, which is total, universal, systemic, and institutionalized.

John describes some of the ideological mechanisms of this system of idolatry (verses 13-17). In the first place, there are the prophetic signs. John introduces the false prophet as an Elijah, performing extraordinary miracles. I believe these miracles or signs are symbolic references to actual events. They are not magic or deceit. These signs appear throughout the apocalyptic tradition, which claims that false messiahs and false prophets will rise up and perform signs and wonders that are capable of deceiving, if possible, the chosen ones (*Matthew* 24:24; *Mark* 13:22). And elsewhere, "the coming of the lawless one is apparent in the working of Satan, who uses all power, signs, lying wonders, and every kind of wicked deception for those who are perishing, because they refused to love the truth and so be saved" (*2 Thessalonians* 2:9-10). A possible interpretation would be that these signs are actions or products of the Empire, introduced in an idolatrous form as miracles. The Roman Empire really did achieve wonders in technology, communications, construction, art, law, and philosophy. These works were presented as the labor of the gods, as extraordinary works, as true miracles of the Empire (today we speak about technological miracles, economic miracles, medical miracles, and so on).

The *image* of the Beast is the ideological apparatus captured with great depth by John. We have already indicated that this image has spirit, which means it has a life that manifests itself in the ability to speak and to kill. We also stated that, for John, the "image of the Beast" probably referred either to the images of emperors shown on Roman coins or to the statues of emperors. John takes this representation to be a typical phenomenon of an idolatrous structure, as being universal and complex. How can we explain the image of the Beast as having spirit, being alive so as to speak and to kill? We have already stated the need to distinguish between institutions and their spirit. John makes such a distinction when he differentiates the Beast from Satan by identifying Satan as the power behind/of the Beast. We have all the institutions of the Roman Empire, but we also have all the supernatural forces of evil behind them (using images from *Ephesians* 6).

The image of the Beast is nothing more than the visible representation of the Empire's invisible spirit. The image is the embodiment of the fetish, of the idol. The image of the Beast is a dead object; nevertheless, it possesses spirit and life when it is transformed into the visible symbolic representation of the spirit or supernatural force behind the Roman Empire. If it is true that the image of the Beast is the imperial representation on Roman coins, it would then follow that Roman currency would be the visible representation of the Empire's spirit. When money becomes a fetish, it becomes a subject with spirit and life, and it has a capacity to speak and to kill. Money becomes the image of the adored Beast, of the worshipped idol, of the revered divinity. Money becomes, in Jesus' words, "mammon"—this world's God, the Lord of the world. Money is an inert thing that the false prophet transforms into a live subject. Money, in itself, does not speak or murder; it is the Empire's spirit, represented by money, that speaks and kills. Money becomes a subject and appears as the visible body of the Empire's invisible spirit. As such, it is alive; it speaks and it kills. In John's *Apocalypse*, Satan gives the Roman Empire its life and power. Monetary currency has become Satan's body.

The transformation of money into a subject transforms the worshipers of the Beast into objects; therefore, they can be marked. Subjects hand their subjectivity over to the Beast, to the money idol, and they become objects. This is the meaning of the mark of the Beast. Worshipers of the Beast find themselves marked by the Beast; that is, they carry the name of the Beast on their foreheads (in their conscience) and on their right hand (in their labor). The mark expresses the Empire's logic or rationality, and those who adore the Beast possess that logic, thereby successfully and joyfully participating in the life of the Empire. To describe this integration or assimilation into life in the Empire, John uses the economic image of buying and selling. But this economic assimilation at the marketplace is also symbolic of an assimilation into all the other structures of the Empire as well. When Christians refuse to idolize money and the Beast, they do not carry the sign of the Beast, and they are not identified as belonging to the Empire. They are excluded and, ultimately, murdered. They are financially sentenced to death by being excluded from the market, and they are sentenced to political, cultural, and spiritual death because they do not recognize the Beast as a god. Christians reject being transformed into Baal's (the god of empire) objects and into mammon's (the god of money) objects.

— main thread that holds the reading together

C. Core: The community that follows the Lamb (14: 1-5).

This passage is at the heart of the entire section under consideration, which itself constitutes the core of the whole of the *Apocalypse*. We are, therefore, at *the core of the core* of the *Apocalypse*. It is not only the literary core of the book's structure; it is also the center of salvation's history. It is the present time, the time between the past and the future, the *kairos* time in which humankind's destiny is played out—here becoming the center of attention in the *Apocalypse*. It is at this core of the core where God's people appear on earth with the Lamb. It is the people who refuse to adore the Roman Empire and who follow Jesus wherever Jesus goes.

This is a small section of the *Apocalypse*, although it is the brightest beacon in the whole work. John portrays the people of God meeting with the Lamb on Mount Zion (14:1-5), just after he has introduced the perverse Trinity of Satan, the Beast, and the false prophet (chapters 12 and 13) and just before the depiction of the judgment on those who worship the Beast (14:6-20). Watching this community follow the Lamb wherever it goes, right in the middle between horrible beasts and a dramatic trial, is an impressive and charged portrait.

The first thing John sees is "the Lamb standing upon Mount Zion." In the *Apocalypse*, Mount Zion does not refer to historical Jerusalem built upon Mount Zion. Neither does it refer to heavenly Jerusalem (chapters 21–22). Zion here is a symbolic designation for the meeting place for the new people of God, now congregating beside the resurrected Jesus. The symbol of Mount Zion certainly reminds us of old Jerusalem and foreshadows the vision of New Jerusalem. The one hundred forty-four thousand mentioned here are not physically in Jerusalem, which at that time had already been ravaged by the Romans. Nor are they in the celestial Jerusalem either, which had not yet descended. Already in the Old Testament, Mount Zion had this symbolic character as an eschatological meeting place of the Messiah and his people.

The people of God who are with the Lamb are made up of "one hundred forty-four thousand who had his name and his Father's name written on their foreheads." The number 144,000 is a symbolic figure identifying the people of God—taking as its model the twelve tribes of Israel. While the number seven symbolizes totality in general, the number twelve symbolizes a social totality. The number 144,000 symbolizes the perfect people of God—twelve tribes of twelve thousand each—meeting, in its totality, with the resurrected Christ. Besides totality and perfection, the number 144,000 represents organization. The people who resist the Beast are very well organized.

In chapter 14, they have the name of the Lamb and the name of their Father written on their foreheads. In chapter 14, the name on the forehead indicates that they belong to God and to the Lamb. This mark is a contrast to the mark of the Beast's name or the Beast's numeral, which was placed on the right hand and on the forehead of those who worship the Beast. This passage makes a clear distinction between the people of the Lamb and the people of the Beast.

Verses 4-5 explain in three phrases the identifying characteristics of the 144,000 in John's vision. First, they "have not defiled themselves with women," for they are virgins. In the *Apocalypse*, fornication and prostitution are recurring and unequivocal symbols of idolatry. Virginity or purity is the total absence of idolatry. An alternative, less offensive translation of 14:4a might be: "these were the ones who were not contaminated with idolatry, because they are pure of heart."

Second, "they follow the Lamb wherever he goes." The verb "to follow" is the same word as the technical term used in the Gospels to depict the disciples following Jesus. There is here a strong opposition between the whole earth who "followed the Beast" (13:3) and the saints who "follow the Lamb" as disciples.

Third, "they have been redeemed from humankind as first fruits for God and the Lamb." The verb "to purchase" or "to redeem" that is, "to purchase as a means to redeem," in its figurative sense means "to rescue" or "to liberate." It appears in 5:9 of the *Apocalypse* and here in 14:3-4. In 5:9, we are told that the Lamb "ransomed with his blood persons of every race, language, people, and nation, and has made them to be a kingdom . . . and they will reign on earth." In 14:4, the redeemed are "first fruits" to God and to the Lamb.

Apocalypse **14:5 to 15:4**. The remainder of chapter 14 includes the announcement: "Fallen! Fallen is Babylon the Great!" And it depicts the beginning of judgment on the Beast and all who worship the Beast. It also includes the call for God's people to "resist," to "hold fast to the faith of Jesus." Then follows the affirmation that "those who die in the Lord are blessed"—they will "rest from their labors, for their deeds follow them" (14:13).

At the core of the *Apocalypse* is the victory of the martyrs over Satan and the Beast. The tone of the final song of the whole section has as its model the song of the victory on the exodus (*Exodus* 15:1-5). This martyr's song of the *Apocalypse* is a song of deep faith and optimism (15:2-5).

> Great and amazing are your deeds
>   Lord God Omnipotent.
> Just and true are your ways,
>   King of the nations.
> Lord, who will not fear
>   And glorify your name?
> For you alone are holy.
>   All nations will come
> And worship before you,
> For your judgments have been revealed.

Conclusion: Resistance Today

The *Apocalypse* is a book of political theology. It provides witness to the practice and the political consciousness of early Christian believers at the end of the first century. The author is not a dreamer or a mystic from "another world" but a political theologian making an analysis of reality and building a practice of resistance inside the Roman Empire.

Today we read the *Apocalypse* in order to discover our own practice and Christian conscience inside our present empire. Our empire is more dangerous than the Roman Empire of old, because for the first time in the history of humankind there is an empire capable of killing most of humanity and forever destroying our planet earth. Today's empire is the empire of the total and absolute market, led by the government of the United States of America and all its political and military systems. The world looks in terror as this empire transforms itself into a Beast (chapter13). The ten horns and seven heads show the complexity of the Beast, who today also has "a great mouth uttering haughty and blasphemous words." We also discover the absolute power of the communication media, and all of the churches and "Christian" theologians serving the Beast. This is the spiritual Beast seducing all people on earth. Today people are unable to buy or sell, that is, to participate in the world market, if they lack the mark of the Beast. In today's world the ones carrying the mark of the Beast in their hands and forehead are the empire's politicians and bureaucrats.

The *Apocalypse* teaches us to resist and to defeat the Beast. It fills us with the hope of a possible new world: a society in which everyone has a place in harmony with each other and nature. Our resistance and struggle is foremost a cultural, ethical and spiritual one. The *Apocalypse* also transmits to us the power of the utopia that steers all history, which even now makes possible a practice of liberation to build it. The *Apocalypse* teaches us to build Christian communities in struggle against the Beast, against its false prophet, and against all those "Christian" churches that dominate the world with the power of the Beast.

The first world will be able to resist the global empire of the market when it becomes aware that the whole bureaucratic, political, and military system of the United States is a great Beast threatening the life of human beings and of the whole planet. This resistance will only be possible when citizens of the empire reject the mark of the Beast and exclude themselves from the market, in solidarity with the wretched of the earth. Only then will they recover the ethical and spiritual power transmitted by the *Apocalypse* to destroy the Beasts and to build a new heaven and a new earth, a new society where everyone may have a place in harmony with nature.

8
For the Healing of the World:
Reading *Revelation* Ecologically

▪ ▪

Barbara R. Rossing

Introduction

This essay interprets the story and message of *Revelation* through the lens of ecology. I write as a white, middle class woman who loves nature and wilderness and the out-of-doors and who also has been profoundly influenced by third-world liberation theologies. Undergirding my work on *Revelation* is the belief that the most urgent crisis facing our planet today is what broadly can be called the global environmental justice crisis—the exploitation of both people and nature reflected in the growing global gap between rich and poor as well as in the widespread destruction of ecosystems. Our world is suffering under a system of globalized injustice and violence that is not sustainable for the planet or for its peoples. I believe *Revelation* can speak to these issues.

I also write as a pastor who loves to preach on the book of *Revelation*, especially for Earth Day, April 22, which occurs each year during the Easter season of the church's calendar. In the Easter season, many of the appointed readings are from *Revelation*. These passages invite hearers into a rich world of creation imagery—a wondrous river of life, a healing tree, and a God who dwells in and with creation and who desires to wipe away its tears. *Revelation* is a profoundly hopeful and earth-healing book, culminating in a vision of life-giving water flowing from God's throne and a life-giving tree providing fruit all year through. We desperately need such an earth-healing perspective to inspire and empower us in the midst of the injustice and environmental devastation of our world today.

The link between nature and human justice is crucial, and it is a connection made by the book of *Revelation*. In exploring this connection in *Revelation*, I draw

upon the interpretive framework suggested by Brazilian liberation theologian Leonardo Boff, who links the cry of the earth to the cry of the poor in the biblical book of
Exodus. There God declares: "I have heard the cry of my people . . . and I have come
down to deliver them" (*Exodus* 3:7). Boff draws a parallel between the discourse of
ecology and the discourse of liberation:

> Liberation theology and ecological discourse have something in common: they
> start from two bleeding wounds. . . . Both discourses have as their starting point a
> cry: the cry of the poor for life, freedom and beauty (cf. *Exod. 3.7*) and the cry of the
> Earth groaning under oppression (cf. *Rom. 8.22-23*). Both seek liberation, a libera-
> tion of the poor . . . and a liberation of the Earth.

In Boff's view, "now is the time to bring these two discourses together."[1]

Revelation is a biblical apocalyptic text that can help us bring these two discourses together. Parallel cries—both the cry of human victims and the earth crying
out to God for justice—can be seen at the heart of the message of the *Book of Revelation*. *Revelation* gives voice to a cosmic lament on behalf of oppressed peoples and
on behalf of the whole created world. It also proclaims God's healing for the world.
To be sure, the author of *Revelation* was not an environmentalist in the modern
sense; nevertheless, he was an astute critic of the insatiable appetites of the Roman
Empire that led to injustices against humans and to devastations of the earth. In
the ancient world, some of the same problems of exploitation that Boff and others identify today—exploitation of colonized lands, of the natural environment, and
of peoples—were familiar problems. They are indicted in *Revelation*'s sweeping
critique of the Roman imperial order. For this reason, the important anti-imperial
critique in the book of *Revelation* can serve us today.

Ecological interests are what first drew me to study *Revelation*. I had always been
an avid hiker and naturalist, and I majored in geology in college. When it came time
to pick a doctoral dissertation topic I assumed that ecological interests could not be
linked to biblical studies. "What do you love in the New Testament?" my professor,
Helmut Koester, asked me. "You must write about what you love." I told him that
what I loved was ecology and God's care for the earth—but that I did not expect to
find that in the Bible.

To my surprise, my professor suggested writing on the vision of the New Jerusalem, which comes in chapters 21–22 near the end of the book of *Revelation*.
I had never read these chapters—or at least, I could not recall reading them. What
I discovered is that the vision of the New Jerusalem offers a profoundly earth-
embracing vision in which God descends from heaven to earth to live with humans
in a renewed urban paradise. *Revelation* 21–22 offers the amazing image of the river
of life watering a magnificent tree of life whose "leaves are for the healing of the

nations." This imagery was drawn from the biblical prophet Ezekiel, and it is imagery that can also speak to the issue of rivers and trees in our world today. Through *Revelation*, I discovered a life-giving vision for our world, a vision that now shapes my own life and commitments.

As I read back through the chapters of *Revelation*, I soon saw that *Revelation*'s wondrous New Jerusalem vision is set over against its evil counterpart, the vision of the city of "Babylon" in *Revelation* 17–18. Babylon represents the city of Rome as well as the entire Roman Empire with its exploitive political economy. *Revelation* portrays Babylon/Rome as a toxic empire, oppressing the world. In the Babylon vision of *Revelation* 17–18, we hear the cry of the poor and also the cry of a world longing to be free from domination. In the final New Jerusalem vision, God hears these cries and answers them.

Thus, *Revelation*'s visions of two cities—the one toxic (Babylon/Rome) and the other utopic (New Jerusalem)—show us contrasting images and scenarios for the world and its future. They also call on us to make an ethical choice between two citizenships. God's people must "come out" of Babylon in order to enter into the blessing of the New Jerusalem. This ethical and political contrast between two opposite city visions constitutes the heart of the ecological reading I am proposing for the *Book of Revelation*.

Methodology

My methodology is both historical and literary. I use historical methods to interpret the *Book of Revelation* in its particular historical context and to understand its message in light of the general background of the first century. I use literary methods to discern the meaning of *Revelation* as a coherent literary document, to appreciate the importance of its literary sources, and to grasp its rhetorical impact upon first-century hearers. In addition, I draw upon liberation theology as a lens through which to explore the particular dynamics of oppression against humans and nature and to understand the particular means of liberation as put forth by the author of *Revelation*. In my approach, all of these methods are brought into the service of discovering how *Revelation* can be liberating for our world today.

In seeking to read the story of *Revelation* in a way that affirms the value of creation, I will emphasize five elements of the book's message, focusing on the final depiction of the New Jerusalem as the world-healing vision toward which the entire book builds:

1. Contrary to fundamentalists' claims, *Revelation* does not culminate either in a so-called rapture or in the battle of Armageddon. Rather, *Revelation* culminates in what might be called a "rapture in reverse." That is, instead of people going up, it is God who descends. In *Revelation* 21–22, *God* is "raptured" down to earth.

2. In *Revelation*, there are frequent statements of "woe" over the earth. The intent of these statements is not to pronounce God's curse against the earth. Rather, these declarations are a divine *lament* or cry on behalf of the world—bemoaning the devastating conquest of earth by the unjust Roman Empire. The Greek word *ouai* is, therefore, best translated not as a pronouncement of "woe" but rather as a cry of mourning: "How awful!" or "Alas!"

3. A strong sense of an impending "end" pervades the entire book of *Revelation*; however, the "end" that the book envisions is not primarily the destruction of the earth or the end of the created world. Rather, *Revelation* envisions an end not to the earth but to the Roman imperial order of oppression and destruction.

4. The plagues of ecological destruction in the book of *Revelation* are modeled on the plagues of the story in *Exodus* of Israel's liberation from oppression in Egypt, with the Roman Empire now cast in the role of Egypt. As with the *Exodus* story, the plagues in *Revelation* are warnings to repent, not predictions of devastation for its own sake. Their goal is liberation, not environmental destruction—and if the oppressors *do repent*, the terrible plagues will *not* be carried out.

5. In terms of ethics, *Revelation* affirms an ethic of healing and renewal for the world, not an ethic of escape from the world. God does not leave the world behind, and neither can we.

I will take up these five points respectively and then conclude by offering an ecological reading of the "water of life" imagery in the final New Jerusalem vision. But first we must address the so-called rapture interpretation of *Revelation* that has become popular among fundamentalist Christians today.

Does the Earth Get "Left Behind" in Revelation?

What could possibly be ecological about the book of *Revelation*? The answer to that question in the minds of many readers today would be "Not much!"—especially if you follow the hugely popular "rapture" industry with its fixation on violence and Armageddon. Authors such as Hal Lindsey and Tim LaHaye tell the story of *Revelation* as necessitating World War III and the total destruction of the oceans, rivers, and entire planet earth. For Lindsey, *Revelation*'s proclamation of a "new heaven and a new earth" parallels the threat of destruction of the earth by intense heat in *2 Peter*—God's plan to destroy the earth by fire, probably through thermonuclear war. "Christ is going to 'loose' the elements of the galaxy in which we live," wrote Lindsey in his 1970s best-selling *The Late Great Planet Earth*. "There will be a great roar and intense heat and fire. Then Christ will put the atoms back together to form a new heaven and earth, in which only glorified persons without their sinful natures will live." In Lindsey's vision, no animals or plants will survive to inhabit this new heaven and new earth—only glorified humans.

The most recent version of this destructive view is the fictionalized end-times thriller *Left Behind: A Novel of Earth's Last Days*, the first book in a twelve-novel series whose sales top 50 million copies, plus kid's books, a board game, a web site, two movies, and numerous spin-offs. Tim LaHaye's and Jerry Jenkins's novels unfold like disaster movies, from the worldwide "Wrath of the Lamb Earthquake" to oceanic plagues and fiery hailstones —all leading up to the final bloody battle of Armageddon that will destroy most of the world, except Israel. It is a gripping story of "earth's last days," as the subtitle of the first novel proclaims. With lurid details the novels tell how God sends bloody plagues to turn earth's oceans and freshwater rivers to blood, killing three-quarters of the world's population.

The prospect of such destruction of the earth does not trouble Lindsey or LaHaye because they do not plan to be here on planet earth when it happens. At the last moment before the catastrophes are unleashed, they plan to be "raptured" up to heaven, from where they will watch the drama of earth's destruction. "Although I grieve over the lost world that is headed toward catastrophe," Lindsey writes in his *The Rapture: Truth and Consequences*, "the hope of the Rapture keeps me from despair." He and LaHaye follow a line of biblical interpretation called "dispensationalism," first developed by a British preacher, John Nelson Darby, in the 1830s, in which Christ is portrayed as returning in secret to snatch born-again Christians up to heaven for seven years before the world is destroyed. Rapture proponents are confident that *Revelation*'s message is this: The world must be destroyed over the course of seven years of tribulation, but they and other "raptured" Christians will get to escape and then watch the terrible destruction from the grandstand of heaven. It is a gripping story.

But this "rapture" version of the storyline of *Revelation* is not biblical. Key biblical passages have been misinterpreted to construct a rapture theology. For example, in regard to *Matthew* 24:40-41, where one is left in a field and the other taken, the saved are not the ones who are taken up from earth while the unsaved are left behind. Rather, it is most likely that those who are being judged are taken away, and the saved are left on earth! In regard to *1 Thessalonians* 4:17, in which the believers rise up in the air at the end time to meet Jesus, they do not rise up in order to go on to heaven. Rather, they rise up in order to greet Jesus as a conquering king coming back to re-claim the earth as his own![2] Rapture theology also twists and misinterprets the message of *Revelation*. Although rapture proponents try to claim that John's visionary journey to heaven in *Revelation* 4:1 describes the rapture, there is no rapture and no seven-year period of tribulation in *Revelation*, and certainly there is no predetermined script for the destruction of the earth. The God of the Bible is not a God who wants to destroy the world after "beaming up"

Christians off the earth. Such a view can lead to an appalling and dangerous theology and ethics.

Revelation does indeed proclaim a new heaven and a new earth, but such a proclamation does not mean that God gives us a replacement for this current earth if we damage it beyond recovery. Rather, the earth will become "new" in the sense of resurrection or renewal, just as our bodies will be resurrected, brought to new life—and yet they are still our bodies. The "whole creation is longing for redemption," as the apostle Paul writes. And this is the sense in which there will be a new creation in *Revelation*'s view as well. The earth will be redeemed, healed, made new.[3] The Greek word *kaine* that lies behind the "new" earth in *Revelation* 21:1 can mean either "renewed" or "new"—but it certainly does not mean a "different" earth.

Rapture proponents like to use the image of a countdown to the end-times, almost like the countdown to a missile launch. A Presbyterian pastor taught me a song from his youth about the rapture that draws an analogy to spaceship imagery: "Somewhere in outer space God has prepared a place for all those who trust him and obey. . . . The countdown's getting closer every day." But this song reflects a key point on which the dispensationalist teaching is so false and reckless. There is *no place* in outer space to which God will take us to escape the earth. That is not the biblical message. We cannot trash this planet and assume there is another.

Consider the now infamous remark of Reagan-era Secretary of the Interior, James Watt, who alarmed environmentalists when he introduced a biblical end-times reference into his 1981 testimony before the U.S. House of Representatives. In response to a question about preservation of the environment for future generations, Watt qualified his answer by stating that "I do not know how many future generations we can count on before the Lord returns."[4] Even more extreme is a recent remark by right-wing pundit Ann Coulter : "God gave us the earth. We have dominion over the plants, the animals, the trees. God said, 'Earth is yours. Take it. Rape it. It's yours.'"[5]

But the rape of the earth is not God's will—not in *Revelation,* and not in *Genesis*, where the command to exercise dominion is expressed as a responsibility given to humans to care for the garden of earth (*Genesis* 1:26). *Revelation* makes clear that the tragic rape of the earth is the result of unjust imperial exploitation and conquest and that such abuse will soon be judged by God—who will destroy "the *destroyers* of the earth" (11:18), not the earth itself. Like the rest of the Bible, *Revelation* affirms the positive value of the created world. Far from being anti-earth, *Revelation* gives us, in its final vision of the New Jerusalem, one of the most earth-centered visions of our future in the whole Bible—an apocalyptic wake-up call that can renew our sense of ethical urgency and deepen our ecological commitments. What *Revelation* offers is the promise of liberation and healing for the world, including the created world of nature, from the devastations of empire. Its theology is the very opposite of rapture theology.

An Ecological Reading of *Revelation*

With this overall orientation to *Revelation* in mind, we now turn to the five specific affirmations that clarify how the book of *Revelation* values the world of creation.

1. God Still Loves the Earth and Comes to Dwell in It

To construct a more ecological reading of *Revelation* we first need to underscore that there is no rapture in *Revelation*, no vision of people snatched up from the earth. Instead, in the culminating vision of *Revelation* 21, it is God who is "raptured" down to earth to take up residence, to dwell with us:[6]

> "And I saw the holy city, the new Jerusalem, coming down out of heaven from God, prepared as a bride. . . . And I heard a loud voice from the throne saying "See, the home of God is among mortals. God will dwell with them as their God; they will be his peoples, and God's very self will be with them." (21:2-3)

The whole *Book of Revelation* leads up to this vision of God's descent to earth and the renewal of the world. Heaven is not mentioned again in the *Book of Revelation* after these verses—a fact especially striking for a book in which heaven has been so central. This is because God's throne moves down to earth. Contrary to the escapism and "heavenism" that dominates fundamentalist interpretations today, *Revelation* emphasizes that our future dwelling will be with God on earth, in a radiant, thriving city landscape. The New Jerusalem comes down out of heaven to earth, and the home of God will be among people. From now on, God "will dwell with them as their God" (21:7). There will be no heavenly or earthly temple in the New Jerusalem, and all the faithful will be priests, because God will dwell with people on earth with an immediacy that eliminates the need for any mediation of God's presence and actions.

Traditional Christian interpretations have viewed *Revelation*'s New Jerusalem as a vision of heaven, a place where we go after we die. The Left Behind authors and other pre-millennial dispensationalists interpret *Revelation*'s New Jerusalem as a future so far off in time that it comes only after more than a thousand years from now, after a pre-determined sequence of global tribulation, the millennium, the last judgment, earth's destruction, and only then "eternity itself." Indeed, for the Left Behind series, New Jerusalem is a future world so remote in time that it is not treated in any of the twelve novels.

In contrast to such "heavenist" or "futurist" views, I want to reclaim the vision of New Jerusalem back from heaven to earth, back from the future to the present, so that it can speak to us today.[7] The visions of *Revelation* give hope for the future, to be sure, but their *ethical* function is to speak an urgent word to those living in the present time. In terms of ethics, the *Book of Revelation* exhorts readers to "come out" of the destructive Babylon *now*, so that they can live already in terms of God's vision for our world. For readers in the first century the vision offered a profound picture of hope. Today, as well, God's New Jerusalem is intended to shape our ethical vision, our desires, and our commitments. The beauty and radiance of New Jerusalem, its open gates, its healing tree, and its river of life invite our entry and participation. New Jerusalem invites us to imagine our world differently.

God comes to dwell with us on earth. This "rapture in reverse" of *Revelation* 21–22—God's coming down to earth—is the first and most important step toward an ecological reading of this book. God still loves the world and even comes to live in it. God will never leave the world behind!

2. "Alas" for Earth, Not "Woe" upon Earth: God Does Not Curse the Earth

A second step toward a more ecological reading of *Revelation* involves a reconsideration of the so-called "woes" of *Revelation*. If God cares about the earth, then how are we to explain the apparent "woes" against the earth and its inhabitants that are so prominent in *Revelation*? The terrifying declarations of "Woe" throughout *Revelation*'s middle chapters have led some interpreters to think the book predicts destruction for earth. Beginning with the fourth trumpet in *Revelation* 8, in the middle of terrifying *Exodus*-like plagues, such announcements of "woe" are frequent—and they are cited by rapture proponents and others to argue that God has consigned the earth to suffer plagues of ecological disaster and ultimate destruction. For example, an eagle flying through mid-heaven cries out "Woe, woe, woe to the inhabitants of the earth" (8:13), and later a heavenly voice announces what sounds like a curse: "Woe to the earth and the sea, for the devil has come down to you in great wrath, because he knows that his time is short!" (12:12).

However, in these so-called woes of *Revelation*, God is not pronouncing a curse but rather offering a lament, bemoaning earth's conquest and abuse by Roman imperial powers. In my view, *Revelation*'s "woes" must be read in light of the book's overall critique of Rome.

The Greek word that is usually translated "woe" (*ouai*) is not easy to translate into English. It is a cry or sound in Greek that can be used to express lamentation or mourning.[8] Spanish Bibles simply use the sound "Ay, ay, ay." In my view, the Greek word *ouai* is better translated consistently as "alas!" or "How awful!" throughout the entire book of *Revelation*. Lamentation or "alas" is clearly the sense of the word *ouai* that is used later in chapter 18 in the three-fold formulaic lamentations pronounced by the rulers, merchants, and mariners weeping over Babylon. For example, the kings of the earth say,

> Alas, Alas, the great city
> Babylon, the mighty city,
> For in one hour your judgment has come

Most translators render their expression as "Alas, alas, alas" (18:10, 16, 19, RSV and NRSV). I argue that this standard translation of *ouai* as "alas" in *Revelation* 18 should inform our translation of other references to *ouai* in *Revelation* as well. The so-called woes then declare not a curse *against* the earth, but rather God's lament *on behalf of* the earth that has been subjugated by evil powers: "Alas for you, earth and sea, for the devil has come down to you in great wrath, because he knows that his time is short!" (12:12).

Although no English word is the exact equivalent of the Greek, the subtle but important distinction between a pronouncement of "woe" and a lament of "alas" makes an enormous difference ecologically. "Alas" conveys a level of sympathy and concern for the earth that the English word "woe" does not.[9] If we translate *ouai* as "alas," God can be understood as sympathizing in mourning and lament over Earth's pain, even while God is threatening plagues as a means to bring about Earth's liberation from injustice. Such a translation is supported by recent interpretations of similar passages in the Old Testament, such as *Jeremiah* 12:7-13, about which Terrence Fretheim has written, "these verses are a divine lament, not an announcement of judgment."[10]

3. End of Empire, not End of Earth: Liberation of Earth from Captivity to Rome

So why does God lament or mourn on behalf of the earth in *Revelation*? In my view, the cries of "Alas" in 12:12 and throughout the middle chapters are best understood as part of the book's larger political critique against Roman imperialism. This leads to my third point for an ecological reading: *Revelation*'s primary polemic is not against the earth as such, but against the exploitation of the earth and its peoples. The voice from heaven expresses God's cosmic cry of lamentation because God is outraged that the lands and the seas have been subjugated by Satan's emissary, the Roman Empire. God cries out in a cosmic lament against Rome's violent military conquests that have enslaved both people and nature.

Crucial to such an anti-imperial reading of *Revelation* is God's proclamation that "the time has come . . . for destroying the destroyers of Earth" (11:18). This statement attributes blame for the destruction of earth *not to God* but to unjust "destroyers" who decimate and devastate the earth. What God plans to destroy, according to this crucial verse, is not the earth itself but rather the idolatrous "*destroyers*" of earth—that is, Rome, with its entire political economy of exploitation and domination. This makes a crucial difference both eschatologically and ecologically for the way we interpret the book.

We must look at the book in its first-century historical context. The *Book of Revelation* was written when Roman imperial conquest was at its height. Britain had been brutally conquered by Emperor Claudius in 43 C.E., and Armenia was conquered by Nero in 63 C.E. Most important for *Revelation* was the recent re-conquest of Palestine and the destruction of Jerusalem at the end of the four-year long Jewish Revolt of 66 to 70 C.E. Rome publicly celebrated its military conquests with coins, triumphal monuments, and other propaganda boasting of the Empire's military victories. The message was unmistakable and would have been known by everyone: Rome was all-powerful and invincible, and any attempt at resistance would be dealt with severely.

The ecological aspects of Roman imperialism are only now receiving scholarly attention. Recently, Robert Jewett has identified concern for environmental degradation as one element behind the apostle Paul's claim that "the whole creation has been groaning" for liberation (*Romans* 8:19-23). Jewett argues that when early Christian audiences heard *Romans* they "could well have thought about how [Roman] imperial ambitions, military conflicts, and economic exploitation had led to the erosion of the natural environment throughout the Mediterranean world, leaving ruined cities, depleted fields, deforested mountains, and polluted streams."[11] Similarly, when audiences of *Revelation* heard the devastations upon nature threatened by God, they may have considered these threats as God's justice paying back Rome for what Rome had done to the lands and waters of so many subject nations. Furthermore, as I will argue below, references to rare woods and metals and other items in the cargo list of *Revelation* 18 may have evoked for hearers connections to experiences of actions in their own lands—deforestation and depletion of natural resources by the Empire.

In the view of *Revelation*, God will not tolerate Rome's destruction of the earth much longer, despite Rome's claim to rule forever. In fact, the author's so-called end-times language was probably chosen deliberately in order to counter Rome's imperial and eschatological claims to eternal greatness.[12] Rome claimed eternal dominance over the entire world, with slogans like *Roma Aeterna*—"eternal Rome." The boast of the Whore of Babylon/Rome reflects this imperial hubris, "I rule as a queen; I am no widow, and I will never see grief" (18:7). This arrogant boast sets up Babylon/Rome for its catastrophic dethronement and destruction only a few verses later. God answers Rome's boasts of omnipotence and eternity with a resounding no. In response to the question of the eternity of Roman rule, "How long, O Lord?" (6:10), *Revelation* comforts the souls who had been martyred by Rome with the message that it will be "just a little longer" (6:11) until God will destroy "the destroyers of the earth" (11:18). *Revelation*'s insistence on the imminent "end" assures its audience that Rome will not rule the earth forever.

Revelation's lament, its "Alas for the earth" (12:12), concedes that Rome's own imperial claims of domination over the earth have come to pass—but only temporarily. Now that Satan has lost the battle in heaven and has been thrown down to earth (12:9), the earth has for a short time become the arena in which Satan's emissary, namely Rome, "makes war" against the earth and against God's saints (12:17).

But *Revelation* makes clear that Rome's domination of the earth is only temporary. Satanic Rome will not last forever. The devil knows that "his time is short" (12:12). Heaven has already become a "Satan-free zone,"[13] even though earth is still under Satan's reign of terror. The cry of "Alas (*ouai*) for earth" (12:12) expresses the certain hope that Satan/Rome will not stalk the earth much longer. In the eschatological vision of this book, *Revelation* promises that the earth will soon be freed from imperial Satanic captivity.

In summary, the God of *Revelation* does not seek to destroy the earth. Rather, God seeks to rescue the earth from the empire that is devastating it—the land, the seas, and the creatures who inhabit them—so that creation can be brought to fulfillment.

4. The *Exodus* Story in *Revelation*: Plagues as Warnings

How will the liberation come about for the earth and its peoples? The fundamental model for liberation in *Revelation* is the *Book of Exodus*, the story of the liberation of Israel from bondage in Egypt. As Elisabeth Schüssler Fiorenza and other scholars have shown, the *Book of Exodus* furnishes the pattern for much of *Revelation*'s imagery, including Jesus as the Lamb who takes on the role of Moses.[14] The entire *Book of Revelation* suggests a parallel between the Christians' journey out of Rome and the Israelites' journey out of Egypt. For example, the author of *Revelation* calls Christians to "come out" of Babylon (18:4). The connection to Moses and the *Exodus* becomes explicit when God's servants sing the "song of Moses, the servant of God, and the song of the Lamb" (15:3). As such, the *Book of Revelation* gives a "re-reading of the Exodus, now being experienced not in Egypt but in the heart of the Roman Empire."[15]

Understanding the profound ways that *Revelation* borrows from the exodus story can also help us to interpret what is perhaps the most ecologically difficult imagery of the book—the plague sequences described in the middle chapters (6–16). As we saw with regard to the "woes," *Revelation*'s terrible plagues can give the impression that the destruction of rivers, burning of trees, waters turning to blood, and other environmental calamities are somehow an expression of God's will to destroy the earth—an impression that the Left Behind novels capitalize on with ghoulish detail. But *Revelation*'s plagues are threats and warnings, not predictions of inevitable destruction. They are modeled on God's threats of punishment against Pharaoh in *Exodus*. The plagues serve as wake-up calls, warning oppressors of the consequences of unjust actions. God does not predict that these ecological disasters *must* happen—they are rather urgent warnings of what *may* happen if unjust oppressors do not repent. The plague visions of *Revelation* are like the nightmarish visions Ebeneezer Scrooge experiences in Charles Dickens' *A Christmas Carol*—they show a terrifying future that will happen if Scrooge does not change his life. But they also make clear that there is still time for change, and that disaster is not inevitable. *Revelation*'s scathing indictment of oppressors who fail to repent even in the face of the first sequence of plagues underscores that the ultimate purpose of the plagues is to effect repentance, for *Revelation* tells us that the rest of humanity who survived these plagues still "did not repent of the works of their hands . . . nor did they repent of their murders or sorceries or their immorality or their thefts" (9:20-21).

The plagues are part of the book's liberating vision—they are "ecological signs" enlisting nature itself in the struggle for liberation. Terrence Fretheim argues that the *Exodus* plagues "function in a way not unlike certain ecological events in contemporary society, portents of unmitigated historical disaster."[16] In our time, it can be especially important to see the threats of polluted waters and other calamities as ecological wake-up calls—that warn of the consequences of disastrous actions and that call for change before it is too late.

Chilean scholar Pablo Richard interprets *Revelation*'s plagues as imperial assaults on the poor, arguing that it is inaccurate even to call the plagues of *Revelation* "natural" disasters:

> In earthquakes and hurricanes the poor lose their flimsy houses because they are poor and cannot build better ones; plagues, such as cholera and tuberculosis, fall primarily on the poor who are malnourished. . . . Hence the plagues of the trumpets and bowls in Revelation refer not to "natural" disasters, but to the agonies of history that the empire itself causes.[17]

Richard draws an analogy also to contemporary imperial situations:

> Today the plagues of *Revelation* are rather the disastrous results of ecological destruction, the arms race, irrational consumerism, the idolatrous logic of the market.

To summarize, I am arguing that both *Revelation*'s plagues and its "woes"—two elements of the book that can seem the most anti-ecological—show us God's cry for a world that needs to be freed from imperial exploitation. As in the *Exodus* story, God calls on people to "come out" of Babylon/Rome, to withdraw from participation so as not to be implicated in its sins (18:4) and so as to be able to participate in the New Jerusalem. Threats of dire consequences await oppressors if they continue in their unjust ways. As *Revelation* 16:5-6 shows, it is "axiomatic" or "worthy" (*axios*) that the consequences of oppression on the earth will come back around in boomerang-like fashion upon those who commit such injustices.

5. The Ethics of Earth-Healing: *Revelation*'s Choice between Two Cities

For us today, the ethical question is: how can the anti-Roman lament of *Revelation* and its vision for a new exodus take shape in our own global situation? Escapist scenarios of a "rapture" can only serve to deflect attention away from the earth and away from the book's primary critique of empire. We need to seek a historical reading of *Revelation* that takes seriously its prophetic critique of empire as well as its compelling vision for the renewal of the earth. We need to listen to the book's urgent wake-up call. As a means to develop this reading, we can draw on the contrast between *Revelation*'s two competing cities in such a way as to see, on the one hand, the depiction of Babylon as the author's ethical critique of oppression and, on the other hand, the depiction of New Jerusalem as the author's ethical vision of utopian possibilities.

The Babylon vision can offer a prophetic critique of environmental injustice and ecological imperialism. *Revelation* 17-18 depicts the Roman Empire as a powerful market economy, a great prostitute that has "seduced" and "intoxicated" rulers and nations with its trafficking.[18] This is not unlike the way in which poor communities experience environmental destruction today—the flooding of rivers caused by multinational logging companies clear-cutting forests in South Asia, denial of access to drinking water because of privatization of water supplies in Bolivia and South Africa, and other crises of deprivation.[19] Like Babylon/Rome, ours is a world of buying and selling, frenetic commerce and accumulation of wealth side by side with abject poverty. Poor people, most of all, are "left behind" in today's globalized economy.

At a time such as ours, when globalization is increasing, we can be attentive to *Revelation*'s astute critique of Rome's tributary economy and unjust trade, including slave trade. The twenty-six items in the cargo list of *Revelation* 18:12-13 indict Rome's extractive economy and militarism, the lucrative transport of human captives, and the natural resources of conquered territories on ships to Rome. Slave trade is specifically named at the culmination of the list—a rare New Testament condemnation of the institution of slavery. Two of the items in the list of cargoes are forest products: "all kinds of scented woods" (*xylon*, citrus hardwood imported from North Africa) and "objects made of ivory and expensive wood."[20] Distant lands and forests were being stripped bare in order to provide for Rome's insatiable appetites. John's apocalypse says no to such unsustainable destruction.

The opposite of the Babylon vision, the vision of New Jerusalem, gives us, in the author's portrayal, God's vision for the future of our world. As a contrast to Babylon/Rome, New Jerusalem offers the promise of a totally renewed urban landscape, in which God takes up residence on earth. At the center of the city is a life-giving river flowing from the throne of God, giving water free of charge. On either side of the river stands the life-giving tree. This tree provides fruit all the year through to meet the hunger of the people. And the leaves of the trees provide healing for the nations. This is the city into which those who "come out" of Babylon/Rome are invited. The New Jerusalem is a city where life and its essentials are given "without money," as a gift, even to those who cannot pay for them.

The ethical contrast of the two cities presents *Revelation*'s audience with the choice to "come out" of the destructive political economy of Rome (18:4) in order to participate in the justice of God's New Jerusalem.[21] Today, the vision of the New Jerusalem can empower a renewed commitment to environmental justice, to the health of our cities, rivers, forests, oceans, neighborhoods, and world. It can shape our vision for addressing our urban and ecological crises—crises such as the global market economy that marginalizes millions of people while decimating forests and ecosystems, crises that sap our moral will as environmental problems become both more complex and more urgent. *Revelation* offers nothing less than God's vision of justice and healing for the entire human and natural world—for all of creation.

The most important verse for an ecological reading of the New Jerusalem vision may be *Revelation* 22:2, the image of the world-healing tree of life and the wondrous river of life:

> On either side of the river was the tree of life with its twelve kinds of fruit, yielding
> its fruit each month; and the leaves of the tree were for the healing of the nations.

This pivotal verse underscores that God's will is to heal the world, not to destroy it. Notice that healing comes not directly from God or the Lamb, but through the created world—through the leaves of a living tree. Again, this is an important counter point to the Left Behind imagery of vast destruction. *Revelation*'s healing imagery of the river and of the tree of life can inspire us to a new, ecological vision for our planet that is urgently needed.

Water of Life "as a Gift" and the Living Waters of the Columbia River Watershed

I want to conclude by exploring one specific image, the river of the water of life, as an example of an aspect of the utopian New Jerusalem that holds great promise for an ecological appropriation of *Revelation*. Water, freely given by God, flows through New Jerusalem's paradisiacal landscape (21:6, 22; 22:17; see also 7:17). In the overall argument of *Revelation*, the invitation to drink from the "springs" of the water of life in New Jerusalem functions as a contrast to the deadly "springs" of waters that turned to blood and became undrinkable (16:4).[22] Twice God extends the invitation to come and receive the water of life "without cost" (*dorean*)—that is, without money:

> To the one who is thirsty I will give to drink from the spring of the water of life as
> a gift (*dorean*). (21:6)

This promise is reiterated in chapter 22:

> Let everyone who is thirsty come. Let anyone who wishes take the water of life as a gift (*dorean*). (22:17)

Why so much attention to the gift of the water of life "without money"? Because the author of *Revelation* knew that poor people lack the money to buy even the essentials of life. New Jerusalem is a vision of a gift economy where creation's resources are available to everyone, not just to people with money. God hears the cries of poor people and the cries of the earth, and God responds with the gift of life-giving water to quench our thirst and the thirst of the whole world.

The "living waters" of *Revelation*'s New Jerusalem vision are not just part of a future visionary world. This vision can speak concretely about life for the real waters of our world now, for rivers and groundwater sources, for endangered wetlands and estuaries. New Jerusalem's promise of access to pure, living water for all can offer a prophetic critique of our damage to ecosystems, of waters polluted by industrial and agricultural waste, of the denial of drinking water to those who cannot pay. We are told that one billion people in our world lack access to clean drinking water, while at the same time "a legacy of factory farming, flood irrigation, the construction of massive dams, toxic dumping, wetlands and forest destruction, and urban and industrial pollution has damaged the Earth's surface water so badly that we are now mining the underground water reserves far faster than nature can replenish them."[23] At such a time when the freshwater reserves on our planet are in danger of depletion and destruction by such human causes, *Revelation*'s vision of the river of life can sustain our commitment to justice and healing for all of creation's waters.

A recent example of such an ecological use of *Revelation*'s "water of life" imagery is a Roman Catholic bishops' pastoral letter that addresses issues of human justice and ecological threats to the Columbia River watershed in the Pacific Northwest. Chaired by Bishop Skylstad of the Spokane Diocese, the letter was signed also by archbishops from Seattle and Portland and by five other bishops representing dioceses in Montana, British Columbia, Idaho, Oregon, and Washington.[24] It offers a vision for the watershed that, like *Revelation*, combines a call for human justice with a call to care for the earth.

The bishops write, "We propose an integrated spiritual and social vision for the watershed." The bishops underscore the beauty and sacredness of the Columbia River watershed, a huge area that encompasses some 259,000 square miles in the United States and the Canadian province of British Columbia. The document cites such ecological problems as the depletion of salmon, chemical and radioactive pollution from the Hanford Nuclear Reserve on the Columbia River, pollution from mine seepage at huge copper mines in Idaho and Montana, along with human crises such as the loss of livelihood and the growing gap between rich and poor. In an earlier draft, the bishops call for efforts to create a "sacramental commons," invoking *Revelation*'s imagery of the river of "living water."

The entire document is organized around river imagery: "The Rivers of Our Moment" (economic and ecological analysis); "The Rivers through Our Memory" (historical overview of the human and biotic communities that populate the watershed); "The Rivers in Our Vision" (biblical and theological visioning); and "The Rivers as Our Responsibility" (ethics). The bishops propose specific ethical commitments, including: a commitment to save salmon as an "indicator" species of the health of the ecosystem, a commitment to honor treaties with indigenous peoples, a commitment to save and promote family and cooperative farming, a commitment to energy conservation and community building, and a commitment to "ecologically responsible logging and mining."

We need such a reading of *Revelation*'s healing vision not only for the Columbia River watershed but for all of earth.

Conclusion:
The New Jerusalem Ecological Vision for Today

The ecological legacy of *Revelation* and other biblical apocalyptic literature is ambiguous, to be sure, in the history of biblical interpretation. I do not deny the problematic dimensions of the book. But *Revelation*'s prominence in our culture is too great to dismiss this book. As such, we need to challenge the escapist and violent rhetoric of Left Behind and reclaim *Revelation*'s vision as a source of liberation and a source of a visionary ethics for healing our earth. We need to listen to the cry of the earth and the cry of the poor in this apocalyptic biblical book. We need to see the connection between, on the one hand, *Revelation*'s anti-imperial critique of the effects of militarism and violence against the earth in Roman imperial times and, on the other hand, the global exploitation of the earth and its peoples today. The earth and its peoples are crying out to God—and to those of us humans who have the resources to do something about it. God laments the devastation of creation. And we ought to lament it also!

Revelation can give a vision of ecological renewal for the Columbia River and for all the rivers and cities of our world. *Revelation*'s tree of life with its leaves for the healing of nations can offer an ethical vision for healing the whole wounded creation. We need *Revelation*'s vision of a river of living water flowing from God through the center of our cities.

Apocalyptic visions like *Revelation*'s New Jerusalem vision serve as visions for the future, but not only for the future. *Revelation* invites us to live in terms of its healing vision even now. In the beauty of a river flowing through the Pacific Northwest, indeed, in every river, every city, and every tree, God wants us to glimpse the renewal of the world, flowing from the heart of God and dawning already in our midst.

Notes

1. Leonardo Boff, *Cry of the Earth, Cry of the Poor*, 104.

2. See "Debunking the Rapture by Verse" in Barbara Rossing, *The Rapture Exposed: The Message of Hope in the Book of Revelation*, 173–80.

3. *Romans* 8:19-23.

4. Watt was speaking before the House Interior Committee. Quoted by Grace Halsell, *Forcing God's Hand: Why Millions Pray for a Quick Rapture—And Destruction of Planet Earth*, 103; see also Paul Boyer, *When Time Shall Be No More: Prophecy Belief in American Culture*, 141.

5. "Hannity and Colmes," June 20, 2001; quoted in "The Wisdom of Ann Coulter," *The Washington Monthly*, October 2001; www.Washingtonmonthly.com/features/2001/0111.coulterwisdom.html.

6. See Barbara Rossing, "River of Life in God's New Jerusalem: An Ecological Vision for Earth's Future."

7. The term "heavenist" was coined by Norman Habel: "'Heavenism' is the belief that heaven, as God's home, is also the true home of Christians. . . . Earth, by contrast, is only a temporary 'stopping place' for Christians en route to heaven." See "Ecojustice Hermeneutics: Reflections and Challenges" in *The Earth Story in the New Testament, 3–4.*

8. So Margaret Alexiou, *The Ritual Lament in Greek Tradition*.

9. Since there is no "to" in the Greek text, the typical translation of "woe *to* the earth" is particularly inaccurate—there is no indirect object in the dative case. The accusative could better be taken, then, as an accusative of reference. In light of this, a literal translation might be: "Alas, with respect to the earth" or "Alas for earth."

10. Terrence Fretheim, "The Earth Story in Jeremiah 12."

11. Robert Jewett, "The Corruption and Redemption of Creation: Reading Rom 8:18-23 within the Imperial Context.".

12. See Dieter Georgi, "Who is the True Prophet?" 100–126, for this "eschatological" reading of *Revelation* 18 as countering Roman imperial propaganda of a utopic "golden age."

13. So Robert Smith, *Apocalypse: A Commentary on Revelation in Words and Images*, 65.

14. For the argument that *Revelation* draws most extensively on *Exodus* traditions, see the works of Elisabeth Schüssler Fiorenza, especially *Revelation: Vision of a Just World*.

15. So Pablo Richard, *Apocalypse: A People's Commentary on the Book of Revelation*, 77.

16. Fretheim, "The Plagues as Ecological Signs of Historial Disaster," 387.

17. Pablo Richard, *Apocalypse: A People's Commentary*, 86.

18. The intoxication accusations against Babylon in 17:2 and 18:3 are paralleled by charges of deceit and sorcery (*pharmakeia*) in 18:23. See Richard Bauckham, "Economic Critique of Rome in Revelation 18," for the argument that Babylon's intoxicating wine in 17:2 and 18:3 refers to the seductive delusion of the *Pax Romana*: "Rome's subjects are . . . taken in by Roman Propaganda. They are dazzled by Rome's glory and seduced by the promised benefits of the *Pax Romana*" (56). Allen Callahan calls the accusation of intoxication and *pharmakeia* a "narcotics charge," for which Babylon is guilty of "poisoning the international community" ("A Note on Revelation 18: Apocalypse as Critique of Political Economy," 7).

19. See Maude Barlow and Tony Clarke, "Who Owns Water?"

20. See Richard Bauckham, "Economic Critique of Rome in Revelation 18," with its discussion of the provenance of each item in the cargo list in terms of conquered lands.

21. For the argument that an ethical contrast furnishes the frame for *Revelation*'s final two city visions, see Barbara Rossing, *The Choice between Two Cities: Whore, Bride and Empire in the Apocalypse*.

22. This is reminiscent of the *Exodus* plague that turned water to blood (*Exodus* 7:18-24; see also *Wisdom of Solomon* 11:5-7), making the water undrinkable. See the interpretation of the plagues of Egypt by Terrence Fretheim as both acts of judgment and "ecological signs of historical disaster. They function in a way not unlike certain ecological events in contemporary society, portents of unmitigated historical disaster" ("The Plagues as Ecological Signs of Historical Disaster," 387).

23. Barlow and Clarke, "Who Owns Water?" 12

24. See www. columbiariver.org.

9

Revelation 13:
Between the Colonial and the Postcolonial,
a Reading from Brazil

■ ■

Vítor Westhelle

Introduction: The Apocalyptic Ethos

Apocalypsis is the Greek word for revelation. Its Latin equivalent, *revelatio,* is the
origin of the English word "revelation." Revelation is a word that often suggests
positive connotations, for it implies the self-manifestation of God's power, glory, and
love. However, the English word "apocalypse," which is transliterated directly from
the Greek, evokes in us peculiar and frightening images: cataclysm, catastrophe,
calamity, devastation, Judgment Day, Armageddon, and so forth. Many of these
images are in fact drawn from the *Book of Revelation* itself. When viewed as a literary
work, the "book" of *Revelation* is commonly accepted as apocalyptic literature.
Its fantastic and rich imagery, its colorful language, and its clear-cut dualism of
opposing sides have long been associated with a given literary genre that we label
"apocalyptic." However it is important to remember that Christians consider all
the scriptural writings to be constitutive of God's self-revelation; so, the *Book of
Revelation* represents only one expression of apocalypticism as revelation, albeit an
important expression.

In considering these popular ways of defining "apocalyptic" as a literary genre
and as a fantastic narration, we should be careful to avoid two pitfalls. First, apocalypticism should not be defined in terms of a literary genre alone. The *Book of Revelation* is only one expression of a larger apocalyptic *ethos* that pervaded the time
right before, during, and for a while after the New Testament writings were penned.
The diverse writings of the New Testament, as I have said, frame an apocalyptic
message about the impending coming of the Kingdom of God in differing ways
and in a variety of genres, representing various expressions of a larger apocalyptic
milieu.[1] The point is this: The manifestations of apocalypticism have less to do with

183

the literary "apocalyptic genre" than with the larger "apocalyptic ethos," an ethos that reflects a distinctive attitude toward reality. Hence, it is more helpful to focus on the apocalyptic ethos in general than on the literary genre by itself. The literary genre is a particular expression within this larger apocalyptic ethos.

The second pitfall to be avoided in defining apocalypticism is that we might get so caught up in the fantastic images associated with the *Book of Revelation* that we end up focusing only on their surface meaning. Hence, we might miss the fact that these extravagant images are "tropes," namely, figurative utterances straining to express an experience of the world that ordinary language and parsimonious prose unable to convey in depth. The apocalyptic experience of the world that these tropes bore in the first century cannot be easily or entirely recouped, because they belong to a context that is different from ours. Of course, this situation complicates our efforts to understand *Revelation*. Nevertheless, the tropes or images in *Revelation* are not totally obtuse, and the first-century experience of the world to which they point is not entirely inaccessible. The historical data assembled is arguably more reliable now than it was for the generations of believers in the decades that followed Jesus' crucifixion.

By seeing apocalyptic images as figurative expressions of an experience of the world, we open up the *Book of Revelation* so that its symbolism serves as an invitation for us to use the same or similar tropes to express *our* experience of the world. Instead of limiting their meaning to a religious allegory created toward the end of the first century to describe the end of time, we can see the power and illumination of these images in such a way that they can apply symbolically in many and different contexts. In other words, the tropes of *Revelation* have symbolic power far beyond their application to first-century realities. To treat the tropes as symbols, instead of allegories, is to apply their dynamics potentially to any and every institution or system, *including our own institutions and systems*.[2] As such, we are invited to employ the images of *Revelation* in fresh ways in our context and to resort to our own ways of employing figurative language in our context to convey the message that John of Patmos was articulating with the imagery he found relevant in his day. Even the fantastic figures that emerge in *Revelation* regain unexpected meanings in different contexts.

In the extended example that follows, we shall see how the richness of the language of *Revelation* played out in the Brazilian context, offering a language to name realities in the experience of the people that the conventional vernacular failed to fully address. This naming of situations far distant in space and time from the context of the "Seer of Patmos" is what Paul Ricoeur called the "surplus of semantic meaning," a phrase expressing the idea that a text has meaning that exceeds the meaning intended by the original author. As we shall see in the case study presented below, "the sense of a text is not behind it but in front of it";[3] that is, the sense of a text is not in the author's intentionality but in the reader's appropriation of the text in a different context and in another semantic field.

The Brazilian Context

As a result of residing first in Brazil, my native country, then in Denmark and in South Africa for several semesters, and most recently in the United States for the last decade, I cannot but regard myself now as a "hybrid" person shaped by very diverse cultural and socio-economic matrixes. The places I carry in me, which have made me who I am today and which continue to shape my being, have given me an experience of the world that I share with an increasing number of people—a situation that accounts for what sociologists call the most significant sociological phenomenon of the turn of the millennium, namely, *migration*.[4] The hybrid nature of my identity has become clear to me many times when going through immigration at an airport in the United States. As an example, in a recent entry into the country I hand over my Brazilian passport, which bears the history of my various residences and visits, to the immigration officer. He looks through the passport and then asks me for my visa. So I give him a plastic card that says "Resident Alien." The officer then gives the passport back to me with the comment: "This is worth nothing." Holding up my plastic green card, he adds, "This is what really counts." Apparently, having lived in and visited many different countries no longer means much. The only thing that counts is that I have *official* permission to be in the United States; my identity is suddenly restricted to what is encoded in that plastic card that says "Resident Alien." The card just states *officially* that I do not belong. Due to their heterogeneity, hybrids do not belong; they are strangers wherever they are, whether they are there legally or illegally.

Hybrid as I am, it is my Brazilian homeland that I wish to lift up here. I grew up in a context in Brazil that was heavily laden with apocalyptic motives and attitudes. The military coup of 1964, along with events that took place during the subsequent military regime in Brazil, shaped for many of us a perception of reality that was filled with stories of persecution, imprisonment, torture, displacement, and exile. For many of us living through it, these were not just stories but naked realities of ourselves and of the names and places of our friends and relatives, realities that shaped and reshaped our attitude toward the world. In this context, we searched for language adequate to express the bewildering experience of such havoc. From this struggle, engaged in the student movement throughout the 1970s, I have learned that one does not really choose to be apocalyptic; rather, one is lured into it by the extremity of circumstances. Later, in the middle 1980s, having finished a Ph.D. and serving as a pastor in a rural area of southwest Brazil, near Paraguay, the extremity of circumstances would shape yet another apocalyptic experience.

During this period of time, I was involved in leading a day-long Bible study with displaced and landless peasants in Brazil. The focus was placed on chapter 13 of the *Book of Revelation*. My purpose here is to provide an account of that Bible study and the larger framework of events that led to it.

The Pastoral Land Commission (CPT) was (and still is) an ecumenical organization originally formed in 1975 by the Roman Catholic Conference of Bishops of Brazil to work with landless peasants.[5] Landless peasants are the largest social group affected by the rise to power of the military regime and by the subsequent enforcement of its economic program and agrarian policies. These peasants were rendered landless by the drastic and devastating agrarian reform instituted by the new military regime, which created incentives for monocultural farming and which set aside extensive areas that deterred small and multicultural farming. As a result of these agrarian policies, one-third of the entire population of Brazil was displaced from their life on small farms on the land. A simple demographic before-and-after comparison demonstrates the drastic dimensions of those policies. In 1965 (at the beginning of the military regime, shortly after the military coup), two-thirds of the population of Brazil lived in rural areas. Only twenty years later, in 1985 (when democracy was slowly being reintroduced), not more than one-third of the population lived in rural areas.

Most of the peasants who were driven from their land swarmed into crowded urban areas.[6] However, a huge number of the peasants who were displaced—a contingent ranging from fifteen to twenty million people—became landless peasants living on occasional work and seasonal labor in large monoculture farms (often these peasants would be working on land that they once owned but that was now incorporated into a latifundium). Upon being displaced from the small farming plots they owned, these peasants did not follow the mass-migration to the cities, because they could not be assimilated into the over-saturated urban areas. Or if they did go to the cities, after awhile they returned to the countryside, now as displaced peasants, when the dire conditions of city slums were no longer bearable. For the most part, however, they became "squatters" living in small communities of fifty to three hundred persons in tents and makeshift shelters on federal land and other unoccupied areas from which they would often be expelled by police and military force.

In the late 1980s, I served as coordinator for the work of the CPT in the southern State of Paraná. Our task in working with this population of displaced peasants was threefold: first, to accompany them pastorally by caring for their spiritual needs; second, to do advocacy work on their behalf; and, third, to engage them in continuing education, which included training in technical skills such as ecological agriculture, natural medicine, political instruction, and biblical-theological formation. This brings us to the Bible study of *Revelation* 13. However, before I move into an account of that event, I want to introduce some concepts that will illustrate the larger political context of our work with these displaced people and that will explain the larger apocalyptic ethos in which we lived and worked.

Some Working Concepts

My work with CPT was done in conjunction with an organized people's movement called the Landless Rural Workers Movement (MST). This movement represented a shift among the peasants from a naïve acceptance of their situation to a profound awareness of the dynamics of the conditions under which they were living. This raising of consciousness represents a transition from *colonialism* to *postcolonialism*. A colonial situation is characterized by two main features. The first feature of colonialism is called *hegemony*,[7] the capability of a dominant group to exercise power over the subjected or *subaltern* group without overt use of force. Hegemony is distinguished from tyranny by the fact that it presupposes the tacit assent given by the subaltern group to this exercise of power. Hence, there is the presence of power but the absence of the need for the dominant hegemonic culture to use overt force to maintain control, which is possible because of the tacit assent by the subalterns. In colonialism, the subaltern group simply accepts their situation as the way things are. The second feature of colonialism is the passive acceptance by the subaltern group of the *representations* or identity that is projected upon them by the dominant group. Again, the subaltern group accepts these representations of themselves as matters of fact.[8]

By contrast, a postcolonial situation prevails when these two conditions no longer apply, that is, when the subaltern group no longer assents to hegemonic rule by the dominant group and when the subaltern group no longer accepts the imposed representations of who they are by the dominant group. In Brazil the latter process is called, after Paulo Freire, *conscientização*.[9] When these new conditions prevail, the oppressed have succeeded in breaking with hegemony and are already engaged in shaping a new world.[10]

However, there is also a transitional phase between a colonial and a postcolonial situation. This transitional phase is like a twilight zone whereby there is a growing awareness by the subaltern group of these two features (namely, tacit assent to hegemony and acceptance of the identity given to them by the dominant group) and a political practice that contests the group's situation—but without yet being able to break totally away from it.

This twilight zone between colonialism and postcolonialism is what creates the conditions for an apocalyptic attitude and an apocalyptic ethos to emerge. As a working definition, I am suggesting that an *apocalyptic ethos* is characteristic of this "being on the way" between colonialism and postcolonialism. The colonial attitude takes the world as it is; the postcolonial attitude is already able to strategize in creating another world. An apocalyptic attitude exists between these two conditions. In the apocalyptic ethos of this transition period, people no longer conform, but at the same time they are not yet able to strategize and build a new world. The distinguishing feature of apocalyptic is neither passivity (as in a colonial situation) nor strategy (as in a postcolonial situation) but tactics.

It is important to distinguish *strategy* from *tactics*. Strategy, which defines the actions of a social group in a postcolonial condition, is the organizing of available resources and power to be expended in achieving a goal that lies beyond the present condition. Strategy, then, presupposes a surplus and allocation of resources. By contrast, tactics, which characterizes the actions of a subaltern group in the in-between state, is the craft of the weak. By becoming aware of their condition, although not yet able to summon any extra resources to use in strategizing, the weak are nevertheless able to create a living space in the midst of the struggle itself. In a postcolonial situation in which strategy can be employed, power has a "territory," a place that can be conquered or negotiated regarding its use. By contrast, in the in-between situation in which one must resort to tactics, power is a network of relations without a proper place (in the system) and without even an external territory to be occupied. There is simply no external location or means to build another world. Tactics is the art of escaping a colonial condition by plunging into the heart of it.[11]

All this is well illustrated by the apocalypticism present in *Revelation*. John of Patmos's apocalyptic perspective represents the transitional state in between colonialism and postcolonialism. On the one hand, the Seer clearly rejects the colonialism of the Roman Empire. He refuses to accept Roman hegemony for any Christian group, and he repudiates the Roman representation of its subjects. On the other hand, John is not yet in a postcolonial situation in which he has access to resources and territory as means to strategize the building of a new world. Rather, John is in the in-between state of weakness with no political leverage of his own. Nevertheless, in this situation, the author plunges into the heart of the situation with tactics designed to carve out the vision of a new world and to give his communities a new identity—even in the midst of the colonial situation.

This act of escape by plunging into the heart of the colonial situation is the case with apocalypticism insofar as it implies the loss of the world, including the surrender of all commerce, all negotiations, all means of exchange—a situation in which one has chosen to relinquish or has lost any possibility of making it in the existing system. In the very demise of these things, in the moment when all these things are relinquished or lost, a new world order is already dawning. When one gives up accepting things as they are, gives up compromising with the prevailing system, then one can begin to imagine a new and different world.

In this regard, it makes sense when the author of *Revelation* presents a vision of "a new heaven and a new earth" in which "the sea was no more" (21:1). The sea (the Mediterranean Sea or the Aegean Sea) represented the maritime commerce and the cultural exchange of the dominant power of Rome as well as a major means by which Rome exercised hegemony.[12] Hence, the "sea" is a metonymy for the modus operandi of the dominant international and imperial economy at the time. What was regarded first and most important in this Roman world will be the last or least—or, more accurately, "no more"—in the coming world of John's apocalyptic vision. The Seer's apocalyptic vision calls for a radical option between these two—to be either hot or cold, but not lukewarm, and to be for this new world rather than against it or indifferent to it. Only those who have resources to trade can afford to be lukewarm ,and, from an apocalyptic viewpoint, this capacity to trade is of no avail (3:15-17). When one has lost or chosen to relinquish all resources and means of trade and exchange, then one can imagine a new world that does not include such means of domination. This awareness of an impending reversal of conditions and values is a fundamental feature characteristic of an apocalyptic ethos. This awareness of a new world is the space opened up by the apocalyptic ethos in the midst of a situation that otherwise could only lead to despair.

What makes biblical apocalyptic different from an apocalypticism of inevitable catastrophe (a cosmic cataclysm, an Armageddon) is that there is no surrendering of hope. This capacity to maintain hope is what is entailed in the craft of biblical apocalyptic. To use an oxymoron, it is a "desperate form of hope," which Paul called "the hope against all hope" (*Romans* 4:1). It is not "the horror, the horror," as in Joseph Conrad's description of the brutal Belgian colonialism in the Congo at the beginning of the twentieth century as presented in his novel *Heart of Darkness*. Nor is it like the film *Apocalypse Now* in which Francis Ford Coppola renders Conrad's tale in the context of the United States war in Vietnam. What is different in the biblical apocalyptic and what we still encounter among people living in the twilight zone on the way from colonialism to postcolonialism is that hope is present. And this hope affords resilience. To express such hope in the midst of a colonial situation requires tactics. The tactics for the sustenance of such hope, however, are not easy to detect by those outside the apocalyptic environment. It is not easy because the tactics employed in an apocalyptic situation are aimed precisely at preventing the detection of the subalterns' new-found awareness by the colonial power. This covert means of expressing the tactics of hope is *dissimulation*.

Dissimulation or dissembling is, in some sense, an act of deception. It is the art or tactic of appearing to defer to those who have power but to do this act of deference in such a way as to express, albeit in covert ways, one's resistance to that situation. It is a survival tactic, an act of self-protection in the face of being confronted by overwhelming supremacy, while at the same time both resisting the hegemony and also preserving an alternative identity, albeit in a hidden way. Dissimulation stands between, on the one hand, total subservience to the dominant narrative of the colonial power and, on the other hand, the overt and explicit naming of the conditions of oppression, which becomes possible only in a postcolonial situation. Surely, the overt naming of the conditions of oppression is the ultimate goal to be pursued. But it is naïve, idealistic, and romantic to engage in the overt naming of oppression in the context of overwhelming supremacy. Many well-intended outsiders who come to "liberate" people fail to grasp the significance of this situation and as such fail to appreciate (or even to discern) the dynamics of resistance that the tactics of dissimulation represent. Outsiders tend to think the native people are being naïvely subservient, when in fact they are cunningly resisting in the only way they can.

Octavio Paz compares the craft of dissimulation to the skill of acting. "Dissimulation," he writes, "is an activity very much like that of actors in the theater, but the true actor surrenders himself to the role he is playing . . . [while] the dissembler never surrenders or forgets himself, because he would no longer be dissembling if he became one with his image."[13] If dissemblers became one with their image, either they would be surrendering themselves or else they would be insane—giving themselves over to an identity that they knew was not their own. Such forms of mental illness are not uncommon among those in transition from colonialism to postcolonialism, which is also the reason why apocalypticism is often associated with madness. A more apt comparison even than that of Paz's analogy with the theater might be the similarity between dissembling and the masks of the carnival. In the carnival atmosphere, an *alter* personality is allowed to jest and make fun of the powers that be, all the while being "protected" by the mask. The difference is that dissembling in real life does not happen in the permissible space of the carnival, where it is tolerated and where it can be easily decoded. Instead, dissembling happens in everyday life, where jesting against the powers is not permissible and where the expressions of resistance dare not be decoded.

The fact that dissembling is not overt is precisely the reason outsiders often view it either as sheer surrender or as a psychological disorder, when in fact it is neither. An outsider who is not trusted by the group (and it takes years of work for an outsider to gain trust) is very unlikely to discover the rules of dissembling—partly because the tactics of dissembling are copious and partly because they keep changing constantly and are therefore elusive. For the outsider, the fine line distinguishing dissimulation, on the one hand, from surrender or mental illness, on the other hand, is extremely difficult to discern, yet very clear for those living in the midst of the apocalyptic ethos.

The *Book of Revelation* engages in such dissimulation. The author does so as a tactic in the in-between state of apocalyptic. On the one hand, John condemns capitulation to Roman hegemony. He excoriates Jezebel and the Nicolaitans—Christians who, for whatever reasons, simply go along with emperor worship and the eating of meats offered to idols. In their acts of political manipulation, there is no resistance to Rome, but only subservience. By contrast, John offers resistance, but he does so covertly. John does not really use language that "reveals" openly and explicitly his own view of the Roman order. He dissimulates. Thus, while John does name the political realities of Roman hegemony, he does so in language that is indirect, either because it is encoded or because it is cryptic. He condemns Rome with bizarre images and with reference to fantastic creatures. He says much that explains why people are enamored with Rome, "drunk with the wine of her fornication" (17:6). He even portrays the glory of Rome in positive ways, but he does this in language that is so configured as to suggest covertly by exaggeration that such glorifying of Rome is idolatry. Yet, in so doing, he remains within the bounds of dissimulation. If you will notice carefully, he never explicitly names Rome or the emperor or the emperor's minions. The Seer uses language designed to reveal the truth to insiders at the same time that it conceals this message to outsiders—which is the art of tactics. As outsiders, we modern readers have to work hard to understand this dynamic, yet when we read *Revelation* under similar apocalyptic conditions, such work becomes surprisingly suggestive and evocative.

The Choice to Study *Revelation* 13

The year was 1987. A group of landless peasants was camped on the side of a major highway linking Brazil to Paraguay in the southwest part of the country—a common scene! The camp was squeezed between the runway and the fence of a well-guarded nearby large farm, near the city of Cascavel. Nearly 150 people—children, women, and men of all ages—lived under black plastic tents that were like ovens under the burning tropical sun. They had been there already for a number of months after being expelled by force from a farm they had occupied. Two of us from CPT, a Capuchin brother and I, were called in to help this group process some internal conflicts in the camp. Dysfunctional communal relations were never surprising under those stressful and dire conditions. Among the activities that took place during the two days we spent with them was a Bible study carried out with the whole camp. Many of those in the group were illiterate or had received little formal education, which meant that the printed text alone was not enough to convey the content of the chosen text. So, in addition to using the printed text, we resorted to storytelling, dramatic performance, and artistic portrayals of scenes.

The text chosen was *Revelation* 13. We selected this text deliberately, for three reasons. First of all, we opted for this book of the Bible because, notwithstanding the spatial and temporal distance, the context of the *Book of Revelation* is framed in a socio-political and economic milieu that bears striking resemblance to the situation of the landless peasants. Second, we chose this particular passage in *Revelation* because it has to do with the naming of one's reality. As we explained above, in an apocalyptic situation, hope resides in striving to name boldly one's own reality—with the recognition that this bold naming will be done in the form of dissimulation, a dissimulation that must not allow the "apparent" deference to authorities to take over one's personality; that is, without forgetting that subservience and madness are always the nearest neighbors of the dissembler. Chapter 13 of *Revelation* seemed to be a text that would allow for this naming to be raised in a contemporary context and even, as we shall see, to bring some surprises. Finally, we chose this particular chapter because the text itself is a lesson on how to use dissimulation as a way to name a reality.

Based on the limited availability of bibliographical resources, we laid out for the people some historical and literary presuppositions of the text we were working with. We needed to do this in order to construct a plausible first-century scenario that would help to explain how the narrative of the passage unfolded. In addition to historical-critical considerations, the grounds for making some of our exegetical decisions were rooted in the narrative itself and were hermeneutical in nature; that is, we were more concerned with how the text was being read in relation to its original context than in what its original intention might have been. Our focus was on what the relation between narration and politics evinced.

We assumed that the text was written toward the end of the reign of the Roman emperor Domitian (81–96 C.E.). Political and personal characteristics of the emperor and of his reign are crucial for understanding some of the imagery used in chapter 13.[14] Domitian was by and large hated by the aristocracy in general and by the senate in particular (members of which, along with his wife, planned and carried out his assassination in 96 C.E.). He was, however, popular among the common citizens. And he was particularly appreciated by the army, because he had raised the salaries of the soldiers to unprecedented heights a number of times during his reign. Also worth mentioning is the image he projected of himself. At the meetings of the Roman senate, for example, he would wear triumphal dress. At the games over which he presided, he wore a golden crown, with his fellow judges also wearing crowns and with his own effigy engraved among the effigies of the Olympian gods. In addition, he insisted on being addressed as *dominus et deus* ("lord and god").

Besides these political and personal characteristics, there are some other features of Domitian's reign that needed to be lifted up in the context of reading *Revelation*. Although Rome had had a long and honorable history of freedom of speech, this commitment started to change at the beginning of the first century C.E. with the introduction of official censorship by the emperor Augustus. But it was only at the end of the century, during the reign of Domitian, that free speech was totally suppressed. A slightly critical reference to Domitian or about him may have been enough for execution (as happened to a historian, as well as to the historian's secretaries who were crucified with him). Dramatists and poets were thrown to the dogs or at minimum banished, practices that might, incidentally, account for our author's own exile on the isle of Patmos (1:9).

This emperor's relationship to Christianity had some remarkable features as well. In 95 C.E., Domitian executed his cousin Flavius Clemens, presumed to be a Christian, on charges of *atheotes*—of being an atheist. Atheism or irreligion was a common accusation against Jews, Christians, and some philosophical groups.

Unlike many of his predecessors and his successors, however, Domitian did not carry out mass executions of common Christian folk. Rather, his instrument of persecution was more subtle and sophisticated. Domitian's most effective measures against Christian communities and other groups were implemented through high taxation, confiscation of property, and economic marginalization. As is the case also today, it is easier to spot and condemn a dictator for his cruelty in taking lives than it is to recognize the brutality and to count the victims of an exploitative economic system. These, then, are some relevant characteristics of the broader political context in which *Revelation* was written.

The Bible Study of *Revelation* 13

During the Bible study, this background information about *Revelation* was conveyed to the camp as a means to place John the Seer in their own company as someone struggling to find a language to express the dynamics of oppression that were so elusive. What John of Patmos *was seeing*, most of his fellow Christians *were not seeing*. Furthermore, John had to express what he was seeing in a language that was coarse enough to wake people from their slumber but skillfully dissimulating enough to elude (Roman) censorship—something, as we have indicated, that subaltern people and those who have lived under military dictatorships would readily understand. In short, the author of *Revelation* was a master at bringing together an apocalyptic attitude with the practice of dissimulation.

The meaning of much of the imagery that John employs in this chapter (and throughout the book) still eludes us, and it is plausible to suppose that contemporaries of John were so much more equipped to discern the meanings and nuances of the images than we are now. Nevertheless, what we were able to identify was enough to fill a day-long Bible study. What follows, then, are some of the characteristics of the text that we lifted up for the landless peasants who participated in the Bible study that day.

First, we dealt with the way in which the text lays out a hierarchy of powers, pointing out that it does so in a way that is encoded. On top of the hierarchy is the dragon—the same dragon that in chapter 12 was persecuting the woman who gave birth to the child. The dragon is the mythical representation of the fallen angel expelled from heaven (12:7-8). Following the description of the dragon, chapter 13 is divided into two parts dealing respectively with two beasts, one emerging from the sea and the other emerging from the land. Finally, there is the creation of an image (perhaps a statue) of the first beast, which the people have to make and which is given life and speech by the second beast. The people must worship this image or else, if they refuse, they will likely be killed.

Decoding the images in the hierarchy for the contemporary situation can be done in two ways, either by reading them allegorically or by deciphering them symbolically. If we treat the hierarchy as an *allegory*, each of the figures would represent a discrete particular person. The dragon would be Satan; the first beast would be the emperor; the second beast would be a consul or governor; the image of the beast would be a local authority who represents the people but whose power derives from the beast. Such allegories are not easy to apply to a different context with different political systems.[15]

The other way of decoding the hierarchy is to treat the images as *symbols*, each of which would stand for realities that are ubiquitous. In this approach, each image can apply to any group or institution as reflecting ambiguous and contradictory characteristics of the different figures in *Revelation*. The dragon symbolizes a power or system greater than any particular authority or power that could be specified or seen as an identifiable entity in itself. The first beast, the one that emerges from the sea (evoking the power of the international trade and political economy at the time), stands for the highest power on earth (call it "the global beast"). The second beast, the one that emerges from the land (which suggests the extension of the empire, its domain), stands for those who minister in lands beyond the center and who are directly accountable to the authority of the center (call it "the colonial beast"). The image/statue of the beast can be anything that *we produce* and that ends up enslaving us. One example of the "image of the beast" given in the Bible study by the peasants was a television set, and another example was a hoe, as the most common tool used by seasonal workers who weed soybean plantations. We left the option open and waited to see which would be the reading they chose, and we were surprised.

Second, we pointed out that in John's dissimulation there are a number of motifs ingeniously at work to provoke some cognitive dissonance in the reader. These motifs also bear dimensions of encoding, because they expose allegiance to Rome as idolatry and they do so cryptically by the means of flattery and allusion. One such dissonant motif is the use of the positive concept of "authority" in relation to the negative image of the satanic dragon (13: 4, 7, and 12). The dragon has authority of his own. The dragon then grants that authority to the beast that emerges from the sea (the global beast), which in turn delegates authority to the beast that emerges from the land (the local, colonial beast). In the text, the Greek word for "authority" is *exousia*. This is the same word that Paul used in *Romans* 13:1, to say that "there is no *authority* except from God, and those that exist have been instituted by God." Paul's view is clearly contrary to the Manichaean view that God and Satan are two independent forces in the cosmos vying against each other. It is hard to miss the irony in John's apparently cavalier remark that *exousia* is being instituted by the dragon, suggesting to his readers that Satan was a reality completely independent from God (rather than a fallen angel) and that there was here what in Latin American theology has been called a "battle of gods." However, John avoids Manichaeism, if barely, by suggesting that this authority is predicated upon the human willingness to worship the dragon and upon the human failure to see the dragon (Satan) for what it really is. The problem is one of idolatry; but in order to say this as provocatively as possible, John himself needed to use the language of flattery in an exaggerated or hyperbolic way such that it would sound glorious to supporters of Rome but would border on blasphemy in a covert manner to the insiders who "had ears to hear."

Another positive motif that causes dissonance in the reader is the coded image of prophecy that is associated with the second beast. John describes the second beast as one that works "great signs, even making fire come down from heaven to earth in the sight of the people" (13:13). The Judeo-Christians whom John was addressing would hardly fail to notice that bringing fire down from heaven was proof of a true prophet, as it is portrayed, for example, in the story of the confrontation between Elijah and the prophets of Baal (*1Kings* 18). Once more, the point of this blunt dissonance in *Revelation* is to send an encoded message, which those (and only those) familiar with the Judeo-Christian Scriptures at the time would recognize. This is the author's cryptic way of talking about idolatry. To be sure, it is subtle. Yet in a world in which Christians were regarded as irreligious, using this imagery of the beast verges again on blasphemy and, if detected by the Roman authorities, could be very dangerous. Nevertheless, this cryptic language involves a risk that John is willing to take in order to sharpen his message. His message is clear (to insiders), but it is not overt (and therefore it is hidden to the powers of the day).

An additional example of a motif that causes cognitive dissonance in the reader is an allusion to the book of *Exodus*. When John depicts the reasons why people from every tribe, tongue, and nation are willing to worship the beast, the author depicts them as saying, "Who is like the beast, and who can fight against it?" (13:4). Anyone who was even barely familiar with the Hebrew Scriptures would not miss the irony. The motif is taken out of Miriam's song of liberation in *Exodus* 15, in which a similar refrain is sung: "Who is like thee, O Lord?" That which the Hebrew people had addressed to God, the people of the earth are now saying about the beast. By means of this cryptic allusion, the author once again suggests to those who can "get it" that worshiping the beast is clearly idolatry.

"Who has ears, hear!" is the refrain repeated in the whole book again and again (2:7, 17, 29; 3:6, 13, 22; 13:9). It is an admonition from John for insiders to discern his true message. John the Seer sees, and what he sees needs to be communicated and must be heard. What he says is a subversive word, but a word that must be said in such a way as to be loud and clear for those who need to hear it, but concealed enough to be hidden to those who represent the hierarchy of powers he describes here in chapter 13.

Let us recapitulate: the Seer of Patmos introduces his vision of the beasts, naming each one of them in cryptic fashion for what they really are. Yet what John sees and what John calls them is not how the people of the earth, who idolize them, see them. John himself gives the clues as to how others see these figures. The first beast is bedecked with diadems—a symbol of royalty, dignity, and respect. The second beast appears to be like a lamb, suggesting meekness and humbleness. The image/statue of the beast is a human production, giving the impression that it is under human control, yet it is nothing but an idol, a fetish. But what you see is not what you get, says the Seer to those who can and will hear: Listen to what the Spirit says, and you will discern the beast behind the adornments. Do you know what you see? Do you see what you know?

Next, an ingenious play of images is posited on the motif of "hearing." It seems that, to John's way of seeing, people are so captivated by the idolatrous sight of the image of the beast that they do not hear. And if they do hear, to whom are they listening? By the command of the (colonial) beast, the one that the emerged from the earth, people are to make an image/statue of the first (global) beast. The (colonial) beast gives breath or spirit (*pneuma*) to this built image of the (global) beast, so that it can speak and persecute those who refuse to bow down to it in adoration (13:15). Again verging on idolatrous blasphemy, the author attributes to the beast the power to give the gift that only God can give. For it is God alone who gives life and breath to humans (*Genesis* 2:7). At creation, God breathed into the creature of the earth (*adam*) the breath (*ruah / pneuma*) of life, a gift that allowed humans to name the world (*Genesis* 2:19-20). Whose spirit is it that they are now listening to? This is the question the Seer of Patmos is asking in an apocalyptic tone. It is a call for discernment—and discernment we will get!

Toward the end of chapter 13, after denouncing the persecution of those who do not worship the image of the beast, John offers a surprisingly blunt condemnation of what today would be the equivalent of the global market. Everyone, rich and poor, freedmen and slaves, had to have a mark on the forehead or on the hand, and no one would be permitted to "buy or sell" unless they had the mark, the name of the beast, or the number of the beast's name. The second beast required that people submit to the first beast in worship and adoration or they would be prohibited from sharing in the wealth of the (Roman) economic system.

Then comes the climatic rhetorical moment of the narrative, for which John has been preparing the reader. This climax is almost a sarcastic way by which John teases the readers into admitting for themselves that all the exotic creatures that the Seer has just displayed are nothing but figments of an idolatrous imagination. After all this supernatural imagery of dragons and beasts, the narrative ends with a riddle. "This calls for wisdom: let the one who has understanding reckon the number of the beast, for it is the number of a human. And its number is six hundred and sixty-six" (13:18). Behold the last surprise: the beast John has been talking about is *human*! Indeed, all too human! The number six symbolizes that which is close to perfection (seven) but not quite. In the words of *Psalm* 8, the human is made just "a little less than" a god. Also, creating humans was the work God did on the *sixth* day, just before the closure of holy Shabbat. And a three-fold six is very likely an emphatic assertion that it is six, it is six, it is six; that is, it is *wholly human* (symbolized by the emphatic threefold repetition), and nothing more than a human. After awakening his readers with jarring language and the use of cognitive dissonance while dodging the censors with the far-fetched imagery of uncanny creatures, the Seer announces in a final ironic move that the incredible beings he has presented are nothing but God's beloved creatures corrupted by power into bestiality!

Rhetorically speaking, the first move of our author was to show the essential wickedness of the powers, the powers that most people of the earth esteemed so highly for their apparent beauty and adornments. John's naming of the wickedness of the powers leads the reader to see that the act of worshiping these beasts really amounts to nothing but a despicable idolization. In his second move, he exposes the beasts as merely human creatures. When he does this, the author undoes the supernatural implications of the imagery that he himself has used in order to accomplish the results aimed at by that first move. In so doing, he clarifies why their adoration is idolatry—because the objects of their devotion are only human beings or human-made fetishes! The trajectory that cuts through chapter 13 goes from alienation (the creature is adorned and worshiped) to dissimulation (it is an extraordinary beast, a supernatural creature) and ends by giving them the clue to the real identity, the *human* identity, of their object of devotion—but just short of explicitly naming it! It is this being "just short of" that signals the author's final relinquishment of his own power of naming in favor of the reader. The Seer undoes his own use of extravagant imagery in a surprising twist. He sets it up so that, here at the end, it is now up to the readers to reckon the riddle and own the naming for themselves!

The Outcome of the Bible Study

This is also how the introduction to the Bible study ended, just short of naming the beast. One of the activities that followed was for people to do the naming of the beast for themselves and for their own situation, following the same tactic that John had used. The discussion groups then formed spontaneously, with no directions as to how they should be organized. When the community assembled again in the afternoon, the groups reported their findings. Some of the naming by the different groups was predictable to us. The beasts they named in their situation included the military, the government, the capitalist system, the rural-based oligarchy, the lumber industry, and so on. These were the beasts that had brought them to this place and the beasts with which they as a community still had to contend. However, this naming involved forces that were all external to the community, and it in no way addressed the issues for which we had come to the camp, namely, the internal issues that were plaguing the community itself. To use the Seer's vision, there was the need not only to name the external beasts oppressing them but also to name the *image(s)* of the beast—those things that the community "worshiped" but that were really of their own making (v. 14).

Then, to our surprise, one of the groups named some of the intracommunal "images" of the beast. This group was comprised only of women (all the other groups were mixed). Their words cut to the chase. In their report, there was *parrhesia*, the boldness that takes a risk by speaking up. Their naming included three related things: pans (a symbol for the arduous work, normally done by women, of cooking over a small open fire under a hot black plastic tent filled with smoke); alcohol (which mostly men indulged in at night); and the "central committee" of the camp (which was ultimately responsible for administering the camp and which, in this particular camp, unlike the others, was comprised of males only). This was the naming that took the courage of a "parrhesiast," a bold speaker. The naming of the beasts by other groups were definitely true, and, due to their political training, these groups were able to identify those beasts—perhaps even without our Seer's help. However, the naming of the *image* of the beast, the human-made idol, was the key that enabled the members of this community to enter into the deeper levels of what structures of oppression are able to produce and to replicate, even among the oppressed themselves. The more subtle mechanisms of the structures of oppression, being of our own making, elude us, and we do not realize that they are nothing but the re-*production* of the very beast in our midst. And indeed, at least to the men, these images had looked rather nice and innocent!

Like Rome, the image of the beast looks good and appealing to us. We may benefit from it greatly, as many people benefited from the Roman Empire in the first century. In so doing, however, it blinds us to the corrupt and destructive reality of the thing and prevents us from seeing the idolatrous allegiance we have given to it. But if we name it out loud—whether it be the Roman Empire or the Brazilian military regime or the patterns of sexism in our very midst—we may be able to see it for what it is and dispel its power over us.

As Paul Ricoeur said, the "sense of a text lies in front of it." Indeed the meaning of *Revelation* 13 for this community of landless peasants lay not in what John the Seer had intended for his particular situation, but in what he evoked by leaving the naming to his readers, beyond his control and even two millennia later and in place even unknown to him. John of Patmos ends his composition of chapter 13 not with a riddle, as it is often supposed, but with an ellipsis. . . . He left it up to his readers to fill it in. That is what those peasants did, and that is what we also are invited to do.

Notes

1. See the influential essays by Ernst Käsemann, "Die Anfänge christlicher Theologie" and "Zum Thema der urchristlichen Apokalyptik," 82–131. His main thesis is that "the apocalyptic was . . . the mother of all Christian theology," 100.

2. Since Goethe, the difference between symbol and allegory is defined in aesthetic theory in the following terms: "It makes a great difference whether the poet starts with the universal and searches for the particular, or beholds the universal in the particular. The former mode of procedure generates the allegory, in which the particular is taken as an illustration, an example of the universal. The latter reveals . . . the truth of symbolism, that the particular represents the universal not as a dream or a shadow, but as a living instantaneous revelation of the inscrutable." Johann Wolfgang Goethe, *Maximen und Reflexionen*, 67–68.

3. Paul Ricoeur, *Interpretation Theory: Discourse and the Surplus of Meaning*, 87.

4. A helpful collection of essays on the social and theological significance of migration in the contemporary world can be found in Gioachino Campese and Pietro Ciallelle, eds., *Migration, Religious Experience, and Globalization*.

5. For more information, see Marcelo de Barros Souza, Vítor Westhelle, and Ivo Poletto, *Luta pela Terra: Caminho da Fé*.

6. See Sérgio Sauer, *Reforma Agrária e Geração de Emprego e renda no Meio Rural*, 30–48.

7. The notion of "hegemony" was developed by the Italian philosopher Antonio Gramsci to describe a situation in which "the supremacy of a social group manifests itself in two ways, as 'domination' [*dominio*] and as 'intellectual and moral leadership' [*direzione*]." *The Antonio Gramsci Reader*, 249.

8. On the question of the representation of the subaltern, see the excellent essay by Gayatri Chakravorty Spivak, "Can the Subaltern Speak?" 271–313.

9. The word is poorly rendered in English as "consciousness raising." It conveys the notion that one produces by oneself the awareness of who one is within communitarian relations of solidarity. See Paulo Freire, *Pedagogía del oprimido*.

10. The literature in the field of postcolonial studies is immense; some of the most celebrated postcolonial writers are Amilcar Cabral, Franz Fanon, Edward Said, Aimé Césaire, Homi Bhabha, Gayatri Spivak. A good collection of representative writers and a comprehensive bibliography can be found in Patrick Williams and Laura Chrisman, eds., *Colonial Discourse and Postcolonial Theory*.

11. This distinction between strategy and tactics is finely elaborated in Michel de Certeau, *The Practice of Everyday Life*, 34–39.

12. For an excellent discussion of the politico-economic significance of this expression, see Barbara Rossing, *The Choice between Two Cities: Whore, Bride, and Empire in the Apocalypse*, 144–47.

13. Octavio Paz, *The Labyrinth of Solitude*, 29 and 42. A similar analysis of the phenomenon of dissimulation is offered by Homi Bhabha, *The Location of Culture*, under the notion of mimicry. See pp. 85–92 on "Of Mimicry and Man: The Ambivalence of Colonial Discourse." For further discussion on the phenomenon of dissimulation, see Vítor Westhelle, "Multiculturalism, Postcolonialism, and the Apocalyptic," 3–13.

14. For more information on Domitian as emperor, see F. E. Adcock Cook, and M.P. Chralesworth, eds., *The Cambridge Ancient History*, vol. 11 S.A. 22–45; and the article "Domitianus," in Hubert Cancik and Helmuth Schneider, eds., *Der neue Pauly: Enzyklopädie der Antike*, vol. 3.

15. The allegory, said Goethe, "transforms appearance into a concept and the concept into an image so that the concept is always limited by the image, but also fully expressed in it." Goethe, *Maximen*, 192.

10

Hope for the Persecuted, Cooperation with the State, and Meaning for the Dissatisfied: Three Readings of *Revelation* from a Chinese Context

K.-K. (Khiok-khng) Yeo

Introduction

Personal Reflections

The *Book of Revelation* has the most "universal" scope of any narrative in the New Testament. Nevertheless, reading *Revelation* from "particular" locations can yield fruitful results. My first encounter with the book of *Revelation* occurred when I was a non-Christian. Born and raised in a Chinese family in Malaysia, I grew up with religious freedom there. I was taught from my youth to stay away from religion and to place my trust in science and self. Yet I was in despair, because I saw that a secular worldview could not provide a peaceful coexistence of multi-racial groups in a nation nor could it empower the human spirit to moral excellence. I was worried that violence seemed to be the consistent means of the human aspiration to peace. I was dissatisfied because I saw that a scientific worldview could neither fulfill the human quest for meaning nor supply the human need for love. As such, I came to appreciate the message of *Revelation* not because I was persecuted, but because I was discontent with an atheist view of life. The visions of Christ in the book of *Revelation* and the descriptions of a world salvation gradually being consummated appealed to me. As a result of my encounter with *Revelation*, I placed my trust in Christ and was baptized as a Christian in high school in 1976.

Oddly enough, the year 1976 was the end of a ten-year period of turmoil in China. This period was officially called the Cultural Revolution (1966–1976), but in hindsight it was really a "cultural destruction." Many of my relatives who had not fled China for Malaysia in the 1940s went through a difficult time. I learned in my home church in Malaysia that *Revelation* was a source of comfort for many

Christians in China. The message of hope, salvation, and faithfulness in *Revelation* appealed to these people who were being persecuted for their faith. I came to realize that my reading of *Revelation* as a way to discern a meaningful life and to discover a reality that "ought to be" was not the same as the reading of those suffering ones who were in need of comfort. While the *Book of Revelation* was difficult to decipher, I, as a young Christian, began paying attention to its message and how it could be read in different ways.

I came to the United States for my theological education in the early 1980s. The historical-critical methods I learned at the seminary added new perspectives to my previous layperson readings of *Revelation*. However, over the last twenty years I have never lost touch with Chinese Christians and intellectuals in China; I make annual trips to visit churches and to lecture at universities in China. Of course, China and the Chinese church are changing, and their responses to the visions of *Revelation* also change.

Chinese Christians and *Revelation*

Chinese Christians have responded to the *Book of Revelation* in different ways amid the changing religious and political situations during and after Mao's era. Christians in China have had an ambivalent attitude toward *Revelation*. On the one hand, as persecuted Christians, they have gained hope from *Revelation*'s vision of the future. On the other hand, they cannot accept the harsh and thoroughly dualistic rejection of the state as presented in *Revelation*. As we shall see, the Roman imperialism of John's time and the Chinese communism of the modern era are not the same, even though they share similar elements. As a result of the differences between the ancient and the modern context, some Chinese Christians have challenged the application of the message of *Revelation* to the Chinese situation. Consequently, some Chinese Christians have responded differently from the first-century Christian audiences of *Revelation*. In addition, some Chinese Christians are drawn to *Revelation* quite apart from the issue of resistance to or cooperation with the state.

In light of this situation, we can identify three different Chinese Christian appropriations of the *Book of Revelation*. First, Chinese Christians have seen *Revelation* as a source of hope and empowerment in the face of persecution by the state during the Cultural Revolution. Second, some Chinese Christians have resisted the thoroughgoing dualism of *Revelation* regarding "church and state," because such a negative view of the state has polarized Chinese Christianity and has prevented productive cooperation with the state. Third, other Chinese Christians, like myself, have found *Revelation* helpful even in situations where there is no active persecution or political oppression. People who experience intellectual dissatisfaction with "what is" can be claimed by the vision of *Revelation* as to what "ought to be." *Revelation* presents a vision of wholeness and meaning to Chinese people today who are searching for meaning in life and who are neither persecuted nor oppressed. It is these three appropriations that I wish to explain and place in their historical context in recent Chinese history.

Eschatology, Apocalypse, and Millenarian Hope

Before explaining the three Chinese Christian readings of *Revelation*, it will be helpful to define key concepts used in this analysis (eschatology, apocalypse, and millenarian hope) and, in so doing, to summarize key aspects of the theology of *Revelation*.

Eschatology

The term "eschatology" is usually understood in three ways. First and foremost, eschatology is, in general, the study of the end-time or of end things. The term eschatology is comprised of two Greek words, *eschaton* (end or last) and *logos* (word or study); hence, eschatology is "talk about end things." In this regard, the *Book of Revelation* deals with end things, such as a final judgment, heaven and hell, and a new heaven and a new earth. Second, in terms of an interpretation of the meaning of history, eschatology refers to the goal and purpose of history, its end or hopeful outcome. In this sense, eschatology is "teleology" or talk (ology) about goal (*telos*). In the case of *Revelation*, the *telos* or end of history is Christ, the Lamb of God (5:6, 8, 12, 13; 6:1, 3, 5, 7, 16; 7:9, 10, 14, 17; 12:11; 13:8, 11; 14:1, 4, 10; 15:3; 17:14, 19:7, 9; 21:9, 14, 22, 23, 27; 22:1, 3). *Revelation* shows that the end of the world will be the beginning of a New Jerusalem (3:12; 21:2-10), namely, the boundary-less, transcendent city of God constructed by the Lamb of God. Third, in terms of a theology of history, eschatology refers to the *coming* activities or *revealing* work of God in the world. Specifically, in terms of a theology of history in the *Book of Revelation*, the author seeks to overcome the problem of suffering caused by Roman persecution. *Revelation* does this by "looking only to God and proclaiming God as 'the Coming One,' by becoming itself a sign of hope in everything it tries to say."[1] Hence, in *Revelation*, we see the rupture of God's redemptive forces at work in the present age, forces that will bring about the complete reign of God on earth soon.

If we were to put these three understandings together, we might think of eschatology as the original intention of God for the consummation of creation. Moltmann argues this syncretistic view succinctly: "Christian eschatology follows this christological pattern in all its personal, historical and cosmic dimensions: *in the end is the beginning*."[2] He argues that,

> *Christian* eschatology has nothing to do with apocalyptic "final solutions" . . . for its subject is not "the end" at all. On the contrary, what it is about is the new cre-

ation of all things. Christian eschatology is the remembered hope of the raising of the crucified Christ, so it talks about beginning afresh in the deadly end. . . . Christ can only be called "the end of history" in the sense that he is the pioneer and leader of the life that lives eternally. Wherever life is perceived and lived in community and fellowship with Christ, a new beginning is discovered hidden in every end. What it is I do not know, but I have confidence that the new beginning will find me and raise me up. . . . In God's creative future, the end will become the beginning, and the true creation is still to come and is ahead of us.[3]

Apocalyptic

In Greek, the word "apocalypse" means "revelation" or "unveiling." It usually refers to a literary work such as the *Book of Revelation* (sometimes called *The Apocalypse*) that describes the end of the world. The typical features of an apocalypse include, among other things, a revelation of the end involving transcendent visions, angelic intermediaries, cataclysmic battles, and conflicts between good and evil.[4] Both eschatological and apocalyptic worldviews see God in full control of the outcome of history, despite the apparent dominance of evil in the present. But "eschatology" and "apocalypse" are not the same: apocalypse, as reflected in a type of literary work, involves violent destruction and end-time messianism as part of the historical process. Eschatology, on the other hand, is a broader concept that may or may not include such apocalyptic elements. In other words, it is not adequate simply to use the broader term "eschatology" to depict the *Book of Revelation*. Rather, and more specifically, *Revelation* is an "apocalypse," its worldview is "apocalyptic," and it has an "apocalyptic type of eschatology." Historically speaking, John's *Apocalypse* is the product of an "apocalyptic movement."[5]

Millenarianism

Many social scientists prefer the word "millenarianism" to "apocalyptic movement," although both terms refer to socio-religious movements that embrace apocalyptic eschatology.[6] The words "millennium" (from Latin) and "chiliasm" (from Greek) both mean "a thousand." The concept of "thousand" in both terms originates from the *Book of Revelation*, where a thousand-year reign of Christ and the martyrs is depicted as a blissful age of heaven on earth. While the adjective "millenarian" derives from the "thousand year reign," it has come to refer in general to movements that embrace end-of-the-world hopes, irrespective of any thousand-year reign. In contrast to speaking abstractly about the theology of *Revelation*, it is more helpful to use social-science models of millenarian, nativistic movements (the uprising of natives against colonizers) and crisis cults (radical religions that emerge from cultural crises) as means to portray the social and political contexts of *Revelation*.[7]

Methods of Analysis

Reading *Revelation* from a Chinese context necessitates that I first take seriously the social, political, and cultural contexts of the time, both the time of *Revelation* and the time of modern China. Then it is possible to show more clearly how Chinese Christians responded to their specific problems with hope and strength. In order to do this effectively, I will be using both the historical-literary analyses of apocalyptic (such as that of H. H. Rowley)[8] as well as the sociological analyses of apocalyptic (such as that of Stephen L. Cook and others) to read and interpret *Revelation* from my cultural perspective.

I will seek to show that the causes for Chinese Christians' millenarian and eschatological hopes are complex. On the one hand, like many millenarian groups, the causes include economic deprivation, political persecution, and personal suffering. On the other hand, the causes also include various intellectual dissatisfactions that prevent people from experiencing personal, societal, or cosmic wholeness. Chinese Christians who experience intellectual dissatisfaction are a "brooding minority" (in Paul D. Hanson's words) that seeks to transform the society by means of otherworldly hopes that are beyond this mundane world.[9] It is important to show how apocalyptic movements can be driven by factors other than deprivation.[10] Cook finds no evidence that millennialists must suffer from psychopathology, resulting from various forms of deprivation.[11] Based on the argument of Hillel Schwartz, Cook argues that:

> The millennial "outbursts," like the new wealth created by an entrepreneur, may stem from newly emergent creative "energy." This more holistic approach allows that a millennial group may result from something as simple as a group realization of the variety of available worldviews. Such a realization would allow for the propagation of a new and radically different symbolic universe. . . . Because people believed that the Messiah had come, their whole world waxed and waned.[12]

It is very appealing to understand *Revelation* from this social-science point of view. To do so may suggest that the apocalyptic movement reflected in *Revelation* was driven not just by political and social deprivation but also by dissatisfaction with "the way things are" in light of a vision of "what might be." Likewise, a social-scientific understanding of the Chinese situation may explain why the message of *Revelation* appeals to intellectual, educated, as well as uneducated Chinese. The message of millenarian hope offers the Chinese an open system of understanding meaning in history—hope for wholeness beyond their worlds of dissatisfaction or persecution. The message of *Revelation* is relevant to both marginalized, persecuted groups *and* those non-deprived millennialists suffering from intellectual dissatisfaction, that is, to those suffering from "cognitive dissonance"[13] or psychological "anomie" and an "absence of meaning."[14] "Cognitive dissonance" or "anomie" describes nihilistic anxiety, a disintegrating world, or the brokenness of self because of conflicting worldviews, feelings, or ideologies that people experience. People of every age, social class, economic status, race, and situation can have this dissonance. The resolution to such dissonance is the recognition that the present world is fallen and evil but that the good is yet to come as a final triumph and perfection.

First Reading:
Faith under Persecution (*Telos* of Salvation)

Revelation depicts the religious, cultural, economic, and political struggles of some Christians in Asia Minor at the end of the first century, probably during the reign of the Roman emperor Domitian. The persecution of Christians by the Roman Empire that is reflected in the *Book of Revelation* arose from their resistance to emperor worship, their exclusive loyalty to Christ without compromising with the synagogue, and their persistent adherence to a faith at odds with the syncretistic practices of Greco-Roman religions. The narrative of *Revelation* manifests a definite progression that offers hope to these faithful believers. The book uses symbolic language to portray stages: first a spiraling cycle that goes back and forth between persecution of Christians by Rome and judgment on Rome by God; then the emergence of the dragon (the forces of evil, chapters 12–13, 20) to be defeated by the return of Christ, who will then reign with resurrected saints on earth for a thousand years; followed by a second judgment and a second resurrection, the arrival of a new heaven and new earth; and finally the appearance of the holy city—the new Jerusalem come down out of heaven from God (chapters 20–21).

In this narrative progression, *Revelation* does not set forth stages of world history; rather, it gives a Christian reading of history with a distinctive emphasis on the Lamb of God as the *telos* of history. In other words, faith in the Lamb of God by the persecuted Christians enabled them to overcome evil and violence by means of sacrificial loyalty in imitation of Jesus, the first and the last of all powers. The "breaking in" of God's kingdom in the present and the destruction of evil forces at the end-time confirm the truth of the faith of the believers. Beyond destruction and persecution come consummated salvation and cosmic wholeness (a new heaven and a new earth) and Jesus as the goal (*telos*) of history.

Chinese Christians in the Cultural Revolution

The Domitian persecution that lies behind the apocalyptic eschatology of *Revelation* has parallels in modern history, especially during the Cultural Revolution in China under the regime of Mao Tse-tung, when Christian pastors and laity were systematically persecuted, imprisoned, and killed. Persecuted Chinese Christians found the end-time message of *Revelation* worth believing, for it engendered faith and hope for them. Chinese Christians believed that John presented a theology of history in which the historical process was under the control of God. Despite persecution and the dominance of evil, Christians saw the present and the final period of history as under the lordship of Christ. In unveiling the eschatological reality of salvation for his audience, the author of *Revelation* claimed that the fulfillment of the promise in the future could be seen and experienced now—an experience that is true for the first audience as well as for later audiences of *Revelation*.

Hence, the political and religious contexts of *Revelation* in the Roman Empire of the first century and of Christians during the Cultural Revolution in China of the twentieth century were quite similar. Yet it is important to recognize that the historical periods and the cultural dynamics of the two contexts were also quite different.

Mao's movement, for example, was initially a resistance movement against Western imperialism. If one comes to understand the imperialism and the feudalism faced by China at the time of the Cultural Revolution, one will sympathize with Mao's vision of nationalism and proletarianism. In so doing, one will sympathize also with his rejection of all religions—at least as Marx and Feurbach defined them, namely, as a tool of the upper class to exploit the lower class.[15] The Western Christian powers colonized China and kept China from modernization.[16] Seen through the eyes of the Chinese, the Treaty of Nanking (1842) and the Treaty of Tientsin (1858) were both totally unjust acts of blatant imperialism in exploiting China's resources and in forcing its people to accept opium grown in India in exchange for tea and silk.

It may be correct that (some) Christian missionaries condemned the opium traffic and that they were never directly a part of the imperialistic or colonial activity against China. Nevertheless, the facts are that the Western imperialists often used the name of Christianity as a justification to conquer, that the preaching of Christianity was often dominated by Western culture, and that the native churches were always tied to Western leadership and under the control of overseas mission boards. Mao Tse-tung considered Christian missionary work in China to be a form of foreign cultural aggression. And it was not only Mao who opposed Christianity, but the people as well. In fact, the Chinese Boxer Uprising of 1900 was the culmination of sixty years of popular antagonism toward *all* foreigners.[17] The Chinese communists therefore viewed religion, especially Christianity, as a foreign imperialist's ideological tool for the exploitation of the common people.[18] Mao himself believed that in the socio-economic realm, religion was used by the oppressor to give the oppressed a false hope of a future world.

Ironically, the anti-religious ideology of Maoism functioned as a religion in its own right, perhaps taking the place of the superstitions and religions that Maoism sought to annihilate. In this regard, the Christian groups in China were threatening not just because of their connection to imperialism; they were also minority groups that stood against Maoism and were persecuted for it. Similarly, in the first century, the Romans sometimes considered Christians to be subversive of the state. The Romans persecuted the Christians in Asia Minor because Christianity was considered to be an "atheist" religion that did not worship the emperor and the city gods. Unlike the Christian God, these Roman gods were gods whose images or "idols" could be *seen* and whose adherents supported the Empire. Unlike Judaism, a monotheistic faith that had legal status in the Empire, Christianity did not always acknowledge the divinity (divine right) and benefaction of the Caesars. Hence, faith in Christ was considered to be politically suspicious, if not subversive, to the *Pax Romana*.

Faith in Christ speaks critically of the political agenda of any and every "empire" that is based on conquest and fear. Thus, the Roman Empire and the Maoist Empire were established by means of the seduction of power, the destructiveness of violence, and the expansion of military might as the means to bring peace and prosperity. Similar to the ideology or "theological politic" of the Roman Empire, Maoism is essentially a religion of de-eschatology, because Maoism denies the working of God in history—a view that results in millenarian hopelessness. The "will to power" of the political reality of Maoism does not view the consummation of salvation as the goal of history; hence, violence and "permanent revolution" become justifiable means to bring about the utopia of communism within history.[19]

Faith in the Lamb of God

In contrast to Maoism, Christians consider the nonviolent Lamb of God to be a better model for the ordering of life. As Yoder puts it, "the crucified Jesus [Lamb of God] is a more adequate key to understanding what God is about in the real world of empires and armies and markets than is the ruler in Rome, with all his supporting military, commercial, and sacerdotal networks."[20] Following this thesis of Yoder, Toole writes regarding the appealing nature of apocalyptic eschatology: "The cross is a political alternative to insurrection because it stands at the end of a path of resistance that refused violence."[21] It is ironic that Mao originally shared a similar hope for Chinese society. He intended to liberate people from the socio-political bondage of imperialism and yet ended up with a totalitarian and oppressive state.

Perhaps the political millenarian state of Maoism became totalitarian because it rejected divine grace and love. The Maoist monolithic ideology emphasized its own consistency and purity. Therefore, in a Maoist political utopia, there was no margin for error. Consequently, various anti-revolutionary campaigns were organized to purge any deviant, alternative views. Many Chinese Christians went through "accusation meetings," because they were suspected of "counter-revolutionary" ideas and activities. Few Christians escaped trial or death (at least when the church did not go underground), because they were accused of subscribing to and being brainwashed by the unscientific foreign religion of Christianity. Even to this day, the communist government in China remains suspicious of religious groups and activities. Christian teaching on eschatology, not to mention apocalyptic thought, is a sensitive, if not prohibited, topic. Therefore, Chinese Christians today still struggle with this doctrine and are hesitant to preach it.

Maoism believed that as the Chinese people's ideological consciousness increased, religions such as Christianity would gradually wane and their role in human society would decrease to zero. For example, Jiang Qing (1914–1991), the wife of Mao, declared during the Cultural Revolution that "Christianity in China has already been put into a museum. There are no more believers."[22] However, hope and history have proven Maoism and Jiang Qing wrong. As Tertullian put it, "the blood of the martyrs is the seed of faith." And it was *hope* that nurtured such faith in Christ. In contrast to Mao's followers, Chinese Christians have seen the whole picture of God's revelation working itself out in history. In the *Book of Revelation*, they have seen a vision of the consummation of history, and such a comprehensive historical vision grants them the assurance of victory, comfort in suffering, and hope in the midst of dismay. From apocalyptic eschatology, they have learned to be open to God and to the future in an attitude of obedience, worship, and confidence.

For many Chinese Christians, *Revelation* assures them that a life of faith and trust in the God who raised Jesus will also reveal a new beginning for them. In the face of the impending end of their world through persecution, they have trusted that God will bring about new life from death.

Second Reading: Cooperating with the State (Resisting the Dualism of *Revelation*)

The Christianity we have described was not the only form of indigenous Christianity in China. While all Chinese Christians found faith and hope in the message of *Revelation* during statewide persecutions, nevertheless some Chinese Christians came to develop a different, positive view of their relationship with the atheist government—a view that was not compatible with the view of the state in *Revelation*. They agreed in principle with the communist government's vision for society, and they determined to work together with the state in bringing about this vision. These Chinese Christians formed the Three-Self Patriotic Movement and registered their churches with the government. Other churches (often referred to, inaccurately I think, as "underground" churches) disagreed with this point of view and refused to register with the government.

The Christian Patriotic Movement

The first step in the development of the Christian patriotic movement in China involved the separation of Chinese churches from Western control. This process of independence was anticipated by the formulation of the "three-selfs" principles, already implied in the work of Campbell Gibson.[23] These principles were formally proposed by Henry Venn (1796–1873) of the Church Missionary Society and Rufus Anderson of the American Board of Commissioners for Foreign Missions.[24] Venn argued that "the elementary principles of [1] self-support and [2] self-government and [3] self-extension be sown with the seed of the Gospel . . . in the Native Church"[25] in China. Anderson in turn called on missionaries "to ordain presbyters . . . and to throw upon the churches . . . the responsibilities of self-government, self-support and self-propagation."[26] These three principles helped make Chinese churches self-sustaining and free of Western imperialism.

In the early twentieth century, these principles began to take an even stronger hold. In light of the 1922 publication of *The Christian Occupation of China*,[27] the conference that year aimed to build more and more independent Chinese churches, such as those founded in Jinan, Qingdao, Yantai, Enxian, and Wiexian, and also to set up schools, hospitals, and centers of service. Then, in the 1920s, some larger independent churches were founded, such as the Little Flock and the True Jesus Church. These churches were unconnected to Western organized denominations and unregistered with the government.

The second step in the development of the Christian patriotic movement in China came when the desire to dissociate from Western imperialism was combined with a patriotic devotion to the Chinese Government, which led to the formation of the Three-Self Patriotic Movement (TSPM). This movement urged not only separation from Western powers but also a commitment to cooperate with the Chinese communist government—and thereby to register with the government as a religious group. The political aspirations connected to this movement would serve to divide registered and unregistered churches in China. Registered churches tended to express patriotism to China, while unregistered churches generally did (do) not believe that nationalism should be expressed explicitly either in private spirituality or in public church life.

In 1949, the government established a sophisticated network to administer religious policy and to supervise religious activities. While the government wants all churches to be registered, not all house churches are registered. The "official church" refers to those churches that are registered. It is precisely this point of government monitoring and control that has led some Chinese churches to choose to be "apolitical" and thus to refuse to register with the government. The question of registration has to do with the relationship between church and state. Many of my American friends argue with me for the separation of church and state, citing the United States as the best example. Perhaps because of such an assumption, the same American friends are puzzled about how it is possible for the registered churches in China to be "Christian" or "biblical." Although I will not go into the historical reasons for advocating for the separation of church and state (as a response to Emperor

Constantine's Holy Roman Empire vision), it is worth noting two aspects to this issue. Regarding the governmental aspect, one could argue that the state has no right to establish or control religious expression. Regarding the church aspect, one could argue that the church has no business engaging in politics. In contrast to both of these views, the TSPM does not oppose either the monitoring and registration of churches by the Chinese government or the idea that the church might cooperate with the government.

The Dualism of Revelation

The radical, dualistic separation of church and state, of governmental politics and Christian spirituality, could be traced to the *Book of Revelation*. The author of *Revelation* seemed to condemn any Christian compromise with or tolerance of the dominant political ideology of the day. For example, in the letters to the churches in Ephesus (2:1-7), Pergamum (2:12-17), and Thyatira (2:18-29), the author warned the readers to watch out for opponents within the churches, whom he referred to as the Nicolaitans. The Nicolaitans were presumably the "apostles" (2:2) who were itinerant missionaries and who, as far as we can tell, had an accommodating approach toward Rome.[28] In the letter to Pergamum (2:15), John reproached the church for tolerating the Nicolaitans. Those who held the teaching of Balaam (2:14) might also be the same group of people who held to the teaching of the Nicolaitans, because of an etymological correlation between Balaamites and Nicolaitans.[29] The Nicolaitans were those who claimed to have knowledge of demonic realities that granted them, on the one hand, the freedom to live in peaceful coexistence both with secular society and with the imperial cult without sacrificing their faith in God and Jesus Christ and, on the other hand, the license to engage in libertine behavior.[30] John uses two phrases to depict the attitude of these opponents: "to eat food sacrificed to idols" and "to practice immorality." Both are references to syncretistic and thus compromising tendencies of these Christians toward secular as well as imperial ideology.[31] In addition, the message to Thyatira accused the prophetess Jezebel of the same vices: eating meat offered to idols and practicing fornication. Elisabeth Schüssler Fiorenza suspects that the Thyatiran opponents are the same group as the Nicolaitans.[32] *Revelation* 2:24 explicitly spells out their teaching as "knowing the deep things of Satan."

The attitude of the *Book of Revelation* toward the Roman Empire is thus one of condemnation (16:19; 18:19). The author identifies the Roman Empire with the beasts and with Satan (2:13; 18:2). He depicts the city of Rome as the whore (17:1, 15-16; 19:2). He condemns Rome's (Babylon's) political alliances and its economic trade as seduction (18:3-20). He exposes Rome's idolatry and violence (11:7; 13:14). He calls for followers of Jesus to withdraw from its political, economic, and social life (2:2-3; 3:4-5; 13:17). He calls followers of the Lamb to conquer by resisting its seduction and violence (3:24-29). The *Book of Revelation* rejects Rome without reservation; the author sees no possibility of the church working together with the government.

Christian responses to the government's relationship to religion vary, even in the New Testament. Differentiating true faith leading to martyrdom from wise faith with compromise is subtle. Other New Testament books, such as *Romans* (13:1-7) and *1 Peter* (2:13-17), do not have a polarizing view of the relationship between church and state. The dualistic understanding of church and state in the *Book of Revelation* is not helpful to Chinese Christians who are seeking to cooperate with the government. By contrast, most unregistered churches in China have taken this dualistic message of *Revelation* seriously, and they refuse to listen to the Chinese government, especially in matters of Christian belief, polity, and identity.

Cooperation with the Chinese Government

Because of differences in the contexts of *Revelation* and of Chinese Christianity, we need to apply the message of *Revelation* carefully. Here, two key considerations are important. First, unlike Chinese Christianity, early Christianity at the time of *Revelation* had not yet become an imperialistic force. Therefore, the author of *Revelation* did not suspect it within Christianity and did not critique it among the churches of first-century Asia Minor. However, having identified itself in recent centuries as one of the Western imperialistic forces, Christianity in modern Chinese history is not without its imperialistic tendency. Therefore, it is necessary today for Chinese Christianity to critique Western imperialism in both its religious and political forms. Second, Chinese communism, though atheist, has had a policy of cooperation and religious freedom (at least in its constitution). Unlike the ancient Roman government, which did not welcome cooperation with early Christians, the Chinese government wanted to work with Christians to rebuild China. The social program of Maoist ideology did not intend to destroy religion so as to free China from the domination of foreign powers and wealthy landlords. Mao's vision was to empower peasants and laborers as proletarians to bring about the socio-economic prosperity of China. Mao also believed in the moral virtues of the new humanity, that people must work hard at their socialist consciousness as a means to rebuild a strong nation. Many Chinese Christians were sympathetic to Mao's socialist vision and able to affirm Mao's social programs of building communes for the sharing of resources among the people, of increasing agricultural and industrial production to strengthen new China, and of Mao's will for Chinese nationalism that the prosperity of Chinese society be in the hands of the people themselves—not in the hands of foreigners nor those of some elitist group.

When the communist government came to power in 1949, they adopted the policy of religious freedom and tolerance. The political purpose of such adoption was not spelled out, but C. M. Chen, an official of the Religious Affairs Bureau, said that the purpose of the government was not outright extermination of religion but restriction, reformation, and control. Chen pointed out that the TSPM had been created to make religion serve politics and to make the church politically non-threatening.[33] To the registered churches, TSPM was a wise religious and political strategy precisely in its courage to cooperate with the Communist Party on the common ground of shared social concerns—based on the understanding that God is above all and that no government has a right to absolute power, but is subordinated under God. In other words, despite the fallenness of government, God can still realize God's perfect will of working toward good through any means, including that of government.

A document called the "Christian Manifesto," which dealt with the relationship between the church and the state, was prepared cooperatively by a Christian leader, Wu Yao-tsung, and a political figure (the premier), Chou En-lai, in 1950.[34] The Manifesto called on Chinese Christians to heighten their "vigilance against [Western] imperialism, to make known the clear political stand of Christians in New China, to hasten the building of a Chinese Church whose affairs are managed by the Chinese themselves." It further stated that Christians should support the "common political platform under the leadership of the government."[35] It called upon churches relying on foreign personnel and financial aid to discontinue these relations and work toward self-reliance. Around the same time, the Protestant Three-Self Reform Movement (TSRM)[36] was officially established in 1951.[37] In 1958, Wu wrote in *Tien Fung (Heavenly Wind)* that "without the Communist Party there would not have been the TSPM or the Christian Church. . . . I love the Communist Party."[38]

Opposition to the Patriotic Movement

Unregistered churches, however, expressed the conviction that the government should not have any control over their Christian identity, freedom, or responsibility. Most of the resistance to TSPM came from preachers like Wang Ming-dao and Watchman Nee, some "underground" house-churches, and the Roman Catholic Church,[39] all of whom were reacting against the more "liberal" theology of TSPM and its cooperation with the Communist Party. Interestingly enough, this position of opposition comes close to the view of *Revelation*. Their assumption was that the Chinese government, being communist in ideology, is "pagan" and satanic, similar to that of the Roman Empire as symbolized by the "evil forces" in the *Book of Revelation*.

Up to this day, Chinese Christianity continues to struggle over the issue of church and state, resulting in conflicts between the registered and unregistered churches. Unregistered churches do not think that Christianity should work with a government that does not love or honor the Christian God. This is the theology of the *Book of Revelation*, which harshly critiques Roman ideology of violence, economical domination, pagan belief, immoral values, a false sense of peace and security, an idolatrous claim of divinity on the part of the emperors, and so forth.

Appropriating the Bible

The question related to this issue for Chinese Christians today has to do with their biblical hermeneutics—the dynamics of their interpretation. With shifting political contexts, how should one be faithful to the Bible and yet true to one's own cultural context? Can one not develop a theology out of the distinctiveness of one's own context?

In that regard, how does Chinese Christianity address the following questions? Is it only for survival that the registered churches supporting the TSPM have chosen to emphasize the common ground between Christianity and communism instead of magnifying their differences? Is it a "collaboration in the humanist cause"[40] that should be considered a betrayal of faith? Or is it not also a positive collaboration? Is God not able to work through the government and beyond the government—even if the government is not sympathetic to the Christian cause and even if the government at times creates obstacles to the Christian witness? Does God work only within the limits of human will? Does God only work through Christians? In other words, even if people wish evil, can God not work good out of evil and unbelief?

It is important to note that *Revelation* does not critique government per se but its "fallenness." *Revelation* critiques principalities and powers whose purpose is to demonize and destroy life. William Stringfellow, a commentator on *Revelation*, argues that these fallen powers take forms in government departments, financial systems, political ideologies, and even religious institutions, and their power of deception is at work pervasively in the world: "Every principality in its fallenness exists in remarkable confusion as to its own origins, identity, and office. The fallen principalities falsely—and futilely—claim autonomy from God and dominion over human beings and the rest of creation, thus disrupting and usurping the godly vocation or blaspheming, while repudiating their own vocation."[41] How the Chinese churches read the Chinese communist government and its departments as "fallen" will determine their differing positions on the church and the state. By and large, unregistered churches hold to a "dualistic position" on the church and the state; they do not think that the Chinese communist government is a trustworthy partner to work with, and they think that its fallenness is unredeemable. They do not believe that God will work through this government. On the contrary, registered churches believe that the state is under the rule of God and that therefore believers should take part in the state. TSPM regards the policy of religious freedom to be "a reasonable one" but has no illusions about communism's atheist views.[42] TSPM therefore works with the state on "common ground," and it does so for the sake of Christ and the benefit of the people.

Initially, in response to persecution resulting from differing views between the Chinese government and Christianity, Chinese Christians found the messages of hope and salvation and wholeness in *Revelation* trustworthy. Subsequently, in response to the communists' view of building a New China, the TSPM has held to political accommodation, thus differing from the dualistic position of church and state in the *Book of Revelation*. Registered Chinese churches believe that if the communist government, though atheist in belief, would want to form a united front with believers of any formal religions in order to construct a socialist China, then Christians can be patriotic and can work toward rebuilding China in ways beyond the political vision and will of the government. Christians find hope in their cooperation with the government. Christians hope that God will use their vision of the Lamb of God as the goal of history. Precisely because of such love for their country and their Christian vision, to be a Chinese Christian (a "both/and" rather than an "either/or") is possible, but not without tension. The *Book of Revelation* can thus offer a message of hope but also of ambiguity—or even challenge and hindrance—to Chinese Christians.

Reading Three: Christians with Cultural Dissonance (Theology of History)

Most scholars assume that apocalyptic thinking is driven only by persecution, and that the *Book of Revelation* was therefore written in response to persecution. The logical sequence of this scenario is: Christian conversion, which leads to persecution, which in turn exposes the evil nature of the state, which then results in John's vision of the future that offers encouragement to the persecuted. Using the social-science model (along with my own experience) to re-read *Revelation* has, however, challenged my assumption that *Revelation* simply addresses a group of persecuted Christians in need of comfort and encouragement. Many Chinese intellectuals today, quite apart from a context of persecution, have a keen interest in the doctrine of eschatology. Such a phenomenon has challenged me to raise a new question about *Revelation*: what if the persecution of these early Christians in *Revelation* was a secondary cause for the author to write the book? What if the author's primary purpose was to present the vision of a consummated future, a vision of meaningful living for all who do not find the current vision of the Roman state to be the way things "ought to be." In other words, the author wanted to reveal an alternative way of life that was different from the culturally conditioned Roman way of life. The author wanted to present a vision of living based on God—the reality of "what ought to be" based on "the Alpha and the Omega"—"who is, and who was, and who is to come, the Almighty" (1:4, 8).

In this scenario, it was the vision of Christ that drove this book, not Roman persecution. An alternative logical sequence might be: the Christian vision of a consummated future of "the way things ought to be" makes apparent the evil nature of "the way things are" in the Roman world, which leads Christians to oppose the way things are and thereby to be persecuted for it. In Christ, John experiences a way of living based on love (1:6), purity, and faithfulness to God. This vision leads him to see the evils in the Roman Empire—the seduction, the violence, the fornication, the destruction, the lying—that have resulted in political hegemony, social bondage, personal despair, and ecological destruction. And the author knew that this newly found commitment to God and to God's future would result in persecution. The author's vision of life offered by Jesus both responded to and created intellectual/personal dissatisfaction, which in turn led to opposition to the state. Correspondingly, the *Book of Revelation* does not begin with persecution; rather, it begins with Christ's love, the eternal nature of that love rooted in God, and its powerful capacity to make people priests of God (1:5-6). It moves from there to the exposure of Rome as evil and then to the consequent Roman persecution of those who do not subscribe to Roman ideology. In other words, the evil of Rome is apparent because all its programs contradict the nature and the works of Christ.

Chinese Christians Seeking Meaning in History

It is this interpretation of history among Chinese Christians that I wish to explain here, namely, that Chinese Christians today continue to find the message of *Revelation* helpful, even though the contextual problem they face has moved from a situation of religious-political persecution to a present situation of "lost-ness" and "meaninglessness" about the future. Chinese Christians now look to the Coming God who provides a Christ-filled *future outcome* to history, a future that is necessary for human existence to be redemptive and meaningful *now in the present*. God's *past* irruption into human history as seen in the death and resurrection of the Christ allows them to discern a process of history rooted in "what ought to be" rather than in "what is." In other words, God's involvement in history is apocalyptic in the sense that the Christ-event reveals the grand narrative that can bring meaning out of chaos, wholeness out of violence, and salvation out of lost-ness. Chinese Christians find the visions of *Revelation* to be meaningful: history and all affairs in this world have a beginning, a direction, and an intended goal (1:8; 22:1-5); salvation, not destruction, is the final destiny of life, and God's presence/glory is the ultimate reality (21:22-27); worship and trust provide stamina for truth seekers to be morally and spiritually strong in the midst of chaos and challenges in the world (5:1-14).

The strength of Christianity in China is a sign that people are finding meaning in its message. The growth of Christianity during the post-Mao era has been dramatic. By 1990, there were an estimated 6,000 registered churches and 15,000 registered "meeting points" for five million believers.[43] The "Christianity fever" took hold after 1989 in intellectual circles and in the academy. The surge in numbers is reflected in the fact that the government continues to have a *phobia* about religion, as Alan Hunter and Kim-Kwong Chan describe:

> Religion gained a higher political profile after 1989. . . . [The government] was aware that religious organizations, especially Christian ones, had been influential in opposition to the communist governments of eastern Europe. Stricter regulations were promulgated, and rumours spread that a crackdown on religious activities was imminent. In 1990, Chinese government officials reportedly feared that 70 per cent of the nation's religious activities were out of control, while Premier Li Peng called for attacks on the underground churches.[44]

What accounts for this surge? After ten years of Cultural Revolution, the Bamboo Curtain was lifted, and exchanges in commerce, knowledge, technology, sports, and the arts were common. At the same time, a desire for spirituality, a religious search for meaning, and a deep moral concern have remained strong. Most Chinese people respect the pragmatism and the Four Modernizations (in agriculture, industry, science and technology, and national defense) under the leadership of Deng Xiaoping in the late 1970s; they yearn for peace and prosperity for modern China. Many people, including government leaders, at one time looked to Falun Gong (a syncretistic religion based on Buddhist and Daoist teachings combined with meditative exercises) to achieve wholeness. The interest in religion was so great that the government exhibited its fear and began to crack down.

Other factors have contributed to the interest in religion in China. In various lecture engagements and visits to the main cities of China in the last ten years, I have witnessed increasing material prosperity, vigorous commercial activities, and the luxurious spending of the rich. University students, Christian and non-Christian alike, have repeatedly told me about their fear that the pragmatism of capitalism, technological advancement, and economic modernization will lead China to a doomsday destruction of ethical and intellectual vitality. They lament the disappearance of hope for the future, community building, integrity of character, and a spiritual quest. These were all part of the early development of Maoism in China, but they are now difficult to find. The context in China has changed, and, as a result, a new way of relating to the *Book of Revelation* is now called for.

The Power of a Utopian Vision

Even though my critique of Maoism is harsh at times with regard to its political and ideological misguidedness, I would not want to deny how essential Mao's vision is for the future of the Chinese people. There is no doubt that the vision itself can be taken too far (particularly, for example, by the leftists). And there is no doubt that Mao's political strategy of realizing that vision by means of violence is unwarranted. Nevertheless, the vision for the future does provide drive and hope for the people. China today lacks the kind of vision that provides hope for the future, a future that is good for the country and society. Instead, China today is preoccupied with individualism and focused on materialism. Individualism and materialism become the means of satisfaction and the goals of existence. In the absence of a utopian vision in the post-Mao era, the presence of a commercial utopia might be self-consuming. To be sure, in the post-Mao era, the Four Modernizations have gone very well. Yet people are well aware of social impasses, leadership corruption, moral deterioration, and political nepotism in China today. People look back positively on the era of Mao. In the popular imagination, Mao remains a moral and political leader who gave the masses of people a ray of hope—"the symbol of an age of economic stability, egalitarianism, and national pride."[45]

The *Book of Revelation* has an explicit view of eschatology. Perhaps that was in part due to the author's conscious effort to contrast his apocalyptic vision with the absence of eschatology in popular culture—especially in the propaganda of the *Pax Romana*, which claimed that Rome and the Emperors were *already* ushering in a millenarial reign at that time on earth. The Empire's vision of reality spoke persuasively to the oppressors and the powerful, because it was a form of realized eschatology that does not wait for future hope. Realized eschatology resists *and* refuses the need for eschatological hope.

The lack of utopian vision in China today presents a similar problem of realized eschatology focused on material prosperity. Most Chinese people think that reli-gion and spirituality are not significant needs for any person. Intellectuals and researchers study religion and spirituality simply as academic disciplines. The fundamental problem of secular utopias rooted in materialism, however, is that they de-eschatologize history by denying that history has a goal and meaning. And the result of treating history as accidental and meaningless is "the discrepancy between the piling up of technological and scientific instrumentalities for making all things possible, and the pitiable poverty of goals."[46] A secular realized eschatology views history in terms of an instantaneous and eternal Now, which does not have a purpose and goal, and thus no meaning either.[47] A materialist realized eschatology masks religion in human desire with the hope that technology and materialism can create a paradise on earth—a kingdom of security and a present without a future.

If modernization and secularization in contemporary China constitute a "religion" with absolute power, many people are seeking to find this religion by searching for democracy and capitalism from the West. However, these things will not bring the meaning they are seeking. In fact, democracy may not really grant freedom, and capitalism may in fact bring with it many societal evils. Many Chinese today want a secularization of religious values that will fulfill their needs and desires. This anti-eschatological ideology of secularization stands in contrast to the Christian hope of wholeness. By focusing on the eternal Now, an anti-eschatological "religion" of democracy and capitalism eradicates hope and dissolves the future.

Implications for Interpreting *Revelation*

Perhaps the question that troubles the author and the audience of *Revelation* is not only the meaning of suffering, but also the meaning of history. In other words, beyond the termination of suffering, is there something more and better and whole? To provide meaning to suffering, John does not narrate the *whole* of world history from the beginning to the eschatological end. Rather, as Schüssler Fiorenza points out, "Revelation consists of pieces or mosaic stones arranged in a certain design, which climaxes in a description of the final eschatological event. The goal and high point of the composition of the whole book, as of the individual 'little apocalypses,' is the final judgment and the eschatological salvation."[48] Even in his explanation of the meaning of suffering, John attempts to stretch human finitude beyond the present to the historical past (Jesus' death and resurrection) and to the future end of time (eschatological hope), thus granting the audience a vision of the past, present, and future.

To explain the meaning (theology) of history, the author portrays a "newness" that is beyond human anticipation. Why? Because what is new—the New Jerusalem, the new heaven, and the new earth—draws human finitude to that which is a radically consummated whole, defined only by the person Jesus Christ. History has a goal; it is moving toward salvation and wholeness, in which the glory of God will fill all in all. Exactly how it is going to turn out, we do not know. But the message of *Revelation* allows the faithful—those who have ears to hear and eyes to see—to be caught up in that eschatological drama of salvation.

The power of apocalyptic rhetoric in *Revelation*, as Adela Yarbro Collins has pointed out, resides in the power of *catharsis* in crisis, that is, in the power of the language of *Revelation* to calls its readers to have feelings of purity and assured victory despite the broken world they live in. Often two sets of symbols are used in apocalyptic rhetoric: one describes "what ought to be," and the other describes "what is." The "ought to be" portrays hope; the "what is" depicts reality. The language of these symbols is primarily "commissive," which calls "for commitment to the actions, attitudes, and feelings uttered."[49] This expressive and evocative language in *Revelation* creates a virtual and emotional experience for the hearers; it expresses a view of history, suffering, and reality. As evocative language, it elicits a response from the hearers in terms of thoughts, attitudes, and feelings by the use of effective symbols and dramatic plot, inviting imaginative participation in a commitment to move from "what is" to "what ought to be."[50] In other words, the *Book of Revelation* generates a catharsis that purges the reader of allegiance to what is and commissions them to live by what ought to be. The promise of the future as portrayed in *Revelation* guarantees "what ought to be." This promise of the future also envelops the past and the present and, in so doing, saves believers from being lost or ambiguous in the present—thereby claiming them as people who belong to the absolute future of history, which is God.

In the midst of capitalist seduction and democratic utopia, many Chinese Christians have continued to look to Jesus Christ. On a recent annual teaching trip to China, I was amazed to see that churches were packed with Christians and seekers.[51] Every sermon that I have heard in China thus far is biblically based, Christ-centered, and a reminder for Christians to be spiritual leaders who provide hope and light to a country that is looking desperately for meaning.[52]

Conclusion

Since the end of history has now been revealed and known in Christ, past and present audiences of *Revelation* are invited to participate in that future by anticipation. It is God, the purposeful actor in history, who alone has the power to bring history to its consummation, "incorporating each temporal present as it occurs"[53] until the end of time. It is for this reason that one can anticipate with assurance that God the Almighty reigns. That is the central message and purpose of *Revelation*.

The imagery of Christ in *Revelation* is intended to give hope and assurance (confident faith) to Christians under persecution and to grant a holistic vision of God's created world to those in search of meaning in God's grand plan in history. The self-surrender of Jesus was a sacrifice of self for humanity, and it serves as an example, albeit a divine and inimitable one, to empower believers to endure in the face of persecution. Meaning in history is constructed not by means of conceit or violence but by the obedience of faith to God's holiness, as the Lamb of God has exemplified. The community is called to believe that it has access to the celebration of the saving work of God by sharing in the present suffering of Christ and by participating in the fullness of Christ's glory in the future. Beasts (6:8; 11:7; 13:1-18; 14:9-1; 15:2; 16:2-13; 17:1-20; 20:4, 10) will arise in history to deceive all who dwell upon the earth, and those who refuse to worship the Beast will be slain (13:11-14). The challenge for the faithful, says John, is to overcome and to conquer (2:7, 11, 17, 26; 3:5, 12, 21) the deception and seduction of the beasts. The only way one can overcome distortion, deception, and persecution is by looking at Jesus. After all, the title of the work is *The Revelation of Jesus Christ*.

Notes

1. Gerhard Sauter, *What Dare We Hope? Reconsidering Eschatology*, 11–20, here 19–20.

2. Jürgen Moltmann, *The Way of Jesus Christ: Christology in Messianic Dimensions*, x.

3. Jürgen Moltmann, *The Coming of God: Christian Eschatology*, trans. M. Kohl, xi.

4. John J. Collins, "Introduction: Towards the Morphology of a Genre," 9: "'Apocalypse' is a genre of revelatory literature with a narrative framework, in which a revelation is mediated by an otherworldly being to a human recipient, disclosing a transcendent reality which is both temporal, insofar as it envisages eschatological salvation, and spatial, insofar as it involves another, supernatural world."

5. See Stephen L. Cook, *Prophecy and Apocalypticism: The Postexilic Social Setting*, 1–54.

6. See the standard definition of these terms by David Aune, "The Apocalypse of John and the Problem of Genre," 67.

7. See Sylvia L. Thrupp, "Millennial Dreams in Action: A Report on the Conference Discussion," 11–12.

8. H. H. Rowley, *The Relevance of Apocalyptic, passim*; Philip R. Davies, "The Social World of Apocalyptic Writings," 255.

9. Paul D. Hanson, *The Dawn of Apocalyptic*, 214.

10. Cook, *Prophecy and Apocalypticism*, 35, mentions the Free Spirit millennial sects in thirteenth-century Europe that included people from privileged, wealthy intelligentsia: the rich and powerful Janko and Living brothers of Wirsberg in the 1450s and 1460s who led a millennial group; Fiorence, the civic reformer Savonarola who at the end of the fifteenth century spoke to political officials and the upper class as well as to the poor; a millennium group in Calabria of the Middle Ages with Joachim of Fiore (c. 1135–1202) as the leader; among other examples.

11. Ibid., 44.

12. Ibid.

13. Leon Festinger, Henry W. Riecken and Stanley Schachter, *When Prophecy Fails: A Social and Psychological Study of a Modern Group that Predicted the Destruction of the World, passim*.

14. Robert Jay Lifton, "The Image of the End of the World: A Psychohistorical View," 151–70.

15. Maoism accepts the Marxist dogma that religion originated in primitive society as a way of dealing with the unexplainable forces of nature. But as society developed, religion had become a tool of the upper class to exploit and control the lower class by taking "the minds of the exploited off their present condition of misery" (G. Thompson Brown, *Christianity in the People's Republic of China*, 76–77).

16. Robert C. Tucker, *Philosophy and Myth in Karl Marx*, 105.

17. Donald E. MacInnis, *Religious Policy and Practice in Communist China: A Documentary History*, 12.

18. Cf. Leslie Lyall, *God Reigns in China*, 126, who elaborates this point.

19. Yeo Khiok-khng (K. K.), *Chairman Mao Meets the Apostle Paul: Christianity, Communism, and the Hope of China*, 18, 20.

20. John Howard Yoder, *The Politics of Jesus: Vicit Agnus Noster*, 246.

21. David Toole, *Waiting for Godot in Sarajevo: Theological Reflections on Nihilism, Tragedy, and Apocalypse*, 214.

22. Arthur Wallis, *China Miracle: A Voice to the Church in the West*, 65.

23. He arrived in Shantou in 1874, and was determined to make the Chinese church there independent, strong, and native, but the principle was not well practiced in Shantou. Of eighty-eight congregations, only twenty-eight were self-supporting by the 1930s. See George A. Hood, *Mission Accomplished? The English Presbyterian Mission in Lingtung, South China*, 296.

24. The idea of "three selfs" was also proposed by two American missionaries, S. L. Baldwin and V. Talmage, in the 1800s. S. L. Baldwin, "Self-Support of the Native Church," and J. V. N.

Talmage, "Should the Native Churches in China Be United Ecclesiastically and Independent of Foreign Churches and Societies," *Records of the General Conference of the Protestant Missionaries of China Held at Shanghai,* May 10–20, 1877, 283ff, 429–31.

25. Max Warren, ed., *To Apply the Gospel: Selections from the Writings of Henry Venn,* 26.

26. R. Pierce Beaver, ed., *To Advance the Gospel: Selections from the Writings of Rufus Anderson,* 37.

27. M. T. Stauffer, ed., *The Christian Occupation of China.*

28. W. Bousset, *Offenbarung Johannis,* 204–6.

29. Nikolaos (*nika laos*) is equivalent to the Hebrew *ms slm* = "he has consumed the people."

30. Elisabeth Schüssler Fiorenza, "Apocalyptic and Gnosis in the Book of Revelation," 569–71.

31. Cf. Num 25:1-18; *1 Corinthians* 8 and 10; A. T. Ehrhardt, "Social Problems in the Early Church," *The Framework of the New Testament Stories,* 276–90; Schüssler Fiorenza, "Apocalyptic and Gnosis," 67–68; and G. B. Caird, *A Commentary on the Revelation of St. John the Divine,* 39.

32. H. Zimmermann also contends that the Nicolaitans had a prominent role in these churches, in "Christus und die Kirche in den Sendschreiben der Apokalypse," 176–97.

33. Lyall, *God Reigns,* 129.

34. *Documents of the Three-Self Movement,* Wallace C. Merviwn, Francis P. Jones, ed., 19–21.

35. *Tien Fung* 423 (July 7, 1954) 1 and 425–27; (Sept 3, 1954): 3–10.

36. In 1954, for the sake of unity, the name was changed to the Protestant Three-Self Patriotic Movement. Compare *Documents,* 4.

37. Lyall (*God Reigns,* 131) critically observes that TSPM is not a spontaneous, free independent body of the Chinese Church, but an organization created by the Communist Party to carry out party policy. Lyall's point is that the late Wu Yao-tsung was pro-communist and a serious student of Marxism.

38. Lyall, *God Reigns,* 131; *Documents,* 184–91.

39. See Brown, *Christianity,* 86–88 for details.

40. Julia Ching, "Faith and Ideology in the Light of the New China," 26.

41. William Stringfellow, *An Ethic For Christians and Other Aliens in a Strange Land,* 80.

42. K. H. Ting, "A Call for Clarity: Fourteen Points from Christians in the People's Republic China to Christians Abroad," 145–49.

43. Alan Hunter and Chan Kim-kwong, *Protestantism in Contemporary China,* 3.

44. Ibid., 4.

45. Geremie Barmé, *In the Red: On Contemporary Chinese Culture,* 320.

46. Frank E. Manuel and Fritzie P. Manuel, *Utopian Thought in the Western World,* 811.

47. See Yeo, *Chairman Mao Meets the Apostle Paul,* 231.

48. Schüssler Fiorenza, *The Book of Revelation: Justice and Judgment,* 47.

49. Adela Yabro Collins, *Crisis and Catharsis,* 144.

50. Ibid., 144–45.

51. For example, in Beijing there are two churches that can seat 5,000 each, three churches that can accommodate 1,500 people each, and seven that can seat 500 each. Additionally, there are more than 200 meeting points, with each accommodating 50 to 100. In China overall, there are more than 2,000 pastors, and more than 350 of them are women.

52. Just to name two: the ministries of the China Christian Council and the Amity Foundation seek to build up China through the body of Christ. The ministries include education, publications, medical services, music resources, ecumenical relations, rural church work, feeding the poor, and so on.

53. Lewis S. Ford, "God as the Subjectivity of the Future," 292.

Appendix 1
Intercultural Bible Study:
Three Principles

Intercultural biblical interpretation can open up new dimensions in the study of the Bible, as you may have experienced from the collection of essays in this volume. Some readers might want to turn the experience of reading this book into an intercultural study of *Revelation* in dialogue with the authors of these essays and with others in a group. The four appendices in this book offer some suggestions for how that might be done.

Several authors have proposed models for doing intercultural Bible study, and I have benefited from their work enormously. Eric Law has written a number of books that are very helpful in outlining principles, guidelines, and dynamics of power in intercultural study groups. Daniel Patte and colleagues have developed a program called Contextual Bible Study, which they illustrate with a study of the *Gospel of Matthew*. Gerald West reports on Bible study with people in South Africa, as does Musa Dube. Insights and ideas may be gleaned from these and other writers idenitfied in the bibliography for Intercultural Bible Study. Here in the appendices of this book, I offer my own model, using *Revelation* along with this volume as the case study.

Our image for intercultural Bible study is the model, first developed by Justo González, of an ethnic roundtable with the Bible at the center and people around the table who come from different cultures and different social locations within cultures (identified by such markers as race, gender, age, economic level). In this model, participants are doing two things. First, they are in dialogue with the Bible. This, in itself, is a cross-cultural experience. Readers of the Bible are like "immigrants" entering into the first century—bringing their own cultural experiences to the task of understanding the text as responsibly as possible in its first-century context and seeking to be changed and transformed by the experience.

Second, the participants around the table are in dialogue with each other. This interaction offers the benefit of insights from people of diverse cultures and social locations. Such a dialogue can involve many cross-cultural engagements as participants encounter and challenge each other and are transformed by these experiences. In making use of this book, participants can also add the voices of these authors as contributors to the conversation—to read and reflect on the essays, to compare and contrast them with each other, to identify what they find interesting and illuminating, and to discover how they might be changed by the challenges these writers offer.

The following three principles may assist in preparing participants for intercultural Bible study.

1. Be open to more than one valid interpretation.

The first principle is to be open to the idea that there is more than one valid interpretation of a biblical writing or passage. If participants enter a Bible study thinking that there is only one Christian way to believe and act or only one way to interpret the Bible, then it will be very difficult to have a constructive intercultural dialogue.

Diversity of belief and ethical practice has been a constitutive dimension of Christianity from the beginning—from the event at Pentecost when pilgrims to Jerusalem from many cultures heard the apostles praising God *in their own tongues*! From these diverse cultures around the Mediterranean came diverse interpretations of the Christ event. The New Testament is a testimony to this cultural diversity, each writing having a distinct view of God, Jesus, the spirit, the human condition, the stance toward politics and empire, the means of salvation, the ethical vision for life, and the mission and structure of the church.

Different expressions of Christianity today are drawn from these different expressions of Christianity in the New Testament. As such, the present diversity among denominations is not so much a sign of the brokenness of the body of Christ as it is an expression of the rich diversity that was there from the beginning. In other words, diverse Christian expressions serve to bear the full breadth of the original good news. Furthermore, new cultural expressions of Christianity have emerged in the contemporary world. The strength of Christianity lies not in its uniformity but in its incredible capacity to adapt to diverse situations and cultures due to its many and varied expressions. The mark of the church and the sign of the universality of the gospel is not uniformity but diversity.

The same principle of diversity applies to diverse interpretations of the Bible. Given the polyvalent nature of the biblical texts and the differences among interpreters, multiple legitimate interpretations are inevitable. Indeed, they are desirable.

The failure to be open to diversity risks loss of the rich possibilities of meaning in the text under study. We have much to learn from each other's interpretations. People from dominant cultures may be struck by how differently others read the Bible. People from suppressed cultures are often transformed by the way people from other suppressed cultures read the Bible. But the failure to be open to diversity may run an even greater risk, namely, that we presume our interpretations are the only right ones and that, as a result, we are unwilling to bring them into critical conversation with others. When we absolutize our interpretations in this way, we lose the challenges others might bring to our interpretations and we risk not being open to the wisdom of others—indeed to the wisdom of God.

Multiple interpretations can occur for many legitimate reasons: the multivalent nature of texts, the variety of methods and approaches, the cultural placement and social location of the interpreter, and the lenses through which readers view the Bible. However, if the study group overrides legitimate diversity by setting uniform agreement as a goal, this could stifle diversity, particularly minority points of view. By contrast, in an intercultural dialogue over interpretation, we should begin with the assumption that people will have different views, that there are good reasons for these differences, that people can learn from them, and that such diversity can be integral to a vital community. However, the goal is not agreement or disagreement but transformations that may emerge from a free and critical sharing of diverse perspectives on the Bible.

It may be helpful for the group to distinguish between interpretation and appropriation. *Interpretation* refers to the meanings we give to a text in its original context. *Appropriation* refers to the applications of an interpretation to modern contexts. The criteria for establishing the legitimacy of interpretations will be different from the criteria that establish the legitimacy of appropriations. Not all interpretations are to be accepted as valid interpretations of the text. Interpretations are explored and weighed (and accepted or rejected, in part or as a whole) based on the evidence in the biblical text and in its first-century context.

However, we may accept a certain interpretation of a text as a legitimate interpretation from a historical/literary point of view and yet at the same time reject its appropriation to contemporary life. We may do so for a variety of reasons—it will lead to abuse or discrimination; it does not apply to modern cultures; it is helpful in one cultural context but harmful in another; and so on. In European and American history alone, the Bible has been interpreted to justify slavery, exterminate Jews, exclude blacks, abuse women and children, vilify homosexuals, suppress resistance to corrupt and tyrannical states, and establish empires. There is no question that the appropriation of these interpretations, whether they are deemed historically valid interpretations or not, should be absolutely repudiated. On the other hand, interpretations have brought healing, courage to resist injustice, freedom from guilt and shame, liberation from tyranny and empire, compassion, transformation, as well as justice and mercy in society. In this regard, participants may well find a range of ethical, life-changing interpretations that illuminate the biblical texts in their first-century contexts and that can also be appropriated responsibly in contemporary situations.

Decisions to appropriate an interpretation should be weighed not on the basis of convenience or comfort, for we may rightfully be challenged and shaken by some interpretations. Rather, we should evaluate appropriation on the basis of the moral power for good or the potential for harm of the interpretation. Furthermore, appropriation is never a one-to-one translation from the ancient context to a contemporary one. Hence, when an interpretation is deemed appropriate, the interpretation will need to be adapted and transformed to apply fruitfully and faithfully to the contemporary situation.

In the effort to secure diversity of interpretations and appropriations in an intercultural Bible study, two further suggestions may be helpful. The first is: Do not let others interpret/appropriate for you. That is to say, discern your distinctive cultural/social perspective, find your own voice, and offer your own insights. This suggestion may apply primarily to groups whose voices historically have been suppressed. The second is: Do not trust yourself to interpret/appropriate alone. That is to say, do not think you have the one correct interpretation or that you have the whole truth. Rather, rely on the insights of others to confirm, challenge, complement, change, or provide a counterpoint to your interpretation/appropriation. This suggestion may apply most appropriately to people from dominant cultures or social locations. *Together* participants will find the best ways to proffer valid interpretations of the biblical writings in their original context and the wisest ways to determine the appropriations for contemporary contexts.

Hence, unity or community should be based broadly on our common humanity or the unity given by the Spirit and not solely on some agreements over interpretation and appropriation. Nevertheless, if the process of intercultural Bible study is to work, there are some fundamental things participants may need to agree upon in order to carry on the dialogue: having respect for one another, being willing to give and take in the conversation, and being open to new possibilities.

2. Recognize the complexity of intercultural differences and relationships.

The second principle for intercultural dialogue is to be aware that interactions between cultures are complex.

Culture itself is obviously a complex matter. At an observable level, a culture is comprised of the language, customs, patterns of interaction, family and social groupings, government, work habits, leisure time, among many other things. At a deeper level, culture also involves the shared beliefs, values, patterns of thought, and myths that give coherence to a culture and that shape how people see life and what they do. People are born into these values and patterns, grow up with them, and as adults live with them and benefit from them. The culture is like the air that the society/community breathes. Although cultures are fluid as a result of internal forces and external relationships, they maintain a continuity of identity amid change. Cultures differ significantly, and people bring their differing cultures to the task of interpretation. Therefore, understanding each other in an intercultural group will involve explanation, clarification, and lots of storytelling.

A healthy attitude to diversity may combine the crucial importance of diversity among cultures with the recognition that all cultures are human constructions. The realization that cultures are socially constructed enables people not only to appreciate other cultures but also to see the relative nature of their own culture. Such an awareness goes a long way in intercultural dialogue to enable participants to be open to one another, to consider the strengths and limitations, the problems and the possibilities, the dangers and the oppressiveness of each culture (including one's own), and to learn from each other. Weighing cultures in this way will prevent us from demonizing or romanticizing any culture. Nevertheless, people from dominant cultures/social locations especially may learn a great deal by seeing their culture/social location through the eyes of others who are affected by their dominance.

Participants may need to be careful not to stereotype or categorize cultures or people from different cultures. Cultures have significant particularity, even when they are part of a larger block of similar cultures. For example, within the larger block of Asian cultures, there are significant differences among Korean, Japanese, and Chinese cultures. Furthermore, internally, each discrete culture will have a different configuration of social locations such as gender, social class, economic level, and so on. Hence, it is best to take nothing for granted about a person's culture or social location and to be prepared to ask in order to understand.

In addition, many people embody the experience of more than one culture. People who grow up in a subordinate culture know both their own culture and the dominant culture. Due to relocation and marriage, some people may be "hybrid" in their cultural identity. The same is true with people having multiple and/or conflicting social locations. People bring these complexities of their cultural/social location to the task of interpretation and to the relationships in a study group.

In dialogue among cultures, it is important to have a sense of one's own culture. In itself, being aware of one's own culture and seeing the world through the distinct lenses provided by that cultural experience is inevitable and can be good. It is important to bring it into awareness so that we are not held captive to its biases or kept ignorant of its impact on other cultures. People in subordinate cultures or marginalized societies are often well aware of their own cultural identity and live out of it in intentional ways, because they have learned it as a contrast to another (usually dominant) culture. On the other hand, people from dominant cultures may be oriented to their own culture without awareness of its distinctive patterns and values. All need to be careful not to take their own culture for granted but to lift it to consciousness so that it can be brought into critical conversation with others. The Reading Profile in Appendix Three may be a helpful tool in identifying cultural and social factors that shape interpretation and cultural interaction.

The group will also benefit by being aware of some tragic dynamics of *ethnocentrism*, the corporate parallel to egocentrism. Ethnocentrism can be destructive in several ways. First, ethnocentrism can be oppressive when people think that their culture is the "natural" and the normative way to live and that everyone else should live this way as well—particularly when such attitudes are combined with the power to dominate. Another unfortunate dynamic of ethnocentrism occurs when people distort the representation of other cultures. People tend to see other cultures in simplistic, stereotypical terms, especially when they do not know much about them.

Also, ethnocentrism leads people to view other cultures only in terms of their own culture. That is, when we encounter one aspect of another culture—patterns of relationship, body language, verbal expressions, or even silence—the tendency is to understand the meaning and impact of it in terms of our own cultural dynamics rather than seeing it in the whole context of the other culture. As such, people can easily misread signals and misinterpret patterns of relating. Another form of ethnocentrism occurs when we take for granted that others will understand our signals and our ways of relating, because they seem so natural and obvious *to us*.

Hence, in cross-cultural conversations, participants should take little for granted and assume that matters are more complex than they seem. We should depend on the people from other cultures to clarify what the complexities of their culture might be. In dialogue, it may be a helpful to give each other permission to speak up when there is a misunderstanding so as to clarify it.

In a Bible study, there is an additional factor that comes into play, namely the relationship between the cultures of the first century and the Christian responses to them in that era. Here, participants may see the ways in which early Christians drew upon and also challenged in quite radical ways the cultures of their time. Through this biblical lens, we may discern the ways in which today the Bible may critique and challenge our contemporary cultures. We may thereby see how the Bible challenges each of us to go against the values of our culture or to seek to change the dynamics of our culture.

In dialogue with the Bible, participants can create the conditions for constructive cultural interaction that will bring justice and equity not only at the individual level and in the Bible study group but also in the larger culture and society.

3. Seek justice in the power dynamics of cross-cultural interactions.

A third principle of intercultural dialogue relates to the importance of attending to the power dynamics in the group. They are always present, for good or for ill and in ways that are just or unjust. Unless the group is aware of them and addresses them openly and constructively, negative power dynamics will probably undermine efforts at dialogue.

People have different experiences of personal power in society. For example, European American males from the dominant cultures within the United States tend to believe that people are equal, that they have the power to speak, and that their words can change things. People from Asian cultures may generally defer to others out of respect and wait to be given permission to speak. People from some oppressed cultures/social locations know that people are not equal, that what they say will make little or no difference, and that they will have to speak strongly and insistently in order to be heard. If each group engages in their own understanding of power within an intercultural dialogue without regard for the ways of others, the dialogue will soon break down and patterns of domination and injustice will simply repeat themselves.

Likewise, different cultures have different styles for dealing with conflict and with differences of opinion. Some cultures may seek to avoid overt conflict out of a respectful desire not to offend. Other cultures emphasize the importance of being nice to each other or of being a non-anxious presence in the midst of conflict. Some cultures consider directness and confrontation as a sign that you are taking the other person seriously or see interruption as a sign that you are listening. Again, all of these styles are laden with power dynamics that can frustrate or facilitate dialogue. The group may need to negotiate these differences and find some equitable way to compromise as a means to agree on guidelines for conversation.

And just because the people in a group are committed to overcome dominance and injustice does not mean that such power dynamics will not still be operative in the group. People in dominant positions with a personal commitment to overcome discrimination are often surprised to learn how they are implicated in institutional and structural discrimination. For example, churches may desire to welcome people of other cultures, but they may not realize how the building, the organizational structures, the worship, and the patterns of relating may lead visitors from other cultures to feel alienated and marginalized. People in positions of power are often unaware of these institutional/structural power dynamics, while those who are affected negatively see them quite clearly.

This same dynamic is also true in the political, economic, and cultural relationships of the colonial domination of first-world countries over third-world countries. People in the colonial powers benefit from these relationships of exploitation and may not understand why those who are in colonized situations experience the dominant country as evil, exploitative, and oppressive. People in first-world countries may disavow personal prejudice yet find that it is not easy to disassociate themselves from being implicated in dynamics of oppression among nations.

Similar dynamics of power occur not only among nations but also among the power roles within any given culture or society: elites and marginalized, men and women, wealthy and poor, differences in social status and formal education, management and labor, assertive extroverts and shy introverts, pastors and laity, teachers and students, and a host of other generally unequal relationships. The power dynamics of such roles within society differ with each culture. In each case, there may be patterns of injustice in the society that will tend to be repeated in group study. One of the key goals of intercultural Bible study is to address and counter such dynamics and create interactions that are just and liberating.

Power dynamics in intercultural relationships are complicated by the fact that relationships of oppression are often multiple and conflicting within the same person and within the same group. People may be oppressed in one set of personal and institutional relationships and oppressors in another. For example, an African American male may experience racial and economic oppression in relation to European Americans, yet he may engage in dynamics of oppression in relation to African American females. Or a Hispanic American may experience ethnic and economic oppression from other Americans, yet as an American in relation to third-world cultures, she may be considered an economic oppressor. The point is that people will have differing positions of power/powerlessness at the ethnic roundtable, depending on those with whom they are in conversation.

How the group addresses these issues can either facilitate or subvert constructive intercultural dialogue. A Bible study group may reproduce dynamics of oppression, marginalization, or colonialism in the very relationships within the Bible study. The implications for intercultural dialogue suggest that the location of the dialogue, the language in which it occurs, the set-up of the room, the composition of leadership, the assumptions made about the gathering, and the practices of conversation—all these involve power dynamics that could be either helpful of harmful. The key is whether the group is aware of these dynamics and sees them as occasions for negotiation, for learning, for changing, for liberation both for those who dominate *and* for those who are suppressed, and for reconciliation.

Being aware of these power dynamics in the group will also lead participants to see power dynamics in the biblical text. Given the impetus of early Christians to reach all people with a gospel of reconciliation and peace, it is not surprising that efforts to overcome inequities and injustices are everywhere in the biblical materials, if we but have eyes to see them. The command to care for "the least" in the *Gospel of Matthew*, the central command in the *Gospel of Mark* not to lord over others, the preferential option for the poor, the marginalized, and the oppressed in the *Gospel of Luke*, Paul's efforts to resolve the conflict between the weak and the strong in the *Letter to the Corinthians*, the prohibition against economic discrimination in the *Letter of James*, and the comprehensive condemnation of empire in *Revelation* are but a few of the most obvious examples. At the same time, the Bible itself may sometimes contribute to unjust and oppressive power relationships, as it often does, for example, in relation to women and slaves. Attention to the biblical dynamics of power will sensitize participants also to be aware of unjust or oppressive interactions within the group itself and to seek to overcome them.

Hence, the goal of an intercultural Bible study is not only to encounter the Bible in new ways but also to attend to the intercultural relationships present in the group itself—and not just to avoid further harm and to seek redress of hurts, but constructively to create a community that models an equitable distribution of power and that shares a common commitment to overcome injustice. To meet this goal in the group dynamics, it would be important that diverse cultural/social groups be engaged in every aspect of the study—organizing, planning, agenda-setting, leading and participating, and any other decision-making—so that all these matters can be negotiated together as the group comes into being and carries out its study.

Conclusion

The purpose of intercultural dialogue at the ethnic roundtable is not only to know and accept each other but to be transformed as a community of interpreters by virtue of the interaction, so that we may somehow be different people as a result of the experience. The importance of learning to engage in constructive intercultural dialogue cannot be underestimated at a time when almost everyone encounters other cultures on a daily basis. It may be crucial for our survival as a human race that we come to some profound appreciation of the differences among us as human beings, that we be prepared to learn from each other, and that we be committed to overcome oppression, marginalization, and exploitation. Intercultural Bible study in the church can help us to promote justice in the intercultural relationships in the rest of our lives also.

Our reflections lead to this: Can we make an intentional commitment to seek out and engage in interpreting the Bible with people from different cultures, social locations, and personal perspectives. Such a commitment will replicate the commitment, indeed the mission, of the early church to re-draw the boundary lines so as to encompass people of different "tribes, languages, peoples, and nations." The earliest churches did this not to create a uniformity of response to the gospel of Jesus Christ but to affirm the particularity of the response out of the culture and life-experiences of those who heard the gospel—so that every nation and people would experience their common humanity through their capacity to glorify God *in their own tongue.*

Appendix 2
Intercultural Bible Study:
Some Suggestions for Group Interaction

■ ■

The purpose of these suggested guidelines for Bible study is to engender "transformation through dialogue" with people from diverse cultures, social locations, and reading perspectives. The process assumes that participants will share agreements and have differences with each other—differences with biblical interpretations and differences in cultural perspectives. The process also assumes that the group will address the power dynamics of oppression, discrimination, and marginalization as they come up in the interpretations and in the intercultural relationships.

Through the exploration of points of agreement and points of difference in the interpretation and appropriation of the Bible and in the articulation of differing cultural perspectives, participants will seek renewal, transformation, and commitment together as a community. Transformations of individuals and the group may include: experiencing God in a new way; changing spiritual, theological, political, and ethical perspectives; seeing the world through the eyes of others (biblical writers and other cultures); finding one's voice; discerning power dynamics between cultures; self-/cultural-discovery; changing views about the Bible and how to interpret it; liberation from dynamics of oppressing and being oppressed; or embracing a commitment to justice in new ways. The group may want to discuss its hopes and goals (and fears) about such a study.

These suggestions focus on parish study groups, but they can be adapted for use in classrooms or other venues. The suggestions also focus on dialogue between people of diverse cultural origins, but they may be adapted to address differences due to factors of social location and subcultures within society, such as race, gender, age, economic status, education, sexual orientation, and so on. The suggestions are oriented primarily for use with intercultural groups in the United States; therefore, each intercultural group will need to adapt them for their own use. Finally, the suggestions are detailed and somewhat comprehensive, and participants will want to pick and choose what is helpful for their situation.

The key to any suggestions given here is that they need to be negotiated by the group, because any "guideline" can either foster transformative dialogue or serve to perpetuate oppression and marginalization. In the course of negotiating these processes, the study group may discover some equitable way in which each culture chooses to relinquish some of its own style of interacting and accepts some other styles of interacting as means to come to a consensus about the best ways to proceed together.

Goals

It may be helpful to clarify and determine the goals of the Bible study. Here are some goals to consider.

Engage the Bible. Discover the range of its plausible meanings, its humane appropriations, and its power to transform—with people from different cultures and social locations. Coming to agreement about an interpretation as such is not a goal. Seeking transformation, renewed commitments, and a shared community of discourse through engaging with diverse interpretations is a goal.

Generate a community of dialogue. It is not enough to have a multicultural presence at the Bible study; there is need also to have a process that engenders interactive involvement leading to transformation and a new sense of community.

Interact in liberating ways. The process leads the group to address the power dynamics of intercultural dialogue so that people may have some liberating experiences from the unjust dynamics of oppressing and of being oppressed.

Covenant Guidellnes

The group may want to create a covenant with some principles and guidelines to follow, which might draw on some of the following suggestions. These suggestions are not meant to soften the persuasive power or passion of anyone's perspective and point of view. Nor are they meant to level differences or to mute engagement among people with different perspectives, convictions, and styles of relating. If they result in this, they may need to be re-negotiated. Rather, they are meant to secure constructive dialogue, to guard a diversity of perspectives, and to avoid conversations that cause harm. Here are some ideas to consider.

1. Genuinely seek to understand Scripture through dialogue with others and be open to multiple interpretations.
2. Give priority to relationships that foster the liberation of all participants as more important than arguing the correctness of views. Respect persons while engaging their views.
3. Agree to share your views and feelings and to explain them to others in persuasive and passionate ways, but without seeking to impose them.
4. Agree to listen empathetically and to ask questions of others for clarification and understanding. Represent faithfully the views of others. Challenge the views of others only after understanding them.
5. Agree to negotiate the ground rules for interrupting or correcting or debating or challenging or criticizing another person or point of view. Be patient with the styles of others.
6. Accept the idea of multiple valid interpretations. Agree to disagree and clarify where those differences lie, where there are difficulties with other points of view, and where interpretations may result in injustice.
7. Seek to be open to learn about other people in terms of their cultural, social, and personal perspectives.
8. Be open for something genuinely new to occur—transformation/change/new insights/new commitments—in light of engaging the Bible and different cultural points of view.
9. Honor confidentiality so as to create an atmosphere of trust. Agree to discuss positively and constructively with other members of the group outside the gathering.

Process: After creating a covenant of principles and guidelines, the group may wish to agree to follow them, to be reminded of them in the course of conversation, and to renegotiate them when they do not foster constructive dialogue.

Creating a Climate of Cultural Belonging

Here the objective is to create a climate of trust in which everyone feels that they belong, an atmosphere in which everyone can speak, and a situation in which people treat each other with respect as guests in their home or as sisters and brothers in Christ—even when those images may mean different things to different cultures. It is important for participants to become full cultural partners in this enterprise so that new visions and realities may emerge out of what the group does together. Here are some ideas for negotiation.

1. How you plan the study may make a difference:

    a. It will help that the make-up of the group planning the Bible study is multicultural. You may want to brainstorm about what cultures, groups, classes, or individuals might come together to comprise the study group.

    b. Consider sponsoring/planning this study jointly with a church (or churches) that has members of another cultural identity.

    c. Consider announcing the intercultural Bible study by means of five or six different avenues or media so as to reach people of different cultures and social locations.

2. Choosing the building/room or home in which to meet may be important:

    a. If possible, choose a site together where everyone feels at home or has some sense of ownership.

    b. Think together about how the decor of the room expresses cultural realities, for example, by bringing a picture of Jesus from each culture.

    c. You may want to change or rotate the location for each meeting

3. The arrangement of the room can foster mutual conversation. Consider the following options:

    a. Use a round or square table or place tables and chairs in a circle.

    b. Try to avoid a lectern or a head table. If the group is large and a lectern is used, it will help if the space is versatile and the seating is moveable so as to allow for small groups to form easily.

    c. Make sure that everyone has access to displays or chalkboards as well as printed materials (provided in advance, if possible). Seek ways to make the displays and materials accessible for people who are visually impaired or who may not read (the language) well.

    d. The set-up of the room may need to account for diverse cultural comfort levels in distance or closeness to others.

4. Negotiate the time arrangements:

    a. Determine an agreed upon number of sessions over the course of so many weeks and determine the length of time for each meeting.

    b. Negotiate the differences among cultures about being present at the starting time and whether to observe a consistent ending time for each session.

    c. Participants may want to discuss whether it is important to be present at all classes and whether to let others know if they are not able to come.

    d. The group may want to decide if it will add new members after the course has begun and if this should require the consent of the group.

5. Setting the agenda together:

    a. Agree together on the plan for each class and the readings for each week.

    b. Negotiate and agree on covenant guidelines.

    c. Choose means of leadership (see below).

6. Provide time in the schedule for acquaintance and process.
   a. As a way to get to know each other, the group might want to fill out the Reading Profile (Appendix Three) and then share the things about their cultural context and social location that especially shape the way they interpret the Bible.
   b. You may also want to build time into the schedule for the group to negotiate, evaluate, and renegotiate the guidelines/processes of the study.

Practices of Conversation

1. It may help to alternate responsibility for group tasks. This strategy is designed to decentralize power. In a sense, the process becomes the leader.
   a. Take turns offering prayers to open and close the session.
   b. When reading Scripture aloud: rotate the opportunity, or go around with each one reading a verse (anyone may "pass"), or read the text in different languages.
   c. Consider bringing songs and hymns from different cultures.
   d. If food is to be made available, members may want to take turns introducing food from their culture.
2. Facilitator: Here are some ideas for choosing a facilitator.
   a. Choose one facilitator who is trusted by everyone to facilitate discussion in a way that fosters equity and mutual respect.
   b. Choose two leaders representing groups of different cultures/social locations working together.
   c. Rotate facilitators from session to session.
3. Facilitator: Consider aspects of the facilitator's role.
   a. Possible traits: spirituality of discernment, humility, a gift of empowering others, comfortableness with conflict, ablility to facilitate negotiations.
   b. A leader can model the process—eager to learn about the biblical subject matter, able to listen well, and manifesting genuine interest in other cultures.
   c. The facilitator can assure balanced time to participants—not letting some dominate and inviting silent ones to speak.
4. Active speaking by all: It is important to find structures and procedures that engender speaking as a gift to share for the benefit of the community. You may want to have an agreed-upon amount of time for each person to speak before another speaks. Consider choosing one or more of the following ways to proceed:

a. Separate into cultural groups or by race, gender, age, and so on in order to allow each group to get a sense of community that empowers voice and then report to the whole group.

b. Or divide into small groups of mixed cultures and social locations for more intimate conversation.

c. Try having only one cultural or gender group speak, while others restate what they hear as a means to understanding.

d. Go around the circle.

e. Pass a baton or talking stick. The person with the stick has the floor to speak and answer questions.

f. Have people share in pairs, and then invite conversation in the whole group.

g. Use mutual invitation. The last speaker picks the next speaker.

h. Let the conversation flow freely. Then invite only those who have not spoken to share. No one may speak a second time until all have had a chance to speak once.

i. Have people take a few minutes to write on some issue and then share what they have written.

j. Give anyone permission to "pass" if she or he does not wish to speak.

5. Active listening by all: It is a gift to choose silence so that others may speak. Listen carefully to what others say and treat them with interest and respect. Consider the following:

a. Seek to see through the eyes of others and ask questions for clarification. The group may need to seek permission from each person to ask them questions.

b. Repeat back what you heard to the speaker's satisfaction. Perhaps invite each speaker to do this before giving her or his point of view.

c. Ask about the background or context or personal experience that informs the speaker's view. Often we can respect and accept other points of view more easily when we see where they are coming from.

d. Be careful not to use silence as a way to disengage or as a way to hold power by insisting that others share while you do not.

6. Here are some suggestions for dealing with different points of view:

a. Share/explain the perspective and reasons for it, without trying to impose it upon others.

b. Listen for understanding, and clarify differences.

c. Clarify what factors in culture, social location, and personal experience contribute to one's point of view.

d. Check to see in what ways other members of the same cultural group agree or disagree.

7. Reflector/evaluation: It may be helpful to have a reflector or evaluator to reflect at the end of each session about how the process is going and whether the group is following the agreed-upon guidelines.
   a. Choose one reflector or consider rotating this role.
   b. Or simply set aside time at the end of each session for group evaluation.
   c. The group may also want to set time aside halfway through the whole study for each person to explain how the process is working or not working for them. This may be an opportunity to renegotiate/recommit to a covenant and the process.

Dealing with Potential Difficulties

Here are some suggestions to address problems if and when they occur. Addressing problems is itself a cultural particularity that may require discussion. People from different cultures have diverse styles of interaction—from respectful avoidance to direct bluntness to passionate confrontation to calm conversation to withdrawal. People from different cultures may feel uncomfortable with or resist any of the following suggestions. A general conversation/negotiation about styles of interaction may help the group to find its own way forward in the face of difficulties in conversation.

1. When differences of interpretation and appropriation of the text become disputes, there may be an impasse of frustration and anger. Here are some things to consider.
   a. Re-emphasize the need to clarify and explain the point of view and the deep values and issues that may be at stake. Assume the sincerity of the other.
   b. Consider asking for more information about each interpretation/ appropriation: what evidence is in the text, what method each is using, what in their experience leads them to their interpretation, what consequences each imagines will result from the appropriation. These are questions of inquiry rather than challenges.
   c. State clearly what you find difficult or offensive, and explain why. Identify the issues of belief and value that are at stake for you.
   d. Be passionate and persuasive without imposing your view. Consider being confessional and explanatory rather than defensive and argumentative.
   e. Respect the right of others to differ.
2. When cultural misunderstandings occur that cause hurt and offense,

offenses may occur due to choice of words, stereotyping, speaking in a second language, body language, gestures, facial expressions, touching, style and intensity of speaking, silence, or people interrupting or "correcting" others. The following procedures may help.

a. Give permission for the person who was offended or hurt to explain what happened to them and how they reacted to what happened. Then she/he can explain what the event means in their cultural context.

b. Give space for the person who triggered the offense to explain what they meant by what they said or did. Then she/he can explain what this word or action means in their cultural context.

c. Seek to determine how the communication might have happened in a way that would not have resulted in offense.

3. When members of a cultural group assume certain privileges without being aware of it—by setting the agenda, making most of the decisions, doing most of the talking, consider the following suggestions for taking a different role:

a. Dominating participants stay engaged but listen while others speak, in order to understand rather than to counter another's point of view.

b. Affirm the relevant processes again, and, if need be, renegotiate them.

c. The group may be reminded of the relativity of each culture and the importance of learning from others and the wisdom that can emerge when everyone is involved.

d. In seeking to redress the balance of participation, be careful not to invert the problem by marginalizing members of dominant cultures so as to eliminate their voices from the conversation.

4. When people assume they have no prejudices because they are committed to overcome prejudice, here may be some things to remember:

a. We are all prejudiced in ways hidden from ourselves.

b. The dominant cultures participate in institutional racism/ethnocentrism just by virtue of their place in the structures of life.

c. We can work together to address these issues constructively.

5. When people may be afraid to make mistakes, say the wrong thing, or offend people when they do not mean to offend:

a. Acknowledge upfront that such offenses will occur.

b. Agree to share with each other when something is offensive.

c. Do not be defensive, but seek to learn from others. Clarify misunderstandings and cultural differences.

d. Identify any issues of injustice between cultures and address them.

6. Some may fear to speak in a group comprised of people with dominant voices, due to either culture or gender or age or personality. It may be

difficult for groups that have traditionally experienced less power in society to have a voice when they have had the experience of being ignored, dismissed, patronized, corrected, and overridden. It is hard to express what they think when they have frustration from past hurts and when they feel as if they have to struggle to be heard. Part of the purpose of intercultural communication is to liberate everyone to have a voice in the process.

a. Acknowledge the history of the problem of marginalization, and seek ways
   to structure the conversation to assure that the suppressed group has adequate time to share and discuss their views. Mechanisms can be developed for suppressed groups to alert the group when they experience marginalization.

b. The beleaguered group may need a critical mass of people from a given culture, gender, or other group, because the suppressed groups may not have power to speak as individuals. Find strength in community.

c. Some cultures, out of respect, wait to be asked before they will speak. They may work out a way to indicate to the facilitator or to the larger group that you have a desire to speak. The group can also agree to invite each person to speak.

d. People process things at different paces and some have to work through a secondary language. The group should occasionally stop to let people think and then invite those who have not yet spoken to share their views.

In this whole process, it may help to repeat the agreed-upon guidelines/covenant at the beginning of each session. It may also help for each participant to choose a partner in the group with whom to process and to debrief the session outside the time of gathering. Then, if hurts occur or trust is broken, the partner can be present to the person and assist in healing and reconciliation.

Finally, it is worth reiterating the sense of deep appreciation that can emerge when people from diverse cultures and social locations have worked through difficulties and learned from each other and come to a new level of shared communal relationships and commitments around the study of the Bible. These are the experiences that can fundamentally transform the way we see the world and how we relate to others. Hopefully, the practices of openness and justice experienced in the group will spill over into the commitments and relationships we have in all aspects of our lives.

Appendix 3
Reading Profile:
Cultural Identity / Social Location /
Personal Perspectives

The items listed here serve as a tool to enable people to reflect on the factors that may shape their reading experience. They should not be used to stereotype or categorize people. If the list does not reflect your cultural experience, please disregard irrelevant items and add others. The profile is most helpful when participants comment on important dynamics of each item. For further reflections on these categories, see the section on "Factors of Cultural/Social Location and Reading Perspective" in the Introduction to this book (page 14).

1. Geographical/Natural Location

2. Cultural Identity/Nationality

3. Social Location within Society

a. Race/ethnicity

b. Gender/sexual orientation

c. Economic level/occupation

d. Religious affiliation/convictions

e. Political affiliation/convictions

f. Social class/vocation

g. Other key factors (education, health, disability, legal status, age, and so on.)

4. Historical Context/Era: Ethos and Conditions

5. Personal Experiences, Beliefs, Values, and Commitments

6. Approaches to Interpretation/View of Scripture

7. Communities of Interpretation

8. Other

Appendix 4
A Study Guide for Ten Sessions of Two Hours

■ ■

Planning Meeting:
Each two-hour session below might be organized in the following way.

Introduction: Greetings. Opening prayer. Review of the Covenant. (10 Minutes)
Part One (45 minutes)
Break(?) (10 Minutes)
Part Two (45 Minutes)
Reflections about the process. Concluding prayer. (10 minutes)
Note: Three sessions are devoted here to introductory matters before the essays in
the book are given as preparatory reading, because it is important for participants
to become familiar first with the *Book of Revelation* and to form some of their own
views about it before they read the perspectives of others. However, Sessions Two
and Three could be combined.

Session One

Part One:
1. Introduce participants and briefly share background.
2. Go over the guidelines for intercultural Bible study and negotiate (confirm/
change) a covenant suggested by the planning committee.
3. Agree to your covenant.
Part Two:
1. Share your expectations and goals for this Bible study. Share uncertainties and
fears.
2. Give your impressions of and past experiences with the *Book of Revelation*.

Session Two

Preparatory Reading:
Read the *Book of Revelation*.
Fill out the "Reading Profile" (see Appendix three)
Read the Appendices of *From Every People and Nation*.
Part One:
1. Give initial impressions of the *Book of Revelation*.
2. Identify questions for exploration in the course.
Part Two:
1. Let people further introduce themselves by explaining some features of their cultural identity, social location, and personal perspective.
2. Explain from the "Profile" the factors that especially shape your interpretation of the Bible and the *Book of Revelation* in particular.

Session Three

Preparatory Reading:
1. Read the "Introduction" of *From Every People and Nation*.
2. Re-read the *Book of Revelation*. It is desirable to re-read the whole *Book of Revelation* in preparation for each session, along with the specific passages suggested in relation to each chapter.
3. Optional: Read a standard (and brief) introduction and/or commentary on the *Book of Revelation*. Consider the entries on Revelation in the *New Jerome Bible Commentary* (Adela Yabro Collins), the *Anchor Bible Dictionary* (Adela Yabro Collins), or the *New Interpreter's Bible* (Christopher Rowland).
Part One:
1. Discuss the Introduction:
    What is intercultural criticism?
    What is the difference between interpretation and appropriation?
    What approaches may be used to give a faithful interpretation?
    How can there be many plausible interpretations?
    What power dynamics are operative in interpretation and appropriation?
Part Two:
1. What are your reflections on the *Book of Revelation* in light of the Introduction and your second reading?
2. What did you learn from the commentary? Can you tell the cultural/social location of the author of the commentary you read? How has that shaped the author's interpretation and appropriation?

Session Four

Preparatory Reading:

1. "The Witness of Active Resistance: The Ethics of *Revelation* in African American Perspective" by Brian K. Blount. *Revelation* 1:1-11.

2. "*Revelation*: Clarity and Ambiguity: A Hispanic/Cuban American Perspective" by Justo González. *Revelation* 17:1-8 (9-15).

Part One:

1. Read aloud *Revelation* 1:1-11. Correlate Blount's cultural/social/personal location with the interpretation offered.

2. Let each one reflect on and evaluate the interpretation of *Revelation* by Blount.

3. How were you challenged by it? How might you and different people from your culture respond to this challenge?

Part Two:

1. Read aloud *Revelation* 17:1-8 (9-15). Correlate González's cultural/social/personal location with the interpretation offered.

2. Let each one reflect on and evaluate the interpretation of *Revelation* by González.

3. How were you challenged by it? How might you and different people from your culture respond to this challenge?

Session Five

Preparatory Reading:

1. "Coming Out of Babylon: A First-World Reading of *Revelation* amongst Immigrants" by Harry O. Maier. *Revelation* 3:14-22.

2. "Polishing the Unclouded Mirror: A Womanist Reading of *Revelation* 18:13" by Clarice J. Martin. *Revelation* 18:9-13.

Part One:

1. Read aloud *Revelation* 3:14-22. Correlate Maier's cultural/social/personal location with the interpretation offered.

2. Let each one reflect on and evaluate the interpretation of *Revelation* by Maier.

3. How were you challenged by it? How might you and different people from your culture respond to this challenge?

Part Two:

1. Read aloud *Revelation* 18:9-13. Correlate Martin's cultural/social/personal location with the interpretation offered.

2. Let each one reflect on and evaluate the interpretation of *Revelation* by Martin.

3. How were you challenged by it? How might you and different people from your culture respond to this challenge?

Session Six

Preparatory Reading:
1. "Power and Worship: *Revelation* in African Perspective" by James Chukwuma Okoye. *Revelation* 11:15-19.
2. "The Heroine and the Whore: The *Apocalypse of John* in Feminist Perspective" by Tina Pippin. *Revelation* 12:1-6.

Part One:
1. Read aloud *Revelation* 11:15-19. Correlate Okoye's cultural/social/personal location with the interpretation offered.
2. Let each one reflect on and evaluate the interpretation of *Revelation* by Okoye.
3. How were you challenged by it? How might you and different people from your culture respond to this challenge?

Part Two:
1. Read aloud *Revelation* 12:1-6. Correlate Pippin's cultural/social/personal location with the interpretation offered.
2. Let each one reflect on and evaluate the interpretation of *Revelation* by Pippin.
3. How were you challenged by it? How might you and different people from your culture respond to this challenge?

Session Seven

Preparatory Reading:
1. "Reading the *Apocalypse*: Resistance, Hope, and Liberation in Central America" by Pablo Richard. *Revelation* 15:2-4.
2. "For the Healing of the World: Reading *Revelation* Ecologically" by Barbara Rossing. *Revelation* 21:22-22:5.

Part One:
1. Read aloud *Revelation* 15:2-4. Correlate Richard's cultural/social/personal location with the interpretation offered.
2. Let each one reflect on and evaluate the interpretation of *Revelation* by Richard.
3. How were you challenged by it? How might you and different people from your culture respond to this challenge?

Part Two:
1. Read aloud *Revelation* 21:22—22:5. Correlate Rossing's cultural/social/personal location with the interpretation offered.
2. Let each one reflect on and evaluate the interpretation of *Revelation* by Rossing.
3. How were you challenged by it? How might you and different people from your culture respond to this challenge?

Session Eight

Preparatory Reading:

1. "*Revelation* 13: Between the Colonial and the Postcolonial: A Reading from Brazil" by Vítor Westhelle. *Revelation* 13:11-18.

2. "Hope for the Persecuted, Cooperation with the State, and Meaning for the Dissatisfied: Three Readings of Revelation from a Chinese Context" by K.-K. (Khiokkhng) Yeo. *Revelation* 21:1-7.

Part One:

1. Read aloud *Revelation* 13:11-18. Correlate Westhelle's cultural/social/personal location with the interpretation offered.

2. Let each one reflect on and evaluate the interpretation of *Revelation* by Westhelle.

3. How were you challenged by it? How might you and different people from your culture respond to this challenge?

Part Two:

1. Read aloud *Revelation* 21:1-7. Correlate Yeo's cultural/social/personal location with the interpretation offered.

2. Let each one reflect on and evaluate the interpretation of *Revelation* by Yeo.

3. How were you challenged by it? How might you and different people from your culture respond to this challenge?

Session Nine

Preparatory Reading:

1. Re-read the *Book of Revelation.*

2. Prepare to give reflections on the discussions in Part One and Part Two of the next session.

Part One:

1. Let each participant reflect overall on the interpretations of *Revelation* encountered in the book.

2. Which interpretations of *Revelation* were most plausible to you? Why? Which interpretations of *Revelation* did you agree with least? Why?

Part Two:

1. Let each participant reflect overall on the appropriations of *Revelation* encountered in the book.

2. Which appropriations of *Revelation* were most influential for you? Which appropriations did you agree with least? Why? Which rejections of the dynamics of *Revelation* were most influential with you? Why?

3. Which did you find most affirming/challenging to you and to your culture? Why?

Session Ten

Preparatory reading:

1. Review and revise your "Reading Profile."

2. Choose what for you is the most meaningful/powerful passage from *Revelation*.

3. Be prepared to explain:

    a. Why the passage is important to you (in relation to your Profile).

    b. What you think this passage meant to original hearers in the context of hearing the whole of *Revelation*.

    c. How you think the passage (as it reflects the whole of *Revelation*) might be appropriated and/or resisted today.

Part One:

1. Let participants identify their chosen passage and reflect on it in relation to their own cultural/social location.

2. Participants may want to demonstrate the relevance of *Revelation* in song, art, poetry, or some other creative expression.

Part Two:

1. Have the group reflect on the experience of intercultural criticism.

    a. What did you learn?

    b. How were you challenged, changed, and transformed by the experience?

    c. What new commitments have you made?

    d. What new things have you learned and experienced as a community?

[Note: For those who wish to view portions or all of *Revelation* as part of the course, see "The Revelation of St. John," a dramatic performance on videotape by David Rhoads. It is available through SELECT c/o Trinity Lutheran Seminary, 2199 E. Main Street, Columbus, OH 43209 (614-235-4136).]

Bibliography 1
Intercultural Bible Study

This bibliography contains articles and books about intercultural education and pedagogy.

Adams, J. Q., and Janice B. Welsch. *Multicultural Education: Strategies for Implementation in Colleges and Universities*. Volume 2. Illinois Staff and Curriculum Developers Association, 1992.

Angrosino, Michael. *Talking about Cultural Diversity in Your Church: Gifts and Challenges*. Walnut Creek, Calif.: AltaMira, 2001.

Anum, E. "Towards Intercultural Contextual Bible Study: A Review of the Adoption of Contextual Bible Study in the West of Scotland." *International Review of Mission* 91 (2002): 224–36.

Arbuckle, Gerald A. *Earthing the Gospel: An Inculturation Handbook for the Pastoral Worker*. Maryknoll, N.Y.: Orbis, 1990.

Augsburger, David. *Pastoral Counseling across Cultures*. Philadelphia: Westminster, 1986.

Barndt, Joseph. *Dismantling Racism: The Continuing Challenge to White America*. Minneapolis: Augsburg, 1991.

Belenky, Mary Field, et al. *Women's Ways of Knowing: The Development of Self, Voice, and Mind*. New York: Basic, 1986.

Bennett, Milton. "Towards Ethnorelativism: A Developmental Model of Intercultural Sensitivity," 27–69, in *Cross-Cultural Orientation: New Conceptualization and Application*. Edited by R. Michael Paige. Lanham: University Press of America, 1986.

Borelli, John, editor. *Handbook for Interreligious Dialogue*. 2nd Edition. Morristown, N.J.: Silver Burdett & Ginn, 1988.

Brache, John M., and Karen B. Tye. *Teaching the Bible in the Church*. St. Louis: Chalice, 2003.

Cassity, Michael, and others. *Living Out Our Deepest Differences: Religious Liberty in a Pluralistic Society*. Boston: Learning Connection, 1990.

Cochrane, James. *Circles of Dignity: Community Wisdom and Theological Reflection*. Minneapolis: Fortress Press, 1999.

Conradie, E. M. "Biblical Interpretation within the Context of Established Bible Study." *Scriptura* 78 (2001): 442–47.

DeYoung, Curtiss Paul. *Coming Together: The Bible's Message in an Age of Diversity*. Valley Forge, Pa.: Judson, 1995.

Dube, Musa. *Other Ways of Reading: African Women and the Bible*. Atlanta: Society of Biblical Literature, 2001.

Eisland, Nancy L. *The Disabled God: Toward a Liberatory Theology of Disability*. Nashville: Abingdon, 1994.

Evans, Alice Frazier, Robert A. Evans, and William Bean Kennedy. *Pedagogies for the Non-Poor*. Maryknoll, N.Y.: Orbis, 1987.

Everding, H. Edward, et al. *Viewpoints: Perspectives of Faith and Christian Nurture*. Harrisburg, Pa.: Trinity Press International, 1998.

Foster, Charles. *Embracing Diversity*. Washington, D.C.: Alban Institute, 1997.

———, and Theodore Belsford. *We Are the Church Together: Cultural Diversity in Congregational Life*. Valley Forge, Pa.: Trinity Press International, 1996.

Friere, Paulo. *Pedagogy of the Oppressed*. Translated by Myra Bergman Ramos. New York: Herder and Herder, 1971.

Gittins, Anthony. *Gifts and Strangers: Meeting the Challenge of Inculturation*. New York: Paulist, 1989.

Hall, Edward. *Beyond Culture*. New York: Doubleday, 1976.

Hofstede, Geert. *Culture's Consequences: International Differences in Work-Related Attitudes*. Abridged edition. Beverly Hills, Calif.: Sage, 1987.

Irizarry, José. "The Religious Educator as Cultural Spec-actor: Researching Self in Intercultural Pedagogy." *Religious Education* 98 (2003): 365–81.

Katz, Judy H. *White Awareness: Handbook for Anti-Racism Training*. Norman: University of Oklahoma Press, 1978.

Kim, Young-Il. *Knowledge, Attitude, and Experience: Ministry in the Cross-Cultural Experience*. Nashville: Abingdon, 1992.

Kohls, L. Robert. *Developing Intercultural Awareness*. Washington, D.C.: Society for Intercultural Education, Training, and Research, 1981.

Law, Eric H. F. *The Bush Was Blazing but Not Consumed*. St. Louis: Chalice, 1996.

———. *Inclusion: Making Room for Grace*. St. Louis: Chalice, 2000.

———. *Sacred Acts, Holy Change: Faithful Diversity and Practical Transformation*. St. Louis: Chalice, 2002.

———. *The Wolf Shall Dwell with the Lamb: A Spirituality for Leadership in a Multicultural Community*. St. Louis: Chalice, 1993.

Levison, John R., and Priscilla Pope-Levison, editors. *Return to Babel: Global Perspectives on the Bible*. Louisville, Ky.: Westminster John Knox, 1999.

Lightfoot, Sara Lawrence. *Respect: An Exploration*. Reading, N.J.: Perseus, 1999.

Martin, Judith, editor. *Theories and Methods in Cross-Cultural Orientation*. New York: Pergamon, 1986.

Musuoka, Fumitaka. *The Color of Faith: Building Community in a Multiracial Society*. Cleveland: Pilgrim, 1998.

Nieman, James, and Thomas Rogers. *Preaching to Every Pew: Cross-Cultural Strategies*. Minneapolis: Fortress Press, 2002.

Paige, Michael, editor. *Cross-Cultural Orientation: New Conceptualization and Application*. Lanham, Md.: University Press of America, 1986.

Patte, Daniel. *The Challenge of Discipleship: A Critical Study of the Sermon on the Mount as Scripture*. Harrisburg, Pa.: Trinity Press International, 1999.

———, Monya A. Stubbs, Justin Ukpong, and Revelation E. Velunta. *The Gospel of Matthew: A Contextual Introduction for Group Study*. Nashville: Abingdon, 2003.

Postman, Neil, and Charles Weingartner. *Teaching as a Subversive Activity*. New York: Delacorte, 1969.

Pui-lan, Kwok. *Discovering the Bible in a Non-Biblical World*. Maryknoll, N.Y.: Orbis, 1995.

Rhoads, David. *The Challenge of Diversity: The Witness of Paul and the Gospels*. Minneapolis: Fortress Press, 1996.

Richard, Pablo. "Interpreting and Teaching the Bible in Latin America." *Interpretation* 56 (2002): 378–86.

Rosenberg, Marshall. *Nonviolent Communication: A Language of Compassion*. Del Mar, Calif.: PuddleDancer Press, 2000.

Ruessman, J. "Teaching the Bible with Respect." *Bible Today* 39 (2001): 294–99.

Segovia, Fernando, and Mary Ann Tolbert, editors. *Teaching the Bible: The Discourses and Politics of Biblical Pedagogy*. Maryknoll, N.Y.: Orbis, 1998.

Sikkema, Mildred and Agnes Niyekawa. *Design for Cross-Cultural Learning*. Yarmouth, Maine: Intercultural, 1987.

Storti, Craig. *Cross-Cultural Dialogues*. Yarmouth, Maine: Intercultural, 1994.

Tracy, David. *Dialogue with the Other: The Inter-Religious Dialogue*. Grand Rapids: Eerdmans, 1990.

Waun, Maurine. *More than Welcome: Learning to Embrace Gay, Lesbian, Bisexual, and Transgendered Persons in the Church*. St. Louis: Chalice, 2001.

Webb-Mitchell, Brett. *Unexpected Guests at God's Banquet: Welcoming People with Disabilities into the Church*. New York: Crossroad, 1994.

West, Gerald O. *The Academy of the Poor: Towards a Dialogical Reading of the Bible*. Sheffield: Sheffield Academic, 1999.

———. *Contextual Bible Study*. Pietermaritzburg: Cluster, 1993.

———, and Musa Dube, editors. *"Reading With": An Exploration of the Interface between Critical and Ordinary Readings of the Bible—African Overtures*. Semeia 73 (1996).

Wolf, Miroslav. *Exclusion and Embrace: A Theological Exploration of Identity, Otherness, and Embrace*. Nashville: Abingdon, 1996.

Woodruff, Paul. *Reverence: Renewing a Forgotten Virtue*. Oxford: Oxford University Press, 2001.

Bibliography 2
Cultural Interpretation

This bibliography contains the information for the footnotes in the Introduction, along with other books and articles relevant to cultural interpretation.

Adam, A. K. M., editor. *Handbook of Postmodern Biblical Interpretation*. St. Louis: Chalice, 2000.

———. *Postmodern Interpretations of the Bible—A Reader*. St. Louis: Chalice, 2001.

———. *What Is Postmodern Biblical Interpretation?* Guides to Biblical Scholarship. Minneapolis: Fortress Press, 1995.

Adedejl, F. "Contextual Exegesis—An Interpretive Method for Biblical Hymnic Texts: A Nigerian Perspective." *Asian Journal of Theology* 17 (2003): 17–25.

Aichele, George, et al. "Ideological Criticism," 272–308, in *The Postmodern Bible: The Bible and the Culture Collective*. New Haven: Yale University Press, 1995.

———. *The Postmodern Bible: The Bible and the Culture Collective*. New Haven: Yale University Press, 1995.

Anderson, Janice Capel. "Feminist Criticism: The Dancing Daughter," 103–34, in *Mark and Method: New Approaches in Biblical Studies*. Edited by J. Anderson and S. Moore. Minneapolis: Fortress Press, 1992.

———, and Jeffrey Staley, editors. *Taking It Personally: Autobiographical Biblical Criticism*. Semeia 72. Atlanta: Scholars, 1995.

Bailey, Randall, editor. *Yet with a Steady Beat: Contemporary U.S. Afrocentric Biblical Interpretation*. Semeia Studies 42. Atlanta: Society of Biblical Literature, 2003.

———, and Tina Pippin, editors. *Race, Class, and Politics of Biblical Translators*. Semeia 76. Atlanta: Scholars, 1996.

Bevans, Stephan. *Models of Contextual Theology*. Faith and Cultures Series. Maryknoll, N.Y.: Orbis, 1996.

Bird, Phyllis, K. D. Sakenfeld, and Sharon Ringe, editors. *Reading the Bible as Women: Perspectives from Africa, Asia, and Latin America*. Semeia 78. Atlanta: Scholars, 1997.

Blount, Brian K. *Cultural Interpretation: Reorienting New Testament Criticism*. Minneapolis: Fortress Press, 1995.

———. *Then the Whisper Put on Flesh: Ethics in an African American Context*. Nashville: Abingdon, 2001.

Boer, Roland. *Last Stop Before Antartica: The Bible and Postcolonialism in Australia*. Sheffield: Sheffield Academic, 2001.

———. *A Vanishing Mediator? The Presence/Absence of the Bible in Postcolonialism*. Semeia 88. Atlanta: Society of Biblical Literature, 2001.

Booth, Wayne C. *The Company We Keep: The Ethics of Fiction*. Berkeley: University of California Press, 1988.

———. *Critical Interpretation: The Powers and Limits of Pluralism*. Chicago: University of Chicago Press, 1979.

Bowe, Barbara. "Reading the Bible through Filipino Eyes." *Missiology* 36 (1998): 345–60.

Braxton, Brad. *No Longer Slaves: Galatians and African-American Experience*. Collegeville, Minn.: Liturgical, 2002.

Brenner, Athalya, and Carol R. Fontaine, editors. *A Feminist Companion to Reading the Bible: Approaches, Methods, Strategies*. Sheffield: Sheffield Academic, 1997.

Brett, M., editor. *Ethnicity and the Bible*. Leiden: Brill, 1996.

Brown, Michael Joseph. *Blackening the Bible: The Aims of African American Biblical Scholarship*. Harrisburg, Pa.: Trinity Press International, 2004.

Bultman, Rudolf. "Is Exegesis without Presuppositions Possible?" 289–96, in *Existence and Faith: Shorter Writings by Rudolf Bultman*. Edited by Shubert Ogden. Cleveland: World, 1960.

Canclini, Nestor Garcia. *Hybrid Cultures*. Minneapolis: University of Minnesota Press, 1995.

Cannon, Katie G., editor. *Interpretation for Liberation*. Semeia 47. Atlanta: Scholars, 1989.

Cardenal, Ernesto. *The Gospel in Solentiname*. 4 vols. Translated by Donald Walsh. Maryknoll, N.Y.: Orbis, 1976–1982.

Carroll R., M. Daniel, ed. *Rethinking Contexts, Rereading Texts: Contributions from the Social Sciences to Biblical Interpretation*. Sheffield: Sheffield Academic, 2000.

Clarke, S. "Viewing the Bible through the Eyes of Subalterns in India." *Biblical Interpretation* 10 (2002): 245–66.

Clines, David. "Biblical Interpretation in International Perspective," *Biblical Interpretation* 1 (1993) 67–87.

———, and Tamara Escanabe, editors. *Telling Queen Michal's Story: An Experiment in Comparative Hermeneutics*. Sheffield: JSOT Press, 1991.

Cosgrove, Charles. "Advocating One Reasonable Interpretation of Paul over against Other Reasonable Interpretations: A Theological Approach to the *Sandweg* Question." In *Another Way? Pauline Soteriology for Jews and Gentiles in Romans*. Edited by Robert Gagnon. Grand Rapids: Eerdmans, 2004.

———. *Appealing to Scripture in Moral Debate: Five Hermeneutical Rules*. Grand Rapids: Eerdmans, 2002.

———. *Elusive Israel: The Puzzle of Election in Romans*. Louisville, Ky.: Westminster/John Knox, 1997.

———. "Rhetorical Suspense in Romans 9–11: A Study in Polyvalence and Hermeneutical Election." *Journal of Biblical Literature* 115 (1996): 271–87.

———, editor. *The Meanings We Choose: Hermeneutical Ethics, Indeterminacy, and the Conflict of Interpretations*. London: T & T Clark, 2004.

Countryman, L. William. *Interpreting the Truth: Changing the Paradigm of Biblical Studies*. Harrisburg, Pa.: Trinity Press International, 2003.

Croatto, Severino. *Biblical Hermeneutics: Toward a Theory of Reading as the Production of Meaning*. Translated by Robert R. Barr. Maryknoll, N.Y.: Orbis, 1987.

De La Torre, Miguel. *Reading the Bible from the Margins*. Maryknoll, N.Y.: Orbis, 2002.

DeYoung, Curtis. *Coming Together: The Bible in an Age of Diversity*. Valley Forge, Pa.: Judson, 1995.

Dietrich, Walter, and Ulrich Luz, editors. *The Bible in a World Context: An Experiment in Contextual Hermeneutics.* Grand Rapids: Eerdmans, 2002.

Donaldson, L. E. "Are We All Multiculturalists Now? Biblical Reading as Cultural Context." Semeia 82 (1998): 79–97.

Donaldson, Laura, editor. *Postcolonialism and Scriptural Reading.* Semeia 75 (1996).

Douglas, K. B. "Marginalized People, Liberating Perspectives: A Womanist Approach to Biblical Interpretation." *Anglican Theological Review* 83 (2001): 41–47.

Dube, Musa. *Other Ways of Reading: African Women and the Bible.* Atlanta: Society of Biblical Literature, 2001.

———. *Postcolonial Feminist Interpretation of the Bible.* St. Louis: Chalice, 2000.

——— and Jeffrey Staley, editors. *John and Postcolonialism: Travel, Space and Power.* Sheffield: Sheffield Academic , 2002.

Eagleton, T. *Ideology: An Introduction.* London: Verso, 1991.

Elizondo, Virgilio. *Galilean Journey: The Mexican American Promise.* Maryknoll, N.Y.: Orbis, 1991.

England, John, and Archie Lee, editors. *Doing Theology with Asian Resources: Ten Years in the Formation of Living Theology in Asia.* Auckland, New Zealand: Pace, 1993.

Felder, Cain Hope. "Beyond Eurocentric Biblical Interpretation: Reshaping Racial and Cultural Lenses." *Journal of the Interdenominational Theological Center* 26 (1998): 17–32.

———. *Troubling Biblical Waters.* Maryknoll, N.Y.: Orbis, 1989.

———, editor. *Stony the Road We Trod: African American Biblical Interpretation.* Minneapolis: Fortress Press, 1991.

Fewell, Dana Nolan, and Gary Phillips, editors. *Bible and Ethics of Reading.* Semeia, 77 (1997).

Fowl, Stephen. *Engaging Scripture: A Model for Theological Interpretation.* Oxford: Blackwell, 1999.

———, editor. *The Theological Interpretation of Scripture: Classic and Contemporary Readings.* Oxford: Blackwell, 1997.

———, and L. Gregory Jones. *Reading in Communion: Scripture and Ethics in the Christian Life.* Grand Rapids: Eerdmans, 1991.

Fowler, Robert, Edith Blumhofer, and Fernando Segovia, editors. *New Paradigms for Biblical Study: The Bible in the Third Millenium.* New York: T & T Clark, 2004.

Gadamer, H. G. *Truth and Method.* Translated by J. Weinsheimer and D. Marshall. Revised edition. New York: Crossroad, 1989.

González, Justo. *Out of Every Tribe and Nation: Christian Theology at the Ethnic Roundtable.* Nashville: Abingdon, 1992.

Goss, Robert, and Mona West, editors. *Take Back the Word: A Queer Reading of the Bible.* Cleveland: Pilgrim, 2000.

Gottwald, Norman, editor. *The Bible and Liberation: Political and Social Hermeneutics.* Maryknoll, N.Y.: Orbis, 1984.

Green, Barbara. *Mikhail Bakhtin and Biblical Scholarship: An Introduction.* Atlanta: Society of Biblical Literature, 2000.

Grenholm, Cristina, and Daniel Patte, editors. *Reading Israel in Romans: Legitimacy and Plausibility of Divergent Interpretations.* Romans through History and Cultures Series. Vol. 1. Harrisburg, Pa.: Trinity Press International, 2000.

Hayes, J. D. *From Every People and Nation: A Biblical Theology of Race.* Leicester: Apollos, 2003.

Hiebert, Theodore, editor. *Toppling the Tower: Essays on Babel and Diversity.* Chicago: McCormick Theological Seminary Press, 2004.

Horsley, Richard A. "Paul and the Politics of Interpretation," 224–41, in *Paul and Politics: Ekklesia, Israel, Inperium, Interpretation.* Edited by Richard A. Horsley. Harrisburg, Pa.: Trinity Press International, 1997.

———, editor. *Paul and the Roman Imperial Order*. Harrisburg, Pa.: Trinity Press International, 2004.

Isasi-Díaz, Ada María, and Yolanda Tarango. *Hispanic Women: Prophetic Voice in the Church*. San Francisco: Harper & Row, 1988.

Jobling, David, and Tina Pippin, editors. *Ideological Criticism of Biblical Texts*. Semeia 59. Atlanta: Scholars, 1992.

———, and R. Schliefer, editors. *The Post Modern Bible Reader*. Oxford: Blackwell, 2001.

Jonker, L. C. "Mapping the Various Factors Playing a Role in Biblical Interpretation." *Scriptura* 78 (2001): 418–28.

Kahl, W. "Intercultural Hermeneutics—Contextual Exegesis: A Model for Twenty-first Century Exegesis." *International Review of Mission* 89 (2000): 421–33.

Kanyoro, Musimbi R. A. *Introducing Feminist Cultural Hermeneutics: An African Perspective*. Cleveland: Pilgrim, 2002.

Keller, Catherine, Michael Nausner, and Mayra Rivera, editors. *Postcolonial Theologies: Divinity and Empire*. St. Louis: Chalice, 2004.

Kelley, S. *Racializing Jesus: Race, Ideology, and the Formation of Modern Biblical Scholarship*. New York: Routledge, 2002.

Kitzberger, Ingrid Rosa, editor. *Autobiographical Biblical Criticism: Between Text and Self*. Leiden: Deo, 2002.

———. *The Personal Voice in Biblical Interpretation*. London: Routledge, 1999.

Lacine, Stuart. "Indeterminacy and the Bible: A Review of Literary and Anthropological Theories and Their Application to Biblical Texts." *Hebrew Studies* 27 (1986): 48–80.

Larkin, W. J. "Approaches to and Images of Biblical Authority for the Postmodern Mind." *Bulletin of Biblical Research* 8 (1998): 129–38.

Lawson, Marjorie, editor. *Women of Color Study Bible*. Nashville: World, 1999.

Lee, A. C. "Returning to China: Biblical Interpretation in Postcolonial Hong Kong." *Biblical Interpretation* 7 (1999): 156–73.

Levine, A.-J. "The Disease of Postcolonial Biblical Studies and the Hermeneutic of Healing." *Journal of Feminist Studies in Religion* 20 (2004) 91–99.

———. "Multiculturalism, Women's Studies, and Anti-Judaism." *Feminist Studies in Religion* 19 (2003): 119–28.

Levison, John R., and Priscilla Pope-Levison, editors. *Return to Babel: Global Perspectives on the Bible*. Louisville, Ky.: Westminster John Knox, 1999.

Liew, Tat-siong Benny, editor. *The Bible in Asian America*. Semeia 90-91 Atlanta: Society of Biblical Literature, 2002.

Liew, Tat-siong Benny, and Vincent Wimbush. "Encountering Texts, Encountering Communities: A Symposium on African and Asian Engagements with the Bible." *Union Seminary Quarterly Review* 56 (2002): 21–81.

Lim, Johnson T. K. *A Strategy for Reading Biblical Texts*. Studies in Biblical Literature, vol. 29. New York: Peter Lang, 2002.

Mailloux, Stephen. "Reader Response Criticism." *Genre* 10 (1977): 413–31.

Malina, Bruce. "Reading Theory Perspective," 3–23, in *The Social World of Luke-Acts: Models for Interpretation*. Edited by J. Neyrey. Peabody, Mass.: Hendrickson, 1991.

Mariaselvam, A. "Biblical Interpretation for India Today." *Bible Bhashyam* 28 (2002): 505–20.

Martin, Clarice J. "Womanist Biblical Interpretation," in *Dictionary of Biblical Interpretation*. Vol. 2. Edited by John H. Hayes. Nashville: Abingdon, 1999.

———. "Womanist Interpretations of the New Testament: The Quest for Holistic and Inclusive Translation and Interpretation," 225–44, in *Black Theology: A Documentary History*. Edited by James Cone and Gayraud Wilmore. Vol. 2. Maryknoll, N.Y.: Orbis, 1993.

McKnight, Edgar. *Post-Modern Use of the Bible: The Emergence of Reader-Oriented Criticism*. Nashville: Abingdon, 1988.

Mesters, Carlos, editor. *The Use of the Bible in Christian Communities of the Common People.* Maryknoll, N.Y.: Orbis, 1993.

Miller, J. H. *The Ethics of Reading: Kant, de Man, Eliot, Trollope, James, and Benjamin.* New York: Columbia University Press, 1987.

Moore, Stephen. *Literary Criticism and the Gospels: The Theoretical Challenge.* New Haven: Yale University Press, 1989.

———. *Poststructuralism and the New Testament: Derrida and Foucault at the Foot of the Cross.* Minneapolis: Fortress Press, 1994.

———, and Janice Capel Anderson, editors. *New Testament Masculinities.* Atlanta: Society of Biblical Literature, 2003.

Mosala, Itumeleng. *Biblical Hermeneutics and Black Theology on South Africa.* Grand Rapids: Eerdmans, 1989.

Mouton, Elna. *Reading a New Testament Document Ethically.* Leiden: Brill, 2002.

Mutheraj, J. G. "Re-reading the New Testament in India: Some Hermeneutical Explorations." *Asia Journal of Theology* 13 (1999): 14–50.

Mwombeki, F. R. "Reading the Bible in Contemporary Africa." *Word and World* 21 (2001): 121–28.

Naluparayil, J. "Reader-Response Criticism: A Theoretical Framework for Multiple Interpretations of Biblical Texts." *Bible Bhashyam* 28 (2002): 558–64.

Nikwoka, A. O. "New Testament Research and Cultural Heritage: A Nigerian Example." *Asian Journal of Theology* 17 (2003): 287–300.

Okoye, James. "Mark 1:21-28 in African Perspective," *Bible Today* 34 (1996) 240–45.

Okure, Teresa. "Inculturation: Biblical Theological Bases," 55–88, in *Evaluating the Inculturation of Christianity in Africa.* Edited by Teresa Okure. Eldoret, Kenya: AMECEEA Gaba, 1990.

———. *To Cast Fire upon the Earth: Bible and Mission Collaborating in Today's Multicultural Context.* Pietermaritzburg: Cluster, 2000.

Patte, Daniel. *The Challenge of Discipleship: A Critical Study of the Sermon on the Mount as Scripture.* Harrisburg, Pa.: Trinity Press International, 1999.

———. *Discipleship according to the Sermon on the Mount: Four Legitimate Readings, Four Plausible Views of Discipleship and Their Relevant Values.* Valley Forge, Pa.: Trinity Press International, 1996.

———. *Ethics of Biblical Interpretation: A Reevaluation.* Louisville, Ky.: Westminster/John Knox, 1995.

———, ed. *Global Bible Commentary.* Nashville: Abingdon, 2004.

———, et al. *The Gospel of Matthew: A Contextual Introduction for Group Study.* Nashville: Abingdon, 2003.

Phillips, Gary. "The Ethics of Reading Deconstructively," 283–325, in *The New Literary Criticism and the New Testament.* Edited by F. McKnight and E. Struthers Malbon. Valley Forge, Pa.: Trinity Press International, 1994.

———. *Poststructural Criticism and the Bible: Text/History/Discourse.* Semeia 51 (1990).

———, and Nicole Wilkinson Durand, editors. *Reading Communities Reading Scripture: Essays in Honor of Daniel Patte.* Harrisburg, Pa.: Trinity Press International, 2002.

Pope-Levison, Priscilla and John Levison, editors. *Jesus in Global Contexts.* Louisville, Ky.: Westminster John Knox, 1992.

Powell, Mark Allan. *Chasing the Eastern Star: Adventures in Biblical Reader-Response Criticism.* Louisville, Ky.: Westminster John Knox, 2001.

———. "The Forgotten Famine: Personal Responsibility in Luke's Parable of 'The Prodigal Son,'" 265–87, in *Literary Encounters with the Reign of God.* Edited by Sharon Ringe and Paul Kim. London: T & T Clark, 2004.

Prior, Michael. *The Bible and Colonialism: A Moral Critique.* Sheffield: Sheffield Academic, 1997.

Pui-lan, Kwok. *Discovering the Bible in the Non-Biblical World*. Maryknoll, N.Y.: Orbis, 1995.

Raisanen, Heikki, et al. *Reading the Bible in the Global Village: Helsinki*. Atlanta: Society of Biblical Literature, 2000.

Raja, J. J. "Democratization of Communication and Biblical Hermeneutics." *Asian Journal of Theology* 17 (2003): 431–41.

Rhoads, David. *The Challenge of Diversity: The Witness of Paul of the Gospels*. Minneapolis: Fortress Press, 1996.

———. "The Ethics of Reading Mark as Narrative," 202–19, in *Reading Mark, Engaging the Gospel* by David Rhoads. Minneapolis: Fortress Press, 2004.

Richard, Pablo. "Interpreting and Teaching the Bible in Latin America." *Interpretation* 56 (2002): 378–86.

Ringe, Sharon. "An Approach to a Critical, Feminist, Theological Reading of the Bible," 156–63, in *A Feminist Companion to Reading the Bible*. Athalya Brenner and Carol Fontaine, editors. Sheffield: Sheffield Academic, 1997.

Robinson, Robert, and Robert Culley, editors. *Textual Determinacy: Part Two*. Semeia 71 (1995).

Sakenfeld, Katherine Doob. "Feminist Reading of the Bible: Problems and Prospects." *Bangalore Theological Forum* 32 (2000): 18–27.

———, and Sharon Ringe, editors. *Reading the Bible as Women: Perspectives from Africa, Asia, and Latin America*. Semeia 78. Atlanta: Scholars, 1997.

Sampathkumar, P. A. "Current Trends in Indian Biblical Studies." *Biblebhashyam* 25 (1999): 64–77.

Sano, R. L. "Shifts in Reading the Bible: Hermeneutical Moves among Asian Americans." *Semeia* 90/91 (2002): 105–18.

Scholz, Susanne. *Biblical Studies Alternatively*. Upper Saddle River, N.J.: Prentice Hall, 2003.

Schottroff, Luise, Silvis Schroer, and Marie-Theres Wacker. *Feminist Interpretation: The Bible in Women's Perspective*. Translated by Martin and Barbara Rumscheidt. Minneapolis: Fortress Press, 1998.

Schreiter, Robert. *Constructing Local Theologies*. Maryknoll, N.Y.: Orbis, 1993.

Schroer, Silvia and Sophia Bretenhard, editors. *Feminist Interpretation of the Bible and the Hermeneutics of Liberation*. New York: Continuum, 2003.

Schüssler Fiorenza, Elisabeth. *Bread Not Stone: The Challenge of Feminist Biblical Interpretation*. Boston: Beacon, 1984.

———. *But She Said: Feminist Practices of Biblical Interpretation*. Boston: Beacon, 1992.

———. "The Ethics of Interpretation: De-Centering Biblical Theology." *Journal of Biblical Literature* 107 (1988): 3–17.

———. *In Memory of Her: A Feminist Theological Reconstruction of Christian Origins*. New York: Crossroad, 1983.

———. *Rhetoric and Ethic: The Politics of Biblical Studies*. Minneapolis: Fortress Press, 1999.

———. *Sharing Her Word: Feminist Biblical Interpretation in Context*. Boston: Beacon, 1998.

———, and Shelly Matthews, editors. *Searching the Scriptures*. Vol. 1: *A Feminist Introduction*. New York: Crossroad, 1997.

———. *Searching the Scriptures*. Vol. 2: *A Feminist Commentary*. New York: Crossroad, 1994.

Segovia, Fernando. *Decolonizing Biblical Studies: A View from the Margins*. Maryknoll, N.Y.: Orbis, 2000.

———. "Intercultural Criticism," 304–5, in *Searching the Scriptures*. Vol. 1. Edited by Elisabeth Schüssler Fiorenza and Shelly Matthews. New York: Crossroad, 1995.

———. *Interpreting beyond Borders*. Sheffield: Sheffield Academic, 2000.

———. "Toward Intercultural Criticism: A Reading Strategy from the Diaspora," 302–30, in *Reading from This Place*. Vol. 2. Edited by Fernanod Segovia and Mary Ann Tolbert. Minneapolis: Fortress Press, 1995.

———, editor. *Toward a New Heaven and a New Earth: Essays in Honor of Elisabeth Schüssler Fiorenza*. Maryknoll, N.Y.: Orbis, 2003.

———. *What Is John? Literary and Social Readings of the Fourth Gospel*. Atlanta: Scholars, 1998.

———. *What Is John? Readers and Readings of the Fourth Gospel*. Atlanta: Scholars, 1996.

———, and Mary Ann Tolbert, editors. *Reading from This Place*. Vol. 2: *Social Location and Biblical Interpretation in Global Perspective*. Minneapolis: Fortress Press, 1995.

———. *Reading from This Place*. Vol. 1: *Social Location and Biblical Interpretation in the United States*. Minneapolis: Fortress Press, 1995.

———. *Teaching the Bible: The Discourses and Politics of Biblical Pedagogy*. Maryknoll, N.Y.: Orbis, 1998.

Segundo, Juan Luis. "The Hermeneutical Circle," 7–38 in *Liberation of Theology*. Translated by John Drury. Maryknoll, N.Y.: Orbis, 1976..

Shillington, George. *Reading the Sacred Text: An Introduction to Biblical Studies*. London: T & T Clark, 2002.

Shweder, Richard. *Thinking through Cultures*. Cambridge: Harvard University Press, 1991.

Smit, D. J. "The Ethics of Interpretation: New Voices from the USA." *Scriptura* 33 (1990): 16–28.

Smith-Christopher, Daniel, editor. *Text and Experience: Towards a Cultural Exegesis of the Bible* Biblical Seminar 35. Sheffield: Sheffield Academic, 1995.

Spivak, Gayatri. "Can the Subaltern Speak?" 277–313, in *Marxism and the Interpretation of Culture*. Edited by Cary Nelson and Lawrence Grossberg. Urbana: University of Illinois Press, 1988.

Stone, Ken. "Biblical Interpretation as a Technology of the Self: Gay Men and the Ethics of Reading." *Semeia* 77 (1997): 139–55.

———. "Gay/Lesbian Interpretation." In *Dictionary of Biblical Interpretation*. Edited by John H. Hayes. Nashville: Abingdon, 1999.

———. "What Happens When 'Gays Read the Bible'?" 77–85 in *The Many Voices of the Bible*. Edited by Sean Freyne and Ellen van Wolde. London: SCM, 2002.

Sugirtharajah R. S. *Asian Biblical Hermeneutics and Postcolonialism*. Sheffield: Sheffield Academic, 1999.

———. *The Bible and the Third World*. Cambridge: Cambridge University Press, 2001.

———. *Postcolonial Criticism and Biblical Interpretation*. Oxford: Oxford University Press, 2003.

———. *Postcolonial Reconfigurations: An Alternative Way of Reading the Bible and Doing Theology*. St. Louis: Chalice, 2003.

———, editor. *The Postcolonial Bible*. Sheffield: Sheffield Academic, 1998.

———. *Vernacular Hermeneutics*. Sheffield: Sheffield Academic, 1999.

———. *Voices from the Margin: Interpreting the Bible in the Third World*. London: SPCK, 1991.

Suleiman, S., and I. Crossman, editors. *The Reader in the Text: Essays on Audience and Interpretation*. Princeton, N.J.: Princeton University Press, 1980.

Tannehill, Robert. "Freedom and Responsibility in Scripture Interpretation, with Application to Luke," 265–78, in *Literary Studies in Luke-Acts*. Edited by R. P. Thompson and T. E. Philips. Macon, Ga.: Mercer University Press, 1998.

Tanner, Kathryn. *Theories of Culture: A New Agenda for Theology*. Guides to Theological Inquiry. Minneapolis: Fortress Press, 1997.

Thiselton, Anthony. *New Horizons in Hermeneutics: The Theory and Practice of Transforming Biblical Reading*. London: HarperCollins, 1992.

Tiffany, Frederick, and Sharon Ringe. *Biblical Interpretation: A Roadmap*. Nashville: Abingdon, 1996.

Tolbert, Mary Ann. *Perspectives on the Parables: An Approach to Multiple Interpretations.* Philadelphia: Fortress Press, 1979.

———. "The Politics and Poetics of Location," 305–17, in *Reading from this Place.* Vol. 1. Edited by Fernando Segovia and Mary Ann Tolbert. Minneapolis: Fortress Press, 1995.

———. "When Resistance Becomes Repression: Mark 13:9-27 and the Poetics of Location," 331–45, in *Reading from this Place.* Vol. 2. Edited by Fernando Segovia and Mary Ann Tolbert. Minneapolis: Fortress Press, 1995.

———, editor. *The Bible and Feminist Hermeneutics.* Chico, Calif.: Scholars, 1983.

Tompkins, J., editor. *Reader-Response Criticism: From Formalism to Post-Structuralism.* Baltimore: Johns Hopkins University Press, 1980.

Upkong, J. S. "Developments in Biblical Interpretation in Modern Africa." *Missionalia* 27 (1999): 313–29.

———. "Models and Methods of Biblical Interpretation in Africa." *Neue Zeitschrift für Missionsschaft/Neuvelle Revue de science missionaire* 55 (1999): 279–95.

———, et al. *Reading the Bible in the Global Village: Cape Town.* Atlanta: Society of Biblical Literature, 2003.

Vanhoozer, Kevin L. *Is There Meaning in This Text? The Bible, the Reader, and the Morality of Biblical Knowledge.* Grand Rapids: Zondervan, 1998.

Weems, Renita J. "Womanist Reflections on Biblical Hermeneutics," 216–24, in *Black Theology: A Documentary History.* Vol. 2. Edited by James H. Cone and Gayraud S. Wilmore. Maryknoll, N.Y.: Orbis, 1993.

West, Gerald O. *The Academy of the Poor: Towards a Dialogical Reading of the Bible.* Sheffield: Sheffield Academic, 1999.

———. *Biblical Hermeneutics of Liberation: Modes of Reading the Bible in the South African Context.* Pietermaritzburg: Cluster, 1991.

———. *Contextual Bible Study.* Pietermaritzburg: Cluster, 1993.

———. "Reading Other-Wise: Re-Envisioning the Reading Practices and Place of the Socially Engaged Scholar." *Scriptura* 68 (1999): 49–66.

———. "White Men, Bibles, and Land: Ingredients in Biblical Interpretation in South African Black Theology." *Scriptura* (2000): 141–52.

———, and Musa Dube, editors. *The Bible in Africa: Transactions, Trajectories, and Trends.* Leiden: Brill, 2000.

———. *"Reading With": An Exploration of the Interface between Critical and Ordinary Readings of the Bible African Overtures.* Semeia 73 (1996).

West, Mona. "Reading the Bible as Queer Americans: Social Location and the Hebrew Scriptures." *Theology and Sexuality* 10 (1999): 28–42.

Wildsmith, A. "Cultural Exegesis: The Bible is Open to Everyone." *African Journal of Evangelical Theology* 21 (2002): 199–209.

Wimbush, Vincent. *Historical/Cultural Criticism as Liberation: A Proposal for an African American Biblical Hermeneutic.* Edited by Katie G. Cannon. Semeia 47. Atlanta: Scholars, 1989.

———. "Interpreting the Spin: What Might Happen If African Americans Were to Become the Starting Point for the Academic Study of the Bible." *Union Seminary Quarterly Review* 52 (1998) 61–76.

———, editor. *African Americans and the Bible: Sacred Texts and Social Textures.* New York: Continuum, 2000.

Yee, Gale A. "The Author/Text/Reader and Power: Suggestions for a Critical Framework for Biblical Studies," 109–18 in *Reading from This Place.* Vol. 1. Minneapolis: Fortress Press, 1995.

Yeo, Khiok-khng. *What Has Jerusalem to Do with Beijing? Biblical Interpretation from a Chinese Perspective.* Harrisburg, Pa.: Trinity Press International, 1998.

————, ed. *Navigating Romans through Cultures: Challenging Readings by Charting a New Course*. New York: T. & T. Clark, 2004.

Young, Iris. *Justice and the Politics of Difference*. Princeton, N.J.: Princeton University Press, 1990.

Bibliography 3
The *Book of Revelation*

▪▪▪▪▪▪▪▪▪▪▪▪▪▪▪▪▪▪▪▪▪▪▪▪▪▪▪▪▪▪

This Bibliography contains information for the footnotes in chapters one through ten, in addition to other relevant books and articles on *Revelation*.

Abir, P. A. "More than Blood Witness." *Indian Theological Journal* 34 (1997): 233–61.

Adam, A. K. *Handbook of Postmodern Biblical Interpretation.* St. Louis: Chalice, 2000.

Alexiou, Margaret. *The Ritual Lament in Greek Tradition.* Cambridge: Cambridge University Press, 1974.

Allen, V., and T. Paul. "Science and Fiction: Ways of Theorizing about Women," 165–83, in *Erotic Universe: Sexuality and Fantastic Literature.* Edited by Donald Palumbo. New York: Greenwood, 1986.

Althusser, Louis. *For Marx.* Translated by Ben Brewster. Harmondsworth: Penguin, 1969.

Ashcroft, Bill, Gareth Griffiths, Hellen Tiffin. *Post-Colonial Studies. The Key Concepts.* New York: Routledge, 2000.

Astorga, C. A. *The Beast, The Harlot, and the Lamb: Faith Confronts Systemic Evil.* Quezon City: New Day, 1999.

Aune, David. "The Apocalypse of John and the Problem of Genre." *Semeia* 36 (1986) 67.

———. "The Form and Function of the Proclamation to the Seven Churches (Revelation 2-3)." *New Testament Studies* 36 (1990): 182-204.

———. "The Influence of Roman Imperial Court Setting Ceremonial on the Apocalypse of John." *Biblical Research* 28 (1983): 5-26.

———. *Revelation.* Word Biblical Commentary in three volumes: *Revelation 1-5.* Dallas: Word, 1997. *Revelation 6-16.* Nashville: Thomas Nelson, 1998. *Revelation 17-20.* Nashville: Thomas Nelson, 1998.

———. "The Social Matrix of the Apocalypse of John." *Biblical Research* 26 (1981): 16–32.

Awkward, Michael, editor. *New Essays on Their Eyes Were Watching God.* New York: Cambridge, 1995.

Backus, Irena Dorata. *Reformation Readings of the Apocalypse: Geneva, Zurich, Wittenberg.* Oxford: Oxford University Press, 2000.

Baker, Houston A., Jr. *Workings of the Spirit: The Poetics of Afro-American Women's Writing.* Chicago: University of Chicago Press, 1991.

Bakhtin, Mikhail. *Problems of Dostoevsky's Poetics.* Edited and translated by Caryl Emerson. Minneapolis: University of Minnesota Press, 1984.

Balsdon, J. P. V. D. *Romans and Aliens.* Chapel Hill: University of North Carolina Press, 1979.

Barlow, Maude, and Tony Clarke, "Who Owns Water?" *The Nation* (September 2–9, 2002), 11–15.

Barmé, Geremie. *In the Red: On Contemporary Chinese Culture.* New York: Columbia University Press, 1999.

Barr, David. "The Apocalypse of John as Oral Enactment." *Interpretation* 40 (1986): 243–56.

———. "The Apocalypse as a Symbolic Transformation of the World." *Interpretation* 38 (1984): 39–50.

———. "Blessed Are Those Who Hear: John's Apocalypse as Present Experience," 87–103, in *Biblical and Humane: Festschrift for John Priest.* Edited by Linda Bennett Elder, David Barr, and Elizabeth Strutheers Malbon. Atlanta: Scholars, 1996.

———. "Elephants and Holograms: From Metaphor to Methodology in the Study of John's Apocalypse." *SBL 1986 Seminar Papers* (1986): 400–411.

———. *Tales of the End: A Narrative Commentary on the Book of Revelation.* Santa Rosa, Calif.: Polebridge, 1998).

———, editor. *Reading the Book of Revelation: A Resource for Students.* Atlanta: Society of Biblical Literature, 2003.

Barthes, Roland. *Mythologies.* Translaed by Annette Layers. New York: Hill and Wang, 1972.

Bartkowski, Frances. "A Fearful Fancy: Some Reconsiderations of the Sublime." *Boundary* 215 (1987-88): 23–32.

Bauckham, Richard. *The Climax of Prophecy: Studies on the Book of Revelation.* Edinburgh: T. & T. Clark, 1998.

———. "Economic Critique of Rome in Revelation 18," 47–90, in *Images of Empire.* Edited by Loveday Alexander. Sheffield: JSOT, 1991.

———. *The Theology of the Book of Revelation.* Cambridge: Cambridge University Press, 1993.

Bauer, David. "A Book with Seven Seals? Introduction to the Revelation of John." *Bulletin Dei Verba* 54 (2000): 4–7.

Beale, Gregory. *The Book of Revelation: A Commentary on the Greek Text.* Grand Rapids: Eerdmans, 1999.

Beaver, R. Pierce, editor. *To Advance the Gospel: Selections from the Writings of Rufus Anderson.* Grand Rapids: Eerdmans, 1967.

Berger, Peter. *The Noise of Solemn Assemblies: Christian Commitment and the Religious Establishment in America.* Garden City, N.Y.: Doubleday, 1961.

Bhabha, Homi K. *The Location of Culture.* London: Routledge, 1994.

———. "Signs Taken for Wonders," in *The Location of Culture.* London: Routledge, 1994.

Biguzzi, G. "John on Patmos and the 'Persecution' in the Apocalypse." *Estudio Biblicos* 56 (1998): 201–20.

Blassingame, John, editor. *Slave Testimony: Two Centuries of letters, Speeches, and Autobiographies.* Baton Rouge: Louisiana State University, 1977.

Bloch, Ernst. *The Principle of Hope.* Translated by Melville Plaice et al. Oxford: Blackwell, 1986.

Bloomquist, L. Gregory. "Methodological Criteria for Apocalyptic Rhetoric. A suggestion for the Expanded Use of Sociorhetorical Analysis." In *Vision and Persuasion: Rhetorical Dimensions of Apocalyptic Discourse.* Edited by Greg Carey and L. Gregory Bloomquist. St. Louis: Chalice, 1999.

Blount, Brian K. *Cultural Interpretation: Reorienting New Testament Criticism.* Minneapolis: Fortress Press, 1995.

———. *Go Preach!: Mark's Kingdom Message and the Black Church Today.* Maryknoll, N.Y.: Orbis, 1998.

————. "Reading Revelation Today: Witness as Active Resistance." *Interpretation* 54 (2000): 398–412.

————. *Then the Whisper Put on Flesh: New Testament Ethics in an African-American Context.* Nashville: Abingdon, 2001.

Boesak, Allan. *Comfort and Protest: The Apocalypse from a South African Perspective.* Philadelphia: Westminster, 1987.

Boff, Leonardo. *Cry of the Earth, Cry of the Poor.* Maryknoll, N.Y.: Orbis, 1997.

Bonhoeffer, Dietrich. *The Cost of Discipleship.* London: SCM, 1990.

Boring, Eugene. "The Theology of Revelation: The Lord Our God Almighty Reigns." *Interpretation* 40 (1986): 257–69.

Boring, Eugene. *Revelation.* Interpretation. Louisville, Ky.: John Knox, 1989.

Botha, Pieter. "God, Emperor Worship, and Society: Contemporary Experience and the Book of Revelation." *Neotestamentica* 22 (1988): 87–102.

Bottigheimer, Ruth. *Grimms' Bad Girls and Bold Boys: The Moral and Social Vision of the Tales.* New Haven: Yale University Press, 1987.

————. "Silenced Women in the Grimms' Tales: The 'Fit' Between Fairy Tales and Society in Their Historical Context," 115–31, in *Fairy Tales and Society Illusion, Allusion, and Paradigm.* Edited by Ruth Bottgheimer. Philadelphia: University of Pennsylvania Press, 1986.

————. "The Transformed Queen: A Search for the Origins of Negative Female Archetypes in Grimms' Fairy Tales," 1–12, in *Gestaltet und Gestaltend: Frauen in der Deutschen Literatur.* Edited by Marianne Burkhard. Amsterdam: Rodopi 1980.

Bousset, W. *Offenbarung Johannis.* Göttingen: Vandenhoeck & Ruprecht, 1906.

Bowe, Barbara. "Visions of Heaven, Dreams of the End." *Bible Today* 37 (1999): 354–59.

Bowers, Susan. "*Beloved* and a New Apocalypse." *The Journal of Ethnic Studies* 18:1 (Spring 1990): 59–77.

Boyer, Paul. *When Time Shall Be No More: Prophecy Belief in Modern American Culture.* Cambridge, Mass.: Belknap, 1992.

Bozon, F. "John's Self-Presentation in Revelation 1:9-10." *Catholic Biblical Quarterly* 62 (2000): 693–700.

Bradley, K. R. *Slaves and Masters in the Roman Empire: A Study in Social Control.* New York: Oxford University Press, 1987.

Brady, David. *The Contribution of British Writers Between 1560 and 1830 to the Interpretation of Revelation 13:16-18 (The Mark of the Beast).* Tübingen: Mohr Siebeck, 1983.

Brasher, B. E. "From Revelation to the X-Files: An Autopsy of Millenialism in American Popular Culture." *Semeia* 82 (1998): 281–95.

Braund, Susanna Morton. "Juvenal," 386–387, in *The Oxford Companion to Classical Civilization.* Edited by Simon Hornblower and Anthony Spawforth. New York: Oxford University Press, 1998.

Bredin, M. R. J. "The Synagogue of Satan Accusation in Revelation 2:9." *Biblical Theology Bulletin* 28 (1998): 160–64.

Broadhead, E. K. "Sacred Imagination and Social Protest." *Review and Expositor* 98 (2001): 77–85.

Brooke-Rose, Christine. *A Rhetoric of the Unreal: Studies in Narrative & Structure, Especially of the Fantastic.* Cambridge: Cambridge University Press, 1981.

Brown, G. Thompson. *Christianity in the People's Republic of China.* Atlanta: John Knox, 1986.

Brueggemann, Walter. *Revelation and Violence: A Study in Contextualization.* Milwaukee: Marquette University Press, 1986.

Bull, Malcolm. *Seeing Things Hidden. Apocalypse, Vision and Totality.* London: Verso, 1999.

Burdon, C. *The Apocalypse in England: Revelation Unraveling, 1700-1834.* New York: St. Martin's, 1997.

Caird, George. *A Commentary on the Revelation of St. John the Divine.* Harper's New Testament Commentaries. New York: Harper & Row, 1966.

Callahan, Allan D. "A Note on Revelation 18: Apocalypse as Critique of Political Economy." Unpublished Paper, 7.

Callahan, Allan. D. "Apocalypse as Critique of Political Economy: Some Notes on Revelation 18." *Horizons in Biblical Theology* 21 (1994): 46–65.

Callahan, Allan. D. "The Language of the Apocalypse." *Harvard Theological Review* 88 (1995): 453–70.

Campbell, G. "How to Say What with Words: Story and Interpretation in the Book of Revelation." *Irish Biblical Studies* 23 (2001): 111–34.

Campese, Gioachino and Pietro Ciallelle, eds. *Migration, Religious Experience, and Globalization.* New York: Center for Migration Studies, 2003.

Cancik, Hubert and Helmut Schneider eds. *Der neue Pauly: Enzyklopädie der Antike.* Stuttgart: Metzler, 1996–2003.

Cannon, Katie G. "Race, Sex, and Insanity: Transformative Eschatology in Hurston's Account of the Ruby McCollum Trial." In *Liberating Eschatology: Essays in Honor of Letty M. Russell.* Edited by Margaret A. Farley and Serena Jones. Louisville, Ky.: Westminster John Knox, 1999.

Carey, Greg. "Apocalyptic Discourse, Apocalyptic Rhetoric." *Vision and Persuasion. Rhetorical Dimensions of Apocalyptic Discourse.* Edited by Greg Carey and L. Gregory Bloomquist. St. Louis: Chalice, 1999.

———. *Elusive Apocalypse: Reading Authority in the Revelation to John.* Macon, Ga.: Mercer University Press, 1999.

———. "How to Do Things with (Apocalyptic) Words: Rhetorical Dimensions of Apocalyptic Discourse." *Lexington Theological Quarterly* 33 (1998): 85–101.

———. "Teaching and Preaching the Book of Revelation in the Church." *Review and Expositor* 98 (2001): 87–100.

Carey, Greg, and Gregory Bloomquist, editors. *Vision and Persuasion: Rhetorical Dimensions of Apocalypytic Discourse.* St. Louis: Chalice, 1999.

Carrell, P. R. *Jesus and the Angels: Angelology and the Christology of the Apocalypse of John.* Cambridge: Cambridge University Press, 1997.

Charry, E. T. "A Sharp Two-Edged Sword: Pastoral Implications of Apocalyptic." *Interpretation* 53 (1999): 158–72.

Ching, Julia. "Faith and Ideology in the Light of the New China." *Christianity and the New China.* South Pasadena: Ecclesia, 1976.

Collins, Adela Yarbro. *The Apocalypse.* New Testament Message 22. Wilmington, Del.: Michael Glazier, 1979.

———. "The Apocalypse." In *The New Jerome Biblical Commentary.* Edited by Raymond E. Brown. New York: Prentice-Hall, 1990.

———. "Apocalyptic Themes in Biblical Literature." *Interpretation* 53 (1999): 117–30.

———. *The Combat Myth in the Book of Revelation.* Missoula: Scholars, 1976.

———. *Cosmology and Eschatology in Jewish and Christian Apocalypticism.* Leiden: Brill, 2000.

———. *Crisis and Catharsis: The Power of the Apocalypse.* Philadelphia: Westminster, 1984.

———. "Early Christian Apocalypticism: Genre and Social Setting." *Semeia* 36 (1986).

———. "Insiders and Outsiders in the Book of Revelation." In *To See Ourselves as Others See Us: Christians, Jews, "Others" in Late Antiquity.* Edited by Jacob Neusner and Ernest Frerichs. Atlanta: Scholars, 1989.

———. "The Political Perspective of the Revelation to John." *Journal of Biblical Literature* 96 (1977): 241–42.

———. "Revelation, Book of," 694–708, in *Anchor Bible Dictionary.* Vol. 5. Edited by David Noel Freedman. New York: Doubleday, 1992.

———. "Villification and Self-Definition in the Book of Revelation." *Harvard Theological Review* 79 (1986): 308–20.

———. "Women's History and the Book of Revelation," 80–91, in *SBL 1987 Seminar Papers.* Edited by Kent Richard. Atlanta: Scholars, 1987.

Collins, J. J. "Apocalypse: The Morphology of a Genre." *Semeia* 14 (1979). Entire issue devoted to subject.

———. "Jerusalem and the Temple in Jewish Apocalyptic Literature of the Second Temple Period." *International Rennert Guest Lecture Series* 1 (1998): 3–31.

Collins, Patricia Hill. *Black Feminist Thought, Knowledge, Consciousness, and the Politics of Empowerment.* 2nd edition. New York: Routledge, 2003.

Cone, James. "The Meaning of Heaven in Black Spirituals," 60–71, in *Heaven.* Edited by Bas Van Iersel and Edward Schillerbecks. New York: Seabury, 1979.

Cook, S. A., F. E. Adcock, and M. P. Charlesworth, editors. *The Cambridge Ancient History,* vol. 11. Cambridge: University Press, 1936.

Cook, Stephen L. *Prophecy and Apocalypticism: The Postexilic Social Setting.* Minneapolis: Fortress Press, 1995.

Coulter, Ann. "Hannity and Colmes," June 20, 2001. Quoted in "The Wisdom of Ann Coulter," *the Washington Monthly,* October 2001. www.Washingtonmonthly.com/features/2001/0111.coulterwisdom.html.

Court, John. *Revelation.* Sheffield: Sheffield Academic, 1994.

Cukrowski, K. "The Influence of the Emperor Cult on the Book of Revelation." *Restoration Quarterly* 45 (2003): 51–64.

Cummings, George C. L. "The Slave Narrative as a Source of Black Theological Discourse: The Spirit and Eschatology." In *Cut Loose Your Stammering Tongue: Black Theology and the Slave Narratives.* Edited by Dwight N. Hopkins and George Cummings. Maryknoll, N.Y.: Orbis, 1998.

Cutler, Jonathan. "Literary Fantasy." *Cambridge Review* 95 (1973): 30–33.

———. *On Deconstruction: Theory and Criticism after Structuralism.* Ithaca, N.Y.: Cornell University Press, 1982.

Darton, Robert. *The Great Cat Massacre and Other Episodes in French Cultural History.* New York: Basic, 1984.

Davies, Philip R. "The Social World of Apocalyptic Writings." In *The World of Ancient Israel,* edited by R.E. Clements. Cambridge, England: Cambridge University Press, 1989.

de Certeau, Michel. *The Practice of Everyday Life.* Berkeley: University of California Press, 1984.

de Silva, D. A. "Honor Discourse and the Rhetorical Strategy of the Apocalypse of John." *Journal for the Study of the New Testament,* 71 (1998): 79–110.

———. "A Sociological Interpretation of Revelation 14:6-13: A Call to Act Justly toward the Just and Judging God." *Bulletin for Biblical Research* 9 (1999): 65–117.

de Smidt, K. "Hermeneutical Perspectives on the Spirit in the Book of Revelation." *Journal of Pentecostal Theology* 14 (1999): 27–47.

De Villiers, P. G. R. "Persecution in the Book of Revelation." *Acta Theologica* 22 (2002): 47–70.

de Zayas, Alfred M. *Nemesis at Potsdam: The Expulsion of Germans from the East.* 3rd edition. Lincoln: University of Nebraska Press, 1989.

Denney, Reuel. "The Poet and the Scholar." In *The Connecticut River and Other Poems.* New Haven: Yale University Press, 1939.

Desrosiers, G. *An Introduction to Revelation.* London: Continuum, 2000.

Donelson, Lewis. *From Hebrews to Revelation: A Theological Introduction.* Louisville, Ky.: Westminster John Knox, 2001.

du Rand, J. A. "A Socio-Psychological View of the Effect of the Language (Parole) of the Apocalypse of John." *Neotestamentica* 24 (1990): 351–65.

du Rand, J. A. "Your Kingdom Come 'On Earth as It Is in Heaven:' The Theological Motif of the Book of Revelation." *Neotestamentica* 31 (1997): 59–75.

Dube, Musa. *Post-Colonial Feminist Interpretation of the Bible.* St. Louis: Chalice, 2000.

Duff, P. B. *Who Rides the Beast? Prophetic Rivalry and the Rhetoric of Crisis in the Churches of the Apocalypse.* New York: Oxford University Press, 2001.

Ecksteins, Modris. *Walking Since Daybreak: A Story of Eastern Europe, World War II, and the Heart of Our Century.* Toronto: Key Porter, 1999.

Ehrhardt, A. T. "Social Problems in the Early Church." *The Framework of the New Testament Stories.* Cambridge: Harvard University, 1964.

Elizondo, Virgilio. *Galilean Journey: The Mexican-American Promise.* Maryknoll, N.Y.: Orbis, 1983.

Ellul, Jacques. *Apocalypse: The Book of Revelation.* New York: Seabury, 1977.

Ewing, Ward B. *The Power of the Lamb: Revelation's Theology of Liberation for You.* Cambridge, Mass.: Cowley, 1994.

Faley, Roland. *Apocalypse Then and Now: A Companion to the Book of Revelation.* Mahwah, N.J.: Paulist, 1999.

Farmer, Ronald L. *Beyond the Impasse: The Promise of a Process Hermeneutic.* Studies in American Biblical Hermeneutics. Macon, Ga.: Mercer University Press, 1997.

Fears, J. Rufus. "The Cult of Jupiter and Roman Imperial Ideology." *ANRW* 2/17.1(1981): 3–141.

Fears, J. Rufus. *Princeps a diis electus: The Divine Election of the Emperor as a Political Concept at Rome.* Papers and Monographs of the American Academy in Rome 26. Rome: American Academy in Rome, 1977.

Fee, Gordon D. "Once Again: An Interpretation of 1 Corinthians 8-10." *Biblica* 61 (1980): 186.

Festinger, Leon, Henry W. Riecken, and Stanley Schachter. *When Prophecy Fails: A Social and Psychological Study of a Modern Group that Predicted the Destruction of the World.* New York: Harper & Row, 1964.

Fitzgerald, William. *Slavery and the Roman Literary Imagination: Roman Literature and Its Contexts.* New York: Cambridge University Press, 2000.

Ford, J. Massingberde. *Revelation.* The Anchor Bible. Garden City, N.Y.: Doubleday, 1975.

Ford, Lewis S. "God as the Subjectivity of the Future." *Encounter* 41 (1980): 292.

Forgacs, David, editor. *The Antonio Gramsci Reader.* New York: New York University Press, 1988.

Frappier-Mazur, Lucienne. "Marginal Canons: Rewriting the Erotic." *Yale French Studies* 75 (1988): 112–28.

Freire, Paulo. *Pedagogía del oprimido.* Mexico: Siglo XXI, 1982.

Fretheim, Terrence. "The Earth Story in Jeremiah 12." In *Readings from the Perspective of Earth.* Edited by Norman Habel. Earth Bible vol. 1. Sheffield: Sheffield Academic, 2000.

———. "The Plagues as Ecological Signs of Historial Disaster." *Journal of Biblical Literature* 110 (1991): 387.

Friedrich, N. P. "Adapt or Resist? A Socio-Political Reading of Revelation 2:18-29." *Journal for the Study of the New Testament* 25 (2002): 185–211.

Friesen, Steven. *Imperial Cults and the Apocalypse of John: Reading Revelation in the Ruins.* Oxford: Oxford University Press, 2001.

Fukuyama, Francis. *The End of History and the Last Man.* New York: Avon, 1992.

Gager, John G. *Kingdom and Community: The Social World of Early Christianity.* Englewood-Cliffs, N.J.: Prentice-Hall, 1975.

Gaibreath, Robert. "Fantastic Literature as Gnosis." *Extrapolation* 29 (1988): 330–37.

Galinsky, Karl. *Augustan Culture: An Interpretive Introduction.* Princeton, N.J.: Princeton University Press, 1996.

Garrett, Susan. "Revelation." In *The Women's Bible Commentary*. Edited by Carol Newsom and Sharon Ringe. Louisville, Ky.: Westminster John Knox, 1998.

Gates, Henry Louis Jr. *The Signifying Monkey: A Theory of African-American Literary Criticism.* New York: Oxford University Press, 1988.

Georgi, Dieter. "Die Visionen vom himmlischen Jerusalem im Apok 21 und 22," 351–72, in *Kirche. Festschrift Günther Bornkamm.* Edited by Dieter Luhrmann and Georg Strecker. Tübingen: Mohr, 1980.

Georgi, Dieter. "Who Is the True Prophet?" *Harvard Theological Review* 79 (1986) 100–126.

Gibbs, Nancy. "The Bible and the Apocalypse." *Time Magazine.* July 1, 2002.

Giblin, Charles. "Recapitulation and the Literary Coherence of John's Apocalypse." *Journal of Biblical Literature* 56 (1994): 81–95.

Gilkes, Cheryl Townsend. *If It Wasn't for the Women: Black Women's Experience and Womanist Culture in Church and Community.* Maryknoll, N.Y.: Orbis, 2001.

Glancy, Jennifer A. *Slavery in Early Christianity.* New York: Oxford University Press, 2002.

Gloer, W. H. "Worship God! Liturgical Elements in the Apocalypse." *Review and Expositor* 98 (2001): 35–57.

Goethe, Johann Wolfgang. *Maximen und Reflexionen.* Frankfurt: Inseln, 1976.

González, Catherine Gunsalus, and Justo L. González. *Revelation.* Louisville: Westminster John Knox, 1997.

———. *Vision at Patmos: Studies in the Book of Revelation.* Nashville: Abingdon, 1991 [1978].

González, Justo L. *For the Healing of the Nations: The Book of Revelation in an Age of Cultural Conflict.* Maryknoll, N.Y.: Orbis, 1999.

———. "Los últimos tiempos en la historia de la iglesia," 87–110, in *La historia como ventana al futuro.* Buenos Aires, Argentina: Ediciones Kairós, 2002.

Goss, Linda, and Marian E. Barnes, editors. *Talk That Talk: An Anthology of African-American Storytelling.* New York: Simon & Schuster, 1989.

Gracia, Jorge. *How Can We Know What God Means: The Interpretation of Revelation.* New York: Palgrave, 2001.

Gradel, L. *Emperor Worship and Roman Religion.* Oxford: Oxford University Press, 2002.

Habel, Norman C., and Vicky Balabanski. "Ecojustice Hermeneutics: Reflections and Challenges." In *The Earth Story in the New Testament.* Edited by Norman C. Habel and Vicky Balabanski. The Earth Bible vol. 5. Sheffield: Sheffield Academic, 2002.

Halsell, Grace. *Forcing God's Hand: Why Millions Pray for a Quick Rapture—And Destruction of Planet Earth.* Beltsville, Md.: Amana, 1999.

Hanks, Tom. *The Subversive Gospel: A New Testament Commentary of Liberation.* Cleveland: Pilgrim, 2000.

Hanson, Paul D. *The Dawn of Apocalyptic.* Philadelphia: Fortress Press, 1975.

Harland, Philip A. *Associations, Synagogues, and Congregations: Claiming a Place in the Ancient World.* Minneapolis: Fortress Press, 2003.

———. "Honoring the Emperor or Assailing the Beast: Participation in Civic Life among the Associations in Asia Minor and the Apocalypse of John." *Journal for the Study of the New Testament* 77 (2000): 99–121.

Harrington, D. J. "Apocalypse: Ten Steps to Help You Understand the Book of Revelation." *Church* 15 (1999) 11–14.

Harrington, Wilfrid. *Revelation.* Sacra Pagina. Collegeville, Minn.: Liturgical, 1993.

Harris, Michael A. "Singing a New Song: The Literary Function of the Hymns in the Apocalypse of John." PhD dissertation. Southern Baptist Theological Seminary, 1988.

Hays, Richard. *The Moral Vision of the New Testament: Community, Cross, New Creation.* San Francisco: HarperSanFrancisco, 1994.

Hemer, Colin J. *The Letters to the Seven Churches of Asia in their Local Setting.* Grand Rapids: Eerdmans, 2001.

Hoch-Smith, Judith. "Introduction," 1–23, in *Women in Ritual and Symbolic Roles.* Edited by Judith Hock-Smith and Anita Spring. New York: Plenum, 1978.

Hood, George A. *Mission Accomplished? The English Presbyterian Mission in Lingtung, South China.* Frankfurt: Verlag Peter Lang, 1986.

Hopkins, Dwight. "Slave Theology in the 'Invisible Institution,'" 14–15, in *Cut Loose Your Stammering Tongue: Black Theology and the Slave Narratives.* Edited by Dwight N. Hopkins and George Cummings. Maryknoll, N.Y.: Orbis, 1998.

Horsley, Richard A. "The Slave Systems of Classical Antiquity and Their Reluctant Recognition by Modern Scholars." In *Slavery in Text and Interpretation.* Semeia 83/84. Edited by Allen Dwight Callahan, Richard A. Horsley, and Abraham Smith. Atlanta: Society of Biblical Literature, 1998.

Howard-Brook, W., and A. Gwyther. *Unveiling Empire: Reading Revelation Then and Now.* Maryknoll, N.Y.: Orbis, 1999.

Hunt, Stephen, ed. *Christian Millenarianism from the Early Church to Waco.* Bloomington: Indiana University Press, 2001.

Hunter, Alan, and Chan Kim-Kwong. *Protestantism in Contemporary China.* Cambridge: Cambridge University Press, 1993.

Hurston, Zora Neale. *Mules and Men.* Bloomington: Indiana University Press, 1978.

Hutcheon, Linda. *Splitting Images: Contemporary Canadian Ironies.* Toronto: Oxford University Press, 1991.

Jack, Alison. *Texts Reading Texts, Sacred and Secular: Two Postmodern Perspectives.* Sheffield: Sheffield Academic, 1999.

Jackson, Rosemary. *Fantasy: The Literature of Subversion.* New York: Methuen, 1981.

Jacobs, Harriet. "Incidents in the Life of a Slave Girl, Written by Herself." In *Slave Narratives.* Edited by William L. Andrews and Henry Louis Gates Jr. New York: Library Classics of the United States, 2000.

Jacobsen, David. *Preaching the New Creation: The Promise of New Testament Apocalyptic Texts.* Louisville, Ky.: Westminster John Knox, 2000.

Jameson, Fredric. *The Political Unconscious: Narrative as a Socially Symbolic Act.* Ithaca, N.Y.: Cornell University Press, 1981.

———. *The Prison-House of Language. A Critical Account of Structuralism and Russian Formalism.* Princeton, N.J.: Princeton University Press, 1972.

Jay, Nancy. "Sacrifice as Remedy for Having Been Born of Woman," 283–309, in *Immaculate & Powerful: The Female in Sacred Image and Social Reality.* Boston: Beacon, 1985.

Jewett, Robert. "The Corruption and Redemption of Creation: Reading Rom 8:18-23 within the Imperial Context." In *Paul and the Roman Imperial Order.* Edited by Richard A. Horsley. Harrisburg, Pa.: Trinity Press International, 2004.

Johns, Loren L. *The Lamb Christology of the Apocalypse of John: An Investigation into Its Origins and Rhetorical Force.* Tubingen: Mohr Siebeck, 2003.

Johnson, Georgia Douglas Camp. "Inevitably." In *The Heart of a Woman and Other Poems.* Boston: Cornhill, 1918.

Johnson, James Weldon, editor. *The Book of American Negro Spirituals.* New York: Viking, 1931.

Jones, Larry Paul, and Jerry Sumney. *Preaching Apocalyptic Texts.* St. Louis: Chalice, 1999.

Joshel, Sandra R., and Sheila Murnaghan, eds. *Women and Slaves in Greco-Roman Culture: Differential Equations.* New York: Routledge, 2001.

Kalilombe, Patrick A. "Spirituality in the African Perspective." In *Paths of African Theology* Edited by Rosino Gibellini. Maryknoll, N.Y.: Orbis, 1994.

Kamboureli, Smaro. *In the Second Person.* Edmonton, Alberta: Longspoon, 1985.

Kangas, R. "The Book of Revelation: The Consummation of God's Economy." *Affirmation and Critique* 4 (1999): 3–13.

Karanja, Ayana I. *Zora Neale Hurston: The Breath of Her Voice.* New York: Peter Lang, 1999.

Käsemann, Ernst. "Die Anfänge christlicher Theologie" and "Zum Thema der urchristlichen Apokalyptik," 82–131, in *Exegetische Versuche un Besinnungen.* Vol. 2. Göttingen: Vandenhoeck & Ruprecht, 1968.

Kearney, Richard. *The Wake of Imagination: Toward a Postmodern Culture.* Minneapolis: University of Minnesota Press, 1988.

Keller, Catherine. *Apocalypse Now and Then: A Feminist Guide to the End of the World.* Boston: Beacon, 1996.

———. "Eyeing the Apocalypse," 253–73, in *Postmodern Interpretations of the Bible: A Reader.* Edited by A. K. M. Adam. St. Louis: Chalice, 2001.

Ketterer, David. *New Worlds for Old: The Apocalyptic Imagination, Science Fiction and American Literature.* Bloomington: Indiana University Press, 1974.

Kim, J. K. "'Uncovering Her Wickedness': An Inter(con)textual Reading of Revelation 17 from a Postcolonial Feminist Perspective." *Journal for the Study of the New Testament* 73 (1999): 61–81.

Kingswell, Mark. *Dreams of Millennium: Report from a Culture on the Brink.* New York: Viking, 1996.

Kio, Stephen. "Exodus as the Central Symbol of Liberation in the Book of Revelation." *Bible Translator* 40 (1989): 120–35.

Kistemaker, Simon. *Exposition of the Book of Revelation.* Grand Rapids: Baker Academic, 2001.

Kittel, Gerhard and Gerhard Friedrich, eds. *Theological Dictionary of the New Testament.* Translated by Geoffrey W. Bromiley. Vol. 9. Grand Rapids: Eerdman.

Klassen, William. "Vengeance in the Apocalypse of John." *Catholic Biblical Quarterly* 28 (1966): 300–311.

Knight, Jonathan. *Revelation.* Sheffield: Sheffield Academic Press, 1999.

Koester, C. "Recent Studies of the Book of Revelation." *Lutheran Quarterly* 14 (2000) 109–12.

Koester, C. *Revelation and the End of All Things.* Grand Rapids: Eerdmans, 2001.

Kovaks, J., and C. Rowland. *Revelation.* Blackwell Bible Commentaries. Oxford: Blackwell, 2003.

Kramer, H. W. "Contrast as a Key to Understanding the Revelation to St. John." *Concordia Journal* 23 (1997): 108–17.

Kraybill, Nelson. *Imperial Cult and Commerce in John's Apocalypse.* Sheffield: Sheffield Academic Press, 1996.

Kristeva, Julia. *Strangers to Ourselves.* Translated by Leon S. Roudiez. New York: Columbia University Press, 1991.

Krodel, Gerhard. *Revelation.* Augsburg Commentary on the New Testament. Minneapolis: Augsburg, 1989.

Kyle, Richard. *The Last Days Are Here Again: A History of the End Times.* Grand Rapids: Baker, 1998.

Lambrecht, Jan. *Collected Studies on the Pauline Literature and the Book of Revelation.* Rome: Editrice Pontificio Instituto Biblico, 2001.

Landy, Marcia. "The Silent Woman: Towards a Feminist Critique," 16–27, in *The Authority of Experience: Essays in Feminist Criticism.* Edited by Arlyn Diamond and Lee R. Edwards. Amherst: University of Massachusetts Press, 1977.

Laws, Sophie. *In the Light of the Lamb: Imagery, Parody, and Theology in the Apocalypse of John.* Wilmington, Del.: Michael Glazier, 1989.

Lee, P. *The New Jerusalem in the Book of Revelation: A Study of Revelation 21-22 in Light of the Jewish Tradition.* Tubingen: Mohr Siebeck, 2001.

Lefanu, Sarah. *Feminism and Science Fiction.* Bloomington Indiana: University Press, 1988

Lifton, Robert Jay. "The Image of the End of the World: A Psychohistorical View." In *Visions of Apocalypse: End or Rebirth.* Edited by Saul Friedlander, Gerald Horton, Leo Marx, and Eugene Sklnikoff. New York: Holmes & Meier, 1985.

Lowe, John. *Jump at the Sun: Zora Neale Hurston's Cosmic Comedy*. Urbana: University of Illinois Press, 1997.

Lupieri, E. "Sex and Blood: Some New Approaches to the Apocalypse of John." *Folia Orientalia* 35 (1999): 85–92.

Luther, Martin. "Preface to Revelation." *Das Neue Testament, Episteln und Offenbarung* 1522/46.

Lyall, Leslie. *God Reigns in China*. London: Hodder and Stoughton, 1985.

MacInnis, Donald E. *Religious Policy and Practice in Communist China: A Documentary History*. New York: Macmillan, 1972.

Maclean, Marie. "Oppositional Practices in Women's Traditional Practices." *New Literary History* 19 (1987): 37–50.

Magesa, Laurenti. *African Religion: The Moral Traditions of Abundant Life*. Maryknoll, N.Y.: Orbis, 1997.

Maier, Harry. "Staging the Gaze: Early Christian Apocalypses and Narrative Self-Representation." *Harvard Theological Review* 90 (1997): 131–54.

Maier, Harry. *Apocalypse Recalled: The Book of Revelation after Christendom*. Minneapolis: Fortress Press, 2002.

Malina, Bruce. "How the Cosmic Lamb Marries: The Image of the Wedding of the Lamb (Rev 19:7ff)." *Biblical Theology Bulletin* 28 (1998): 75–83.

Malina, Bruce, and J. Pilch. *Social Science Commentary of the Book of Revelation*. Minneapolis: Fortress Press, 2000.

Malina, Bruce. *On The Genre and Message of Revelation: Star Visions and Sky Journeys*. Peabody, Mass.: Hendrickson, 1995.

Manaparampil, J. "A Spiral-Teleological Literary Structure of the Book of Revelation." *Biblebhashyan* 27 (2001): 44–75.

Mangan, C. "The Bible: Salvation or Creation History?" *Priests and People* 14 (2000): 55–59.

Manuel, Frank E., and Fritzie P. Manuel. *Utopian Thought in the Western World*. Cambridge, Mass.: Belknap, 1979.

Marr, A. "Violence and the Kingdom of God: Introducing the Anthropology of Réne Girard." *Anglican Theological Review* 80 (1998): 590–603.

Marshall, I. H. "The Christian Millenium." *Evangelical Quarterly* 72 (2000): 217–35.

Marshall, John W. *Parables of War: Reading John's Jewish Apocalypse*. Waterloo: Wilfrid Laurier University Press, 2001.

Martin, Clarice J. "Biblical Theodicy and Black Women's Spiritual Autobiography: 'The Miry Bog, The Desolate Pit, A New Song in My Mouth.'" In *A Troubling in My Soul: Womanist Perspectives on Evil and Suffering*. Bishop Henry McNeal Turner Studies in North American Black Religion. Edited by Emilie M. Townes. Maryknoll, N.Y.: Orbis, 1993.

———. "'Somebody Done Hoodoo'd the Hoodoo Man': Language, Power, Resistance, and the Effective History of Pauline Texts in American Slavery." In *Slavery in Text and Interpretation*. Semeia 83/84. Edited by Allen Dwight Callahan, Richard A. Horsley, and Abraham Smith. Atlanta: Society of Biblical Literature, 1998.

———. "Womanist Biblical Interpretation." In *Dictionary of Biblical Interpretation*. Vol. 2. Edited by John H. Hayes. Nashville: Abingdon, 1999.

———. "Womanist Interpretations of the New Testament: The Quest for Holistic and Inclusive Translation and Interpretation." *Journal of Feminist Studies in Religion* 6/2 (1990): 41–61.

Martin, Joan M. "A Sacred Hope and Social Goal: Womanist Eschatology." In *Liberating Eschatology: Essays in Honor of Letty M. Russell*. Edited by Margaret A. Farley and Serene Jones. Louisville, Ky.: Westminster John Knox, 1999.

Mathewson, Dave. "The Destiny of the Nations in Revelation 21:1-22:5: A Reconsideration." *Tyndale Bulletin* 53 (2002): 121–42.

———. *A New Heaven and a New Earth: The Meaning and Function of the Old Testament in Revelation 21:1–22:5.* London: Sheffield Academic, 2003.

Mattern, S. P. *Rome and the Enemy: Imperial Strategy in the Principate.* London: University of California Press, 1999.

Maurier, Henri, *Philosophie de l'Afrique noire.* 2nd edition. St. Augustin: Anthropos-Institut, 1985.

Mbiti, John S. "African Concepts of Christology." In *Christ and the Younger Churches.* Edited by George F. Vicedom. London: SPCK, 1972.

———. *African Religions and Philosophy.* London: Heinemann, 1969.

———. *Bible and Theology in African Christianity.* Nairobi: Oxford University Press, 1986.

———. "Eschatology." In *Biblical Revelation and Africa's Beliefs.* Edited by Kwesi Dickson and Paul Ellingworth. London: Lutterworth, 1969.

McGinn, Bernard. *Antichrist: Two Thousands Years of Human Fascination with Evil.* San Francisco: HarperSanFrancisco, 1994.

———. "Symbols of the Apocalypse in Medieval Culture." *Michigan Quarterly Review* 22 (1983): 265–83.

McIlraith, D. A. "For the Fine Linen of the Saints: Works and Wife in Revelation 19:8." *Catholic Biblical Quarterly* 61 (1999): 512–29.

McVann, Mark. "The Apocalypse of John in Social-Scientific Perspective." *Listening* 28 (1993) 3.

Meeks, Wayne A. "Apocalyptic Discourse and Strategies of Goodness," *Journal of Religion* 80 (2000) 461–75.

Meeks, Wayne A. *The First Urban Christians. The Social World of the Apostle Paul.* New Haven: Yale University Press, 1983.

Melchoir-Bonnet, Sabine. *The Mirror: A History.* Translated by Katharine H. Jewett. New York: Routledge, 2001.

Merviwn, Wallace C., and Francis P. Jones, editors. *Documents of the Three-Self Movement.* New York: National Council of the Churches of Christ, 1963.

Michael Coogan, editor. *The New Oxford Annotated Bible: New Revised Standard Version with the Apocrypha.* 3rd Edition. New York: Oxford University Press.

Michaels, J. R. *Revelation.* Downers Grove, Ill.: Intervarsity, 1997.

Míguez, Nestor. "Apocalyptic and the Economy: A Reading of Revelation 18 from the Experience of the Economic Exclusion." In *Reading from This Place.* Vol. 2. Edited by Fernando Segovia and Mary Ann Tolbert. Minneapolis: Fortress Press, 1995.

Minear, Paul S. *New Testament Apocalyptic.* Nashville: Abingdon, 1981.

Mitchell-Kernan, Claudia. "Signifying, Loud-Talking and Marking." In *Signifyin(g), Sanctifyin', & Slam Dunking.* Edited by Gena Dagel Caponi. Amherst: University of Massachusetts Press, 1999.

Moers, Ellen. *Literary Women.* London: Women's Press, 1978.

Moise, Steven, editor. *Studies in the Book of Revelation.* London: Continuum, 1999.

Moltmann, Jürgen. *The Coming of God: Christian Eschatology.* Translated by Margaret Kohl. London: SCM, 1996.

Moltmann, Jürgen. *The Way of Jesus Christ: Christology in Messianic Dimensions.* Translated by Margaret Kohl. London: SCM, 1990.

Montgomery, Maxine Lavon. *The Apocalypse in African American Fiction.* Gainesville: University of Florida Press, 1996.

Moore, Stephen D. "The Beatific Vision as a Posing Exhibition: Revelation's Hypermasculine Deity." *Journal for the Study of the New Testament* 60 (1995).

———. "Revolting Revelations," 173–99, in *God's Beauty Parlor and Other Queer Spaces in and around the Bible.* Stanford: Stanford University Press, 2001.

Morrison, Toni. *Beloved.* New York: Penguin, 1988.

———. *Playing in the Dark. Whiteness and the Literary Imagination.* New York: Random House, 1992.

Morton, R. "Glory to God and the Lamb: John's Use of Jewish and Hellenistic/ Roman Themes in Formatting his Theology in Revelation 4-5." *Journal for the Study of the New Testament* 83 (2001): 89–109.

———. "Revelation 7:9-17: The Innumerable Crowd before the One upon the Throne and the Lamb." *Ashland Theological Journal* 32 (2000): 1–11.

Mounce, Robert. *The Book of Revelation.* Grand Rapids: Eerdmans, 1977.

Murphy, F. J. *Fallen Is Babylon: The Revelation of John.* Harrisburg, Pa.: Trinity Press International, 1998.

Nakhro, M. "The Manner of Worship according to the Book of Revelation." *Bibliotheca Sacra* 158 (2001): 165–80.

———. "The Meaning of Worship according to the Book of Revelation." *Bibliotheca Sacra* 158 (2001): 75–85.

Nee, W. "The Holy City, New Jerusalem." *Affirmation & Critique* 5 (2000): 66–74.

Newport, K. G. C. *Apocalypse and Millenium: Studies in Biblical Exegesis.* Cambridge: Cambridge University Press, 2000.

O'Leary, Stephen. *Arguing the Apocalypse: A Theory of Millennial Rhetoric.* New York: Oxford University Press, 1994.

Olsen, Lance. *Ellipse of Uncertainty: An Introduction to Postmodern Fantasy.* New York: Greenwood, 1987.

Olson, D. C. "'Those Who Have Not Defiled Themselves with Women': Revelation 14:4 and the Book of Enoch." *Catholic Biblical Quarterly* 59 (1997): 492–510.

Painter, Nell Irvin. *Soul Murder and Slavery.* Waco, Tex.: Markham Press Fund, 1993.

Palumbo, Donald. "Sexuality and the Allure of the Fantastic in Literature," 3–24, in *Erotic Universe: Sexuality and Fantastic Literature.* New York: Greenwood, 1986.

Patrides, C. A. and Joseph Wittreich. *The Apocalypse in English Renaissance Thought and Literature.* Ithaca, N.Y.: Cornell University Press, 1984.

Patte, Daniel. "Biblical Scholars at the Interface between Critical and Ordinary Readings: A Response." In *"Reading With": African Overtures.* Edited by Gerald West and Musa Dube. *Semeia* 73 (1996).

———. *Ethics of Biblical Interpretation: A Reevaluation.* Louisville, Ky.: Westminster John Knox, 1995.

Patterson, Orlando. *Slavery and Social Death: A Comparative Study.* Cambridge: Harvard University Press, 1982.

Paz, Octavio. *The Labyrinth of Solitude.* New York: Grove Weidenfeld, 1985.

Pendergast, Mark. *Mirror, Mirror: A History of the Human Love Affair with Reflection.* New York: Basic, 2003.

Peterson, Eugene. *Reversed Thunder: The Revelation of God and the Praying Imagination.* San Francisco: Harper & Row, 1988.

Pilch, John. *What Are They Saying about the Book of Revelation?* New York: Paulist, 1978.

Pilgrim, Walter. *Uneasy Neighbors: Church and State in the New Testament.* Overtures to Biblical Theology. Minneapolis: Fortress Press, 1999.

Pippin, Tina. *Apocalyptic Bodies: The Biblical End of the World in Text and Image.* New York: Routledge, 1999.

———. *Death and Desire: The Rhetoric of Gender in the Apocalypse of John.* Louisville, Ky.: Westminster John Knox, 1992.

———. "'And I Will Strike Her Children Dead': Death and Destruction of Social Location." In *Reading From This Place: Social Location and Biblical Interpretation in the United States.* Edited by Fernando Segovia and Mary Ann Tolbert. Minneapolis: Fortress, 1995.

———. "The Revelation to John." Pp. 109–30 in *Searching the Scriptures, A Feminist Commentary*. Volume 2. Edited by Elisabeth Schüssler Fiorenza. New York: Crossroad, 1994.

Prevost, Jean-Pierre. *How to Read the Apocalypse.* New York: Crossroad, 1993.

Price, S. R. F. *Rituals and Power: The Roman Imperial Cult in Asia Minor.* New York: Cambridge University Press, 1984

Prigent, Pierre. *Commentary on the Apocalypse of St. John.* Tübingen: Mohr Siebeck, 2001.

Propp, Vladimir. "Structure and History in the Study of the Fairy Tale." *Semeia* 10 (1978): 57–83.

Raboteau, Albert L. *A Fire in the Bones: Reflections on African-American Religious History.* Boston: Beacon, 1995.

Ramsey, Michael. *Interpreting the Book of Revelation.* Grand Rapids: Baker, 1992.

Records of the General Conference of the Protestant Missionairies of China Held at Shanghai, May 10–20, 1877. Shanghai: Presbyterian Mission Press, 1878.

Reddish, Mitchell G. "Martyr Christology in the Apocalypse." *Journal for the Study of the New Testament* 33(1988): 85–95.

———. "Reclaiming the Apocalypse." *Perspectives in Religious Studies* 42 (1997): 125–38.

———. *Revelation.* Macon: Smyth & Helwys, 2001.

Resseguie, J. L. *Revelation Unsealed: A Narrative Critical Approach to John's Apocalypse.* Leiden: Brill, 1998.

Richard, Pablo. *Apocalypse: A People's Commentary on the Book of Revelation.* Maryknoll, N.Y.: Orbis, 1995.

Ricoeur, Paul. *Interpretation Theory: Discourse and the Surplus of Meaning.* Fort Worth: Texas Christian University Press, 1976.

Rissi, Mathias. "The Kerygma of the Revelation to John." *Interpretation* 22 (1968).

Robbins, Vernon K. *Exploring the Texture of Texts: A Guide to Socio-Rhetorical Interpretation.* Valley Forge, Pa.: Trinity Press International, 1996.

Roloff, Jürgen. *The Revelation of John.* Translated by John E. Alsup. Continental Commentaries. Minneapolis: Fortress Press, 1993.

Rorsch, F. "Revelation as 'Subversive Literature.'" *Bulletin Dei Verbum* 54 (2000): 13–15.

Rosinsky, Natalie M. *Feminist Futures: Contemporary Women's Speculative Fiction.* Ann Arbor: UMI Research, 1984.

Rosner, B. S. "The Concept of Idolatry." *Themelios* 24 (1999): 21–30.

Rossing, Barbara R. *The Choice Between Two Cities: Whore, Bride, and Empire in the Apocalypse.* Harrisburg, Pa.: Trinity Press International, 1999.

———. *The Rapture Exposed: The Message of Hope in the Book of Revelation.* Boulder: Westview, 2004.

———. "River of Life in God's New Jerusalem: An Ecological Vision of Earth's Future." *Currents in Theology and Mission* 25 (1998): 487–99.

———. "Standing at the Door of a New Millenium: Economy, Eschatology, and Hope." *Dialog* 37 (1998): 263–68.

Rotz, C. J., and J. A. DuRand. "The One Who Sits upon the Throne: Towards a Theory of Theocentric Characterization according to the Apocalypse of John." *Neotestamentica* 33 (1999): 91–111.

Rowe, Karen E. "Feminism and Fairy Tales." *Women's Studies* 6 (1979): 237–57.

———. "To Spin a Yarn: The Female Voice in Folklore and Fairy Tale," 53–74, in *Fairy Tales and Society: Illusion, Allusion, and Paradigm.* Philadelphia: University of Pennsylvania Press, 1986.

Rowland, C. "Reading the Apocalypse." *Way* 39 (1999): 349–60.

———. "Revelation." In *The New Interpreters Bible.* Vol. 12. Nashville: Abingdon, 1998.

Rowley, H. H. *The Relevance of Apocalyptic.* London: Lutterworth, 1944.

Royalty, Robert. "The Rhetoric of Revelation," 596–617, in *Society of Biblical Literature 1997 Seminar Papers*. Atlanta: Scholars, 1997.

Royalty, Robert. *The Streets of Heaven: The Ideology of Wealth in the Apocalypse of John*. Macon, Ga.: Mercer University Press, 1998.

Ruah, Nicholas K. *The Sacred Bonds of Commerce: Religion, Economy, and Trade Society at Hellenistic Roman Delos, 166-87 B.C.* Amsterdam: Gieben.

Russ, Joanna. "The Image of Women in Science Fiction," 79–94, in *Images of Women in Fiction: Feminist Perspectives*. Edited by Susan Koppleman Cornillon. Bowling Green: Bowling Green State University Popular Press, 1972.

Sauer, Sérgio. *Reforma Agrária e Geração de Emprego e renda no Meio Rural*. São Paulo: ABET, 1998.

Sauter, Gerhard. *What Dare We Hope? Reconsidering Eschatology*. Harrisburg, Pa.: Trinity Press International, 1999.

Schillebeeck, Edward. *Christ: The Experience of Jesus as Lord*. New York: Seabury, 1980.

Schnabel, E. J. "John and the Future of the Nations." *Bulletin of Biblical Research* 12 (2002) 243–71.

Scholes, Robert. "A Footnote to Russ's 'Recent Feminist Utopias,'" 86–87, in *Future Females: A Critical Anthology*. Edited by Marleen S. Barr. Bowling Green: Bowling Green State University Popular Press, 1981.

Schüssler Fiorenza, Elisabeth. "Apocalyptic and Gnosis in the Book of Revelation." *Journal of Biblical Literature* 92 (1973): 67–68.

———. *The Book of Revelation: Justice and Judgment*. 2nd edition. Minneapolis: Fortress Press, 1998.

———. "Composition and Structure of the Book of Revelation." *CBQ* 39 (1977): 344-66.

———. "The Followers of the Lamb: Visionary Rhetoric and Social-Political Situation." *Semeia* 36 (1986): 123–46. Republished in *The Book of Revelation: Justice and Judgment*. 2nd edition. Minneapolis: Fortress Press, 1998.

———. "Redemption as Revelation (Revelation 1:5-6 and 5:9-10)." In *The Book of Revelation: Justice and Judgment*. 2nd edition. Minneapolis: Fortress Press, 1998.

———. *Revelation: Vision of a Just World*. Proclamation Commentaries. Minneapolis: Fortress Press, 1991.

———. *Rhetoric and Ethic: The Politics of Biblical Interpretation*. Minneapolis: Fortress Press, 1999.

Segovia, Fernando F. *Decolonizing Biblical Studies: A View from the Margins*. Maryknoll, N.Y.: Orbis, 2000.

Shelton, Jo Ann. *As the Romans Did: A Sourcebook in Roman Social History*. 2nd edition. New York: Oxford University Press, 1998.

Slater, T. B. "On the Social Setting of the Revelation of John." *New Testament Studies* 44 (1998): 232–56.

Slater, T. B. *Christ and Community: A Socio-Rhetorical Study of the Christology of Revelation*. Sheffield: Sheffield Academic, 1999.

Sleeper, Freeman. *The Victorious Christ: A Study of the Book of Revelation*. Louisville, Ky.: Westminster/John Knox, 1996.

Smith, Jonathan Z. "Cross-Cultural Reflections on Apocalypticism," 281–85, in *Ancient and Modern Perspectives on the Bible and Culture: Essays in Honor of Hans Dieter Betz*. Edited by Adela Yarbro Collins. Atlanta: Scholars, 1998.

Smith, Robert. *Apocalypse: A Commentary on Revelation in Words and Images*. Collegeville, Minn.: Liturgical, 2000.

———. "'Worthy Is the Lamb' and Other Songs of Revelation." *Currents in Theology and Mission* 25 (1998): 500-508.

Söding, T. "Heilig, Heilig, Heilig: Zur politischen Theologie der Johannes-Apocalypse." *Zeitschrift für Theologie und Kirche* 96 (1999): 49–76.

Souza, Marcelo de Barros, Vítor Westhelle, and Ivo Poletto. *Luta pela Terra: Caminho da Fé.* São Paulo: Loyola, 1990.

Spatafora, A. *From the "Temple of God" to God as Temple: A Biblical Theological Study of the Temple in the Book of Revelation.* Rome: Editrice Ponificia Università Gregoriana, 1997.

Spencer, R. A. "Violence and Vengeance in Revelation." *Review and Expositor* 98 (2001): 59–75.

Spivak, Gayatri. "Can the Subaltern Speak?" 271–313, in *Marxism and the Interpretation of Culture.* Edited by Cary Nelson and Lawrence Grossberg. Urbana: University of Illinois Press, 1988.

———. "Displacement and the Discourse of Woman," 169–95, in *Displacement: Derrida and After.* Edited by Mark Krupnick. Bloomington: Indiana University Press, 1983.

Stauffer, M. T., editor. *The Christian Occupation of China.* Shanghai: China Continuation Committee, 1922.

Stevenson, G. *Power and Place: Temple and Identity in the Book of Revelation.* Berlin: de Gruyter, 2001.

Stone, Kay. "Feminist Approaches to the Interpretation of Fairy Tales," 229–35, in *Fairy Tales and Society.* Edited by Ruth Bottigheimer. Philadelphia: University of Pennsylvania Press, 1986.

———. "The Misuses of Enchantment," 125–45, in *Women's Folklore, Women's Culture.* Edited by Rosan Jordan and Susan Kalcik. Philadelphia: University of Pennsylvania Press, 1985

Stringfellow, William. *An Ethic for Christians and Other Aliens in a Strange Land.* Waco, Tex.: Word, 1979.

Sweet, John. *Revelation.* Harrisburg, Pa.: Trinity Press International, 1979.

Talbert, Charles. *The Apocalypse: A Reading of the Revelation of John.* Louisville, Ky.: Westminster John Knox, 1994.

Tatar, Maria. *The Hard Facts of the Grimms' Fairy Tales.* Princeton, N.J.: Princeton University Press, 1987.

Tavis, Anna. "Fairy Tales from a Semiotic Perspective," 195–202, in *Fairy Tales and Society.* Edited by Ruth Bottigheimer. Philadelphia: University of Pennsylvania Press, 1986.

Taylor, J. V. *Christian Presence amid African Religion.* 2nd Edition. Nairobi: Acton Publishers, 2001 [1963].

———. *The Primal Vision: Christian Presence amid African Religion.* London: SCM, 1963.

Taylor, Mark Lewis. *The Executed God: The Way of the Cross in Lockdown America.* Minneapolis: Fortress Press, 2001.

Terrell, Joanne Marie. *Power in the Blood? The Cross in the African American Experience.* The Bishop Henry McNeal Turner/Sojourner Truth Series in Black Religion. Maryknoll, N.Y.: Orbis, 1998.

Thimmes, P. "Women Reading Women in the Apocalypse: Reading Scenario 1, the Letter to Thyatira." *Currents in Biblical Research* 2 (2003): 128–44.

Thompson, Leonard. *The Book of Revelation: Apocalypse and Empire.* New York: Oxford University Press, 1990.

———. "Cult and Eschatology in the Apocalypse of John." *Journal of Religion* 49 (1969).

———. *Revelation.* Abingdon New Testament Commentaries. Nashville: Abingdon, 1998.

———. "A Sociological Analysis of Tribulation in the Apocalypse of John." *Semeia* 36 (1986): 147–74.

Thrupp, Sylvia L. "Millennial Dreams in Action: A Report on the Conference Discussion." In *Millennial Dreams in Action.* Edited by S. Thrupp. The Hague: Mouton, 1962.

Ting, K. H. "A Call for Clarity: Fourteen Points from Christians in the People's Republic of China to Christians Abroad." *China Notes* 19 (Winter 1980–1981): 145–49.

Tolbert, Mary Ann. "The Politics and Poetics of Location." In *Reading from This Place*. Vol. 1: *Social Location and Biblical Interpretation in the United States*. Edited by Fernando Segovia and Mary Ann Tolbert. Minneapolis: Fortress Press, 1995.

Tombasco, Anthony, ed. *The Bible on Suffering: Social and Political Implications*. Mahwah, N.J.: Paulist, 2001.

Toole, David. *Waiting for Godot in Sarajevo: Theological Reflections on Nihilism, Tragedy, and Apocalypse*. Boulder: Westview, 1998.

Townes, Emilie M. *Breaking the Fine Rain of Death: African American Health Issues and a Womanist Ethic of Care*. New York: Continuum, 1998.

Tucker, Robert C. *Philosophy and Myth in Karl Marx*. Cambridge: Cambridge University Press. 1972.

Turner, Harold. *Profile through Preaching: A Study of the Sermon Texts Used in a West African Independent Church*. Edinburgh: Edinburgh House, 1965.

Turner, W. L. *Making Sense of Revelation: A Clear Message of Hope*. Macon: Smyth & Helwys, 2000.

Ukpong, Justin. "Reading the Bible in a Global Village: Issues and Challenges from African Readings." In *Reading the Bible in the Global Village* by Justin Ukpong et al. Atlanta: Society of Biblical Literature, 2002.

Ulgard, H. "Reading the Book of Revelation Today: Respecting Its Originality while Recognizing Its Lasting Message." *Concilium* (1998): 31–39.

van Henten, Jan Willem. "Dragon Myth and Imperial Ideology in Revelation 12-13." *SBL Seminar Papers* 130 (1994): 496–515.

Vasconcellos, P. L. "Apocalypses in the History of Brazil." *Journal for the Study of the New Testament* 25 (2002): 235–54.

Vassiliadis, P. "Apocalypse and Liturgy." *St. Vladimir's Theological Quarterly* 41 (1997): 95–112.

Vinson, R. B. "The Social World of Revelation." *Review and Expositor* 98 (2001): 11–33.

Volf, Misroslav. *Exclusion and Embrace: A Theological Exploration of Identity, Otherness, and Reconciliation*. Nashville: Abingdon, 1996.

von Franz, Marie-Louise. *The Feminine in Fairytales*. Dallas: Spring, 1972.

Voortman, T. C., and J. A. du Rand. "The Worship of God and the Lamb: Exploring the Liturgical Setting of the Apocalypse of John." *Ekklesiastikos Pharos* 80 (1998): 56–67.

Voorwinde, S. "Worship: The Key to the Book of Revelation." *Vox Reformata* 63 (1998): 3–35.

Wainwright, Arthur W. *Mysterious Apocalypse: Interpreting the Book of Revelation*. Nashville: Abingdon, 1993.

Walhout, Edwin. *Revelation Down to Earth: Making Sense of the Apocalypse of John*. Grand Rapids: Eerdmans, 2001.

Walker, Alice. *In Search of Our Mother's Gardens: Womanist Prose*. New York: Harcourt Brace Jovanovich, 1983.

Wall, Cheryl A. *Zora Neale Hurston: Novels and Stories*. The Library of America. New York: Literary Classics of the United States, 1984.

Wallis, Arthur. *China Miracle: A Voice to the Church in the West*. Eastbourne: Kingsway, 1985.

Warren, Max, editor. *To Apply the Gospel: Selections from the Writings of Henry Venn*. Grand Rapids: Eerdmans, 1971.

Weaver, J. Denny. *The Nonviolent Atonement*. Grand Rapids: Eerdmans, 2001.

Weber, Eugen. *Apocalypses: Prophecies, Cults and Millennial Beliefs through the Ages*. Toronto: Random House, 1999.

———. "Fairies and Hard Facts: The Reality of Folktales." *Journal of the History of Ideas* 42 (1981): 93–113.

Weems, Renita. *Battered Love: Marriage, Sex, and Violence in the Hebrew Prophets.* Minneapolis: Fortress Press, 1995.

Wengst, Klaus. "Babylon the Great and the New Jerusalem: The Visionary View of Political Reality in the Revelation of John," 189–202, in *Politics and Theopolitics in the Bible and Postbiblical Literature.* Edited by Henning Graf Reventlow, Yair Hoffman, and Benjamin Uffenheimer. JSOT Supplement 171. Sheffield: JSOT Press, 1994.

Wengst, Klaus. *Pax Romana and the Peace of Jesus Christ.* Translated by John Bowden. London: SCM, 1987.

Wenig, Lauren. *The Challenge of the Apocalypse: Embracing the Book of Revelation with Hope and Faith.* Mahwah, N.J.: Paulist, 2001.

West, Traci C. *Wounds of the Spirit: Black Women, Violence, and Resistance Ethics.* New York: New York University Press, 1999.

Westhelle, Vítor. "Multiculturalism, Post-Colonialism, and the Apocalyptic," 3–13, in *Theology and the Religions: A Dialogue.* Edited by Viggo Mortensen. Grand Rapids: Eerdmans, 2003.

Wilder, Amos. *The Language of the Gospel.* New York: Harper & Row, 1964.

Williams, Bernard. *Shame and Necessity.* Berkeley: University of California Press, 1993.

Williams, Patrick, and Laura Chrisman, eds. *Colonial Discourse and Post-Colonial Theory.* New York: Columbia University Press, 1994.

Wink, Walter. "The Apocalyptic Beast: The Culture of Violance," *Concilium* (1997): 71-77.

———. "Biblical Theology and Social Ethics." In *Biblical Theology: Problems and Perspectives.* Edited by Steven Kraftchick, Charles D. Myers, and Ben C. Ollenberger. Nashville: Abingdon, 1995.

Witherington, Ben. *The Acts of the Apostles: A Socio-Rhetorical Commentary.* Grand Rapids: Eerdmans, 1998.

Worth, R. H. *The Seven Cities of the Apocalypse and Greco-Asian Culture.* New York: Paulist, 1999.

———. *The Seven Cities of the Apocalypse and Roman Culture.* New York: Paulist, 1999.

Wright, N. T. *The Millenium Myth.* Louisville, Ky.: Westminster John Knox, 1999.

Yeo, Khiok-khng. "What Has Jerusalem to Do with Beijing? The Book of Revelation and Chinese Christians," 523–24, in *Society of Biblical Literature 1998 Seminar Papers.* Atlanta: Scholars Press, 1998.

Yeo, Khiok-khng. *Chairman Mao Meets the Apostle Paul: Christianity, Communism, and the Hope of China.* Grand Rapids: Brazos, 2002.

Yoder, John Howard. *The Politics of Jesus: Vicit Agnus Noster.* Grand Rapids: Eerdmans, 1994.

Zahan, Dominique. *The Religion, Spirituality, and Thought of Traditional Africa.* Chicago: University of Chicago Press, 1979.

Zampaglione, Gerardo. *The Idea of Peace in Antiquity.* Translated by Richard Dunn. Notre Dame, Ind.: University of Notre Dame Press, 1973. *Buch der Civitas Dei*, 2. Auflage. Berlin/Zürich: Weidmannsche, 1965.

Zanker, Paul. *The Power of Images in the Age of Augustus.* Translated by Alan Shapiro. Ann Arbor: University of Michigan Press, 1990.

Zerbe, G. "Revelation's Exposé of Two Cities: Babylon and New Jerusalem." *Direction* 32 (2003): 47-60.

Zimmermann, H. "Christus und die Kirche in den Sendschreiben der Apokalypse." In *Unio Christianorum: Festschrift Jaeger.* Paderborn: Schöningh, 1962.

Zipes, Jack. "Marxists and the Illumination of Folk and Fairy Tales," 235–43, in *Fairy Tales and Society.* Edited by Ruth Bottigheimer. Philadelphia: University of Pennsylvania Press, 1986.